CW01335531

Letters to His Wife

Freiburg .26. IV. 16.

Meine Teuerste, ich denke Dir mit
innigstem Herzen — lass mich wiedersehen
in Deinem gütlichen Wesen —
Fügung ist alles u. die grösste alles,
dass ich Dich habe.

Komme — u. ich kann mich freuen

Dein lieber

MARTIN HEIDEGGER

Letters to His Wife
1915–1970

Selected, edited and annotated by
Gertrud Heidegger
Translated by R. D. V. Glasgow

polity

First published in German as *"Mein liebes Seelchen!" Briefe Martin Heideggers an seine Frau Elfride 1915–1970* © Deutsche Verlags-Anstalt, 2005

This English edition © Polity Press, 2008

Polity Press
65 Bridge Street
Cambridge CB2 1UR, UK

Polity Press
350 Main Street
Malden, MA 02148, USA

ISBN-13: 978-0-7456-4135-5
ISBN-13: 978-0-7456-4136-2(pb)

A catalogue record for this book is available from the British Library.

Typeset in 10.5 on 12pt Sabon
by Servis Filmsetting Ltd, Stockport, Cheshire
Printed and bound in Great Britain by Biddles Ltd, Kings Lynn, Norfolk

The publisher has used its best endeavours to ensure that the URLs for external websites referred to in this book are correct and active at the time of going to press. However, the publisher has no responsibility for the websites and can make no guarantee that a site will remain live or that the content is or will remain appropriate.

Every effort has been made to trace all copyright holders, but if any have been inadvertently overlooked the publishers will be pleased to include any necessary credits in any subsequent reprint or edition.

For further information on Polity, visit our website: www.polity.co.uk

The translation of this work was supported by a grant from the Goethe-Institut that is funded by the Ministry of Foreign Affairs.

Contents

Acknowledgements   vii

Preface   viii

Editor's Note   xiv

Translator's Note   xv

Letters, 1915–1970   1

Afterword by Hermann Heidegger   317

Life of Elfride Heidegger   318

Life of Martin Heidegger   323

Heidegger Family Tree   328

Annotated Index of Names   329

Index   339

*I dedicate this book to my two grandmothers
and with all my love to my husband and our children,
Florian, Cornelia and Brigitte*

Acknowledgements

I thank my grandmother for the trust she put in me by giving me the letters, and I hope I have done justice to it. I thank my father, Jörg Heidegger, who patiently helped me during my initial difficulties with my grandfather's handwriting and contributed many of the photos of the family and the Cabin. I thank my husband and my children for the loving support they gave me with this project over the years.

I thank my uncle Hermann and my aunt Jutta Heidegger, who went to the great trouble of collating all the letters and helped me with information and names.

I thank Dr Alfred Denker, who knew the answers to many questions. By the same token I thank Professor Friedrich-Wilhelm von Herrmann for his records of my grandmother's memories of her life, which he put at my disposal. Heinrich Heidegger willingly provided me with information from the estate of his father, Fritz Heidegger, and his brother Thomas put photos at my disposal.

Additionally, I thank all those people who undertook a critical reading of my manuscript, in particular my goddaughter Kerstin Pistorius.

Above all, however, I should like to thank Christiane Schmidt and Jürgen Horbach of the Deutsche Verlags-Anstalt for accepting my conception of the book without reservations and allowing our collaboration to take such a trusting and felicitous form.

Rötebuck House, July 2005
Gertrud Heidegger

Preface

My personal family history began in Wiesbaden in 1907. Two girls, Elfride Petri and Hedwig Stein, were in the same class at school and became friends. The course their lives were to follow was closely bound up with the chequered history of Germany in the twentieth century.

Elfride chose one of the professions then open to women and became a teacher. As this failed to fulfil her, she took her bearings with further studies at the Universities of Kiel and Berlin and subsequently studied economics in Freiburg. She married the philosopher Martin Heidegger and had two sons. The older one, Jörg, is my father.

Hedwig followed the usual path taken by daughters from middle-class families and attended a girls' boarding school in French-speaking Switzerland to learn home economics and French. In World War I she became a nurse. Her only brother fell in the conflict, and she nursed her fiancé, a doctor who was gravely wounded, through to his agonizing death. After the war she married the Protestant pastor and member of the Landtag and Reichstag, Karl Veidt, and bore six children. The youngest daughter, Hedi, is my mother.

In 1933 Martin Heidegger was appointed rector of the University of Freiburg and, like his wife Elfride, that same year joined the Nazi party. At the same time, Karl Veidt became involved in the *bekennende Kirche* (the Christian resistance movement) in Frankfurt and was arrested in 1937 and again in 1941. As a consequence of their conflicting political views, contact between the Heidegger family and the Veidt family broke off. It was not until after World War II and the death of Karl Veidt that the two friends, Elfride and Hedwig, met again in Wiesbaden.

On a visit to see his godmother Hedwig in Wiesbaden in spring 1954, Jörg met his future wife Hedi. They were married by August.

My mother was a nurse, and my father a mechanical engineer who later went into teaching. They spent the first two years of their marriage in the Heidegger household, where I was born the eldest of five children. Following the birth of my sister Friederike, space became short and the commotion too great for my grandparents, so we moved into another flat in the same part of town.

In the following years, I enjoyed regular contact with my grandmother, less so with my grandfather, who either needed peace and quiet to work or was away travelling, at conferences or at his brother's in Messkirch. Even so, I retain fond memories of the rare hours we did spend together in his study, where we would listen to Prokofiev's *Peter and the Wolf*, read poems by Johann Peter Hebel, and I would be given peppermints and dark chocolate from his desk drawer.

Grandmother held cherry festivals with us grandchildren in the garden of their house on Rötebuck, taught us to swim in their own pool, and corrected and criticized us plentifully. We also experienced both the softer and severer sides of our grandmother at story time or doing handicrafts, as well as during our stays at the Cabin in Todtnauberg.

I was a shy, dreamy girl with black pigtails. I was not particularly good at school, but enjoyed reading and read a lot. As I was set on going into a caring profession, I decided to follow the family tradition and become a nurse. After training in Heidelberg, in 1975 I returned to work in Freiburg, where I now engaged my grandparents increasingly in conversation. We talked about such topics as our shared interest in art, family tales and my profession. Furthermore, I was able to help my grandparents in their day-to-day lives. After my grandfather's stroke in 1970, from which he made a complete recovery, they built a house in the garden that was better suited for the elderly, and lived there from 1971 onwards.

My career in nursing meant that from an early age I was confronted with the finite nature of life, and I was deeply moved by the calmness with which my grandfather faced his own death. He died in the early hours of 26 May 1976. My grandmother, who thought he was just unconscious, called me. I established that he was dead and attempted to console my grandmother. Together with my cousin Almuth, I tended him one last time. The subsequent period of mourning was especially difficult for my grandmother, as she had felt their final years together to be the best years of their marriage. They had hardly been apart during this time.

My regular visits to see my grandmother gave rise to detailed discussions. During this time she spoke a great deal of the letters Grandfather had written her in the course of their long life together, and which she had preserved. On 13 January 1977 she gave me an old key. It belonged to the wooden chest in which she kept Grandfather's letters. Attached to the key by a silk ribbon was a handwritten label: 'After my death this key belongs <u>exclusively</u> to my granddaughter Gertrud Heidegger.'

Her wish at the time was to keep the letters under lock and key until 1989, the centenary of my grandfather's birth. She wanted to leave it to me to decide what should be done with them, feeling that there was no telling how great the public interest in my grandfather's life and work would be in later years. I could publish the letters in whatever way I saw fit, she told me, but I could also burn them. Having herself gone through times of need – and as the two of them had financed their retirement home by selling the manuscript of *Being and Time* – she did not rule out the possibility of putting the letters up for sale either.

At this stage I was not fully aware of the significance of this legacy. I was conscious only of my grandmother's absolute trust in me as a granddaughter and a woman. In December 1978 she also gave three cassettes and a folder containing written materials my grandfather had given her at various times to the German Literature Archive in Marbach. Among them were three letters from the collection of his letters to her.

In the years that followed, my life was fully taken up with moving to Heidelberg, starting a family and working. In March 1979 my husband Albrecht, our 1-year-old son and I were lucky enough to move into the house on Rötebuck. The chest full of letters remained under lock and key, upstairs in the loft. My grandmother lived close by in her retirement home and took great delight in her great-grandchildren, Florian, Cornelia and Brigitte. It was characteristic of her that she objected to the non-German names we had chosen for our children. To the end of her days she did not essentially change in her nationalistic and anti-Semitic views.

After her 90th birthday, my grandmother's physical and mental condition deteriorated so much that in 1987 she moved into an old people's home in Freiburg. In 1988, she asked me not to make the letters public until 2000. On the advice of my uncle, Hermann Heidegger, that same year I opened the wooden chest with a view to entrusting the letters to a safe in the bank. In it, I found seven boxes, specially made by a bookbinder for my grandfather's letters and cards. It was only now that I realized the full extent of the collection.

After a long period in care, my grandmother died on 21 March 1992 at the age of 98.

From autumn 1999 onwards, my family and professional situation allowed me to concern myself intensively with the legacy of letters, and I felt a deep obligation to do justice to the trust my grandmother had placed in me. With my father's help, I got used to deciphering my grandfather's handwriting and began to copy out the letters. In the course of this work, I grew even closer to my grandparents. My grandfather's personality, in particular, showed itself to me in a new light, and with hindsight some of his behaviour has become easier to understand. Only with the help of the letters did it become possible to arrange some of the things my grandmother had told me in a proper chronological order. On other occasions I had to make comparisons with other sources or work things out for myself.

As far as I could, I have researched the names and events that appear in the letters. In this, I was given willing support by other members of the family and by those who were well informed about Heidegger and his work. I also read the correspondence and biographies of my grandfather and those around him. I was astonished to find that my grandmother is virtually never mentioned in them. It became increasingly clear to me that publication of the letters would arouse great interest, as almost nothing is known about my grandparents' marriage. It is in the nature of such things that there are also many letters that convey matters of less interest. And so the idea was born to publish a book that was not too vast in extent, but informative and easily readable.

In December 2001, my uncle Hermann Heidegger kindly set about the task of comparing and correcting my copies against the handwritten originals.

During this time, I read *My Wounded Heart*, in which Martin Doerry uses selected letters with explanatory notes to tell the deeply shocking tale of his grandmother, Lilli Jahn. As well as leaving a deep impression on me, Doerry's book reinforced the ideas I had formed in planning this one, and directed me to what was to be its German publisher, the *Deutsche Verlags-Anstalt*.

The biggest task now was to select from more than 1,000 letters and cards written between 1915 and 1970 the most important and the nicest ones, as there would only be space for a seventh of them in a handy-sized book. With time, a procedure for making this selection emerged. I read the letters a number of times, among other things taking public interest into consideration, and assessed them in terms of their significance. I underlined the most important passages in different colours according to their themes (red for love, marriage and family; green for philosophy, religion and university matters; blue for food, dwelling and clothing; yellow for the army, war and politics), and found that it was not all that difficult to make a selection. The early letters in particular reveal an intensive exchange of ideas between my grandparents on philosophical, religious, socio-political and university issues.

The letters were addressed on a very personal level to Elfride as a friend, fiancée and wife, and although there are so many of them, they are snapshots that can only sketch an incomplete picture of this long-standing relationship. Not least interesting is also what was hushed over. Even so, the letters provide a unique opportunity to gain an insight into my grandparents' life together.

From the year 1918, when my grandfather was a soldier, 127 letters and cards have been kept, whereas from the year 1947 there is just one letter. Such variations in the number of letters can be explained by the different periods of separation. On the other hand, I know that in 1933 – during his rectorship – my grandfather was frequently away travelling. Since there is nonetheless only a single letter from 1933, I can only assume that some letters are missing from the collection I found in the chest. Whether they went astray or were destroyed and, if they were destroyed, by whom and when, can no longer be clarified today. In a letter from 27 October 1939, my grandfather wrote to my grandmother: 'The letter from R. has been burnt.' And on 22 November 1939 he told her: 'Only you have a copy, which you'd perhaps best destroy, as I shall be giving the final thing a different & broader form.' As there was no corresponding enclosure, my grandmother had clearly complied with his wish. Beyond question is that she read through all the letters once again, arranged them in order and in some cases added comments before she placed them in the chest.

I am aware that any selection of letters, cards and excerpts from texts is always contentious. With the selection of letters I have chosen for this book, I should like to convey the highpoints and turning points, the crises and day-to-day occurrences of a relationship that lasted 60 years. It was inevitable that in copying out and selecting the letters I would have to take a good look at my family's past. Yet I also feel that the gap in generations and time is an advantage. To forestall possible speculation, I have included in the book all the letters in my possession from between 1933 and 1938. Moreover, every one of the small total of anti-Semitic remarks or political comments regarding National Socialism is cited. Undeniably, the compilation selected here will not be sufficient for the reader with scholarly research interests. In due course, I plan to make all the letters and cards fully available to the public in a critical edition.

My grandmother was an intelligent and, for her time, extremely emancipated woman. By 'emancipation', she doubtless did not understand the same as the women of today. For her, the *Frauenfrage* or 'issue of women's rights' had to do with a broad education for girls and an independent and responsible role for women in society. Without her drive and support, the philosophical work of my grandfather would not have been possible in the measure it was. I experienced my grandmother's highly contradictory and difficult personality and had many an argument with her. At times she was extremely jealous, yet she never spoke of the cause. It is only after reading the letters that I now know she had every reason to be, for Hannah Arendt was only one of Grandfather's many close women friends in the course of their marriage. Among the collection of letters, my grandmother included a dated letter she had drafted to her husband in 1956, full of despair. Various comments appended to the letters in her own hand-writing provide hints about his relationships with other women. In this way, she clearly wanted to ensure that these painful experiences came to light after her death. I believe that in publishing this book I have thereby duly served my grandmother's bequest.

Editor's Note

In order to provide contextual information, explain persons or events referred to in the letters and above all shed light on the personality of my grandmother as the recipient of the letters, I have added a commentary that also serves as a link between texts. In this way, I was also able to provide relevant facts and quotations from the letters that I have omitted.

Omissions have been made within the letters in order to safeguard the personal rights of living family members, but also to leave out matters of minor importance and avoid repetitions. These are signalled by […].

Translator's Note

The translator has followed the German text in seeking to maintain the character of the letters. As in the German, abbreviations of proper nouns have been left as such where considered unambiguous (e.g. 'Frbg.' for 'Freiburg'), and square brackets added only where ambiguity was felt to exist (e.g. 'Hu[sserl].' instead of 'Hu.'). Where other words were abbreviated by Heidegger, the translator has attempted to find a roughly equivalent abbreviation of the English word (e.g. 'philos.' for 'philosophical' or 'philosophy') provided this did not result in any additional ambiguity. The symbol '&' has been used throughout wherever Heidegger used 'u.' instead of 'und'. Passages or words underlined have likewise been underlined. Italics have not been used for foreign words or the titles of books or newspapers. Following the German edition of the letters, simple slips of the pen have been corrected without further remark, although misspellings of certain names have been maintained. Passages where the writing is difficult to decipher have been signalled by [?].

The translator has also tried to maintain the character of Heidegger's punctuation: the frequent dashes, which are often indistinguishable from full stops or commas, have only been replaced where necessary in order to avoid confusion. On a number of occasions the translator has used square brackets either to provide background information for an English-speaking reader or to draw attention to wordplay in the German original or the use of specifically Heideggerian concepts. Where such clarifications might threaten to disturb the flow of the text too much, a brief footnote has been provided. The translator would like to thank Winni Schindler for his generous help and support. He would also like to thank Nicholas Walker for his expert suggestions.

Letters, 1915–1970

Elfride 1912

'To my Dearest Soul!' Frbg. 10 Dec. 15 Mart.

1915

Dear Fräulein Petri,

As I was speaking to you this morning, I saw how the look on your face turned reflective and grave and anxious.

My duties made me rush & so I had to leave you in a state of distress and disquiet.

No, you cannot have forgotten what I gratefully confided to you – that those wondrously reflective hours were <u>repose</u> for me.

And much, much more than that – I felt with all my heart that my thoughts soared on within your own attentive soul – there has been an aura of solemnity in my study ever since – and your unaffected gratitude – God, it sprang so deeply from the source – that I shall never forget these hours.

Today I know that we were both <u>bound</u> to think of the 'Saint and Her Fool';[1] & if we provoke disquiet in one another then it is of a sort that words remain powerless to capture.

I beg you, dear Fräulein Petri, do not worry yourself at all about me & above all do not torment yourself with reproaches that are without foundation.

Even if I am rather overworked, I am quick to recover because I can suddenly take pleasure in things. What a delightful thing the sun is.

I don't need to give you reasons why you <u>should </u>come – 'Dearest Soul'.

Best wishes,

Your thankful
Martin Heidegger.

---

[1] *Die Heilige und ihr Narr*, a best-selling novel by Agnes Günther (1863–1911), published posthumously in 1913. The orphan princess in this book is often referred to as *Seelchen*, the affectionate diminutive form of *Seele* (soul) subsequently used by Heidegger.

Come,[2] Dearest Soul, and rest against my heart, I want to look for ever into the depths of your fairy-tale eyes and <u>thank</u> you – Dearest Soul – it is given to me to experience ever new, wonderful things in you – you are mine – & am I to bear this unutterable happiness, are my hands sacred enough tremblingly to clasp yours, is my soul, harried through all the throes of doubt, a worthy shrine wherein your love may dwell for all eternity?

My great happiness weighs me to the ground – in the end, it is above all those of a philosophical nature who experience such uncommon happiness in all its fullness. The philosopher sees the ultimate in all things, experiences the deepest foundations of all existence, thrills in this god-born wondrous happiness – Dearest Soul, I can only accept this wonderful thing with the painful reverence that is ultimately deeper than what we call joy; why do people often weep for happiness? why, when I read your angelically pure poem drenched in the sunshine of fairy-tales, intoxicated with the felicity of childhood, could I not help but fling myself down & close my eyes? – were they the throes of eternity that chased wildly through my soul & then suddenly left behind in me that silence of the stormless mountain, in which all objects grow towards the infinite?

Yes, & so, Dearest Soul, let me accept all happiness with great reverential, prayerful humility & always be ailing with this happiness, for then I am gladdest, happiest & <u>strongest,</u> in this great weight of experiencing I can feel the problems lie heavy on my soul like gigantic boulders; and this burden, which draws its force from the eternal, unleashes the opposing force in me & I feel my sinews tauten & I reach for the heavy hammer of the interminable search for knowledge which gropes forward through dark tunnels of abstraction – & suddenly it comes whistling down & the rock face cracks asunder, the shards fly into the depths & the blue of the sky laughs in on us & profusion of blessing gushes over us & <u>you,</u> Dearest Soul, lean trembling on my shoulder & can still feel the shake of my arm, which is yet infused with the weight of the hammer –

Dearest Soul, and now I must go down on my knees before you, lay your wondrous hand, transfused with blessing, on my tortured brow – and <u>forgive</u> your boy, <u>forgive</u> me for being so full of restlessness on Sunday, I am human & as such hurled into the antagonism of the sensual and the spiritual; but with <u>you</u> it is given to me to experience <u>what is beyond the antagonism,</u> where all tensions are resolved,

---

[2] In this letter Heidegger has switched from the courtesy form of address *Sie* to the more familiar *Du*.

where everything is only sacred & all darkness is banished – Dearest Soul, I'll for ever be your debtor –

I ought to rest now, but no, I cannot. Resting on your bosom, I would gladly recount every last detail of my modest life –

But perhaps you have already beheld me in the intuition of your soul – a simple boy, living with modest, pious people in the country, a boy who could still see the glass globe by the light of which his grandfather sat on a three-legged stool and hammered nails into shoes, who helped his father with the cooperage & forced the hoops into place around the barrels, the hammer-blows resounding through the small, winding alleys; who savoured all the wonderful poetry open to a sexton's son, lay for hours up in the church tower & gazed after the swifts & dreamt his way over the dark pine forests; who rummaged about in the dusty old books in the church loft & felt like a king among the piles of books which he did not understand but every one of which he knew & reverentially loved.

And when that boy, who would get the key to the tower from his father & could choose which of the other boys was allowed up with him & so had a certain prestige & power & was always the leader in all the raids and games of soldiers, the only one allowed to carry the <u>iron</u> sabre; when that boy came home from Latin at the young vicar's and often brought mistakes with him, he would cry his heart out on his good mother's shoulder, though she herself could not give him any help – the little brooder had to 'study' & was allowed to go to grammar school on Lake Constance & in the fifth form when he brought home nothing less than a 'Schiller' as first prize, he was even in the local paper & from then on, as people still say today, he was never again seen in the holidays without a book. And he delved & sought & became quieter and quieter & already he had a vague ideal – the scholar – in his mind – though his pious, simple mother hoped for a 'priest' – it was a struggle for him to win the right to live purely on knowledge, to make his mother believe that the philosopher too can achieve great things for men & their eternal happiness – how often did she ask her son, 'what is philosophy, do tell me', & he couldn't give an answer himself –

And his father, whose brooding taciturnity he inherited, was proud & is so to this day, however strange and incomprehensible all his son's work might be to him & when he got his doctorate summa cum laude, it was in the local paper & for the small town this was cause for celebration, it had never happened in living memory & his old godmother said, 'why, I always knew it, his great-grandfather was just the same, always busy with books; in the Danube Valley where his estate lay among the towering castles of the von Zimmern, he would sit on Sundays with the books he had picked up at the market in Ulm' –

5

You ask how they came to the Danube Valley and the von Zimbern [Zimmern]? The trail leads to South Tyrol, where my ancestors in Switzerland came from – which included a theologian famous at the time [Joh. Henricus Heideggerus] whose many books are catalogued even today in the Freiburg University Library & right below them is his descendant's clumsy dissertation –

How it came about that he might write it & rose further & gained access to the university, without having all the wealth & abundance of a refined spiritual education, without the so powerful & much-used expedient of patronage, how it came about –

it is a wonder to himself & a reason for deep gratitude & childlike humility; perhaps it is for this very reason that he experiences this priesthood in all its depth, because it long lay dormant within him as a distant ideal to which no path seemed to lead, because to him it is much, much more than an office, a position within society, a career – because to him it is a priesthood, something to which only the 'ordained' may gain entry & this ordination proceeds only from a struggle – from complete submission to its ideal, tortured & full of privation – and whosoever has been ordained in this way – can never be proud, but relates all things in his life back only to his innermost mission – everything apart from this is but a cipher to him –

And this lofty, solemn, timeless mission has now been placed in the angelic hands of a 'saint', the whole torrent of deepest experience engulfs the hard struggle – my Dearest Soul scatters the roses on the steep mountain path up to the towering peaks of pure knowledge & most blissful experience in these two creatures whom God was leading along their paths, his inscrutable path, until suddenly, filled with the pangs of holy craving, they found one another; the two of them will build themselves a happiness in which spirit, purity, goodness rush together and, overflowing, pour forth into the languishing souls of those who thirst –

Dearest Soul, clasp your pure hands together & place them in mine – take my soul, it is yours – you saint – and let the flames and glowing heat come together and as they flare up consume one another in the longing for

αὐτὸ τὸ θεῖον καλὸν μονοειδές

'the divine itself in its unchangeable beauty'.

From 1905 Elfride grew up in Wiesbaden, where she attended the girls' high school. For health reasons, her father had to spend the winter of 1907-8 in Nice, where Elfride learnt French. The following summer, armed with a 1909 Baedeker, she travelled alone to London to improve her English and went on a tour of England and Wales. After finishing high school, she spent four years at the Oberlyzeum, *or upper high school, in Wiesbaden, where she took the first part of her teacher training examination in 1913, passing the second state exam after a further year's course in 1914. In the summer semester of the same year, she started an advanced course at Kiel University to qualify her to teach at girls' high schools. When the First World War broke out, she moved to Berlin, where she worked with the National Women's Service. In 1915, studying as an external student at a Kassel grammar school, she passed the school leaving exam that would subsequently allow her to study without restriction.*

In the winter semester of 1915/16, at the age of 22, Elfride moved to Freiburg to study economics. She was keen to deepen her knowledge of the social questions and was particularly interested in the Frauenfrage, the issue of women's rights.

Elfride became a member of the Freiburg Sorority and joined the 'Cabin Guild', founded by female students in 1910. Whenever she could, she visited their cabin on the 1,000-metre-high Silberberg, which was more than an hour's walk from Hinterzarten Railway Station. Having been given a pair of Norwegian skis by her parents in 1913, Elfride was an enthusiastic skier. Her father Richard was a colonel on the inactive list, who managed half of an inherited canvas factory in Alfeld an der Leine. Her mother Martha ran their middle-class household.

At the time Elfride entered university in 1915, the number of registered students at Freiburg had fallen to five or six hundred as a result of the war. A quarter of these were women.

As part of her course, Elfride attended a philosophy seminar on Kant's Prolegomena *given by the 26-year-old Privatdozent Martin Heidegger, and after one of the sessions the two of them got into conversation. When Elfride was due to present a paper, Martin offered to help her and invited her to visit him at home. At the time he was living with an aunt at Hohenzollernstrasse 1.*

For health reasons Martin was considered unfit for active service, but as a member of the Landsturm, *the German National Guard, he was assigned to the postal supervision centre. When not on duty, he pursued his new teaching activities as a* Privatdozent *at Freiburg University, using the rest of his time to work on philosophy.*

Martin came from a humble background and was acquainted with poverty and shortage of money. Throughout his years at school and university he had always depended on grants and often had to borrow money. Elfride was frugal by character, although she was never faced with financial worries.

Guild cabin on the Silberberg

16 Dec. 15

Dearest Soul, I know you won't mind me coming to you quickly – I have to tell you something, I disobeyed you – but I'm sure it'll make you happy – last night I worked till almost 1 o'clock – on a completely new problem that suddenly flashed through my mind – I suddenly felt secret powers grow within me & entered that state of creativity which I hadn't felt since the war began – which I had been awaiting all the time & now it came all of a sudden, like a revelation, the elemental force of the creative, you know, Dearest Soul, whoever's spirit is seized by <u>this</u> will experience something unutterable – perhaps <u>a mother's happiness</u> is the only analogy for it. And who summoned these forces of creation? <u>You</u>, my Dearest Soul – your great service to me – you who know of all things deep with the intuition of your soul – are you happy? – take this deep awareness of happiness with you on your mountain walk & take delight in the great meaning of the great and rich life you lead as a woman. How good you are – the people outside will thank you for it – Do you know what moves me so? That you serve me by imposing silence upon yourself – Dearest Soul 'must write no more', yet the invigorating, sun-like influence she exerts is all the more wonderful – how I'm looking forward to this Christmas Eve! Now I'd just like to have the whole days to myself to take full advantage of my living disposition to create. Dearest Soul, your care does allow me to work longer at night, doesn't it? – <u>I must</u>, & don't know how long I can in these anxious times. Do not be afraid, my love, that I am working rashly or excessively – Seidel was there till 1 o'clock this morning – poor chap – I fear people come to university rather too

8

young, too immature – there is a lack of sound work – of scholarly conscience; people have too many theories & programmes & things in their little heads which they aren't up to yet. When 22-year-olds are editing journals it's just nonsense – what colossal task awaits us – Dearest Soul?

Come back bright and cheerful with plenty of mountain air, the scent of firs, & sun –

Elfride wrote to her father to tell him that she had found the man who, like her, was 'a searcher, but full of vigour and strength'. His answer was very understanding. Elfride was close to her father. Her mother was affectionate and eager to help, but not held in such high regard by Elfride, who considered her superficial and felt she had failed to escape from the traditional role of the bourgeois wife.

Martin was the very antithesis of Elfride's ideal of a tall man with fair hair and blue eyes. He was slightly shorter than Elfride, had black curly hair and was quick to go brown in the sun, for which reason he would subsequently sign his letters with 'Boy' and later with 'Little Blackamoor'. The two of them differed not only in their origins and development, but also in their confession: Martin was Catholic, and Elfride Protestant.

Freibg. 30. XII. 15.

As I've had no news, I'd like to go home after all, Dearest Soul (Friday 3.58).

I presume you made it to the train on time. Much as I wanted to dream yesterday evening, I threw myself into my work bravely and cheerfully. It feels as though I might never ever lose this momentum again.

And certainly not once we're living together in our little house.

Picture to yourself that wondrous scene from yesterday – how in the twilight we sat nestling side by side at the window & you told me about our little house – it was a quite delightful moment & I live on it the days we are apart – though we're not really apart – it's just a pity we're not celebrating the New Year together, but I don't get any other leave. Yet our tree must light up once again & when I'm back I'll write and tell you when you're to come.

Don't torment yourself too much with the Prolegomena.

An ardent kiss to end the year
                    from your
                        happy Boy
If I can, I'll write you something.

1916

[Freiburg] 1. I. 16

It was a full evening, the last one of the year – and the wealth of things that the Christmas tree tells me in moments of contemplation I find so overpowering that I can only close my eyes and find myself lost in reverie – I shall do my utmost to ensure that your quite complete trust in me finds its fulfilment, you must know you are in perfectly safe hands – perhaps we'll have to search quite a lot more, your soul must open out even further, you have yet to grasp the full breadth & depth of problems – receptive, not on your own & brooding – that goes against the nature of a woman & it is typical how you sought a resting point in complete accordance with your feelings yet had to admit how suddenly a hopeless taxing emptiness spread through your delicate soul – feeling & a trembling sensitivity is an unlosable possession of the soul, but – it only has a really deep & unlosable substance if it is saturated, as it were, with ultimate and certain insights that lie beyond any change & becoming, embody the pure being of the idea, and – even more – are the most real reality of all. You will one day view your experience of nature in a quite different light & be surprised that you could see it as something ultimate. No, Dearest Soul, there are things still much deeper – & man is so utterly separated from everything natural that he in himself represents a value of his own – the very fact that he has the power to spiritualize his own nature, which is not bad in itself, raises him above everything natural –

If everything were but bondage to nature & natural soul, would there then really be <u>happiness</u>, this profoundly innermost experience? – would it then ever make sense for us to experience our love as something divine? – if it were not the creation, the free and conscious creation & exaltation of our spirit –

10

If it were not something infinitely higher, deeper, altogether heavenly that makes our heart quiver in the most blissful embrace rather than the animal's rut – then I'd rather be swallowed up by Nothingness today –

It does not bear thinking about – we are guided by, and within us lives, our ownmost <u>consciousness</u>, which finds expression in veneration & devotion; these are experiences that give man his unique position among everything else that is real –

can you imagine devotion without thereby experiencing everything that is timeless; you intertwine, as it were, your innermost experience with the consciousness of your existence as a human being who knows of the deepest riches & treasures – you quaver in the fullness of the experience – so powerful it may almost seem like a cry of woe – the Good in itself descends & shines from the depths of your eyes – in beauty your wonderful body trembles.

Child, don't you sense that only the infinite, most personal spirit of God in his absolute fullness can be the final goal & end for us & our existence –

Why do we experience our happiness so quite extraordinarily <u>deeply</u>, with such extraordinary delicacy – nobility – veneration – & beauty? Surely for the simple reason that we <u>know</u> of the ultimate <u>values</u> & are far beyond merely physical urges – & these physical urges are blind & lead as such to the outrageous excesses we encountered in the symposium, which for us belittle the whole value of this creation for all the pearls it may contain –

Dearest Soul, why do I call you this – why do your eyes shine so wonderfully –

Dearest treasure of my heart, I should be near you this evening – tomorrow I'm coming to you again – I'm tired – yet so glad of heart – good night – Dearest Soul –

You rest against my heart & become quite still –

[Freiburg] 3. I. 16

I haven't got round to writing again until today. In the meantime your memorable letter has come & the 'help'. Many thanks for both.

My question about what you thought of philos. seemed like an assault to you – it was only meant in the dialectical sense, as an approach to the task of somehow bringing experience & knowledge into harmony with one another. What I said about the lack of a foundation was perhaps expressed misleadingly – I did <u>not</u> mean that you lacked the disposition – how could I?

Rather, what I meant was the clarity, the conceptual luminosity, the differences in words & distances of things – your experience was too much <u>just</u> experience for me & perhaps you demand too much of it; 'true experience of God' is a wondrous and rare grace of which one only becomes worthy through suffering, as you have done.

This experience is just as possible for the mystic as for the rational man. Both are extremes; & the intertwining & interpenetration of the two possibilities is the ideal – and this is also a foundation for our inner happiness – for we realize both possibilities yet not in an extreme way, but <u>each with an urge towards the other</u> & this also explains why we can never become superfluous to one another. Never fear that I shall encroach upon the mystical in you in the destructive sense; but I should like to clarify, deepen it.

In my case, as you quite rightly suspect – the path is the opposite one – knowledge, ultimate clear comprehension & interpretation of the meaning, this is what the urge tirelessly pursues – & this urge itself is an innermost experience, which can just detect within itself the refinement & irrational way of the mystical, but always finds it too much of a disruption to pure knowledge, too much of a darkening – this harsh antagonism extends & reaches right into the deepest realms of my spiritual life.

& much as it always strikes asunder what, as the ultimate, I should like to see & experience in glorious luminosity & mystical darkness, it works equally as a spur, prevents creativity from ever coming to rest – & thus, as conflict & disunity, represents maturity & happiness after all, because it is <u>within</u> the antagonism, in the difference, that I first become deeply aware of the coincidentia oppositorum.

Let us thank God that we are people who find life hard to bear – this is no pessimism – but everything great & deep has something of the tragic about it.

Let us be glad, Dearest Soul, that in coming days we shall be able to talk & confide in one another so much – a life of great pain is always a great life & anything that wants to grasp life & reality & the sun must pass through the pain, & every day let us prepare for <u>your</u> & my great long hours of bearing & creating –

Spiritual creation always requires a dying, a gradual dying [of] everything that betokens light & sound & joy & love & happiness & rest – it is always a painful, excruciating loneliness, a casting off of everything changeable; yet this ascent is only ever successful when one has fortified oneself spiritually & one knows that wandering over those bleak heights where the air is thin will not wear us out, but there is always a descent back into the fullness of life, to which one may bring the treasures from the heights. Resting & gathering strength & at the same time dispensing and receiving treasures, this is what I shall find in your wondrous presence – the deepest experi-

ence is what you give to me, in which all antagonism is resolved –
Dearest Soul, <u>you</u> – afterwards I shall light a candle on the tree &
then on an angel's wings the most delicate memory of sacred
moments will come to me & I shall drown in them & give thanks to
you –

And joy will be near me & it will then wander through the mountains to the cabin & at your bedside hover above your brow & the hint
of severity around your mouth will fade away, a blissfully happy smile
will light up your face like the little candle on the tree – you will over-
flow with happiness & a blissfully fervent tremor will glide through
your body & in the most blissful expectation you will feel the yearning well up within you & in the distance behold your most blissful
hour & at the same time you will realize that I've taken you by the
hand to lead you along the mountain paths of pure knowledge – we
shall yearn all our lives and wander & as we yearningly wander we
shall pick the roses by the wayside & where necessary also reach
among the thorns –

Soon you'll be with me again – I'm well.
Your Boy
(I'm sending this with the forces' postal service!)

*Martin was keen to publish his habilitation thesis and when off duty
worked intensively on his lectures. He was unable to meet Elfride
often, and did not want to, for their relationship was to remain a
secret. Martin was afraid that his connection with a Protestant woman
might prove an obstacle to a university career in Freiburg. Even within
Freiburg, their contact was frequently restricted to letters.*

*Elfride was very worried about Martin's health. Fearing he was
overworking, she asked him to avoid tobacco, alcohol and working
too late at night. Martin had the feeling that ideas were 'fermenting'
within him, and the lack of time left by his military duties was a source
of suffering to him. Elfride was on the lookout for an early opportunity to set up home together with Martin. In their letters they dreamt
of their future family life.*

Frbg. 22. I. 16.

I just want to tell you quickly, Dearest Soul, how happy I am – the
snow – I've suddenly turned into a different person, jolted out of the
dust, the constant daily routine – which I have no option but to endure
& do endure – it's turned winter now after all – & I experience all the
pleasures of young days and – you can imagine – what I'd most like
now is to have a snowball fight with you & really let myself go – this
freshness & immediacy that I feel –

what wonderful winters we'll have when the white light of the snow outside shines into our room & we gaze after the swirling flakes in calm joyful peace & happy security – when the stakes of the garden fence carry their heavy bonnets of snow & the titmice fly up to the window & when evening comes quite softly from the mountains, & when our little boy taps at the window with his little fingers & his eyes light up – <u>your</u> dear mountain-lake eyes – in his joy at the twinkle & shimmer of the evening gold – when, trembling, you gently lean your head, quite free now from brooding torment, against my shoulder – & I know that you're in safe hands with me – & that behind me on my desk a great work is maturing towards a great end – this is when the mysterious hour of <u>our</u> happiness will awake –

Much, much love from your happy
                                                    Boy

[Freiburg] 1. II. 16.
I must break off my work, Dearest Soul, and be with you for a few moments. I don't know why I am dreaming of our little house so much these days and all the silent love & joyful happiness – almost as though I were yearning myself away beyond the petty day-to-day routine – I keep having to think over everything it has been given to me to experience this semester, I cannot speak of our primal experience, for me it is something so inexhaustibly rich I cannot think it through – I can only feel elation at it, & how often that happens – almost so I only wish to <u>live</u> at all for moments –

You have given me back my faith in human beings & you have taught me that searchers are grateful for the smallest gift. Dearest Soul – do you have any inkling what powers you have awoken in me?

A life of great worth awaits me, in which I can throw myself fully into my problems & yet you are around me – & vouchsafe me a resting place when I return tired from the distant land of the great questions –

And in your care, you brave creature, I'll gather new strength for the ascent & each time I'll bring you back treasures from my wanderings & your innermost heart shall grow ever richer & <u>more assured</u> & all the two of us will want is to share with glad hands & laughing eyes among those who are searching & want to find their way back from paths that lead astray.

Dearest Soul, the sound of your name does not fully reveal your real being, the deep knowledge you share & your intuition of the great things, your inner power within a great life – when I really feel your spiritual closeness, I want both to create & to revel in all our happiness & thus grow rampant for the finding of truth. –

14

I haven't thanked you yet for your sunny understanding letter from the mountains. I can't do so completely until tomorrow. And I'm as excited as a child at the prospect of those magical moments when I can really be released from all the petty trivialities of life again – and we two lucky things can seize life in its ultimate depths.

I'd so have loved to speak to you after yesterday's seminar – you saw that I heard all <u>your</u> questions & that they proved fruitful, if not for everyone, then at least for those who keep up.

And when the young field surgeon came up to me afterwards & thanked me, I immediately invited him to come to the next few classes; I could see in his eyes how he longed for these ultimate things – & then [he] said to me, this time next week I'll probably be 'out' again. My heart almost stood still as the contrast came home to me in this single moment & all I could do was squeeze the young man's hand. –

Tomorrow we'll talk about many things, fall silent and be glad & happy & become strong once more.

Isn't that right, my child?

I'll come to you at about 7 o'clock. For after the lecture I'd like to rest a little – I'm on leave – & above all I don't want to make you walk all that way home on your own late at night in these troubled times.

Will you prepare a little supper?

Have my bill ready for me too – You see, child, I'm already writing as though we were living in our little house – but there it'll be quite, quite different, this land of happiness is perhaps even beyond the reach of my dreams.

I tremble with joy when I think of it.

I must do a little more work now & when evening next comes I'll be with you, Dearest Soul –

Your happy Boy

Frbg. 10. II. 16

For a moment I must be with you, Dearest Soul, & give thanks to you, just thanks – if I could only hide myself now in a Black Forest cabin & live fully to my inmost being & in my inmost being completely fuse the utterly profound, wonderful, mysterious thing it was given to me to experience with the rhythm of my soul. With your holy sacrifice – for that is what it was, & that's what makes me so small & poor – you brought something deep into my soul, something unattainable – fruitful – a new wellspring of experience has gushed forth & at its waters I'll never quench the holy thirst for the fullness of life, because it is eternal, & because this wellspring only bestows its fullness upon those reprieved by God – though we always live within antagonisms – & yet – I've never felt so restlessly, vibrantly, glowingly and blissfully the absence of antagonisms, the attainment of peace of mind – the capacity for complete and utter rest – of course, I'm just writing words & come nowhere near what is alive in me – but every day I shall come closer to it & interpret this great chaste hour more deeply too, just as I experience it – for I am constantly striving for meaning & am dying from this will to meaning – to philosophy – And how did <u>it all</u> come about, such elegance, delicacy, devotion, reverence – & all things full of beauty & enchantment – Dearest Soul, that I might look on as you dressed, even today I don't know what to make of it, all the ringing & chiming, all the beauty that hovered around your figure as you did so & that floated on into my soul. You must forgive your boy, he won't find it easy – no, he'll never come to terms with these most beautiful, most mysterious experiences of ours – & you have the soul of a woman from whom everything is born full of beauty, so each time everything lights up in fullness – & kills off part of us in daily routine & habit. Thank God, we're rich enough against it. I'd like to talk so much with you about all these holy matters –

Sweet dreams, my Sweetheart – tomorrow I'm coming to you, Dearest Soul –

Your blissfully bewildered
Boy

Frbg. 5. III. 16.

Reading on 'Kunst' by candlelight or
by the birch-tree in the sun . . .

It may perhaps not be entirely clear to you why I so absolutely and necessarily had to promise a letter to you, Dearest Soul, & our dear Friedel –

Perhaps it's that in the last few days my soul has become so full to the brim that it re-gives everything it has found and experienced as a new gift, a good part of a deeply happy & great life certainly consisting in this constant re-giving & re-living & re-savouring & re-creating of gifts – the true <u>quantitas animae</u> of Augustine.

Perhaps it's that by letter-'writing' – the writing of course is just the <u>instrumental</u> part of the action – by experiencing the letter I unchain myself from everything painful, sharp-edged, from everything that has an end & a limit –

that I now have the semester 'behind' me – it <u>is</u> that, but it's not behind me as a burden cast off, as an unpleasant disturbance & interruption in the vacation, as the race of 'professors' is wont to say – I have it <u>within</u> me, truly as a part & force of my soul & its creativity – I have found what I was ultimately looking for & what I was constantly suffering from, the first & the last lecture of the semester have merged into a single reality within me – what before was a barrier, a problem, something dubious, remote, is now immediacy to me, certainty, conviction, liberation –

The urge to work, which, undermined by a nagging scepticism, I had to hold back within me & in the holding-back of which I consciously & knowingly had to consign my inmost intent to the grave – this urge is freely flowing & flooding through me

today I know that there <u>can</u> be a philosophy of vibrant life [*des lebendigen Lebens*] – that I <u>can</u> declare war on rationalism right through to the bitter end – without falling victim to the anathema of unscientific thought – I <u>can</u> – I <u>must</u> – & so I'm today faced by the necessity of the problem: how is philosophy to be produced as living truth & as a creation of the personality valuably & powerfully.

The Kantian question is not only <u>wrongly</u> put – it fails to capture the problem; this is much richer & deeper.

We must not give our young heroes stones instead of bread when they come back hungry from the battlefield, not unreal & dead categories, not shadowy forms & bloodless compartments in which to keep a life ground down by rationalism neat and tidy and let it moulder away –

The philosopher always suffers from life, because the questionableness of life is real in him – but when he takes pleasure in something, this pleasure is richer & more overflowing than anywhere else, because it draws its fullness & fineness from the ultimate depths of one's interpretation of life.

Life had come to me – & being allowed to accompany you two fresh-sunny creatures on your climbing expedition lit up this life for me – there was a chiming & singing in me, all the hidden sources of delightful experience burst open – all because I bear the semester within me – thus was it possible for your end of semester to become a silent joy for me.

Now I take this little joy around with me like a little boy with his new picture book: dwarves and elves, Snow White & Mrs Holle & Rübezahl[3] & all the delights of sunny childhood, but I take deep pleasure when I see before me that I have a living philosophy to be lived – & it is no coincidence that yesterday I worked out & wrote down my theory of consciousness so felicitously, purely intuitively –

On your dear friend I congratulate you – you said as well I was to take a good look at our Friedel – I've already seen into her soul – a living poem; to complete the picture all that was missing was the – guitar.

---

[3] Mrs Holle is a figure in the Grimms' tale by the same name. Rübezahl is the spirit of the Sudeten Mountains.

My Dearest Soul & a living poem somewhere in the Black Forest mountains – I can only be overcome with joy –

Do write & you <u>must</u> get a snapshot of the two of you taken as a souvenir of the W.S. [winter semester] 1916 [1915/ prefixed by Elfride].

Kind regards, your Boy & Friedel's friend.

Many thanks, child, for the flowers on my desk & the sweet things.

This evening I'm going to see Krebs – even though he hasn't replied.

'Kunst' was the name given to the bench around a tiled stove. Friedel Lieber was a friend from Elfride's youth. Her father, a parish priest, had taught Elfride Latin when she was studying in Kassel for her school leaving exam in 1915. First as a guest and subsequently as a member of the Cabin Guild, Friedel often went and stayed at the Silberberg cabin with Elfride. Every day the postman would bring the mail to the cabin, coming on skis if snow had fallen.

Engelbert Krebs was a Catholic priest and member of the Catholic Faculty, who had been a friend of Martin's since 1913.

On 6 March, Martin wrote a letter to Elfride's father to ask for her hand in marriage. The engagement was not official. For Martin's parents, a Protestant daughter-in-law was inconceivable.

In the vacation, Elfride travelled to Wiesbaden to visit her mother, who was concerned about Martin's uncertain financial prospects. Elfride paid frequent visits to the Liebers' parish house, which she greatly admired for its refinement and took as a model for her own future household. She helped out in the day-home for schoolchildren that she had herself helped establish in the winter of 1914/15 as part of her work for the National Women's Service. These day-homes were urgently needed for looking after the many children whose mothers were forced to work as a consequence of the war.

Elfride tried to learn Greek, Martin's favourite language, and continue her studies of philosophy. Her parents, who at this point were very kindly disposed towards the engagement, were keen to meet Martin and invited him to Wiesbaden for Easter. First, however, he visited his own parents in Messkirch. On 3 April he wrote: I now also realize the reason for my parents' silence – they still haven't got over the fact that we're of different denominations; but you mustn't be dismayed about this – it's just that my parents have their own thoughts about these things & you needn't worry that I won't get matters under control calmly & amicably, even though there is no little resistance – I wasn't actually expecting it at all, because of course I myself see everything from other points of view. But now you must obey me & not suffer or be afraid about this episode.

Yet Elfride also received other post from Messkirch:

Messkirch, 5. IV. 16.

Could it be the living closeness, the fresh scent of your figure, the lost happiness of being able to find rest within your eyes, being able to throw oneself into your arms, in order then to live <u>within life</u> & cast off the gruelling world of objects –

Is it the wonderful stillness here – or because it's Wednesday – that I am so strangely restfully restless & can feel the mysterious happiness follow me along all the paths I take – Or is it weighing on me like a cruel deprivation that for weeks now I haven't been able to lay my hand on your brow, haven't been able to say 'Dearest Soul' – haven't experienced such little lovely things as a supper with you, by candlelight, with flowers, you in your smart dress, happiness in our eyes, full of delightful joy, the restrained glow of our souls, pulsating with the expectantly glowing timidity of beauty, the completion of life – child, what harmony of life you have or rather <u>are</u>, a <u>Real</u> figure – a part of the stream of life that is not incessantly splintered & destroyed by conceptual lacerations – my beginning is Titanic & it ends in concepts – the world falls from my trembling hands, cold, unexpressive, unimpressive, a piece of lava growing cold, & within me I feel the bubbling & welling up of the fiery, surging energies –

you artist of my self, dispelling homesickness – I am straining my powers of imagination to have your image alive before me – it is just an 'image', remains just an image – I'd like to force it inside me, recast it into my ownmost existence, not the image, you yourself, or are <u>you</u> that most sacred vessel into which I am sinking, into which <u>we</u> are sinking, or again are these all just aims; if the teleological in its givenness is at the same time already taken from us, does it then just for ever <u>flee</u> before us as we go along?

And yet my memory tells me that once, or more often, all these rifts were no more; that all the darkness turned into bright daylight – & all the streaming flux into a calm as deep as a mountain lake & all the tired struggling into an unshackled blissful floating – when you presented me with abundance, fullness & beauty in a golden bowl –

And today all I have left is memory – longing – & energy, & deep thankfulness, to you my Dearest Soul –

For two days now I've had a quite terrible headache above each temple; it's a complete mystery to me how I came by this affliction. Perhaps with the calm now an adverse reaction. But do not worry –

about your Boy, who actually just wants to send you his love with this long-winded letter. Do you have a picture of your room?

On 6 April Martin wrote: I know, Sweetheart, that in your case it's not egoism but caring love when you press for the marriage to be soon – you must bear with me. [. . .] Like you, I only intended to broach the

19

question of confession in the context of other great problems that will always preoccupy us. I don't believe for a minute that we differ from one another in any way, because we have found one another in our innermost & deepest hearts & so we'll also find harmony over secondary questions.

Martin's visit to Wiesbaden did not take place. He evidently shrank back from the encounter as a result of the resistance from his parents. Elfride's parents took umbrage at this and forbade their daughter further contact with Martin. Yet she stood by her fiancé.

Freiburg, 26. IV. 16

My Dearest Soul, I thank you from the bottom of my heart – let me find rest in your divine nature –

Providence is everything & the greatest of all is that I have you.

Come – & I can be happy

Your Boy

The situation was not easy for the secretly engaged couple. Martin found it difficult to stand by Elfride in the company of his friends and acquaintances and at the university.
He was hoping to be given a lectureship at least.

Frbg. 13. VI. 16.

Now I'm the one who's happy, my Dearest Soul, because you are so happy – you ask why I was so communicative. Well, because I still had the sun in my heart from our hours together, because I was fresh, & because I'd had a success. This consisted in my discovery of a fundamental problem with the theory of the Categories – the solution comes of its own accord, in research it's always the way of posing the problem that is decisive – as to where the white hair comes from, I know nothing of that, I think it just 'happens'. At any rate I wasn't worrying enough for that to be the cause of it. I'm also pleased to have this week to do my work & have some peace & quiet. The fact that in your circle I of course find a response to my problems contributes to my liveliness. – I don't know whether I've already told you what I announced for the winter: Aristotle & Scholasticism.

If conditions remain as they were, I'll lecture on this, because it's less work for me – if I'm freer, I give a systematic lecture.

If you stay here, then perhaps I'll come & see you on Thursday evening & we'll go for the walk on Saturday. The last hours we spent together were so wonderful that everything is still present in my mind & to me your poem is a deep legacy of your great love –

Somewhere spring waters rush
Dreamily into the night –
Somewhere a girl has daydreamt
Away the hours of light –
Somewhere a soul searches,
Among beech trunks and birches –
Somewhere that soul finds,
Drunk with God, the world left far behind.

May 1916   Kind regards,
                                        Your Boy –

                                                        Frbg. 18. VI. 16
My Dearest Soul!
I don't know what suddenly made you so sad – at any rate I'm to blame for it & do apologize most sincerely – actually I wasn't at all prepared for talking about the things you wanted clarified, as I'd been working all afternoon on Hegel, who in the end did get an opinion out of me, but in quite a different context.

    Do not be angry with me, I'll see to it that I can clarify things tomorrow.

    I'll come to you after 6 for supper. On the way into town I'm meeting Ochsner, who's back, whereas my friend [Laslowski] is staying on – how much longer is uncertain.

    Much love from your Boy.

Heinrich Ochsner, though a student of Catholic theology and philosophy, was on friendly terms with Elfride. Ernst Laslowski, by contrast, evidently disapproved of Elfride.

                                                        Freibg. 1. VII. 16.
I only have one request, believe in me, in every last part of me, & forgive me, there's no ill will anywhere – & you probably saw more than would have happened if you'd been impartial. This morning, before I had your letter, I spoke with Ochsner about the discussion you'd had together & came to the conclusion that in the last few years my friend has gone down paths that are completely foreign to me, that he's long since ceased to keep pace with my philos. development. At present I am neither able nor willing to argue the matter out

with him – I want to keep such things at a distance from me & am positively yearning for the days when I can bury myself in my work. It's perhaps my bane that I have a philosophical gift which when activated makes everything else sink away & I neglect my personal concerns, treat them as irrelevant. I must not saddle myself so much with relations to all sorts of people – these days I've often unconsciously dreamt of our little house, where I shall produce my life's work within your great understanding. But first I must still wait patiently, & categorically keep at a distance the bustle into which I let myself be dragged & which is perhaps suitable for historians.

Once again I beg you, my dearest, believe my innermost heart & my love for you – but don't ask me now to remember everything – otherwise I might suffer a decisive check in my creativity, forced as it is – let me at least bring to a close the semester, which of course increases in difficulty with every lecture even as my energy is flagging. Do it for the sake of the task to which I'm bound, and afterwards we'll sort everything out. I beg you, my Dearest Soul, think of me as a man struggling, who also experiences the antagonisms between speculation & everyday life – in a metaphysical sense I suppose I may have a maturity & assurance whereas I completely lack this in natural life precisely on account of my highly speculative attitude – perhaps because I've never lived, associated, exchanged ideas with people a great deal. –

Rickert wrote me a letter today which I'll bring tomorrow. I'll turn down my talk to the girl students. The 'celebration' speech I'll just have to obey orders and give, it'll be the first & last one.

I don't yet know whether I'll be able to give the seminar next Monday –

All these experiences, the toing and froing of plans, news, controversies make what is best in me die.

I'll be with you tomorrow afternoon around 4 o'clock.

Regards, your Boy full of contradictions

Martin was due to give a speech to celebrate the birthday of Grand Duke Frederick II of Baden on 9 July.
Martin had successfully presented his habilitation thesis in 1915 under Heinrich Rickert at Freiburg. In December that year, Rickert was appointed as a full professor in Heidelberg.

Freibg. 4. VII. 16.

Deepest thanks, my Dearest Soul, for your kind letter. Unconsciously I did celebrate your birthday so dearly & deeply that we should be glad – and my dearest gift to you is my love & veneration, the peace and unity I find in you. Indeed, you've shown me such a deeply serious conception of your great vocation that I can say no more on the matter: just the one thing, which must keep the joy, happiness & spirit alive in you, which is that I have deeply bound you to me in my soul, so as not to return to you each time anew, even from the furthest & most abstract heights – for all ascending to the heights is distance, separation, antagonism – & all comprehending, all living in the 'concept' is at the expense of the rich immediacy of innermost experience tangible now – every 'concept' has its limit, must have it, if it wants to 'grasp'[4] – to touch – & all contact is already the beginning of destruction – of inner contradiction.

I kiss your brow to thank you for our time together on the eve of your birthday. I have calmed down & will take the weeks through to the end of semester in my stride. Afterwards I'm determined to get down to printing my habilitation thesis, with which you are to help me.

This week it will hardly be possible for me to come, perhaps on Sunday – or the beginning of next week.

The cake was very good & Friedel's rose, which <u>you</u> gave me, brings me joy.

I'd like to write to Friedel some time this semester after all – please let me know her address.

With deepest love,

Your

happy

Boy

In August, Elfride and Martin spent a happy holiday together on the island of Reichenau on Lake Constance and made their engagement official. A friend of Elfride's, Gertrud Mondorf, accompanied them as a chaperone. Elfride, who loved family heirlooms, was given her grandparents' gold wedding rings by her mother. During a boat trip on Lake Constance, Martin's ring slipped from his finger and was lost in the water. A new ring had to be bought. It was engraved with the words 'Seelchen 1915 Bodensee 1916' ('Dearest Soul 1915 Lake Constance 1916').

Martin's poem 'Evening walk on Reichenau' was written during this trip. It was published for the first time in a slightly different form in the book Bodenseebuch 1917.

In September Elfride went to visit her mother in Wiesbaden. There followed a lively exchange of letters and parcels between Wiesbaden

---

[4] Heidegger here plays on the German words *begreifen* ('to comprehend') and *Begriff* ('concept'), which – minus the prefix *be-* – denote 'grasping' in a more literal or physical sense.

Evening walk on Reichenau.
Seawards flows a silver radiance to distant dark shores, and like a muted word
of love night falls in the summer-weary gardens, damp with evening. And one
last bird-call from the old tower roof is caught among moon-white gables – and
what the bright summer's day brought me lies heavy with fruit – ever a
transcendent freight – in the grey desert of a great simplicity.
12. August. 16.

and Freiburg. Food supplies in Germany were becoming increasingly scarce, so Elfride found it more difficult to provide for her 'Boy'. She also kept up correspondence with friends from her youth and student days who were involved in the war, providing them too with parcels. The manuscript of Martin's habilitation thesis on 'Duns Scotus's Doctrine of Categories and Meaning' had to be proofread before going to press with the publisher J. C. B. Mohr (Paul Siebeck). At the request of Heinrich Finke and with the help of an official recommendation from Edmund Husserl, Martin was awarded a grant for the sum of 400 German marks in view of the high printing costs.

On 26 September it was Martin's birthday.

Freibg. 27. IX. 16.

My Dearest Soul,

First a birthday kiss to thank you for all the lovely things you have lavished on me – the little picture of you is wonderful & is now in distinguished company – I've taken Privatdozent Lotze down from the wall & put him on my desk – next to him Dearest Soul looks over to greet me – the Reichenau picture is a particular delight to me – when I've done enough work I sit down in front of it – & dream – only I've not yet worked out for sure who drew it – & I shan't even mention all the sweet and fine things – I'll write to say thank you for Mother's excellent birthday cake separately.

Your letter delighted me most of all – because it's so utterly free & unencumbered by gloomy things, because you share my pleasure in my work & you have every right to do so – over the last few weeks you've done me a great service with the proofreading <u>& the comments</u> almost all of which I was able to comply with. You will always be my dear, understanding helper with a fine feeling for these things. I need this all the more because my work is of greatest interest to me & gives me a quite curious pleasure only during the creative process itself, in other words when I'm not yet writing. The writing itself I find laborious, because I constantly see the distance between what is to be formulated & the final formula, & because this never seems succinct enough. The 'conclusion', for the pleasing & rapid completion of which I also thank you especially, actually is concise & nonetheless it still lacks that classical serenity – but I'll probably never attain that because I keep on seeing the other side of things.

Certainly I've made 'leaps', but in fact only back to myself. I've returned to the position I had in mind in my earliest semesters – but which I repressed because everything was still too unclear in my mind & without the conceptual means in full sharpness – and perhaps I'd have gone on for a very long time struggling to prime these &

held myself back from facing the great things. Now I've found the courage to do so through you & my first two semesters as a university teacher. – You can imagine how urgently I'm looking forward to the winter, when I'll really be able to throw myself into my work on these problems. The Lotze seminar will also serve as a commemoration of the 100th anniversary of his birth (17 [21] May 1917).

I've just received the final page proofs from the printer's; I don't think we should change anything more except misprints that obscure the meaning & punctuation, should there be any that require correction. I think the book will be quite nice as it is. Read everything carefully once again & send the proofs straight to Siebeck.

A few days ago Father wrote a letter to thank me sincerely for the offprint & enclosed a valuable document – the first picture you drew of him when you were a child – I shall keep it in a safe place. I've just received a card congratulating me on the lectureship. –

Forgive me for forgetting the thing about the index – I also think it's better to separate the subject index from the index of names, a hotchpotch of the two wouldn't work so well [. . .]

By the way, up to the eighth year Ochsner went to a middle school & his grasp of <u>Greek</u> & Latin is shaky too.

Friedel congratulated me very nicely as well & told me that [her brother] Karl is pretty sure to come to Freiburg. –

The other day I met Finke in the library – he was very eager to learn – surely he'll soon realize that he isn't dealing with a student any more.

My letter is a muddle – I'm living too deeply in my problems & so I always forget the half of it. Though times are getting ever more oppressive – & one almost oughtn't to be happy any more with all this misery – we're looking forward to winter with the joy that great tasks arouse. – Tell little Ursula to be good – & you mustn't forget the boys – I wonder if they're 'little blackamoors' too?!

I intend to solve the problem of my coming in October. On the 1st we [the postal supervision centre] are moving yet again, this time into Wagner's printing works in Bertholdstr. – we're getting a very bright & cheerful room. On 5 Oct. Bühler's coming & then I'll be able to leave on the 9th or 10th, at any rate I'd like to come in the first half of Oct. so afterwards I can keep on working. Lectures are beginning in general after 1 November, I suppose. If I've forgotten a few things now, you'll have to remind me in your next letter. My work is progressing at a good pace.

This evening I'll come to you & then we'll talk of great things & be glad about the small ones & be happy.

With deepest love, my Dearest Soul,
Your Boy.

P.S. I think the book will be out by the beginning of the semester. The main part of the work is now done.

From 7 to 10 October Martin was on leave, and he finally took the opportunity to pay his first visit to Wiesbaden, where he let Elfride and her mother spoil him. Elfride's father was otherwise engaged in his capacity as a colonel in Borna, near Leipzig.

Freiburg 11. X. 16.

Your Boy, Dearest Soul, is safely home again – so you are relieved of that worry. I still have to assimilate many new & above all very pleasant impressions, which of course does no harm to my newly regained freshness. – I thank you once again with all my heart, my dearest – you managed everything with such foresight & understanding – you have grasped quite intuitively the art of providing me with successful rest & recovery in a short time – it could not be otherwise; for your great & understanding love gives your inner heart second sight. And you can well imagine what your love – quite apart from the ultimately personal values – means to me for my inner life of creation & the inner surmounting of problems. What is it other than this ideal of fullness that makes us so expectant about this winter – let innermost personal life & great dedication to eternal goals sprout up from a single root & flow together in an ultimate life-purpose – beat together like flames. I'm absolutely bubbling over & am glad when I can read so as to release my inner urgency. And the very fact that in this, my first systematic course of lectures I must leave so much open & problematic & nonetheless have an intuitive grasp of the ultimate foundations & aims gives the whole task an initial momentum. – There's said to have been a meeting yesterday, – so it is going to be a two-hour lectureship – which is what I prefer; even without service 4 hours would have been hectic. – My poem for the Lake Constance book has been accepted – the whole print-run is already printed for 8 sheets of the Scotus book – Geyser wanted to visit me on Sunday. I met him today – looks like a Chinaman, inordinately conceited, implacably one-sided, thinks Windelb[and]. & Rickert are nonsense, Husserl absolutely unoriginal – value philosophy – in short a narrow-minded pedant who goes around peddling his second-hand, cramped textbook philosophy & almost makes me feel sorry for him – is looking for a flat with 11 rooms & can't find one, is depressed because fewer students attend his lectures here – so a good sign for the Faculty – I'm not having Ochsner doing his doctorate with him –

I, by contrast, feel light of heart in my little room & before your dr. picture. –

Now I want to work a little more. Then I'll come to you again &
kiss your dear eyes & be glad.

Regards to the little house & everyone in it. With deep love, Dearest
Soul,

Your

Boy.

*Martin had hoped for the chair of Catholic philosophy at Freiburg,
which had been vacant for two years, but his hopes were dashed with
the appointment of Joseph Geyser, 20 years his senior. For the time
being, this put an end to all talk of a wedding, for Martin's professional prospects were too uncertain. At the end of October Elfride
visited Freiburg again with her friend Friedel, with whom she stayed
in Tivolistrasse.*

*By now the war had reached even Freiburg, with air engagements
taking place above the city's houses. Martin still had to serve in the
postal supervision centre. Supplies became even scarcer, and there
were no prospects of an end to the war, let alone a German victory.*

On 18 October Martin wrote: The jewification of our culture &
universities is certainly horrifying & I think the German race really
should summon up the inner strength to find its feet again. The question of capital though! *Elfride maintained an anti-Semitic outlook all
her life, although this had no bearing on her friendships.*

1917

Friedel was Elfride's best friend. Friedel's brother Karl and his wife Gertrud were now also part of the circle of friends in Freiburg.

In this, the last letter that Martin wrote to Elfride before the wedding, he once again emphasized what letter-writing meant to him.

Freiburg, 12 March 17

My Dearest Soul!

I must thank you with all my heart for your letter. Why does a letter from you always have such a lasting effect upon me & as it were release something in my soul? Today, when I read it through often enough, it was to become clear to me – there's something absolute about the letters between you & me – as long as we still don't truly possess the real conditions for an unrestricted life spent hour by hour in living closeness.

The letter is a form of communion of the soul-spirit – one that is faded & yet unimpeded, complete. To me your letters are always a symbol of our real life in our own house – that life-long togetherness freely and actively shaped from the ultimate depths of our ownmost personal being.

You find within yourself as a woman a limit – with respect to me – but only because I myself have a limit with respect to your own Self, so venerable to me.

And after my lectures in our small circle, from my far-reaching lone-liness I inwardly cried out for your truly living, calm presence –

I couldn't say in front of other people what my request for a 'discussion' ultimately meant – I'd have liked to rest against your heart & gaze into the calm and calming starlit clarity of your eyes. I found it difficult to go home instead of staying quietly with you & letting my

29

hands rest contentedly in yours. And you probably suspected as much too – but custom & circumstances – which up to now have mainly curbed our real life, admonished me to go.

All this I had to bear, simply because my 'innermost being' is a living unity with the individuality of my soul as such – without this unity, personal life & the unity of souls in love would be a harrowing tragedy destined never to be overcome. And for you, my love, it would be a constant sacrifice, and a great one at that on account of its goal. But let it be happiness, albeit not in the popular sense, but the happiness that grows up out of depths & is not just passively accepted.

And you know: the quiet ways of your working within our marriage, your womanly existence within the most immediate reality of my creativity, your motherly mission within our metaphysical destiny, these are powers in my existence that cannot now be lost & the living background to our love in its working & living – they are the metaphysical-historical element of our life's unity. –

And what God decrees is well done. The two of us would have been strong enough to live together with K[arl]. & G[ertrud Lieber]. – but perhaps for this very reason we'd have suffered more silently & more deeply – not for bourgeois reasons – but spiritual-metaphysical ones. However kind & nice Fr[iedel]. is about me, she's foreign to me in what is decisive – however animatedly one can talk with G[ertrud]., she lacks what is intuitive-great – however friendly K[arl]. appears, to me he comes across as empty & clumsy (in inwardly spiritual terms) – however experienced & understanding O[chsner]. appears, he distinctly lacks that activity, that spiritual ruthlessness, that strength –

Why, all the connections that come with this little club are such that I could jettison them at any moment without feeling deprived in the innermost life of my soul –

There is a gulf separating them from the spiritual sphere of influence that <u>your love</u> means to me – not that this necessarily has its effect exclusively in what is only spiritual, problematic, in a concern with my own most personal work, in the capacity to empathize with the temporary & constant tensions & complications – no, but because in you, my love, in the most childlike look of your eyes & the truest kiss, in the most motherly admonition & in the most womanly request your whole soul leaves a living impression upon me – because you are mine – & I am yours – because coming from God in an individual creative oneness we belong to Him – we also require an actual reality of our own – an unrestrained being-for-ourselves.

And the 'security' of our own unitary metaphysical reality is not abstractly teleological, but <u>spiritually historical</u> & thus the first as well, only in the aliveness of deed & experience, i.e. life in wholeness, depth, goodness, <u>love</u>.

For the most part we think of life, even the deeper life we would attain, too statically – according to schemata, instead of in its historical uniqueness and fullness – Not only does it mean a realization of meaning in general, but in its uniqueness & shapeability from within an individual centre there also lies an original special value; & for this very reason dispositions & inner powers are bestowed upon us, which enter our life more intensely & more richly each day.

As soon as the various & manifoldly valued connections within such a life are felt & directed within their central unification & then again in their emanation, the rich security will be there that may be considered strong enough for the proximity of the absolute.

This innermost growing-upward brings with it a noble humility before everything spiritual & every creation only enhances the possibility of an intensification of value – inner upheavals no longer turn into catastrophes – but their otherwise unrestrained violence gathers itself together to form positive impulses & new approaches.

Life within such a structure must have an inner relation to the history of spirit & the soul – an inner one, i.e. a free one, which can always choose the breadth & decisiveness of a standpoint that vanquishes.

And the extent of such choices is determined by the metaphysical vocation of the individual personality – is <u>grace</u>. The metaphysical vocation protects one from falling back into the value-indifferent sphere of merely being driven & overwhelmed within the realization of life. It relieves one from the pressure of merely natural being

May the Lord protect us, i.e. preserve us in this vocation – in faithfulness to ourselves – the pledge of our strong, ardent love and cheerful joy.

When you feel overcome with happiness, my Dearest Soul, I kiss you

with heartfelt love & devotion,
Your Boy

On 20 March, Elfride and Martin were married in a registry office. The next day Martin's friend Engelbert Krebs performed the simple, Catholic war-time wedding ceremony in the University chapel in Freiburg Minster, though the wedding celebrations did not take place until after the Revd. Lieber had also married the couple in a Protestant service on 25 March in Wiesbaden. Elfride's mother laid on a reception, which unfortunately could not be attended by the bride's father, who had to remain on duty in Borna. Elfride's half-sister, Else Presting, went to the reception with her 6-year-old daughter Elfridchen, the bride's goddaughter, who was allowed to scatter flowers.

Wedding morning, 1917

The newly married couple moved into two furnished rooms in Karlstrasse. Every day they had lunch in the local Kolping House.

Martin's parents tried to come to terms with the 'mixed marriage'. They sent food parcels and kept in contact with the young couple by letter.

Elfride made constant visits to her beloved Black Forest and enjoyed cabin life on the Silberberg. The war had by now turned into a world war.

As yet, Martin had not had any close contact with Edmund Husserl, who in March 1916 had been appointed as the successor to Heinrich Rickert's chair at Freiburg.

Freibg. Whit Sunday 1917

My Dearest Soul!
Out of the valley come best wishes to you from your Boy. A symbol too. I can't find a way up into <u>my</u> mountains; I only have the 'point of

32

approach' & <u>that</u> now in its most fully problematic nature. It would give a false idea of philos. creativity if I were to characterize this condition, which has already lasted several weeks, simply as a waiting – it is partly the highest activity of feeling one's way – approaching things, putting them in perspective. That I got to see Husserl is just one episode in a process that comes to me largely out of the darkness & leads on into the darkness. I said once this winter that setting limits to cognition was absurd, but rather cognition should be pursued as deeply as possible. For those who have persuaded themselves that there are limits to cognition, their house is built & all further work a not partic. difficult matter of minor repairs to the inside. In the other situation of positing the ideal, there arises a double possibility: on the one hand simply to deny limits absolutely in this sense & then, unworried by problems, set about cognizing & solving everything – or on the other to set the limits as fluid ones & see the crucial achievement precisely in shifting & destroying them, one might call this 'standpt.' optimistic irrationalism.

I cannot accept Husserl's phen[omenology]. as a final position even if it joins up with philos. – because in its approach & accordingly in its goal it is too narrow & bloodless & because such an approach cannot be made absolute. Life is too rich & too great – thus for relativities that seek to come close to its meaning (that of the absolute) in the form of philos. systems, it's a question of discovering the liberating <u>path</u> in an absolute articulation of relativity. Anyone who is <u>only</u> a logician is thus confronted with a fundamental absurdity – but the logician, standing on the insulating stool, is a great helplessness in philos. At the beginning of his philosophizing, Hegel wrote the well-known essay 'Difference between the Fichtean & Schellingian Systems of Philosophy'. The implacable necessity of a comparable engagement cannot be evaded today, though the setting of the problem is a completely different one & more complicated; the difference between phenomenology & value philosophy. And in fact as a <u>critique</u> in principle, which overcomes in principle, not merely with respect to parts & elements, & becomes <u>positive</u>. Since I've been lecturing, up to now I've constantly experienced these sudden reversals – until 'historical man' came to me in a flash this winter.

But now the bare idea is all I have left, due to the ever sharper criticism.

The objective criticism of system & the self-criticism & the attitude thus produced have largely dominated my thought over the last few months – until I now came to the fundamental realization of their necessity. In addition to this, I've overcome the tendency to overhastiness & can thus engage myself with full critical force unhindered & not driven.

This is why I've been so unproductive over all the last few weeks & haven't got involved in conversations & points of view either. I myself have suffered from it for you, my love, though on the other hand I know you to be strong enough to be able to bear such a period of growth. Through it I've acquired great assurance in the approach & continuation of my next work & every day I'm grateful to you for this great creative opportunity, without explicitly telling you so. The military service hinders me in the actual implementation of this critical work – but unmolested by it I enter ever more confidently into the real frame of mind, which is indeed an unconditional requirement for philosophy. This service remains a hindrance to my personal life at any rate, undeniable though it is that this relatively small sacrifice simply must be made.

And you'll have certainly seen by now that – even when I've been at <u>my</u> work the whole day long – I do keep inwardly more cheerful & relaxed & can really participate in the joy that springs from our silent happiness.

Since you've been wholly mine 'outwardly' as well, life – I mean here in the immediately daily & not unimportant things – has become rounded for me; i.e. I now possess <u>with great assurance</u> the soaring ranges of the soul – & there is such a great wealth of spiritual value inherent in this that I can be grateful to you every day.

A marriage based on bourgeois infatuation must be an abomination – equally incomprehensible to me is the so-called marriage of convenience. I don't yet know what real love in its plenitude means, but I am certain that we both carry it with us. And this is why I'm looking forward to us really being something in our house to our children & – in a broader sense then – to the young people at university & raising them into a spiritual community, the 'invisible church'. I should like to think that mysticisms & the ideas of secret societies will be kept completely at bay – ; if you remember Sohm's concept of the Church you'll know what I mean. –

Fräulein Giesert, our house philosopher, said this morning: 'Isn't it right, Dr Heidegger, you're happy when you can work all on your own for days on end & that's part of your nature just the way Frau Heidegger beams at the very thought of getting out into nature to be with the flowers.' And as she talked she was preparing my mid-morning snack, which true to form I went & forgot. On my way, at Schneck's, I remembered & I realized how much you always care in the smallest things.

Fortunately, we were out by ½ past 11, so I could have an early lunch. It was paltry & poor. But I've just had the roll & will have enough to eat all right. Yesterday I was with Karli [Lieber] at the 'bench', we had a nice chat & I'm looking forward to this evening (Bach!).

Dr [?], Prof. Bühler, the painter Bissier and Martin, Luisenhöhe, May 1917

Mother's parcel came yesterday morning; I gave Karli the letter to take with him. Cheese is taken care of.

[Brother] Fritz has written, he sends his best regards. No news otherwise. There's increasing talk of finding & not without documents. The little picture comes from the Luisenhöhe.

I slept well & woke up in good time. I'm looking forward to tomorrow.

You must have a quite wonderful time up there – bring me back plenty of sun & the radiant splendour of flowers & openness of the soul.

I think of you a great, great deal, my Dearest Soul, & send many affectionate kisses to you in the mountains & am looking forward to your letter.

Wholly your happy Boy.

Kind regards to Friedel & enjoy yourselves.

pto

I am also sending you the little article by Ri[ckert]. Please consider it carefully.

From it you can gauge the spirit that lives in our school & how Rickert behaves in comparison to Pfeilschifter's depiction.

On 7 July Martin was a day-guest at the guild cabin for the first and

35

only time. For Elfride too it was the last time, as from the winter semester on she was called up for compulsory service, could no longer continue her studies and thus forfeited her membership.

At the beginning of August Elfride and her friend Friedel Lieber attended a meeting of the Freideutscher Bund *(the 'Free German Association') on the Lorelei. They crossed the River Rhine at night in a small boat and slept at an inn. Elfride sympathized with the ideals of the* Wandervogel *movement, their ideas on reforming modern life and their advocacy of rambling, healthy food, abstinence from nicotine and alcohol, and the wearing of 'reform' clothes.*

Afterwards, Martin and Elfride together went to visit his parents in Messkirch. Elfride was introduced to a great number of relatives from both his mother's and his father's side of the family and on excursions with Martin became acquainted with his home region. A completely new experience for Martin was their long rambling expeditions, which he learnt to love through Elfride.

After the summer holidays, Elfride had to work as a teacher, for Freiburg was short of roughly 100 teachers as a result of military service, whereas the number of pupils remained the same. Initially she was at a boys' elementary school; then she taught French and Protestant religious instruction at the girls' high school on the Holzmarktplatz. Elfride's salary as a teacher improved their financial situation. Martin's income from his two-hour lectureship and his service pay were low. Elfride found the teaching a strain: the classes were large, and she lacked the teaching experience to fall back on.

It became increasingly difficult and time-consuming for Elfride to get hold of food, clothes, linen and fuel for heating, even though, as was then customary, she did have a domestic help.

In the autumn she finally found an attic flat at Lerchenstrasse 8, which they furnished with inherited furniture and using Elfride's dowry. The flat was three floors up, but was quiet and sunny.

Around the couple a circle of friends, the Klübchen, *or 'Little Club', had formed, cultivated in particular by Elfride. Martin enjoyed the attentions of the young female students who were on friendly terms with Elfride.*

1918

In February 1918, Martin was enlisted in the Karl Barracks, but he was able to sleep at home. A further medical examination declared him fit for active service, and on 11 March he reported for duty as a Landsturm recruit at the army training centre at Heuberg. Martin initially saw being a soldier as an adventure, but before long he found it hard living together in a confined space with his comrades. He had little time to himself, could only write cards and longed for post from Elfride to arrive. On 16 March, Martin finally received a 'succinct' telegram from his wife.

Heuberg, Sunday 17. III. 18.

My Dearest Soul!

It's just the time of afternoon when we have our 'little cup of tea' together – & all my thoughts are with you in the sunny study. Today a particularly beautiful ray of sunshine came my way: your first letter! Of course, I never doubted that you'd soon send me such a nice message. But all week long I waited in vain for my name at the post distribution point. Gradually I became uneasy & when I retired in the evening I kept going over & over it in my mind. And then all of a sudden your telegram. I can only assume you also get my post this late – it really is a dreadfully sluggish business. From the cards & letter of mine that have arrived by now you'll see we had the same thoughts with respect to health & later life. Only the day before yesterday it snowed & the battalion had an interesting night-time exercise in the snow – today it's quite hard, deep blue sky, glorious sunshine & the air, quite wonderful, Mother couldn't get over it just now, even though she knows the climate. Next Sunday now it's our wedding anniversary & the first day of spring – I'm looking forward to it like a child – & I think now of all the love you've given me over the year & I want to work on constantly improving myself so I really deserve it all. –

I was of course pleased about Mother & [sister] Marie's visit – how they marvelled at their strapping soldier & the way he looked – Mother has the old freshness & vigour, looks good – Marie is somewhat troubled – yet does take the matter more lightly now – then we spoke about it – it was so kind how they brought food all that way with them – butter, bacon, egg dainties – unfortunately they had to be off again just now, as they have a journey of 4½ hours home. We wrote you a card; I told them a lot about you & Mother asked me the way she does if you'd really liked it at our house & if you wanted to come again & if the bed had been alright as well. I reassured her fully & asked her to send us butter & milk even if the former is rather expensive. They'll also take care of the eggs.

Our Fritz is very well, at the moment they're at a quiet spot. –

Father, they said, had been quietly waiting every day in case something came from Berlin (re Marburg) – it's moving how pleased the man is & I'm relieved to be able to ease some of the worries my parents had on my account during my student days.

My love, I carry the snowdrop around with me in my ammunition pouch so that it always beams a cheerful greeting to me whenever I'm anywhere on duty – lying in the woods as a gunner or going along a bright country road between the brown fields singing the stirring marching songs with my comrades. Recently we returned home to the accompaniment of music – how it entered our tired bones, a positively blissful feeling. – I've handed over the forged text, the captn was very pleased with it & said thank you – he'll report the matter to the battal. & take it from there. The officers treat me extremely kindly – the batt. commanding officer Baron v. Villiez himself talked with me for quite a long time. He said it was very much to my credit that I was joining in with army service in these surroundings & finding my feet. I already have to do squad leader duty (i.e. as corporal). Physically I feel splendid – today I've a bit of a cold, but it's already passing. We're leaving early on Friday.

With much love, my dear,
                    Your radiant Boy.
    I've also written to Trudchen.

Trudchen, Gertrud Mondorf, was a student friend of Elfride's who also attended Martin's lectures in the winter semester. On 22 March Martin returned to Freiburg, but on 5 May he had to report back for duty at Heuberg.

My Dearest Soul!

Up to now army service has been quite pleasant. In so far as first years are here, we're trained separately – which has many an advantage. My bad teeth will finally be sorted out after my return now too – though this will take a certain time. Nothing will come of Hanover for the time being, as the artillerymen are given preference. But I haven't given up hope that I might land there some time if I pursue the matter vigorously now.

This time I'm missing spiritual communion more keenly than the first & the heart-to-heart talks we have. Only now do I again feel particularly strongly how much the two of us have grown inwardly again & how much we've given one another particularly in the last few weeks.

When we were recently casting our minds back on the story of our love, I felt particularly strongly that our shared destiny is one guided by God & is developing each day into something more valuable.

My most beloved Soul, there's so much sun in our hearts that I cannot be grateful enough for it all.

And it's perhaps precisely because such great outward demands are now being made upon us & each of us makes his sacrifice that the soul comes to life in a very much more elemental & primordial way – it positively bursts forth from us. Being in harmony with one another as a way of life becomes so pervasive that sometimes, gratefully looking back, it's as though I'm seized by an inner tremor & everything within me becomes utterly clear.

And this is perhaps the aptest way of putting it: this growing clarity in my soul – this sincerity of being is something I owe to your sweet presence, your immediate being – I often feel as though in care & devotion & self-sacrifice you're so far ahead of me that I'll always lag behind.

But you know, my love, even though I may sometimes seem as though I have no regard for the value of such things, you know very well that my whole being is ordained towards an understanding and valuing gratitude. You must give me time to cast off completely everything that counts as false for our innermost being, everything that represents an inner restraint on my work itself. –

The fact that we're both drawn from within towards theology again & again is surely hardly a coincidence – but on the contrary an immediate guarantee that one day we'll succeed in building up an elemental religious life of our own within our family, one which radiates its powers of influence over all personal work, over our circles of friends & fellow human beings.

And this constantly arouses within us a special joyfully serious mood of life, for we bear within us the certainty of growth into the whole – & this certainty is <u>our</u> specific form of life only because we've aroused it in one another.

And this spiritual atmosphere of the soul is sure to be so strong that those living with & around us are affected by it.

All the more is poor Theophil to be pitied now that his worthy being is so wholly isolated, so bereft of bridges – rejected, even – superiority in education alone or even in mere knowledge is indeed no higher level in the sphere of the values attaching to personality. And I think it's our duty to maintain this splendid person in the vitality of his values & not abandon him to inner breakdown. –

Now your little Blackamoor has one further request: enjoy your free time, take pleasure in the chestnut candles, the sun, & a good book.

And if you will be sad in the evening on your own – as happens with me now, then just take a walk through my room, where I've spent [many?] a fruitful hour working, & you'll feel how close I am to your heart.

With much love and best wishes

Your Boy.

P.S. Kind regards to good old Theophil & the Liebers.

Theophil Rees was a medic and a good friend from Karlsruhe. He was working at the University Hospital at Freiburg.

Heuberg, 12 May 18

Dearest Soul! Your letter came yesterday just before we set out on a night exercise & so I could devote my attention to it calmly & undisturbed on the march. Above all I'm glad you had such a wonderful Ascension Day together with the Rees lot (I'm happy for good old Theophil that the little woman pulled herself together). I find it wonderful – or at any rate basically quite primordially necessary & genuine – that you also feel such a great need for reflective solitude. This is how both of us return to the depths of our souls in order to release in a living & effective form what has manifested itself in our life together especially in the last few weeks. Here too there are particularly intense episodes & layers of deeper experience, where the inner core throngs forth all the more genuinely & this thronging at the same time sweeps everything with it as it goes – ennobles each hour & enhances it in its intrinsic historical value. And we'll succeed in the creation of a quite elemental religious life of our own & all our work will grow forth from this. I wish with all my heart that you could <u>read</u> Lotze's Metaphysics over the coming days – even though I suspect you won't find it – it is precisely the <u>spirit in its</u>

<u>history</u> that is absent (as a systematic element) from his philos. as a whole.

Religious tolerance is only possible & valuable where a truly religious consciousness is alive – one that sees with the intuitive understanding that shifts everything back to the elemental.

From within such an atmosphere of personal coexistence with the constantly effective perspectives of religious interiorization I shall develop the true philosophy of religion & philosophizing in general.

With your comment about the character of my as yet unformulated work you've once again given voice to your understanding of myself, & reading it I experienced as deep a feeling of gratitude as in the very first days of our love. If you do indeed want to take a step back I can only tell you again today that God has brought into my life's destiny a person whose being both carries mine with it & determines it in its movement.

Such unity within the diversity of life-currents is an unfathomable boon in life. And the trusting help that constantly keeps watch & fights off all atrophy, the calming & radiant giving of joy that often goes unnoticed, the silent devotion that comes & gives – the most tender glow of the soul & the strongest impulses of will & resolve, all these are a fabric of values that we read from one another's eyes & feel in a squeeze of the hand, unformulated in words & all the more immediate.

How wonderful that now of all times the 'greenkin' is suddenly back again, like a good *Ganeisterlîn* [middle high German: 'little spark'], at a time when inwardly I'm suffering so dreadfully on account of my surroundings – the worthlessness that erupts here can hardly even be put into words & the worst thing is one cannot escape – & one's there in the middle of it & has to go along with it as a mere number – you can hardly imagine what a letter from you means to me then – how deeply I'm overcome by the thought of life at home with our goals & values & things of beauty & then struck all the more forcefully by the contrast afterwards.

What the state in its present form & its lack of ethical-metaphysical orientation has already curbed, poisoned, inhibited & destroyed in the way of the inner wealth & potential of personality cannot be calculated in terms of the national debt – nor can it be measured using the prevailing yardsticks – & perhaps we acquire our worth precisely by renouncing any original valuation on the part of the state anyway.

Our university in Fr. must be left to its own devices – we have to gain the necessary distance from it – a lack of concern with its proceedings, which are mainly the work of people who don't have the least awareness of its limits. You going to Finke I understand merely to mean that you rightly need a bit of a change again. But otherwise I

41

myself still succumb too much & too often to the temptations of such occasions – one is not yet refined & reserved enough. If Finke really did speak about Schlegel, this is a deadly sin among scholars given his complete lack of understanding of the modern history of ideas, one for which he can be forgiven all the less as he committed it in his office as pro-vice-chancellor.

For the rest, such proceedings & gestures won't fail to have their effect upon the public.

We must definitely go to Göttingen or Berlin together after the war.

I'm enclosing a little flower for you (for yours I send a thank-you kiss) which I recently found during a battle. Take pleasure in it & send my regards to the daisy.

I kiss you with all my heart, my darling, & am looking forward to seeing you again.

Wholly your little Blackamoor.

P.S. From home I've had neither parcel nor news. I've written a card to the Husserls.

Regards to the Rees lot & the Liebers.

Heinrich Finke was a Catholic historian who had been a professor at Freiburg since 1899. He was Martin's patron early on.

Almost every day Martin wrote at least one card to his wife describing daily life in the army. On 17 May he returned to Freiburg. On 5 July he had to report for duty again, travelling to Berlin with the troops in a group of 20 academics and teachers. On the way he wrote to Elfride as often as possible. On 7 July he arrived in Berlin at the regional weather station command in Charlottenburg. He had forgotten to bring his gas mask with him, but had brought the front door key.

Berlin 8. VII. 18. evening.

Dearest Soul!

This evening I'll get some peace – & be in your presence with all my soul. First the story:

Kassel is dreadful – the journey through the Harz new and interesting: big mines – Kyffhäuser – Mansfeld etc. Luther memorials – but otherwise dreadful – the Mark [Brandenburg] wonderful – the endless ripening cornfields with their sleepy windmills in the evening sun – the birch forests & lakes – I've never taken such great pleasure in a new landscape. Entering Charlottenburg, change to suburban railway – what bustle & reliability – briskness & order; impressive the same feeling overall e.g. esp. the Underground –

And so arrival at ½ past 10 in the evening – then we camped for an hour in the streets – afterwards accommodation in the storehouse of the cmd. building – didn't sleep – in the morning:

Information: we have to cater for ourselves & find our own accommodation so let's be getting on with it: from 9 in the morning till 8 in the evening up & down stairs, dead tired & not eaten anything decent as we didn't yet have any vouchers. I'm now living in a very clean room at a Frau Wolff's, who has a son in the navy, touchingly concerned – there's a bath – only overlooking the backyard, but this is nice & green – good bed – but the board is bad: 2300 g. bread for a <u>week</u> – & on top of that middle-class cooking – much of which I find revolting – tomorrow I'm telegraphing home for food.

Could I perhaps have some potatoes sent to me? –

To have a look round cultural Berlin I first need a good sleep – tomorrow's completely free – Wednesday for kitting out – the course is due to last 8 weeks & begin on the 16th – milit. activity very nice & decent. Afterwards we're to go to the weather stations at the headquarters – life there interesting – not dangerous – pleasant.

Today I met [in the] cmd. building an old acquaintance from my youth who was also with me at gramm. school in Frbg. – he's a long-serving second lieutnt with us – so very convenient – we've been assigned to the airshipmen.

My room costs 45 marks, of this the municipal authorities pay 24. We get 2 marks board money – middle-class cooking: costs 90 pfennigs. I could have had a cheaper room for 30 marks – but unclean & the people less pleasant; on the 5th floor.

My comrades are for the most part paying the same rent or more – today they're already complaining about bugs – whereas meticulously clean & nice at my place.

Dearest Soul! So for the weeks I'm here I'm going to have to keep on rather making demands on you with money – I'll save what I can – but now & again I'd like to eat a little better like the others – Otherwise one gets to the front fatigued.

I admire the people of Berlin, how they accept and understand that they must go <u>hungry</u>. – Discipline – to the point of being impressive. Police constables on horseback at the crossroads – yesterday there were races – <u>what</u> bustle towards Grunewald.

The Berlin student has his own yacht on the lakes – I've already been invited. Tomorrow I intend to go to the library & university.

Could you perhaps get me some jam from town – or through the Reeses! And I want to try & get some bread from home – will you ask Rombach, I'll write to him myself as well. At the moment I must muster all my strength to get through the weeks here somehow.

I often thank the dear Lord that everything has turned out like this & above all that you now have more peace & quiet – you don't need to worry about me – I think I'll get something from home all right – it's just awfully far away – perhaps we should send some money so they can always post me things express. I live a great deal in my memories & now above all thank you especially for the lovely precious weeks & months we've spent together since we married.

What a precious possession such togetherness is – precious in the <u>historical</u> repercussions of its significance for the present & the future. I think I'll learn a great deal in the next few weeks.

Good night, my love – I am with you & with our dear little Jörg. Be of good cheer, both of you –

With deepest love

Your Boy

Regards to our acquaintances.

Elfride was still working as a teacher and was two months pregnant. Martin referred to their unborn child by name in his letters to her.

Martin was by now an airshipman, and had to take care of the day-to-day things of life himself, which he did not find easy. His course in meteorology started on 15 July. On 20 July he gave the following account: So that's one week of the actual work over – I've learnt many new things & take more pleasure in it each day. With this terrific heat everything is very strenuous & I wasn't so used to sitting on school benches any more either – I need the time in the evenings for work as well (consolidation, expansion, specialization). We prob. won't stay here too long – as the individual armies are now each getting their front weather stations in turn. The set-up is probably only a month old – before that there were just isolated stations near the actual airships – now the observations of temp. barometer, wind etc. are to be expertly & systematically provided for the artillery & air force by us. One station is usually under a ltnt. or staff sergeant & 5 more men – one of them, with scientif. training & previous experience, is the assistant (actual) observer –

I'd like to get the odd scien. book on meteorol. & take it out with me.

Elfride was concerned about providing for Martin and sent him parcels with linen and food. She was even more worried about their finances, as Martin was proving rather liberal when it came to spending money on books and food. Their parents in Messkirch and Wiesbaden as well as friends also sent food parcels.

My Dearest Soul!

It's a lonely Sunday afternoon; rainy outside – but it's hardly advisable to go outside anyway. I have the little picture of you on my desk – & would like to be with you now – though I haven't half got a cold – so you couldn't come too close – ; often I find myself suddenly with you in Lerchenstrasse & it's so vivid that not being there is almost painful. My darling, 'I'm longing to see you terribly' – I've only ever been as homesick as this when I first went to grammar school in Constance as a little boy.

If you were here I'd be able to take pleasure in many things, but as it is everything is diminished – we've grown too close for the currents of our experience to be able to run their course at full strength in complete isolation. And it'd be good & fruitful if we could now be together from time to time with our little Jörg. I'm glad above all that the holidays are now coming ever closer for you – when you can have a complete rest for once – ; even after this short time I can feel what it means when one can really shake off something oppressive & stuffy – which is why I'm also looking forward to getting away from Berlin again.

You know, I don't make friends easily with my comrades – well, now I have one – he's from Oberkirch in the Black Forest – has been studying mathemat. & chemistry for just 2 semesters in Heidelberg – very clever, unspoilt – awkward – but very receptive in matters of the spirit –

Yesterday evening we did something special, travelled to Berlin & had a look at the bustle on Friedrichstrasse – we didn't have the courage to go into a bar – at ½ past 11 we came home again, both of us disgusted to the marrow – I presume we only saw the surface – but it is wilder than I could have ever imagined. I'd never have believed such an atmosphere of artificially cultivated, most vulgar & sophisticated sexuality was possible, but now I do understand Berlin better – the character of Friedrichstrasse has rubbed off on the whole city – & in such a milieu there can be no true intellectual culture – a priori there cannot – & even if every perfect remedy were to hand – it lacks what is simply Great and <u>Divine</u>. When I think of Freibg. & its Minster & the outlines of the Black Forest Mountains – ! The war hasn't yet become frightful enough for us. The people here have lost their soul – their faces don't have any expression at all – at most one of vulgarity, there's no staying this decadence now – perhaps the 'spirit' of Berlin can be overcome by a home-grown culture at the provincial universities – at any rate our youth will only be restored to health from this quarter – <u>if it's still possible at all</u>.

With deepest love, your little Blackamoor. Kind regards to Mother. Tell me, what's the news about my glasses?

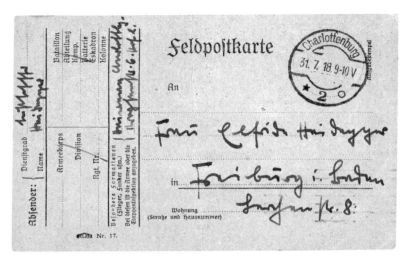

Forces postcard, 30.07.18

At the beginning of August Elfride travelled to Wiesbaden to visit her mother. With her friend Friedel she went rambling along the valley of the rivers Main and Tauber, and afterwards went on to see her parents-in-law in Messkirch.

By mid-August front-line action was imminent for Martin, and he needed money to stock up with supplies for the battlefield. He was hoping he might be better catered for at the front. On 23 August his unit set off for Montmédy in Lorraine. Martin wrote every day during the journey, which lasted until 27 August, when they arrived at the small village where his unit was stationed.

Nouillon-Pont, 28. VIII. 18.

My darling Soul!
I'm now sitting in the nice little hut we've built ourselves, which is fitted out very prettily – (in the near future you'll be getting a picture of it along with a description). Our journey here was very interesting – On Sunday we arrived at Longwy via Luxembourg – from there to Longuyon – which is in a wonderful location – but badly shot up – from [there] we went to Montmédy & stayed there 2 days – until we received further information from the army weather station there – I think Berenberg-Gossler was hit during an air-raid in Montmédy – I saw the military hospital – which is situated right next to the station – i.e. irresponsibly & ineptly – yesterday we came here with our instruments in a goods wagon – nearby I immediately met people from the 28th res. div. (Baden reg.). We're located somewhat outside the village

46

'Dearest Soul – looking for sunflowers to bring them to you. Freiburg –
11.12.1915.'

(350 inhabitants, 80 are still here) 18km north-east [of] Verdun –
lovely plateau with woodland & lovely meadows – a clear air health
resort where I also come for rest-cures – on 1 Sept. we start duty properly – I get every 4th day completely free & can work – otherwise duty
is not that strict either – as the people work well – the ltnt. is a res.
officer geologist – took his doctorate in Tübingen this spring & poss.
wants to do a postdoctoral thesis later – he told me he'd make sure I
can work well –

Now the greatest joy in store for me is: letters from you at long last;
I've come to terms with patiently waiting & the joy will then be all the
greater, purer & more deserved. There is something strangely serious

– & yet peaceful – open – trusting – about existence in the field –
there's probably hardly any danger for us – not even from planes, as
we're quite off the beaten track –

Above my bed (sack with wood-wool on wire mesh, strip of canvas
on top & woollen blanket) I have a small bookcase – a few cards of
Dutch masters from the Kaiser Friedr. Museum, to go with them I'd
now like a picture of you (the shot of the two of us – I don't suppose
I'll get the little wedding-day picture, will I? & a little frame – & then
also the little picture of you standing by the sunflower in the
Worpswede dress –

And then would you be so kind as to ask if there's an edition of
Dostoyevski's The Brothers Karamazov – the books are all in good
hands here.

In the evenings I'm always wholly with you, my love – we're eating
together – sitting on the balcony – chatting in the evening sun &
beaming – & now I'd especially love to be with you & listen to you
telling me about little Jörg – of course soon now I'll be experiencing
much that is deep & mysterious & dear – I hold you silently in my
arms & gaze long & deep into your dear eyes – & kiss you fervently
– if only I could hear your dear voice again – good night, my love –

Wholly your little Blackamoor

Fried potatoes are being prepared right now! – the catering doesn't
seem to be bad. As we often get 150g. jam a day I'd like a little dish
for butter too.

We get the washing done in the village.

N[ouillon-].Pont 30. VIII. 18.

My darling!

This morning I'm on duty – but in the meantime I just want to say
good morning to you – the sun's coming fresh & clear across the
plateau – a slight ground mist is wafting its way across the meadows
– a slight hint of autumn; the mood is strange: reassured joy about
one's present existence – yet at the same time trusting hope for one's
own true existence – serious acceptance of the sacrifice of many previous comforts & in all this, restrained longing & the certainty that
we are thinking of one another – a deep feeling of happiness & wonder
for a spaceless & timeless love – knowledge of one's innermost &
absolute belonging with the most beloved person among the living –
above all the absolute, simple pleasure in this possession in the midst
of the destruction, primitiveness, harshness & impoverished meaning
of one's surroundings has a deeply invigorating effect & latently so,
moreover – not merely upon the base of expressly summoned up acts

of memory & attitudes of longing from the daimon of love – also, today, the knowledge of the coexistence of this love with one's most sacred life's work – of the mutual interpenetration of the two & the advance towards the greatest fulfilment possible – 'He who has thought what is deepest, loves what is most alive' we read in a poem by Hölderlin –. Höld. is currently turning into a new experience for me – as though I were approaching him wholly primordially for the first time.

This whole configuration of moods & emphases will specifically influence my own work – I hope, as soon as things are running properly, to make real progress.

Incidentally I feel a great need to do some writing here – though I'm not yet sure whether to let it take effect.

Hour by hour I'm approaching the moment when I finally have your letter in my hands. We get the post once a day in the evenings –

If you send me anything, above all biscuits & sugar (perhaps I'm better getting that from home), please also enclose some Hoffmann's Drops or something like that; it's rather difficult to get used to the food & it causes all kinds of indisposition – we also have rats under our hut & fleas in the wood-wool – so we really have to put things in order –

We get soup once at midday (with pearl barley & meat in it), in the evening coffee with butter or jam or sausage – I'll just see how it all works out – whether we get by – I think so, if we sleep a lot & there's time for that all right – we have a lot of telephone duty & complex too – I enjoy it a lot & I'll be able to telephone properly by the time I come back.

How wonderful it must be this morning on our little balcony – if only I could sit beside you again – and you'd bring our little cup of tea – How is little Jörg? – recently I had such a nice daydream about how I'll play with him one day – I'm looking forward to getting the picture of you – tell me lots of things

I am very very fond of you, my Dearest Soul
With deepest love,
Your Boy

With her parents-in-law Elfride once again had to confront the issue of the Catholic faith. Although Elfride and Martin had also had a Catholic wedding, she was keen to give their child a Protestant upbringing.

N. P. 4 Sept. 18

My darling Soul!
Many thanks for your 3 letters – I was prepared for what they contain in the way of decisive matters – and for me too the decision has already

been taken – & from the bottom of my heart at that – from the direction of my life, my sense of purpose – perhaps when we've spoken about it we've lacked the necessary seriousness & failed to appreciate the magnitude of what was called for – but today and in the last few weeks, seeing oneself reduced to one's simplest & most elemental existence, petty standards & anxious considerations have all ceased to apply – in the primitiveness of existence issues of ultimate significance approach one another with due immediacy, strength & clarity.

All my earlier insecurity, untruthfulness & casuistry are the simple consequence of an ultra-Catholic education, which on the other hand I always sought to break out of with inadequate means. And the same factors are still present in my parental home (I'm not here reproaching my parents) especially as it's so much a part of the parish house – but ultimately everything is down to the Catholic system's inner lack of freedom – & the pious-acting despotism of conscience.

All this I see today completely clearly.

All argument, therefore, is utterly futile, & would be so even if my parents had a higher level of education – you see, they've grown up into a distorted form of life from which no one can extricate them. If I ask them for their trust in my serious will & resolve, they won't even be able to take that fully seriously & will accordingly judge me to be thoughtless, weak, ungrateful & disobedient. Because they are unacquainted with such a thing as the possibility of a free inner decision & such a thing as the corresponding will to bear responsibility, they regard any deviation from their own will (itself unfree) as disobedience. And at the same time this is then the measure of my ingratitude & neglect of duty.

Of course, you see what is tragic about the whole thing – there's no way out & no mitigation either.

But there is the truthfulness & inherent value of one's own decision & even if this did not itself bring all the benefits of spiritual emancipation, of shared vitality, of rich opportunities for shaping our future family life, the intrinsic value of the decision in the face of the system imposed & passed on would call for this tragedy to be gone through. It is futile & inappropriate to search for grounds for consolation, for it will constantly have to be borne anew by incessantly seeking & following the direction of one's ownmost personal development.

And it's my innermost conviction that we shan't go astray in the process – which goal we reach, if any at all, let's leave that open. I live in large part from my joy at your happiness & your soul's lack of inhibition & all I want is to be together with you again for a little while, holding you in my arms, and to gaze into your eyes and vow with you to receive, lead & guide the newly glowing young soul of our child & provide him with <u>the</u> most valuable of life's opportunities ordained by

50

God in such a way that the life that grows forth from ours & carries it on is one inhabited at root by an orientation towards God together with a powerful will to action within the frame of influence of meaningful human existence.

Now let this vow be taken in a different form – far from you, in the midst of a sphere of existence where life is no longer worth anything, where every man's face bears one particular feature, a characteristic look of having settled the score & being ready, where comforts have ceased to exist – the most painstaking discharge of duties & sense of responsibility are the prevailing content of day & night – where simple, great gratitude bursts forth for each flower & each ray of sunshine, each moment of harmless laughter & each comradely favour – where one first fully feels the blissful happiness that is encapsulated within the thought of one's dearest & most beloved one – where one first experiences what 'home' means: let the will to true humanity & the education & upbringing of human beings as ordained by God be set fully free & henceforth made stronger & constantly enhanced in its value.

And may this vow be one with your life's will & make us both glad & strong.

With devoted love,
Your Boy.

[. . .]

In the summer the German Western Offensive had come to nothing, and the last hopes of victory were yielding to ever-growing concern. In Freiburg there were rumours of the threat of bombardment or a French invasion.

Martin was positioned behind the front, but could hear the sound of fighting going on. On 13 September he described his situation in the following terms: It's still very early in the morning, you'll still be pleasantly 'nodding' – & the little Blackamoor's long since awake – sitting at the telephone & passing huge quantities of numbers on to the artillery, airshipmen, gas officers etc. & as he does so the heavy artillery rumbles & the bombs thunder, making everything in the hut shake – it'll probably get livelier yet – but you don't need to worry about me – we already have the truck for retreat too – but I don't think we'll need it as there are good people stationed there – I'm very well – taking pleasure in the new things I see – your inquisitive Blackamoor is getting his money's worth now – in the village the convoys go close behind one another in threes – assault battalions march through, young rather pale sharp faces – resolute looks in their eyes – no laughing, no singing, even less diffidence or despondency – but quite unflagging strength – I've seen some strange sights, 20m from us is a country

Martin second from left

road that runs from north to south – we look westwards – the glow of the sunset was behind the woods when an assault battalion came marching along the road at a pretty brisk pace – with steel helmets & all loaded up, the men bent forwards somewhat – the muzzles of their rifles pointing sharp into the air – the individual groups standing out clearly, black against the red of the sunset – heavy artillery moves over the crossroads, wonderful horses with tautened muscles, battery commanders jump along the convoy – commands are called through – cars tear along the road, motorcycles in the other direction – the men are all silent, lost in thought, a few kilometres & they're in Hell.

Martin wrote almost every day, read books and tried to philoso-phize when not engaged in his duties. On 22 September he sent Elfride a photograph of himself. You can see the whole hut – with its 'obser-vation tower' – the part to the left of the door is the work & telephone room – to the right is where we live – we're looking towards [Fort] Douaumont, which is clearly visible – at night from the tower we can watch the muzzle flashes & even more the impact of the bombs – which make everything in the hut shake – but you get used to it, and even keep on sleeping. At the gable end, where the steel helmet is on the bricks, you can see the fuel for our oven, which we collected from a barn that had been pounded to pieces.

The soldier farthest right with the pipe is the schoolmaster from Mannheim, next to him is the elementary school teacher from the

Rhineland – the lance corporal next to me is the merchant from Berlin, a nice man –

Not only did Martin receive parcels from Elfride, their relatives and the 'Little Club', but he also sent cocoa and soap from the front back home.

5 Oct. 18. 1 a.m.

My darling Soul!
For you the quiet days of contemplation have now begun – with their rich opportunities for a precious inward life – replete with soul & spirit – the grateful enjoyment of happiness brings a certain lingering peace to existence & basically it is highest activity. In many cases today people – even among the 'intellectuals' – have become especially insensitive to the inner powers & deeds of spiritual struggle & experience – they preach a more outwardly oriented, seemingly 'active' lifestyle – & would reproach philosophy for being out of touch with & turning away from life. The criterion they use here is a false one – rather it can only be won from the innermost unfolding of the spirit itself.

Spirit finds whomsoever it is meant to find, & from those found one wave after another sweeps forth, rousing, agitating & keeping in agitation, into the many who are lethargic & massive in quality & number. This innate vehemence of spirit renders superfluous everything which as a practical philosophy of life abuses the term philosophy – Once we have regained full trust in spirit, we'll reach a position to allow unreflective creative culture to rise up again & continue to exert an influence. But never will cultural artillery, however far it is taken, bring us one step closer to immediate life & experience. Everyone who in future wishes to 'have an effect' at our universities must have understood this – our young artists have penetrated furthest into these basic insights, intuitively & more by feeling –

Unfortunately I had to break off here so as to get the letter away.
With much love,
Your Boy

Starting from 1 October, Elfride was happy to be granted leave of absence from her teaching work on the grounds of her pregnancy.

On 6 October Martin wrote: [In the picture] you can see our living space – in the front left-hand corner you can see part of a bed, but I've moved next to the window – as it was too hot by the oven, especially now a brick oven is being built. On the whole you can probably form an impression of it. Perhaps I'll also get a shot of my corner some time.

Inside the hut

Military camp with wagons & tents

There were rumours and hopes of an armistice offer from the Americans. Martin was keen to dispel Elfride's worries and acted optimistically.

Right at the outset of the war the Husserls had lost one son, and now their son Gerhard received a serious head wound too. As soon as he learnt of this, Martin set out for Sedan, where he looked for him in the military hospitals. Informed that Gerhard had already been transported home, Martin returned to his post without having achieved anything.

Freiburg was in the grip of a wave of acute influenza, which was taking a heavy toll. Husserl and his wife had gone down with it too. A young girl from one of the neighbouring houses in Lerchenstrasse succumbed to it, and Theophil Rees was to lose his pregnant wife Marta.

In a long passage written on 17 October, Martin described the social situation: Only the young will save us now – & creatively allow a New Spirit to be made flesh in the world – Come what may, we must keep our belief in the spirit so surely & trustingly alive within us that we are capable of building up – building perhaps in outward poverty and privation – with many a hindrance – but only times such as these have ever awakened the hour of the birth of spirit – we're bogged down in a horribly deformed culture with a spurious appearance of life – in most people all root connections with the fundamental sources of true life have withered away – superficial existence prevails everywhere, but is all the more brazen, insistent, demanding – we lack the great enthusiasm of the soul & spirit for the true life & experience of valuable worlds – which is why the people from the front today lack any truly rousing sense of purpose – given the sufferings of 4 years, great maturity of spirit & a radical awakening are required to rouse people to sacrifice for true values. Instead, people have been systematically nauseated by pan-German pipe dreams, & as the instruments of power for realizing them are now failing they're faced by a hollow-eyed aimlessness – they labour under a sense not of national belonging based on true love & helpfulness – but of being deceived & abused for the selfish purposes of spiritually misguided or indeed completely unspiritual, backward power groups. In recent decades or even during the whole of the last century we've not taken enough care – if any at all – of the inner human being in ourselves <u>& in others</u>. Values such as soul & spirit have been lacking, their meaning could no longer be experienced – or at most as a perfect object of destruction for exact scientific (both natural sci. & 'histor.') analyses – This whole aimlessness & hollowness & alienation from values has dominated political life & the concepn. of the state in general. The only thing that can help here is the appearance of new human beings who harbour an elemental affinity with spirit & its demands, & I myself recognize ever more urgently the necessity for leaders – only the individual is creative (even in leadership), the masses never – our people today is already much much more impoverished in terms of spirit & soul than it will be in future in material terms – Hardship must at most be an external cause

& stimulus but never a reason & motive for a change in direction of spirit & soul – for this an original turning inwards is required, which we are still very far from grasping & which is oppressed virtually to the point of impotence under the burden of external, technically & quantitatively sophisticated stimulants & gratifications.

in the field 27. 10. 18. 2 a.m.

My darling Soul!
Yesterday three of your lovely letters arrived at once (from the 19th, 20th & 22nd) & so I was amply compensated for the long wait. But I find that the individual letters have a more immediate & rounded effect when each one turns up on its own & not several rushing in at once – but they're welcome any time.

Yesterday evening I went to bed early & enjoyed them all again – & there I was entirely in the little room, could see every detail, could positively feel what was around me & again had such a strong feeling of your closeness, with the love, charm & intensity that come particularly alive to me in many a letter. How little Jörg will look around the room & how his Mummy will conjure up an enticingly sweet-smelling baked apple – & how he'll acquire a feeling for the secret & special nature of every thing in our house, his soul infused with the family home, childhood happiness, sunshine & peace – as well as with life's clarity & prophetic certitudes & true religiousness. Rich moments from the time of our engagement now come back to me with strange frequency & on reflection I experience the wonderful teleology of this time – I experience the individual things not as distinct in time – but as a stage & stratum within the development of an individual life – & all the joys woven in, the moments of abandon, of trust, of self-oblivion in the other, in the Thou – now reveal their life-exalting & creative significance.

However difficult I very often find being separated now of all times, just as sure is my clear conviction that these weeks will have an effect on our entire future & this will be all the purer & more lasting, indeed more deeply-rooted, emerging from the situations imposed upon us, the more intensely, the more confidently we live. When in quiet moments, often pausing in the middle of my work, I drift away, imagine myself in your presence, picture what you might be doing – this to me is like a consecration for the heightened return of our togetherness. And our rich future already is even today, undifferentiated in particulars, veiled in each moment's constellation of values, seemingly in a distant time, yet in a creative present, so that it forms part of our life's innermost centre as it were – & every present is only ever the precious aliveness of past & future life – i.e. truly historical –

In the empirical exploration of life & consciousness conceived in this way you hit upon quite new fundamental insights – (for this the language & concepts first have to be discovered & created in silent contemplation – rough descriptions analysed in their mysterious structures – the condition for all of which is a radical self-emancipation from previous patterns of thought specific to the theory of being & nature). The whole problem of the ego leads not to a pure, empty ego but to one that is filled out & primordially alive & to its constituent elements – being filled with values is based upon being intrinsically opened to values, & this takes us back to the essence of personal spirit, which I conceive as a 'calling' – only thus can the eternal possessions of spirit & its absolute confusions be conceived – such is the ground covered by the problems I've come up against out here, as a continuation of the principle of the historical consc.[iousness] – these problems, which proceed, strictly analytically, wholly in the sphere of values, are gradually also giving me the proper perspective upon the unity of research, teaching & education which is to be created. Partly because it can only be accomplished in a living personality, however, it must & can be philosophically interpretable just to the extent that the living consciousness itself is recognized as the ultimate goal & sphere of interpretation –

When I'm with you we'll have a lot to talk about on the subject. I'd like to lay particular emphasis on bringing the problem of the sacred into these new considerations of principle – not only because they're completely lacking in Otto,[5] but for purely substantive reasons –

And then (you know how the little Blackamoor's always making plans) especially in the first decade straight after the war & probably for good I'd like to give a course of one-hour lectures on the essence of university & academic study – starting from the basic orientation described above – I have an inner conviction that it would help make young people inwardly awake & strong & they will go out as a 'leaven' into the future life of the state & the people – undivided attention to what is positively creative – casting off everything merely short-lived & determined by the milieu – and fostering instead the great critique of principles. For this task all the material from the Academic Volunteer Corps [akademische Freischar] & the Free Germans in general would be extremely useful to me – perhaps Friedel could provide me with some, & anything you know of, please collect it even now.

However gloomy & threatened by fate things are around us, I hold out joyful hope for the assured creative reawakening of our entire

---

[5] Rudolf Otto's work *Das Heilige*, an examination of the experience of the sacred, had appeared in 1917. It was translated into English under the title *The Idea of the Holy*.

existence – only we must finally work our way through to the precious standpoint where we create from <u>within</u> ourselves & do not allow what others think to carry any weight, whether they hold us in contempt, outwardly seem to muzzle us – & rob us of old & now empty institutions –

Our press is a wretched business & an impediment, governed by spiritual adolescents – In spite of everything though it's a joy to be alive, because we're facing completely new horizons, because we've been called to break through these horizons & discover new territory.

You're quite right, my love, if one could only act right now & had those concerned in front of us – . Prince Max is undoubtedly one of the new people & you've interpreted his letter & all the fuss & bother about it quite rightly to my mind. To the problem of piety, which you've sensed is fundamental to Dostoyevski, I'll return another time. –

Yesterday I went sawing wood, we cut up trunks with a great band saw you know – that was fun & left us very hungry & tired. I'm very relieved to hear you got over the flu so quickly – I almost thought as much. The paste is eaten – the little roll was off & quite inedible – I'm glad you have Frau Manzoni there again, I feel very sorry for Fräulein Malenberg. You'll be glad now a proper little blackamoor was in the post box again – my own greatest Sunday joy today is to have brought you an hour of sunshine. With deepest love & kisses

Your Blackamoor

Many thanks for the little garland

Very best wishes to dear Hilde. Regards to the Reeses, the Liebers, Fräulein Mallenbg, etc.

The last letter from the front:

in the field, 10. 11. 18.

My darling Soul!

There was no post again today & they say the postal service as a whole has come to a halt – the wildest rumours are going round – dates for an armistice deal are mentioned, but one after another they prove to be false – the gunfire goes on the same as ever – pointless sacrifice of human lives – what our wretched politics has on its conscience – though disaster now seems to be well on its way – only through this quite radical purification will there be anything to hope for – & only through radicalism – complete commitment of the human being as a whole – will we ourselves advance as real revolutionaries of the spirit.

Every hour now seems useless out here – & one is kept away from where one could & should be helping. I've approached my comrades

58

a little & tried to suggest quite crudely & unphilosophically what the new demands of the spirit will be – I met with alarming standards – with a bourgeois mediocrity & an attitude to life I really wasn't prepared for –

Certainly, our effect will at first be limited to just small circles, & there it will continue to grow of its own accord, quantity isn't what counts at all in the early days anyway, but rather the force & devotion with which it asserts itself –

The new issue of Logos seems to contain quite worthwhile articles – but there is no sign of the Radically New to be seen here – indeed not even the inner needs of the soul seem to be awake to it – though they certainly are to compromises, 'new orientations' etc. – all these things are half-measures, especially when they lack a grounding in philosoph. principles –

Again and again I wish you as peaceful & pleasant a time as possible – & I feel so sure that you'll get our little child, & even dear Hilde, safely through the perils of the coming weeks as a true child of peace. [. . .]

One hears & reads that the troops are to be discharged straightaway to their district commands – that would be splendid – for now I really wouldn't feel like going to Berlin. –

I wonder what the gentlemen at our universities are thinking – & whether the young lecturers are capable of forming a genuine association animated by new convictions & gaining acceptance – though in this respect I'm pessimistic & for the time being pin all my hopes on the students themselves. –

Once the armistice takes effect, you of course won't write any more – for then the forces' postal service will cease to exist – What with all this confusion the return from the front may not be too rosy as far as board & accommodation are concerned. But even that will still be bearable – one has already got used to everything.

Now sleep well, my love, sweet dreams –

soon I'll be with you again & happy moments will be ours.

Wholly your Little Blackamoor.

On 11 November, on the instructions of the German Supreme Army Command, the politician Matthias Erzberger of the Centre Party signed the armistice agreement with the Allies. The world war was over, leaving around 10 million dead, more than 20 million wounded and more than 6 million in captivity. Martin was discharged and sent home.

1919

On 21 January, Jörg was born. The supply situation facing the German population was bad. There were shortages of basic foodstuffs and fuel for heating. Elfride's half-sister had sent her a layette for the baby, and in Messkirch a bassinet was built.

From 1 January, Martin was Husserl's private assistant. He gave a lecture on 'The Idea of Philosophy and the Problem of Worldviews'.

Frbg. 22. I. 19.

Dear Mummy!

The letters came this afternoon – I had a nice nod till ¼ to 4 & then did even nicer work. Before the meal I wrote to Friedel, Trudchen, Lisi, Vetter (Constance), Rombach, Krebs, Finke, Cohn.

There's such pure & utter joy in me that I constantly want to sit quite quietly at little Jörg's basket and thank you. A wholly new element of experience has entered our love, one so strange that I cannot yet grasp its primordial character at all.

It's as though we'd received a new consecration, one that flows through every moment of life anew. If you now ask me from time to time why I'm so quiet, it's the quietness of a deep, reverent joy.

Good night, my love – remember me to little Jörg – Soon I'll be coming into your room again full of happiness & winter sun.

With deepest love,
Your grown-up Little Blackamoor
[. . .]

Martin visited Theophil Rees in Constance, where Rees was working as a doctor in the hospital and mourning for his late wife.

My darling Soul! – dear Little Blackamoor!

From Lake Constance I send you Easter greetings today – it looks as if there won't be much Easter sunshine – but inside us let it be all the purer & brighter.

I've been thinking from time to time recently about the weeks that have passed since the little Blackamoor arrived – both of us have lived intensely, haven't we, each on our own path – from the summer though I'm hoping for one more thing – that we can talk things through with one another once again, can 'chat' – Yet our milieu is so strong that I'm missing it now – for work – perhaps owing to fatigue I was expecting new stimulation from new surroundings – but in vain so far – on the first day I worked a little – but by the next everything was going wrong – there's nothing disruptive – and yet nothing stirring either – a certain easy way of drifting along – whereas productive work takes high tension, from which the phenomenologl. intuition can as it were discharge –

When I look back on the semester, I can still feel the basic mood of harmony in which I lived & I just wish for this state of mind in greater measure for the next one – I've learnt one thing: to immerse myself in concrete problems – this is now the great task: to make concrete problems the focal pnt. & guiding thread of the lecture & let the connections emerge from the analysis itself – For I suddenly caught myself once again indulging in construction – an old vestige of Rickert's philosophizing, yesterday I again tried to work through Rickert's 'Object of Cognition' once more for the lecture course – but with the best will in the world I couldn't go on reading – it was like an inner hostility towards this unparalleled style of constructive & yet unmethodical thought – for this reason in the lecture course I'll now try a positive elaboration of the problem & leave the critical grappling to one side – I now also have an increasingly clear idea why Husserl finds it so difficult to spend time & energy in critical discussions with others at all – the problem areas are so broad that one really shouldn't lose a moment.

I do hope to get into my work in the next few days.

I try to stimulate myself a little by reading, but I find I don't have the peace for receptivity at all – at the same time there's always a certain reluctance to read valuable things because I know that problems that crop up must not distract me & sooner or later I'll have to leave what I've begun – because in that situation my current sphere of problems calls for attention once again [?].

At Theophil's I had a look at the new edition of Eckhart's writings (Diederichs), which is much more thoroughly edited – apart from the worthless introduction – Did you know by the way that Adam Petri first printed Tauler's sermons in Basel in 1521 & along with them some of <u>Eckhart's</u>?

Theoph. has some theosophical writings here – the movement is very widespread here due to a Protestnt. priest – I regard it all as a great danger – but at the same time as an admonition to the Churches to turn back again to primordial life & cast off all levelling, bureaucratization & routine. Th. & I are now discussing Windelband's Preludes together – in the process it becomes increasingly clear to me how weak all this philosophy of worldviews seems with its empty concepts; where philosophy is absolute science, by contrast, it becomes a real experience for the investigator – a type of personal life as such – And only where all valued meaning becomes creative life & finds its actuality there, is it truly meaning – I observe this here in Theophil's sphere of activity too – anyone who has an aptitude for it, as he does, can achieve great things – But in his profession too the majority just seem to know their trade and no more.

And now to come to the little country-boy; such a shame I don't have a picture of him with me – I wonder if the Easter bunny has already come to visit him too – ; his inner cheer & little life has already had a really deep influence on us, hasn't it, & we always leave his basket with a joyful ringing in our hearts – I miss you both very much – you see, the solitude that is fertile ground for research work doesn't consist in merely being undisturbed outwardly – but in fact in coming out from & being able to go back into a rich 'environment' – be happy together, best wishes,
      Your Daddy.

Martin worked on his course of lectures on value philosophy and went on excursions with Theophil to the island of Reichenau and to Überlingen.

In mid-August Martin went to Bernau in the Black Forest to see Husserl, returning to Constance at the end of the month. There he also visited the Vetter family, who were relatives of his, and worked intensively. On 30 August he wrote: I'd like to write in full about my work – what you felt was right in one respect, in that I've inwardly been giving intense thought to this question in recent weeks – above all, the fact is that H[usserl]. does not exactly come bothering me with every new issue & disturbing my independence – for me scientific philos. goes further than H. too. As you once correctly commented before, I'm already certainly beyond him & with much broader horizons & problems. But even at the age of 30 one isn't yet fully fledged & still enjoys kicking over the traces, even if only in private – here H. is a good counterbalance in spite of the unmistakable signs of age. All the same I've decided to collaborate with him, for a start because in

Martin with Jörg, 1919

science what is most personal manifests itself only in the most utterly objective devotion to & shaping of the subject matter & then for <u>practical</u> reasons since appearing on the same title page as H. might well mean something – in the smaller circle of Frbg. Univ. but also in the acad. literature in general. I'm not anxious about the continuity & steadiness of my own developmt. – these forces work & grow in strangely unconscious ways – my relig. phenomenological problems are resolving themselves with each passing month & I'm also structuring my lecture course so as to retain an intimate connection with them & use them as the concrete examples; –

In the coming weeks I'll work splendidly, I can feel it for certain – my productivity is such that I can hardly control it & just have to write all the time & hold on.

A crisis was looming in Martin's relationship with Elfride, and on 1 September he wrote from Constance: Your letter came this morning & I knew beforehand what it contained. Saying many words about it & analysing it all is fruitless. It's enough that you've told me in your plain, assured manner. Mind you, I don't <u>understand</u> your 'inner conflict', nor do I ever want to be presented with any psychological demonstrations in the matter – not out of indifference – but because I want to have you directly the way I can have you, and that Friedel loves you I've known for a long time – asking you about it would have seemed petty to me – from time to time I've been surprised you didn't tell me sooner. It's also characteristic that Friedel felt inhibited by me, & all the more natural as in me he sees merely the clumsy, awkward, narrow-minded armchair scholar who's just a hanger-on. It'd be naive of me & a waste of energy if I were to hold it against him even in the slightest. On the contrary: I've sought & still seek to be good to him & encourage him, even though sometimes this dutiful spiritual ministration isn't easy for me when one never meets with a reaction on the same level (spiritually speaking). When ordinary people give encouragement they preen themselves on the fact – & those who receive the encouragement take it accordingly too & one assumes the role of the grocer woman who brings certain vegetables to the market which you don't get as snugly placed in your basket elsewhere. This brings me to the problem of social intercourse in general, which has been on my mind particularly over the last few days as I've been meeting new people. And I notice: basically they're all indifferent to me – they go past outside as though in front of a window – one gazes after them & perhaps remembers them again some time.

Friedel Caesar, a friend from Elfride's youth, worked as a doctor in the University Hospital in Freiburg.

Martin recalled the journey they had made together when they were first engaged: Yesterday morning Theoph. & I went to Reichenau, hired a boat & rowed to the 'Cove', where we went bathing from the side of the boat & had a sleep – all the lovely Reichenau days from 1916 came back to me again – the evenings in the boat – the walks – out in the Cove, where we read Meister Eckhart on Sundays – the trip to Constance – the little ring in the lake, [. . .] in this way the usual distance from life turns into absolute closeness & from these perspectives only <u>ultimate</u> things are visible – ultimate in the most personal sense too, & your Thou, to which I know myself eternally bound & which – becoming absolute – accompanies me in an ultimate form & to this extent also in the most objective creativity & precisely here shares in what is most personal. For you today, on the other hand, it can only enhance your peace of mind now that you know yourself assured of my understanding trust – & your intuition was genuine when you asked me not to speak much more about it – let's leave everything to the greater course of our marriage – & see it & expend our whole selves in goodness – even if we're aware that these are undeserved gifts to which one isn't entitled – which <u>we ourselves</u> perhaps never get just <u>dropping into our lap</u> like this – but see at a distance in the greater suffering of creativity & self-abnegation. The great calling to a timeless task is always necessarily a condemnation to solitude too & it's in the nature of it that others are unaware of it, but on the contrary understand the loner as the rich man, one honoured, exalted, heeded & talked about, & are then surprised when they meet with boundless contempt on his part (a shoving aside in the higher sense). I'm glad that you now feel inwardly peaceful & lucid – I trust you & your love with the distinctive certainty that my own love for you has – even if I don't understand everything – & cannot fathom the source from which your manifold love draws its sustenance.

Martin now found himself obliged to move into an inn in Wollmatingen, for the senior consultant at the hospital in Constance refused to allow him to stay any longer in Theophil's office.

Wollmatingen, 9 Sept. 19
My Dearest Soul! A lot of things have become clearer to me through your kind letter, & I thank you for it. I've never despised Friedel – it wasn't a positive rejection – but an acceptance of someone who doesn't properly belong with me – but this may be connected with one's completely different background & development, which you indeed got just right – although you overlook the fact that not everything fell into my lap – my student years were hard – full of sacrifices – which I admittedly found easier to bear than others owing to my natural disposition – Of course we must never seriously speak of having deserved anything – but I didn't get where I am today without doing my work – even though it will again be said that I've always had plenty of 'luck' – ; but this very awareness is not at all reassuring – for a start it's in a certain sense uncanny – in the sense of the mysterium tremendum, one comes to live within a specific certainty in one's calling, yet every hour one experiences such a falling-behind that at times one knows oneself to be facing insurmountable difficulties, i.e.

one makes no progress at all – one feels empty – what one has achieved recedes, becomes pointless – or on the other hand – & I've now spent 3 weeks in such a situation – the views, horizons of the problem – genuine strides in fertile solutions – seeing the principles anew, possibilities for the most surprising formulations & coinages, forging genuine connections – all this is so overwhelming, simply brimming over, that physically & in terms of time one is virtually incapable of capturing, detaining, systematically turning the torrent to account –

This absolute productivity likewise has its uncanny side: <u>it</u> is what seems to do the creating & yet one feels oneself to be absolutely present in the process – especially when the condition subsides & the weariness comes & one tries to find one's way back into one's environment – then I know I've been wholly & absolutely present to myself & above all present to the objective world of problems & spirit – here there's nothing alien to oneself – here nothing goes past outside – but one moves along with it oneself & generates the movement – in creative life all alien distance has disappeared – all the more wrenching & churning then is the standing-on-the-other-shore in the natural environment – but: all the more gripping, manifesting the absolute, is the striving & wanting-to-bridge-the-divide in natural life – the moments when the surges of the heart pound together – the sense that 'we've found one another again' – It's a wholly mistaken conception of love to believe that it's nurtured & fostered by shared contents & objects – the way the bourgeois love – they have their shared domesticity – go on journeys together & through their simultaneous and common bonds with the fortuitous contents of a life they come to believe that they love one another & are utterly happy in the process – though their whole life may never experience a genuine eruption of love – And this, after all, is where life transcends the world, that it bears these great opportunities within itself: to be able to find and hold on to the Other among the forms of relative life for a few moments – & what does 'moment' mean here, at bottom it's an inappropriate designation – one borrowed from relative life & transpos[ed] into the absolute – the having-found-one-another is absolutely valuable in itself – the duration is immaterial – by contrast time & duration has its true, valuable function at the stage of expecting & hoping – of trustingly being-prepared for the recurring unification – or at the stage of gratefully recollecting, of joyfully holding on to & holding <u>out</u> with the gifts one has received – ; those who 'live' by expending themselves on ever new contents – objects, goods & people – & see this as life – have never felt life's unbroken torrent of activity. – Times of abandonment [*Ver-lassenheit*] & seeming distance from God are only lived genuinely if they are times of trusting composure [*Gelassenheit*] – that is, of the strong, God-assured mastery of life. Since I read

Luther's Commentary on Romans, much that before was troubling & dark to me has become bright & liberating – I have quite new understanding of the Middle Ages & the development of Christn. religiousness; & wholly new perspectives on the problems of the philos. of religion have opened up to me – Otto, for example, seems to me to be on the wrong track – something I had only a very muddled idea of in the field – & I now understand why Friedel [Lieber] had a certain dismissive attitude towards the book & is still trying in vain to come to terms with it. –

As to Ochsner, you were probably right that he isn't getting anywhere in M. either & is now apparently on the way to abusing & profiting from my mysticism lectures. (If he comes, don't let him in my room). The fact that Fräulein Walter is going to Munich because I'm not lecturing on mysticism is also typical – people would, after all, have experienced & enjoyed the course as something of a sensation albeit without responding in a manly-strong manner or actively getting to grips with an infinite set of problems. It's enough to drive one to despair – here too one stands alone – & expending one's energy & effort upon others is a trespass against spirit. – yet even so I'm looking forward to the coming semester – because apart from the lecture course it's my first productive one in an exclusive sense – & because I feel that after the recent months of clarification the two of us are about to ascend to a new level in life – & to become Absolute & come closer to God is the meaning of existence. – Schwenninger has invited me for a few days as well – I'll have to see how I arrange that – I'm still always hampered by people in my work too much – tomorrow, Wednesday, I have to go to Donauesch[ingen] again. – presumably for the last time. I still haven't got anything from Hu[sserl].

With deepest love, your Blackamoor. Love to the Little Blackamoor as well –

Have a lovely time with him.

Martin had to have a set of dentures fitted, which it took him a while to get used to.

Messkirch, 13 Sept. 19

My darling Soul! I arrived here yesterday evening & made myself at home in my little room – I do find it somewhat easier to find rest here than in the constant toing & froing between Theophil & the Schwenningers. Yesterday Theophil got a card from Habakuk [?], who it seems is interceding with the government on my behalf, according to which my post as assistant has been approved – 'further measures

67

are in progress'. Good old Theophil has taken care of things again. I was happy to give up a few more hours for him in the evening – so we were able to talk together a lot after all.

So, my love, your plan is just wonderful – I don't begin my lectures until 7 Oct. – for I have to practise a lot with my teeth so I can speak fluently again. I'm so looking forward to the happy days when we're completely relaxed once again. I wasn't angry with you about your recognition [*Erkenntnis*] – how could I be when every day I must experience the ruthlessness & severity of cognition [*Erkennen*] with absolute matter-of-factness – but as you've probably seen from my last letter, there are deeper solutions for such severity which are not simply tailored according to the needs of the heart – but which spring from a deeper understanding of the meaning of such conflicts. Life in its elemental power is deeper & fuller than cognition, & all our philosophy indeed suffers from the fact that it allows its further problems to be pre-determined by what is already cognized [*Erkanntheiten*] – with the result that they are disfigured & afflicted with paradoxes from the outset. – I'm so glad within about my constant, steady growth – which grows out of the deep interconnection of my life with you – with the steady orientation towards ultimate radical tasks – everything great is rooted in radicalism alone.

This morning I was outside & walked along the pathway & in the wood where we saw the deer & were so happy that time – so wonderfully relaxed – & I was filled with a great yearning & kept thinking you should have been beside me with your beaming eyes –

My love, how glad I am – especially now I've become somewhat freer & more assured with my tasks & jobs.

And then we'll make things quite wonderful for ourselves & open up anew a rich source of our love which will nourish us with its sacred waters through the busy months ahead. There's such jubilation & joy in me – that what I'd most like is to fly over to you right now. When do you think I should come? Around the 25th perhaps? I'd like to spend my 30th birthday with you really. I wonder what the little man's doing – sometimes I feel homesick for him & his calming presence. –

About Trudchen [Mondorf] I cannot say much – it all seems so incredible to me & after all I'm not close enough to her to have been deeply affected by the new turn of events. My overriding impression is such that I reproach myself & make resolutions as regards my behaviour towards young people who are studying – no longer to reinforce them in their convictions about themselves – if they've really got it in them, they'll attain certainty about themselves of their own accord. Up to now Ochsner has always lived from other people's liberality – even his papers, which he only just managed to produce,

I spoon-fed him. And I have serious doubts as to whether Trudchen is the person to help prepare him for possible work. Above all I don't want to hurt Trudchen – but I've no idea what to do in the face of such a mess. –

I'm hoping to get round to some steady work here in order to put at least the first 5–6 lectures down on paper and thus get slightly ahead. The advantage with this semester is that I don't have to give two different lecture courses as well as a seminar – but can work on everything in one & the same go.

Have a nice rest my love & enjoy the anticipation of our days together, as I do.

Lots of love to the little man.

With deepest love & kisses from your Blackamoor.

Kind regards from my parents & Marie.

As Martin had become estranged from the Catholic Church, his parents now found it extremely difficult to understand their son. Martin was hoping that Elfride could come to Messkirch for a few days' rest and some walking together. Unfortunately, Elfride could not find anyone to look after Jörg for so long. With the help of his parents in Messkirch, Martin arranged for various items of food to be sent by train to Freiburg. He arrived back in Freiburg just in time for his birthday. Jörg was baptized a Protestant.

In the winter semester Martin gave a two-hour lecture on 'Fundamental Problems of Phenomenology'.

1920

Martin spent early January 1920 together with Karl and Gertrud Lieber and the Szilasis, who had invited him to stay at their house in St Märgen not far from Freiburg for a skiing and working holiday.

On 4 January he wrote: My truest happiness is being certain that you can find yourself fully & freely at my side – indeed everything else is artificial & fundamentally false. We're on the way to achieving a genuine, simple & more elemental grasp of life – the creation of a new style – not according to programmes, but to motives awakening from the innermost self. This is also what puts me such poles apart from Husserl today, & – simply to support us financially – I must now find the possibilities for going along with him without violent conflict or emphasis upon such conflict – Up here – along with the spatial distance – I've also acquired an inner distance in considering my situation & I must again admit you were right months ago when you suspected that I shouldn't spend so much time & energy on the young people – because philos. simply must not & cannot be demonstrated to people – anyone who stays the course & is genuine will stand firm of their own accord – after all, we didn't get this spoon-feeding either, as I allowed Husserl to suggest to me. Frau Szilasi said the same thing to me yesterday quite independently – that even in the first weeks she'd noticed the great contrast between Huss. & me – how appalled she was by H[usserl]'s mathematical ethics – how surprised she was that I should associate thus with the little rogue –

At the end of February Martin stayed in St Märgen again, seeking to concentrate on his work.

My darling Soul!

Today has been a glorious Sunday & I've so often wished to myself that you were here with the little man – I'd love to know how you are – couldn't you drop me just a short line every once in a while – I often feel such a longing to see you – especially when I get up from my work, & it always feels as though you should be there – my work's going very well – I'm now working systematically through Bergson & then want to move on to Jaspers, I feel so freely & independently creative at present – I now also have a clear position with respect to Husserl – now all that's required is the offer of a chair, then I can draw on all of my resources & you too will then breathe rather more freely & be able to come out of your shell.

Would you mind sending me the picture soon – most of all I'd like to have the two of you – I've been racking my brains in vain to remember which book I put it in – I think it was definitely an 'Insel' volume, – please do have another look. – [. . .]

Brecht's staying on another week – but the Szils. have not invited him for any longer – he's living with the teacher & eating in another inn – I keep everything at arm's length. The professor's wife is very nice to me & thoroughly restrained – I myself am glad of it – I see plainly again & again – something I always firmly believe in & trust – that our marriage represents something very rich & strong even if it does perhaps lack that love which I cannot really picture anyway. But there are limits everywhere –

May you get completely well again – take joy in the little man – deepest love to you both,

Your Daddy

Has he learnt anything new again?

The Szils. send their regards, the apple purée is very good – perhaps Prof. Szil. can bring some more with him.

There's a washerwoman here.

Franz-Josef Brecht was a student of Martin's. On 11 February Martin wrote: I'm learning a great deal studying Bergson – what I told you just a few weeks ago, about how little we know the French – I find confirmed more & more – problems that Huss. often brings up in conversation as terrifically new were already clearly set out & resolved by Bergs. 20 years ago.

Elfride was pregnant again and suffering health problems. Martin had to interrupt his stay and return to Freiburg as Hedwig Stein, a friend of Elfride's, was unable to help her with the housework. After a good week he returned to St Märgen and remained there until the end of February.

At the end of March, during the Easter period, Elfride went on ahead to Wiesbaden with Jörg, and Martin prepared a talk on 'Oswald Spengler and His Work', which he was to give in Wiesbaden on 14 April as part of the 'Scholarly Week'.

[Messkirch 28. 07. 1920]
Dearest Soul! Putz [Jörg] slept very well all night long, after being ceremonially put to bed by the whole family. It's moving how much pleasure the folks take in the child – They were both standing & waiting up on the hill – he made friends at once – early in the morning when he was awake, his grandfather came to his little bed & looked at him in silence. Marie is very proud & trying hard to do everything of course by the book. I'm still with him & things are still rather slow & awkward, he has a very sweet little bed, in which I've slept too. He also has a rocking-horse – this he's still afraid of.

The big stove with the doors is wonderful, he gets really engrossed in it – but it's even better when I hide <u>behind</u> the stove & can play peekaboo. Marie is just clearing out the cupboard –

He was very good on the journey – at about 11 o'clock in Neustadt he got tired & was still sleeping when we changed trains – afterwards I fed him – it all went very nicely – I think people were amazed how skilfully I looked after the little lad. Afterwards he slept some more – otherwise he sat next to me & had plenty to look at, all the bow-wows going by outside.

In between times he talked with people & flirted – finally from Stockach there was a sweet little girl with whom he played very nicely. – Otherwise he's doing very well – he's just having a bit of trouble doing his business at the moment – but otherwise you wouldn't know he'd had the journey.

I'm well myself – only I am noticing the weariness now & I intend to have a good rest; there'll be no option anyway – as Marie does have to help now & again & looking after everyone is too much for Mother on her own.

It's rather cool up here – but Putz is provided for – I take great delight again in my homeland, the meadows & fields, & gradually I feel what it means to have one's roots in the soil – in fact this only fully struck me through Dostoyevski & I find a very great contrast with people like Afra Geiger & others, who only live in relationships.

It's a great pity you cannot be here with us & we must definitely make it possible for next year. I don't know whether I could work here – in the long run it'd be too quiet. It's too small for our Fritz as well. He cracked a good joke this morning: Marie was just washing the little lad's nether regions & I said she shouldn't beat about the bush but do it properly; and he said she wouldn't do that, otherwise she'd have to go to confession! –

Didn't you pack the little beaker? I'll write a card to Mother today & some time later in rather more detail.

I wonder what you're up to. First of all having a rest & enjoying life – I've very often seen this summer how intensely you now live for yourself as a mother & feel superior to the women who merely search around in other things. I hardly need worry that you'll ever take on airs & graces like Frau Husserl, who recently read out to me from two (newly published) books only the passages that were about her husband.

On the other hand, of course, it is touching how she must have borne with him in the time prior to the Logical Investigations; he said that for 13 years he had driven his wife to distraction. – I don't really know what you think about my work at the moment – & it's probably difficult to say too, as you hardly know what I'm working on & how. I'm looking forward to the unbroken time after my return until the beginning of semester – Husserl also told me I needn't worry about opportunities for publication, the Jahrbuch[6] will be open to me automatically & with 'carte blanche'.

But I always tell myself now that I mustn't do anything half-baked in the coming publications & that they must be of a sort that provides something decisive, well-rounded & distinctive.

Although one has to fend entirely for oneself, the faith of those who are closest to us is more than something external & accidental provided that other people aren't objects but exert an influence as living incentives & do so powerfully from within their own life.

If you have time, do try to read Dost[oyevs]ki's political writings, they'll make a big impression on you – I meant to tell you before we left, and then, if you're able to, with respect to present-day culture, consult the essay by Hermann on dogmatism, in the thin volume lying on the small table.

Write me a long detailed letter soon. It'll make Daddy & Putz happy.

With deepest love, Dearest Soul,

And Putz sends you lots & lots of love & cuddles.

Your Blackamoor.

Kind regards from my parents, Marie & Fritz.

The strap on the back of the rucksack broke when we were changing trains – it was packed too full – it didn't really matter though.

---

[6] The *Jahrbuch für Philosophie und Phänomenologische Forschung* (*Annual for Philosophy and Phenomenological Research*).

The food supplies in the cities were now bad enough to justify talk of famine. Elfride was awaiting the birth of her second child in Freiburg, where she was looked after by friends, while Martin and Jörg were taken care of in Messkirch. Once Jörg had settled down in Messkirch, on 1 August Martin visited Beuron Archabbey with Theophil Rees. The following day he wrote from Messkirch: Here I really am quite free & far away from any surroundings that remind me of university & the philosophical business of the Schools, of discussions & chatter. I'm gradually beginning to feel physically fresh again too. When I now think back on the semester, it was like an assault where one cannot stop & think things over but keeps on running & thus gains ground – ground that I'm now cultivating – one needs this discipline of lectures & the corrective of an advanced audience until one finally has oneself safe in hand. Since the war I've already learnt a great deal concerning the technique & structure of a lecture too, & can now [?] see how my investigations are gradually knitting together. It would be a disaster if earlier or now I'd been roped into a civil service job. And you've accompanied me quietly through everything, & I thank you for it, Dearest Soul.

Messkirch, 6. VIII. 20.

My darling Soul!
Your letter made me very happy & I also see it as an expression of the fact that you've now found some peace & quiet – at a time when you urgently need it.

I also think that the more mature students see you as you are, although they won't grasp the whole truth – because with you it always takes a very long time to break the outer shell, which is in fact often tailored to keep others at bay.

You need hardly envy the women who study, for they're never fully involved & have thus from the outset already given up on grasping what is essential. And for me it's still difficult – though no longer as difficult as it used to be – to find the limit for them – to go as far as it makes sense & is one's duty to do so & then break off ruthlessly.

Mostly one goes too far – or one doesn't take them seriously at all – which again would be irresponsible bearing in mind that they could change courses & still take something with them into the 'other life' after all.

And this is precisely what is strangely new & great about the new type of woman – 'the knowing woman' as you call her – it perhaps <u>sounds</u> just a bit rationalistic yet is meant differently – her whole existence has within itself the same elemental forces & unbroken naturalness, perhaps even more healthy & freer than in the 'Gründerzeit woman'[7] – at the same time though everything is raised to a higher level of spiritual trans-lumination [*Durchleuchtung*]. But even here there remain strange differences – it thus struck me, when I was at the Nelsons' recently, how Frau Nels[on]. really is much more naturally bound up with the children <u>& looking after the children</u> – this too is rather trans-luminated – but in such a way that it's more illuminated [*beleuchtet*] – lit up by Something beside it – an Other that lies outside it: the woman who is loved – it lacks the inner spiritual light that doesn't reorganize everything, doesn't destroy its own meaning – but does loosen things up – so one can oneself always have that distance towards oneself. –

I was glad that you yourself saw a danger in yourself – that in the matter of upbringing you might lay down the direction too much yourself – the same thing has crossed my mind now & then – but I didn't say anything, because I know you're much too clever not to notice it yourself one day. It's delightful to see how Putz now pays attention to everything – he loves listening to the dicky-bird in the Hofgarten park – once he's been somewhere, he knows his way about – Yesterday he was weighed: 24½ lb. Marie & Mother are very careful with him & there's no harm in me going away for a few days – I always keep informed – I often think if only you could be here too – it's so wonderfully peaceful & fresh up here & I love the country so much & am noticing this time more than ever how deeply rooted I am after all in the soil & local character –

As for the great inner joy that you now bear within you & will accompany you all through your life – I don't need to tell you much – you know how I understand, & I keep feeling within myself that you've come even closer to me –

I've gradually become clear about my work – Husserl recently told me he had lived in constant uncertainty & had an opinion about whatever he did – what to make of this excessive modesty & yet pride I don't know – at any rate I answered him – that I was certain what lay ahead of us as a philosophical achievement & human task & for this very reason the surest thing was to be able to keep oneself open to developments & protect oneself from premature conclusions & dogmatic paralysis – I see one of the most difficult tasks facing the philosopher himself as being not to fall by the wayside prematurely and then just plant his cabbages – but to keep up – not with every trend that obtrudes itself from outside, but with the living tendencies that his own creations must necessarily still harbour within them if they are genuine – I always feel these inner revolutions very intensely – the way,

[7] The 'Gründerzeit' refers to the decades of rapid industrialization following the foundation of the German Empire in 1871.

always with a jerk, one undermines oneself – & the strange thing is that what one discovers then is never unfamiliar – but laid down in advance – it's always just a more genuine explication of one's possession, which is an unmerited grace, and which one must neither squander nor leave untouched & ineffective. –

I can still remember very well our last phenomenological talk – as well as my astonishment – which has been on my mind again & again. To me it was a most living confirmation that phenomenol. understanding entails more than just being quick on the uptake & having a sharp intellect. I notice this in the students. There are only very few who can keep up & feel their way into the real intentions – many of them get absorbed by the words & sentences.

I'm very much looking forward to my winter lecture – outwardly too we now have freer possibilities & can shape our life & dealings with people accordingly – above all I'm slowly managing to articulate what is concerning me most deeply & it's important to me to make the presentation as impersonal as possible. –

I'm hard at work once again – in the mornings the new lectures – in the afternoons the reworking of the old lectures & towards evening dictating.

Today I'm going to Beuron until Tuesday & hope to come back with considerable spoils. –

You don't need to send me the mss. [manuscripts] for the time being – it depends how I get on in Beuron.

With deepest love, Dearest Soul,

From the Grown-up Little Blackamoor

A kiss from afar to his dear Mummy from Putz.

Kind regards from my parents & bro. & sis.

Back from Beuron Martin wrote from Messkirch on 12 August:

I came back here yesterday evening. Little Putz was already asleep – but then at 10 I took him upstairs. This morning he was sitting in his little bed & laughing with glee. He's turning into a proper little chubby chops – I have a job picking him up – I don't know if he's being overfed. They just feed him until he's had enough – how about sending further 'instructions' – or is it all right as it is? – He's very lively & rather unruly – everyone thinks he's 3. –

On 20 August Martin reported:

I'm very well – I'm working rather less at the moment as I do now get rather fidgety thinking about how you'll be – but work is going well – the typing up is faltering, as I've got into reworking what I've done –

which helps me a lot – & I'd also like to have my lecture for the winter ready to be able to rework it – I'm right in my element. The Luther edition has already become indispensable to me – the Descartes too I now see quite differently from in the 1919 S.S. [summer semester] when I held a seminar on it – [. . .] Here there's a lot of talk about how many cattle now get bought up from the villages by the Jews & how that'll then be the end of buying meat in winter. Don't you think that if possible we should buy some in advance? Though Mother says it'll be very difficult to get anything out of the farmers – it also depends on what we can spend. [. . .] Next Sunday here it's the harvest dance – Fritz will be right in the thick of things – the harvest has turned out well – but the price won't be low – the farmers are gradually getting insolent up here too & everything's swamped with Jews & black marketeers.

On 20 August Hermann was born.

Messkirch, 23. VIII. 20

My darling Soul!
I'm glad now I know where you are & how you are. I can come to you often now & share in your great joy.

And what I give you – without talking much – in the way of real love, is yours. And one becomes strong oneself in such a love – a giving that is not a giving-away, in the very act of which one first finds oneself & returns to oneself from the sphere of constant distraction & estrangement.

I often find myself thinking how pale, untrue & sentimental everything is that is usually said about marriage. And whether we aren't giving shape to a new form of it in our life – without a programme or intention – but just by letting genuineness come through everywhere. – I can't tell you how much I'm looking forward to the winter. Though my lectures haven't got far yet – the best thing is probably for them to be written during the semester again. In the last few days I haven't got down to much work, after all I've been rather restless, & now I won't be able to sit still properly until I return either.

For a few days now it's been very cold & raw up here – it's very good for me – but it wouldn't be right for Putz in the long run. Today we had to heat the house, he has a slight cough, but otherwise he's cheerful, sings & plays with the blocks of wood. But it's good that we don't have to be here any longer in the raw days of September, as he's still too small for that. The leaves are falling from the trees already & people are predicting an early & hard winter.

I probably will come back here again though – for in spite of everything I'm least disturbed here – I've now said hello to all my acquaintances etc. & have also been together with my parents & bro. & sis. more than otherwise through Putz – so I'll then be able to withdraw completely – this way I also avoid the danger of getting stuck for a week in St Märgen or otherwise chattering away the time.

I must make sure that I get far enough with my preparations, as I do have to be even more 'active' as an 'assistant' – for the ones who were 'passed over' will be watching me closely –

Let's hope there won't be so many different sorts of people & the whole thing will be rather more uniform than last semester – when along with a good set of regulars it swarmed with people who seemed just to have happened by.

Now, you have a very good & quiet rest in the clinic – I don't want you coming out too soon –

Tell me, was Friedel [Lieber] still there when it started?

And what does the 'little man' look like?

I'm really curious to find out. [. . .]

With deepest love and a thousand kisses, my Dearest Soul,

Your Little Blackamoor.

Putz also sends his love and kisses & a special kiss for his little brother.

My parents & bro. & sis. are delighted & admire you for dealing with everything so effortlessly & with such vigour

On 30 August Martin returned to Freiburg with Jörg. Elfride was still in hospital. It was decided that Martin would return to Messkirch to continue preparing for the semester. After a week he was back there so he could work undisturbed. Hilde, a friend of Elfride's, helped the young mother. Food parcels continued to be sent from Messkirch to Freiburg.

In his brother Fritz Martin found someone with a great understanding for his philosophy. Fritz began typing up Martin's manuscripts.

Messkirch, 8. IX. 20.

My Dearest Soul! I really must take the time now & sit down at your bedside with you for an hour or so. I [am] not all that calm after all, even though I tell myself it isn't serious – but I do worry that this way you miss out on the proper time for convalescence while Hilde's still there & that it's all a strain on you. Don't you think Hilde could stay a little longer after all?

Well now, first I must tell you a few things, nothing big, but something that makes me happy: that I'm working so well <u>and steadily</u>; I'm at least partially out of the woods, mainly the old woods, & now the path is free for further ascent. I'm now working – in a quite different intellectual position, admittedly, one of assurance – like I did when I was a student – in one go & with the enthusiasm of moving 'forwards' & 'through'. In the mornings from 7 to 12 & then after a little 'nod' from 2 to ½ past 6, completely free from interruptions for lectures & seminars & visits – and above all increasingly fresh – it's all so important to me – because with this free run-up I'm quite certain to get into it & consolidate my position – & I was thinking the other day – in the evening when I go along the pathway at ½ past 6 in the early autumn, which I love so much, these are wonderful years that lie ahead of me now – that in this way I have the opportunity to live a life of undisturbed silent preparation & research & then each semester enter into lively engagement & my own distinctive production – for only afterwards does it become clear to me where I was successful in the semester in spite of all the imperfections – but the lectures are there before me & this makes it easier for me to get a precise grasp upon what is still unformed.

And now I just have one wish – that in the next few years – as far as the little lads will allow – in your way you can accompany me more closely in forming a strong spiritual milieu.

Perhaps I might also have the good luck some time to find an eminent academic person of my age as a friend, who is not exactly in the same field – but moves within the same spiritual orientation. But perhaps I'm not to have everything & must get along by myself in somewhat harsh independence. And how much I'm discarding in the way of what is false or determined by my limited origins & isolated developmt I notice with each year that passes & owe it to no one but you. I always resist at first – until I've clarified matters in my own mind – but that which is unsettling has its effect in secret – It's thus clear to me today – now I'm working through Harnack again but with quite different horizons – how ridiculous are the diatribes of Häcker, who hasn't produced a fraction of what Harnack achieved, & I'm gradually coming to doubt the genuineness of these Christian [?] men of letters too. Whenever I'm somewhat further away from the bustle of university, these things become clear to me almost of their own accord – standing in the midst of the hotchpotch of all manner of people I'm often still subject to vacillation – albeit only in matters that are peripheral –

I hope you enjoy the Hauptmann – I know you like him a lot – the old heretic impressed me myself with his psychological analysis & development & also in dramatic terms – never before have I found such a portrayal of the elemental power of nature. Yesterday I finally heard from Ragoczi that the Pushkin edition I had asked for is out of print – there's now only the G. Müller edition, which is so expensive that you'll have to be content with a paperback present – but I would like to give you the Pushkin. – [. . .]

Whenever I go for my evening walks now, I always imagine you're with me & I'm always grateful to you for suddenly opening my mind to the beauty of my home region.

Formerly, as a student indeed I had no 'time' for it – now I take new delight each day – & I don't feel happy unless I've been outside either just before the meal or in the evening.

And the only person I usually meet is my old teacher from my first year at elementary school & I find the respect with which he greets me puts me to shame.

When I'm weary in the evenings I play – don't be startled! – '66' with Father & Fritz & get quite involved, like when we played with Mother in Wiesbaden – this way I'm distracted before sleeping – otherwise I'm too deeply preoccupied by philos. –

Manasse [?] -Hölderlin is so grotesque one can only laugh – one wonders whether from this contamination we'll ever get back to the primordial freshness & rootedness of life again – sometimes one could really almost become a spiritual anti-Semite. [. . .]

With deepest love & many kisses, my Dearest Soul – get well again soon & be happy with our lads.

Give them both a tender kiss from me.

Your Blackamoor.

Kind regards to Hilde.

many happy returns to poor Gertrud on her birthday.

The folks send their regards & tell me to ask whether you'd perhaps like to have some butter & bread for next week.

Martin worked hard, but had difficulties with his preparations for the two-hour lecture course 'Introduction to the Phenomenology of Religion'. Elfride had fallen ill, and as a nursing mother was in urgent need of food. Elfride's mother came to stay with her and help out for a while. Before the start of the semester Martin returned to Freiburg again, laden with butterfat and a crate of books. As Elfride was unable to bring in any additional income, their financial situation was very difficult, and they depended upon support from the family and the generosity of friends. Martin's wishes for books could not be met.

Above all through Friedel Lieber, Martin and Elfride gained insights into movements such as the Freideutsche Jugend *(Free German Youth) and the* Deutsche Akademische Freischar *(German Academic Volunteer Corps), an organization founded in Göttingen in 1907 by students seeking to pursue the ideals of the Youth Movement for the reformation of modern life.*

Elfride with Jörg and Hermann, November 1920

1921

The year 1921 was uneventful, Martin's professional future remaining uncertain and the financial situation critical. In February, Martin was invited by the Szilasis on a skiing holiday in the Walser Valley.

[Postcard]

Mittelb[er]g. 2. III. 21.
My D. S. It's quite magnificent up here – skiing, eating & sleeping, one after the other. It isn't as comfortable as in the Black Forest – the snow is quite different too – we're very spoilt by the Feldberg – I'm learning a lot of new things here & what one thinks one has mastered – one learns even better – we must definitely come up here some time – when we can. The post seems to be very slow – I still haven't got anything from you. I wonder what the lads are doing – Frau Heimstadt is up here with her 4 and they're fine. Frau Cohn has also been here for a few days now, she does seem to be pretty ill. There's plenty of milk & cheese here – I'll bring some ch. back with me. During the day the sun's so strong that one can hardly bear it around midday. I am looking forward to being back with you – When I think of Reichenau, I don't fully enjoy it here after all. We'll probably return on Sunday.
    Love to you & the lads.
    Your Bl.

In the summer Martin pinned his hopes upon an associate professor-ship in Heidelberg, but this came to nothing. In August with Elfride he visited his parents and brother and sister in Messkirch.

1922

At the beginning of January 1922, Martin, with a new pair of skis, undertook a strenuous cross-country skiing expedition to Todtnauberg, where he met up with the Szilasis. Elfride went down with flu and was therefore unable to join them there. Once Martin had returned to Freiburg, he too fell ill. Elfride's condition deteriorated to such an extent that she had to go to hospital. Their circle of friends rallied round to look after the family.

Elfride had taken up her economics studies again with a view to doing a PhD in the subject. In this way, she hoped, she would be able to go out to work again if Martin did not receive a chair. On 24 January Martin wrote the following lines on the matter: But 'if I'm to say something too for once', then it's this, that the way I love & know you, I see your studies as something – in their current form, which is perhaps still a tentative one – that hinders you from giving yourself the womanly integrity that you can have in the contxt. of your life with me & the children.

You know I don't want glorifications & womanish idolization & what 'makes a man' – But there's a kind of womanly & above all strong participation – which no manly friendship can replace –

26. I. 22.

My Dearest Soul!
This morning I got up, but had to lie down again, as I'd hardly slept; I don't sleep any more now the trouble has shifted more onto my heart; but I don't want to take any drugs. My temperature's gone, only now I've got a cold; Friedl[änder]. thought it was too cold in the house; but I get it well heated & check it myself; I've already thought about putting the lads in my study. The little chaps are well & I can tell you

honestly that they don't stir all night long. The Privy Councillor's wife came this evening on your behalf; she told me off for being up; of course lying down is best – but I'd like to sleep again at night & not have sleepless weeks & months. It's a similar sort of situation to 1911, only mentally I feel completely fresh, though even a short conversation tires me out. For this reason I don't read much either. My appetite is better again; you needn't worry at all – but I can tell that I'll have to take a little break before launching the assault that's preparing inside me.

I've gained such great assurance that in fact I can learn nothing more from contemporary philosophers & to pursue my own enquiries just have to battle my way through enquiries into what for me are the decisive philosophers in history.

But I also sense the difficulty of the task I'm setting myself; yet one cannot make the goal high & simple enough. I can hear the voice ever more clearly; be true to yourself now & to your goals as they develop, pursue the substantive task, & don't look right or look left – the effect one has depends on other forces – a strong feeling of servitude towards a task that is forming within oneself – & I cannot help myself – this dreadful feeling of isolation – / not springing from a consciousness of being exceptional or suchlike / but from the realization that no one can help & the task that has been glimpsed must be done by sacrificing the possibility of all relaxation or repose.

And this is why in such situations I feel your love most deeply – because – strong as it is – it comes towards me factically of its own accord – because it 'is there' more than aesthetically as a possibility of pleasure.

And it's perhaps no coincidence that your hardness, which causes suffering to yourself, is there for me, as otherwise it would often be unbearable for me to see you living beside me – I mean, the fact that the two of us vigorously & incessantly develop & pursue our marriage anew as a task makes it one that is genuine, human – marriage is a 'haven' for the idle, who close their eyes to themselves & invent one illusion after another, who eschew their marriage & always replace it with something to live for with some prospects of success & gain (children that have turned out well, a role in society, income & a livelihood – the picture of the 'happy marriage'.) –

Friedländer informed me today that I've been voted onto the Faculty (there's perhaps no harm in me coming into greater contact with the gentlemen in this way), his business with Schwörer has fallen through, he's very dejected. His lecture yesterday evening is said to have been excellent, according to Löwith – it's said to have been very successful; let's hope it does him some good; I can well understand how he feels in his situation particularly at the moment.

If possible, please give Helen a menu to bring with her the next few days. She takes good care of me otherwise, the nurse now only comes briefly in the mornings.

This evening Gertrud washed the little chaps & put some fresh things on them – they're proper lads now, especially once they've been given a good haircut.

I think it is better that you stay on & have some peace & quiet <u>and milk</u> – much though I wish you were here. It feels very much more difficult to be here in Lerchenstrasse without you than e.g. several weeks in Messkirch.

I don't yet know how I'll deal with my lecture. In any event I don't want to wreck my creative capacity for the months of March & April.

When I now think it through objectively, it's actually much too much that I'm offering in my lectures.

Yesterday the increased residence allowance came, 908 mks – 90.80 tax. That makes 817.20. / Don't you want anything to read? I'll send you the Madame Councillor [Goethe][8] with this – . So have a nice rest & be glad – Jörg still talks about the 'Little Birthday Man' – the Little One looks splendid & is getting more & more assertive. This could be good.

With deepest love,
Your Little Blackamoor.

During their slow convalescence Martin and Elfride were supported by their friends, who visited them and brought them dainties.

Karl Löwith had been studying under Martin since the summer semester of 1920 and went on to receive his habilitation under him at Marburg in 1928.

During a skiing weekend in Todtnauberg in February, Elfride hit upon the idea of building a cabin there. From the local district of Rütte, she came across a carpenter by the name of Schweitzer who had enough well-seasoned timber, was happy to take on the job and also found them an area of uncultivated land belonging to Pius Brender, commonly known as Black Pius.

On 13 March, Elfride's half-sister Else died at the age of 41 following the stillbirth of her fifth child. Elfride travelled to Leipzig-Gohlis for the funeral and then on to Wiesbaden to console her father. Antonie Runge, Else's mother, had been Richard Petri's first wife and the love of his life. She had died of a haemorrhage at the age of 22 in 1880, two weeks after the birth of her daughter Else.

[8] The much-read letters of Johann Wolfgang Goethe's mother, Katharina Elisabeth Goethe, who as the wife of an Imperial Councillor was commonly known as *Frau Rat Goethe* or Madame Councillor.

For the construction of the Cabin, Elfride requested 60,000 marks from her parents in anticipation of her inheritance. She needed the money immediately and in cash, as the carpenter wanted to turn his pay into natural produce such as leather and flour in view of the inflation. Elfride had drawn an outline of the Cabin, influenced by her experience of the cabin on the Silberberg. It was to be ready to move into by 1 August, as their flat in Lerchenstrasse had been sublet on a fixed-term basis to an American couple in exchange for dollars. Yet there were delays in the construction, and transporting the cooker, bedding and household articles to Todtnauberg also called for considerable ingenuity and energy on Elfride's part. On 9 August, the family moved into a cabin in a state of near completion. The spring had been curbed, but there was still no fountain, no shed and no toilet. Construction of the Cabin was a long-cherished dream that had come true for Elfride, while for her husband it represented a place of contemplative retreat.

In September, Martin visited Karl Jaspers in Heidelberg for the first time. They had met in Freiburg on the occasion of Edmund Husserl's birthday on 8 April 1920 and been in correspondence ever since.

[Postcard]

[Heidelberg] 11 Sept. 22

My D. S.

A quick greeting before work.

I'm really progressing now; I must say, when I look at my Cabin manuscripts, which I have with me, they've turned out anything but badly.

Even so, I now need an unbroken spell for once when I can plough through the whole thing.

I get on very well with J[aspers]. I am acquiring new insights & learning a lot – in terms of material.

He has a very big library, though not one I'd like to have, and I don't let it disturb me much.

You're possibly having the nicest weather now; here it's rainy & foggy.

We work almost all the time, as Jaspers cannot go out much.

In the next few days I'll go & see Rickert some time.

Best wishes to you & the boys

Your Bl.

Kind regards to Herr Maass.

After his stay with Jaspers, Martin went to Freiburg, as he was unable to work properly in the Cabin on account of the children. His friends regularly invited him round for lunch. Inflation was further exacerbating the shortages. For his birthday, Martin was given 30,000 marks by Frau Szilasi, which he hoped to use to buy himself books and paper.

27. IX. 22.

My Dearest Soul!
Yesterday I received a card from Husserl: 'Please come'. Once I was there, Malvine [Husserl] read me a long letter from <u>Natorp</u>. They're <u>determined</u> to have me; Natorp mentions Hamann, who is fully informed of my effectiveness (obv. by Jantzen) – and further that he's recently heard the very best things from Marburg students (PhD students who have been with me here in the last two semesters) – in Marbg. they want a phe[nomeno]logist – & also someone with a critical command of the Middle Ages (those theologians)! Nat. asks H. for a report on teaching activ. – as well as a report on forthcoming publications.

So now I have to produce an excerpt – which Frau Husserl will be kind enough to transcribe.

And then I'll set about transcribing my <u>mss.</u> so Natorp has even more documents. So I've no choice but to stay down here – difficult though it is for me to go even longer without seeing you & the little lads – Every day is valuable now – but I think I'm working with great momentum & 1 or 2 days will then perhaps be enough after all. Bauer too might poss. have to do without me.

Today Besseler writes from Karlsruhe – on behalf of Gurlitt – that Nohl has written to him – the matter will be decided in Göttingen in the very first faculty meeting (at the end of October!) & he hopes for sure to get me through. So somewhere it will work out this time. [. . .]

Mother has written from Messk. – they're expecting me – I replied straightaway to tell them of the situation I'm in – Mother enquires whether she should send potatoes <u>before</u> 1 Oct.; I answered <u>yes</u> & at the same time sent the money.

What am I to do if the potatoes come now?

I was recently at Ebb[in]g[haus]'s; his wife looks <u>very</u> ill; I think they'd like to come up for a night some time.

My Dearest Soul, I'm really longing to see you – & it <u>isn't at all nice</u> – alone in the flat – but <u>marvellous</u> for working – I have to come to terms with this contrast. Fortunately I don't have much time to ruminate on it.

Don't you think it'd be good to send the <u>crate of books</u> again before 1 Oct. – I could <u>really</u> do with it (!) – I can pay for it with Szilasi's money, can't I – get an errand boy to deal with it.

I've got the Augustine – marvellous – Waibel was very decent – about the 9,000 marks – today! when a volume of Nietzsche (pocket edition – used to be 5 marks!) costs <u>560</u> marks. With the money I'll buy the most necessary books as well – <u>Kant</u> etc.

Do you need to have the whole 9,000 marks back? Or are you content with 6,000?

With much love to you & the little lads

from your Little Blackamoor

The bell doesn't work – either upstairs or downstairs! excellent for me – but it bothers the others.

What am I to do? What should I do if Springer were to break into the flat? [. . .]

Martin's hopes of a chair in Göttingen came to nothing; in Marburg a decision was still to be reached.

From now on, the family would often spend the vacation up at the Cabin.

1923

Reaching the Cabin in Todtnauberg was an arduous business, particularly in winter. There were various ways of getting to Todtnauberg: by train to Hinterzarten and from there on foot or by ski over the Rinken, Feldberg and Stübenwasen; by train via Lörrach up the Wiesen Valley to Todtnau and from there on foot up a steep slope; by train to Kirchzarten and from there by carriage via Oberried and Notschrei; or by tram to Freiburg-Günterstal and then on foot or by ski via Horben up the Schauinsland, and over die Halde and Notschrei. All these routes were arduous, especially in adverse weather conditions.

Inflation was making everyday needs prohibitively expensive to meet. Fuel was in particularly short supply. In March, Jörg was taken to Feldafing (on Lake Starnberger) by the Szilasis, Martin joining them there later. On 15 March he told Elfride: Jörgele met me at the station with a beaming face. He's very cheerful & looks very fresh. His little legs & arms still the same – but he's become a bit stronger all right – he's looked after well & meticulously. At table he eats heartily – especially when he's been outside beforehand. The first thing he did was take me to see the nanny-goats in their pen – to which I immediately had to give some hay – he then asked straightaway if Mother was at home again, if Hermännle was still with Frau Leber & if the chuff-a-chuff was on the cupboard. They say he was very homesick at the beginning & the little lad wanted to go home again. He's quite settled in now – yet I'm still glad I'm here.

Martin's hopes for a chair at Marburg fell through, and the situation now became critical, for his term as Husserl's private assistant was also running out.

My Dearest Soul!

Many thanks for your nice letter. It seems that mine crossed paths with yours in the post.

That certainly is a marvellous result & it does Berlin great credit – there's no point in trying to puzzle it out – but Scheler is behind all the 'agitation' against me – for Hartmann didn't take the initiative of his own accord. The whole thing is just like the Kiel affair.

As regards my associate professorship, your view is too optimistic – esp. if my Aristotle is out by then, they'll take care not to set a fox to catch a thief – & on no account will I myself accept any old substitution for this chair.

Now, my Dearest Soul, if it'd worked out, such speedy external advance wouldn't have suited what I've done & want to do – I have time – & we won't be starving just yet either, will we.

The only decisive thing is: I am inwardly assured of my task – & at the same time have so much quiet joy with you & the boys – home & the ideal peace for work. I'll manage even without a change of air –

Surely you don't believe that after this treatment I'd ever accept another chair in Prussia – unless out of sheer need – i.e. out of consideration for you & the children – I had to accept one.

Your news didn't shock me for a moment – I'm completely alone & self-contained with my task & nothing else in the world gives such support as that. The only thing is the pressure from Husserl.

And another thing: I've been too kind with the students & given my time & effort for their sake – when I hear how comfortably the gentlemen run things for themselves here. But I cannot do otherwise – after all, I am a Dozent, a <u>teacher</u>.

I've been very kindly received at Löwith's – the young man has a splendid library – much bigger & better than mine – though at bottom it doesn't have any use – something for sophisticates.

The old man is a petty bourgeois 'schoolmaster' (painter) – he received me in his studio – as the enclosed didn't turn out well – twice again today. [. . .]

Szilasi (husband) constantly runs him down – but the man has worked a bit & can do something – whereas Sz. literally lazes about – you cannot but feel sorry for the wife, especially when you see the way she's tyrannized.

She shows a touching concern for Jörgele – he's already quite burnt, as I am – the weather here is marvellous day after day.

I'm really looking forward to being with you again soon. [. . .]

Löwith has shown me the most beautiful parts of Munich – in particular the collection of Greek vases – this is one of the things that has left the deepest impression on me so far.

For the rest I've had more than enough of the city & will be glad to be out of it again –

Today I bought a pair of Haferl [shoes] for 58,000 – very nice & solid – from a shop mentioned by Herr Löwith – in others they cost 78,000 – there weren't any black market ones. [. . .]

Please don't say anything about the associate professorship to Husserl – you know the old man only goes in for silly utopian fantasies – perhaps it'll now occur to him off his own bat to get me the title.

Our government here in Baden really is so damn stupid that they'd rather appoint Berlin schoolmasters (cf. Heidelberg) than their own lecturers.

The publication wouldn't have helped me either – what does the government care about academic faculty reports –

Anyway, enough of that –

I now have another nice week's work in Feldafing ahead of me with little Putz – here there was nothing doing –

With love and kisses to you –

and love to the little lad as well.

Your real Blackamoor.

Just before Easter Martin wrote:

I work all day long & wish to myself that the whole appointment business would come to an end. It's disgusting the way they're conjecturing, wangling & scheming around – ; that in Berlin I'm regarded as the phen.logist is obviously an empty phrase – & is worth just as much as if I profess my great respect for someone & at the same time spit in his face – . If the appointment of 2 Freiburg lecturers can amount to an obstacle, then they're not serious about me either. Geyser's chair is a very difficult matter – the particular teaching post is only for the history of scholasticism – which Geyser of all people never fulfilled – & which I could probably fulfil as well as anybody – but the question is how great are the demands the theolgs. make on the teaching programme otherwise – I believe indeed that even the government wouldn't dare appoint me for fear of the fuss from the Centre [Party]. It's enough that we get by with our children; otherwise I have more important things to do than strive for a big career or such-like.

On 5 April Martin travelled to Messkirch with Jörg, having been well fed and showered with presents. Martin's father had by now aged considerably, but his mother was fresh and cheerful. On the same day, Martin's sister Marie gave birth to her only child, Clothilde. On 12 April, Martin and his son Jörg were back in Freiburg.

Elfride had meanwhile given up her studies in economics, as she had more than enough to do running the household, looking after the children and organizing their supplies of food.

The family spent the summer up at the Cabin, with Martin making visits to Freiburg. He had by now been appointed to the associate professorship at Marburg. On 8 July he wrote: On Saturday I was at Husserl's; <u>he's staying</u> & wants me later to be his successor; but <u>nothing at all must be said about it</u> – otherwise his negotiations in Karlsruhe will break down – so the motto is – 'he will go'.

To earn money Martin gave private tuition to the Japanese aristocrat Kuki Shuzo. He spent August with the family in Todtnauberg, and in September he was invited to Feldafing again with Jörg. In the meantime, Elfride attempted to solve the problem of their accommodation in Marburg, where the acute housing shortage caused by war and inflation meant that a flat could only be procured through a highly complicated three-way exchange that was liable to break down.

                                                    Feldaf[in]g. 1 Oct. 23
My Dearest Soul!
Yesterday the enclosed card from Hüther came. Also one from Fritz saying that Father isn't at all well. His eyesight has suddenly declined so much that he can no longer go out alone. I suppose it'll be a gradual death over the winter. Under these circumstances it'll be a burden on dear Mother if I come with Jörg. All the same, Father will be happy to have the little lad once more. And I can more or less look after him.

I'll leave here on the 3rd or 4th & be with you on the 6th or 7th – I'll let you know from Messkirch –

I'm really looking forward to still having a few days with you & the children.

In the last few days I've come to a standstill with my work – in the long run the conditions here are unbearable. The Szs are exceedingly kind & nice with me & Jörg.

The money arrived today – as well as the notification from the registrar.

Perhaps something will now come of the other flat. I'll manage to battle through to Christmas all right. I'll have so much to do that I won't have time for brooding. [. . .]

I'm really looking forward to the autumn days with you in Lerchenstr.

With best wishes and fondest love,
                              Your Little Blackamoor.
<u>Lots</u> of love and kisses from Jörgele & from both of us for the little one.

92

*On 12 October Martin moved into two rented rooms in Marburg.
The accommodation had been organized for him by Hans-Georg
Gadamer, who had studied under Martin during the previous summer
semester and was to become a close friend of the whole family.*

Marburg 14 Oct. 23

My Dearest Soul!
It's Sunday evening & I'd like to come & talk to you for a little while.
I can't write to you about business matters until tomorrow afternoon
– I'm not seeing the registrar until then.

The little town is quite delightful – it's just right for me – Yesterday
afternoon the sun came out & I strolled through the bumpy streets with
their pretty little houses – each one looks different & they're all huddled
together like the Hessian girls going shopping in their finery. The Lahn
has plenty of water & flows through between great willow trees – from
one bridge there's a view like in Heidelberg up the Neckar. I have the
feeling that everything will be all right with my work here. But even so
I am sad that you aren't here & we cannot enjoy it together – let's hope
I'll soon be able to show you round. Perhaps you'll see even more.

My little lady is very nice & Trienchen is doing well. For these two
rooms I'm paying 5 unrationed loaves, currently 320 mill. a loaf – a
student room costs 4 loaves.

The lady does ask me to bring bed linen though, this is now generally the done thing – towels as well? I'd also like some cocoa for the
mornings, can you send me some? the same with tea – Frau Hartmann
has been lending me up to now – Furthermore I don't have a standard
lamp – Gadamer can only lend me his for the time being. But I intend
to work during the day whenever possible so as to save light. I'm also
without the waistcoat that goes with the tails – I haven't found the
tram ticket despite a thorough search – please could you just have a
look in the outside side pocket of the grey suit – or in my ski jacket.

The bread coupons are to go on, you know; so I'll need a deregis-
tration form – soon I'll also have to look for coal.

Next Sunday it's the rectorship inauguration ceremony – on 1 Nov
I begin the lectures.

The Hartmanns are charming – I have to go to lunch each of the
next 3 days – I think I get on well with him – their little daughter is
already looking forward to meeting the boys – I had to tell them all
about the Cabin & show them the pictures.

Today I was at Natorp's – tomorrow we're going for a walk together
– his wife is rather loud & effusive – but nice even so – Jaensch is away
for a few days. This afternoon I was at the Gadamers' – the old gentleman very nice – I immediately met the new rector there & Prof.

Busch (modern history) – who was in Freiburg for a time in the 90s – the people are all very warm –

people are very sorry for us for having such bad luck – I dropped something of a hint about Uhlenhuth – they say his wife likes it very much here & has no inclination to move & Dold incidentally is sure to get the flat. Zopke's house I only saw from the outside – it isn't vulgar at all – definitely the nicest –

Dold lives in Orleanstrasse – the Vogels' flat doesn't have a garden at all.

On Saturday I got 2½ billion marks separation allowance – on Tuesday there are supposed to be new ones – ; I wanted to buy myself some jam – 700 million a jar – so I didn't bother. In the evenings I'm still living off the meat & the sausage – lunch costs 200 mill. Here the lecturers queue up at the cash register & pick up their money – I don't think this way will work either once the semester is under way.

The lecture fee is to be 50 gold pfennigs – so 2 gold marks for a four-hour lecture – something at least – if only it were paid out at once.

Student life used to be much easier than now with just a little money – I'm really looking forward to it coming to an end very soon & the removal materializing.

There are no more subscriptions for food of course – but the prices are to remain as stable as possible for a week at a time.

As soon as I have some money I'll send you what I can spare.

I have the removal costs, there's no objection to the approval for the allowance – but it has to go to Berlin – the registrar will see to it with all haste, Prussian style!

In the end I will have to go to Jaensch's after all – which I'm quite glad about because of the heating – he has central heating & it's due to be turned on.

Ruhr refugees had already been assigned to my present flat by the housing office.

For the time being though write to Weissenburgstr. 22, I. Jaensch lives really close by.

The registrar explicitly assured me that the University is very much awaiting me, especially the Theolg. Faculty.

I now just have one wish – that you are well & the boys are & that you can come really soon.

With love and kisses to you & the little lads.

Your Little Blackamoor.

Bed shoes & wristlets please!

Wait until next time I write before sending off the things.

After Martin had changed rooms a number of times, the family was finally in a position to plan its move to Schwanallee 21 in Marburg.

94

My darling Soul!

You're a real brick for bringing it off now after all! I can't tell you how glad I am – especially for you as well.

And now my only wish is that you really can create a home for yourself & realize those long and silently cherished plans.

It'll be a very nice place for us – a lovely garden – No doubt you'll get around to cultivating it too – The wood very near – nice high ceilings. Frau Nidderehe – along with Frau von Behring the wealthiest woman here – has a cow – Frau Zopke says we'll get milk there – if not, whenever we like from the nearby village of Ockershausen – Frau Z. will also pass all the other tradesmen on to us – Frau Gadamer is here & will take on the job. What a small world it is, Frau Zopke – a quite splendid woman – was a friend of Aschoff's in her youth!

On Wednesday I'm being offic. introduced in the Faculty. Today I'm having lunch at the Gadamer seniors'.

Frau Hartmann has been away with her daughter since yesterday. The Szilasis are coming on 3 Nov. at the latest. One of the boys could be put up at the Gadamer juniors'. And you here if need be – only I don't know how it'll be with my work – I've hardly managed to do anything yet & the lecture's just around the corner. Hartmann would be delighted to take you in – I don't know if we can accept – as he's up to his neck in work – but perhaps you'll manage all right there on your own – He doesn't work until the afternoon & night, you know. So when you come, you'll be looked after all right (either here with me or at the Hartmanns').

This morning I bumped into Loewith & Marseille in the Univers. – they arrived yesterday – right off I was able to offer them two rooms that Frau Hartmann had found for me – & in the course of our conversation it emerged – when the name von Rohden was mentioned – that the young woman had had the elder Rohden brothers who were killed in action staying with her & that the Academic Association had been founded in her house – Rohd. is coming tomorrow evening & is to stay there too – very near to us & the Hartmanns.

Everything is resolving itself so nicely now – after the nasty first fortnight – & every day now the responsibility of my task weighs more heavily on my mind & I hope to myself that I at least partly meet the expectations & can be totally committed to my work – then we'll build up a vibrant life here – I often like to think of our engagement at the moment – as silently cherished plans grow & ripen – & now we're coming to an age when we can both really give & ourselves receive such wonderful things from our two boys.

I kiss your dear brow & take your hand once more, so that you may accompany me along this new path.

I was overcome with happiness today – Tanabe [a Japanese student] wrote me a lovely letter from Paris.

But down to business:

On 25 Oct. I sent you <u>three</u> times 20 billion – which I presume you now have.

Yesterday there was supposed to be money again – we came away empty-handed, as there was no means of payment there.

I dealt with the transfer this morning at the registrar's – I asked for the money to be wired to you.

Everything's all right with the Zopkes & the housing office – the Zopkes intend to load up on Tuesday at the latest. The little girl is very happy.

Don't overexert yourself Dearest Soul – I'm afraid you're quite exhausted – will Frau Paul come with you now?

Much love to you & the boys

Your Little Blackamoor.

Soon it'll be: 'Off at Marburg!'

In November 1923 the currency was finally stabilized, and the Reichsmark (equal to one trillion, i.e. a million million, paper marks, or one gold mark) was introduced.

1924

*The Heidegger family settled down well in Marburg. On 2 May 1924
Martin's father, Friedrich Heidegger, died in Messkirch.*

My Dearest Soul! I arrived safely – Father is lying at rest & looks very
peaceful among lots of wreaths – Fritz told me the death throes were
dreadful, from 1 o'clock at night until the following lunchtime at ½
past 12. Haematoma the cause & Father was no longer conscious
thank God. Shortly after the stroke Father slept calmly for another
hour & then his absolutely healthy heart made its presence felt &
refused to give up the fight. Father had been up in the afternoon – ate
with the best of appetites & smoked two more cigars. Half an hour
before the end he then went all quiet. Fritz held Father's hand & could
feel his pulse stop beating. It was lucky for Father that he was unconscious when he died – he's said to have been terribly afraid of Hell.

Father's holding a lovely posy of wild flowers & a simple 'funeral
cross' among them.

Tomorrow at ½ past 2 we'll take Father up to the graveyard. The
boys who ring the bells want to give an especially good performance
for him –

Dear Mother is wonderfully composed – Marie & Rudolf arrived
in Radolfzell just before 2 o'clock – the child [Clothilde] with them –
that way Mother has a little sunshine right away.

I assume you'll write to your parents for me. Mother Marie & Fritz
send their regards.

With love to you & the boys.

Your Bl.

3. V. 24.

Marie will stay with Mother for a fortnight to 3 weeks.

Summer 1924

In the spring Martin received from Japan an offer of a three-year scholarly post at an institute for the Japanese aristocracy and high finance world.

He had by now struck up what was to be a fruitful friendship with the Protestant theologian Rudolf Bultmann. Martin gave a lecture to the Marburg theologians on 'The Concept of Time'.

At the beginning of the vacation Elfride went up to the Cabin with the boys.

Marbg. 2 Aug. 24

My Dearest Soul!
It's become very quiet at home. It won't be that easy for me not having you & the little lads around.

Last week I played faustball twice & had a lot of fun. We want to play every Wednesday morning. The day before yesterday Natorp was there. He isn't at all well & is very depressed at not being able to work. This month he's going to take a cure in Wiesbaden for 4 weeks & is hoping for an improvement. Before then he's speaking at the Quaker meeting in Rothenburg.

From what Bultmann & von Rohden tell me & what I otherwise gather, my talk went down well – particularly with the sort of people who up to now have kept a distance from me. The trouble was that too many people squeezed their way in. In this way a good many things can be said more simply – albeit less precisely – . But I do have confidence in the subject matter itself – not as something finished, but as a concrete directive for real work. At any rate the theology lecturers are very excited & that is good.

Incidentally Natorp said I shouldn't go to Japan – he said he'd be very sorry if I were to abandon Marburg.

The Hartmanns have definite hopes of being offered a chair in spring (either Cologne or Berlin) –

Since you've been up at the Cabin, I've been keeping an eye on the barometer – it's rising nicely again now. Do write soon & tell me how everything was when you arrived.

A few days ago I was visited by the current Prefect of the Vatican Archives – a Franciscan (Katterbach), who was with you in my first Kant seminar back then & sends his regards. He told me some very interesting things about the recent research. [. . .]

The 'Youth Meeting' here is pretty unpleasant & the Founder's Day celebrations are still continuing. The A[cademic]. A[ssociation]. is performing (ancient motets) on Wednesday evening in the Luther Church.

With love to you & the boys

Your Little Blackamoor.

[. . .]

Martin remained alone in Marburg while their flat was being renovated, with Lieschen running the household. On 10 August he wrote to Todtnauberg: Recently Jakobsthal too was with me at Hartmann's – (Little Paul!) The conversation turned to my salary – he was appalled – he said <u>Bremer</u> his assistant got that much. And he explained that he (Jak.) had acted as follows (these Jews!): Bremer was supposed to be getting a better paid assistant post in Giessen – this was not official & only communicated privately – Jak. had this correspondence & took it to Richter in Berlin – said they had to keep Br[emer]. & give him a better salary & that's what happened. Jak. himself has never officially been offered a chair but is in the highest salary bracket. Just before that we'd been talking about Switalski's rejection & I said the Faculty would like to have me – the Dean had expressly asked me – Jak. said I should get a corresponding statement from Huss. to the effect that they wanted me – but would <u>only</u> appoint me if I were certain to come – & should take it to Berlin. According to Jak. such bargaining is the order of the day. Everyone's chasing such opportunities for an appointment outside Prussia. But I have the feeling it's a shady business – because I wouldn't accept the offer anyway – unless I were quite independent of the Catholics. – It also goes against the grain to ask Husserl for that sort of thing. At best he'd have to enquire again himself.

On 17 August Paul Natorp died unexpectedly in a Marburg hospital. Natorp had played an active part in securing Martin's appointment in Marburg. On 23 August Martin wrote: Yes – Natorp – I wander around here & now know that I no longer have anyone here at the University to whom I could look up with admiration. They say I am a severe critic – yet when I find someone whom I can admire & venerate I'm the first to do so. I told you already that at the beginning of August N. suddenly came to me one afternoon – he sat in the leather armchair for a long time – & we spoke of his plans – his kind, animated eyes were hoping & searching for friendship. I accompanied him home as well – the next day he went to give a talk with the Quakers.

At the beginning of September Elfride travelled with the boys from the Cabin to Messkirch to visit her mother-in-law. On 9 September Martin wrote: Now you'll be sitting in Messkirch, – I'd like to come & see you for an afternoon, & have a little cup of tea & a walk up to the graveyard & my beloved forest, on the beautiful pathway. You really must show the little mites the deer outside. Let's hope my youthful escapades don't come back to life in Messkirch at the sight of the boys. [. . .] The boys will give Mother & Fritz a lot of pleasure & bring all the noise & commotion of the past back to the Mesmer House again.

1925

In April 1925 Martin gave lectures on 'Wilhelm Dilthey's Research and the Struggle for a Historical Worldview' in Kassel and Fritzlar. On 18 [?] April he reported: My lectures are pretty well attended by 60–70 – great interest – & I've met a few quite splendid people – a young clergyman called Schaft, who is a friend of Barth's. I now also have the feeling that I speak 'freely' – calmly & not too hard – the next few lectures will be rather more difficult, [. . .]. Bröcker arrived on Thursday on the fast train fr. Hamburg & is staying with Boehlau – a few other students from Marburg have also come, inc. Weizsäcker & wife.

Elfride visited her parents in Wiesbaden with Jörg.

Marburg a/L. 30. VI. 25.

My D. S.

I wish you many happy returns of the day. I should like to thank you on this day for your care for me & your collaboration. After all – along with the phenomenological critique – this involves just what is hardest: renouncing and waiting & believing. And when I consider such a semester from your point of view, this calls for great effort. Here there's still a difference between what duty calls for & what you bestow over and above that in the way of goodness & strength.

And if I don't speak of this, you do know I think of it, don't you? Disagreeable though it is in itself that you're now away even on this day too, it gives me the opportunity to express my gratitude to you more fully than otherwise. And conversely I'll be glad if through my sacrifice I can make you & your dear parents happy.

Hermann is quiet, but instantly happy if one plays with him. On Sunday morning I took him on my little walk to Schwanengasse; he was very proud & suddenly said to me: You <u>have</u> married a lovely

Mother, haven't you – . The delightful thing is that now he really was thinking of you. On Sunday he was in Ockershausen & came back overjoyed. He'd come to my bedside at the very crack of dawn. He often now says vehemently that when Jörg is back he'll then also go to Wiesb. This morning after the lecture I cycled with him towards Kappel & then took him to Kindergarten.

This afternoon he's at the Bultmanns', who also invited me for supper yesterday evening. Afterwards Frau B. sang something from Gluck & he accompanied her. They clearly wanted to give me a special treat.

Heitmüller's talk on Friday tried to mediate between Barth & H[usserl]'s old line of thought – elegantly & clearly – without really getting hold of the subject. The discussion was postponed to Saturday morning. I didn't intend to go because I didn't want to attack an elderly scholar who has rendered outstanding services to the sciences in front of the students. But Bultmann himself came to see me beforehand & so I went along out of friendship; it transpired, as I thought it would, that Bult., a student of Heitmüller's, like Barth – who actually was attacked – now also elegantly yet incisively set out their differences. Von Soden also spoke, then old Jülicher & finally I did too – ; I touched on nothing theological, but tried to bring out the methodological problem, adding purely substantive points without criticism and thereby furnishing an implicit defence of B[ultmann]. from the perspective of philosophy. H[eitmüller]. himself hardly answered the objections – but even so the debate was valuable for the many students who had turned up & was received as such too. The students want to publish it. So I'm very satisfied after all. And the main share of the success is due to the figure of Heitmüller – who spoke elegantly & calmly & said what he understood – without the loud-mouthed counterfeiting of Brunner. In the evening Bultm. had invited the Theolog. Faculty & Heitm. to his house. B. told me that there he'd been set upon by Hermelink (& thus indirectly the latter's wife) & others – they said that he was spoiling the students & making them arrogant & turning other colleagues into second-rate lecturers – that in general only Bult. & Heidegg. counted any more. –

In the meantime Husserl has written 'strictly confidentially' to say that through Jaensch the Commission has enquired into his view as regards the Heidegger-Mahnke pecking order. He furnished this question with a series of exclamation marks & will now of course answer accordingly.

He did want to know, however, what I thought of the Mahnke-Becker relation, so he wouldn't spoil my plans by the way in which he formulates his assessment. I will of course give Becker first place. Huss. explicitly remarks that he had written his assessment of M. solely with regard to the associate professorship.

So the next meeting won't be fixed until Husserl's answer has arrived. I wrote by return of post.

H. writes that Kaufmann will be receiving his habilitation in Freiburg with his revised work on Yorck & is already there.

I've written to the Szilasis, but nothing about an invitation, as I didn't know whether you still want to go ahead with that idea.

The money's taken care of; I received 540.55 marks.

I haven't got hold of the wood yet, as I lost my Saturday morning work time on account of the debate.

Hermann sends you a kiss for your birthday.

The two of us send our very best wishes to you all

and hope you have a lovely time.

Your Bl.

Martin stayed on in Marburg while his family went up to the Cabin. On 31 July he wrote: The invitation to the Faculty meeting on Monday reads: 1. Request of the Theological Faculty that one of their representatives be heard in the matter of the new appointment to the Chair of Philosophy. 2. New appointment to the Chair of Philosophy. As point 1 is a question of basic principle with the most far-reaching implications – which for the moment is independent of me personally, & I'm the only expert in the Faculty for clarifying the matter, Schaefer, Hartmann & Jakobsthal have asked me in the strongest terms to take part in the meeting at all costs. I already had everything packed – & now for the sake of this business have to forgo the immediate departure to which I was so very much looking forward. I feel sorry for you & the boys, who are sure to be waiting. [. . .] Jakobsthal told me & Schaefer confirmed that Otto has the greatest influence with Becker [Prussian minister of education and the arts] & that if he's heard in our Faculty quite a few really will go along with him. But apart from the question as a whole, at issue – as I clearly see it – is a matter of principle. Today Hartmann gave his last lecture. Lectern decorated with roses – Gadamer thanked him on behalf of the students – I myself spoke briefly too.

In August, Martin was proposed as the first-choice successor to Nicolai Hartmann.

In October, Martin went to see his mother in Messkirch and also paid a visit to his friend Theophil, who by now was remarried, had a young son, and was running a practice in Constance.

On 15 October, Fritz married Elisabeth Walter, generally known as Liesel, in Messkirch. Afterwards Martin travelled on to see Karl Jaspers in Heidelberg.

Hdbg. 22 Oct. 25

My Dearest Soul!
Thank you for your cards. The letter to the Rector is taken care of.

I'm spending some very pleasant & rewarding days with Jaspers. And I wish you could share in part of this inner joy of mine.

Such living impulses are irreplaceable – & if I don't have anything of the sort among my colleagues in Marburg – apart from Bultmann perhaps – I'm thankful that I do have Jaspers. There's a reciprocal struggle for the friendship which may prove uplifting for me.

And the weeks up at the Cabin, weeks to which I keep coming back in my mind, have become even more precious to me through this conclusion to the vacation.

If from time to time I now compare Husserl & Jaspers – looking at their philosophical <u>existence</u> – then it's like night & day: on the one hand – to exaggerate – interest in the school – acknowledgement of the master – lack of understanding for destiny & decisions; on the other hand – sovereignty – modesty – personal commitment & a real sense of a man who takes action.

I have to tell him a lot about you & the boys. And today I told him how we met.

And so today I'm especially happy & grateful – Even when I think of the semester. I don't believe it has to be like this – i.e. that we shan't – for all my isolation through work – still find a higher form for our closeness after all.

Your silent help with my work will make me always a debtor – but I also know that you're strong enough to be happy when you see me grow inwardly & become free – apart from academic achievement – which cannot be separated philosophically.

I'm looking forward to being with you again – & I wanted to come on Saturday – but it's the rectorship ceremony on Sunday – so I'll travel on Monday & come on the usual train.

Much love to you & the boys.
Your Little Blackamoor.

The Jasper<u>s</u> (not Jasperrs as you write both times) send their regards.

At Christmas the family again went via Freiburg up to the Cabin at Todtnauberg, which by now was more homely and had a shed and a fountain.

1926

Martin was working hard on his work Being and Time. *In the summer Elfride found a new flat in Marburg at Barfüssertor 15, which was better suited to the family and had a beautiful garden.*

In August, Martin visited the Husserls at Silvaplana in Switzerland, where they spent several days together while Elfride was organizing the removal.

The family spent the late summer together up at the Cabin. Martin had his desk at the Brenders' farm further down from the Cabin, however, where he had more peace and quiet for work on his book.

1927

In the New Year, Elfride visited her schoolfriend Hedwig Veidt née Stein in Herborn, while Martin sought an exchange of ideas with Jaspers in Heidelberg. Martin gave Jaspers the manuscript sheets of Being and Time *to read. The chair of philosophy at Marburg, which Martin had high hopes of being offered, remained unfilled.*

Heidelbg. 2 Jan. 27

My Dearest Soul!

Even though the journey has been planned for quite some time, it feels strange to be here all of a sudden. The controlled regularity of work in recent months has been broken & now I actually first have to collect my thoughts. And the first thing I felt was the joy & anticipation of the holiday months.

As I came 'south' again now I was overcome by homesickness for the Black Forest & I don't know whether I should give up my plans for the Alps after all to be fully with you & the children up there.

J[aspers]. & his wife are still very depressed, although he did become more cheerful as we talked & didn't let anything show. His 76-year-old father is very seriously ill, the brother a serious worry; the nephew (the sister's son) shot himself on 8 Dec. at the age of 18.

Today on top of this the maid here has now fallen seriously ill too so Frau J., who is very delicate & sickly, is without any help; I was going to leave at once; but they asked me to stay all the same. I'll just wait & see. Everything's become rather complicated now & I haven't got down to any transcription yet.

So it's possible I might turn up again earlier than planned. You know Mother doesn't disturb me.

J. is studying my work & becoming more enthusiastic with every sheet & above all he sees the work that's behind it.

Only now am I myself again coming to realize what attention & stimulation mean. New things are awakening & above all I see more sharply the limits & necessities of what has been achieved. And so I really am very happy with my stay.

J. told me that Ri[ckert]. is in regular correspondence with Otto & Jaensch, who has become friends with R. J. said that the way R. spoke about me was quite incomprehensible without constant incitement coming from them.

There seems to exist such a racket economy that it's quite impossible to fight it. Jasp. does think though that such things are only a matter of time & circumstances. –

J. also has the other great work on death masks. We talked about what we ourselves were discussing recently & J. completely shares our opinion that the death mask generally produces the most random face of all – it can happen that the greatness of the person appears once again – to this effect he showed me three photogrs. of Max Weber on his deathbed – Marianne [Weber] has a mask – the only one – it's a dreadful countenance – the severity of the suffering of this existence & at the same time the force of the energy – here one could speak of the demonic. –

Marianne's coming on one of the next few evenings. I mentioned that you were giving a paper on the book. She's now devoting more time again to poverty & help for women students along the lines you agreed when you spoke with her. – People are enthusiastic about my suit & J. said he assumed it was a case of the wife dressing her boy.

I have to tell them lots about you & the children.

I hope you have a nice relaxing time with Hedwig. Here the weather's relatively clear & yet the wind somewhat stronger than in Mbg.

My dearest, much love & a kiss to you & the boys.

Your grateful Blackamoor.

[. . .]

As the family continued to want to go up to the Cabin during university vacations irrespective of whether there was school or not, Elfride obtained permission to teach the boys herself. From time to time they attended the village school in Todtnauberg.

Early in February, Martin was informed that his mother was on her deathbed. On 5 February he wrote from Messkirch: I am of course a great worry to the poor thing & she keeps saying that she's responsible for me. I've reassured her – but nonetheless she finds it hard to bear. So strong are the powers, after all, that they make themselves felt particularly at times such as these. Mother was very serious, almost hard even – as though her true nature were concealed. 'I can no longer pray for you', she said, 'for I have enough to do for myself'. I must bear this, & indeed my philosophy shouldn't only exist on paper, should it. [. . .] I now feel even more strongly than ever that nothing ties me directly to the world here any more; what I received from my parental home & my home town has passed into my work.

Martin went back to Todtnauberg, returning to his mother's deathbed on 19 April. On 21 April he wrote: In the short time I've been here Mother has grown visibly weaker. Her pulse is fading too. For a week now the poor thing has been living only on wine & water. Vomiting every few hours as well. It's a pitiful sight & Mother herself wants it all to end.

M[other]. was very happy when she saw me – was very concerned about whether I'd been picked up & had a proper room for studying. She's enquired about you & the children several times. Most of the time she spends dozing – & has no pain apart from the unpleasantness of the whole condition. At all events I'll stay until Monday. *Johanna Heidegger died on 3 May.*

Being and Time *was published by Niemeyer.*

The family spent the summer up at the Cabin again. Martin went to Freiburg and stayed at the Husserls'. On 17 October he wrote: The article on 'Phenomenology' for the Encycl. Britannica, which Husserl had already sent off to Oxford to be translated, was in my view simply <u>hopeless</u>. Sprawling, full of repetitions, unstructured & without a short & clear presentation of the central point. I considered it to be in the interests of the matter itself to tell Husserl my opinion openly. He took it in very good part & M[alvine]. in particular was glad. The translation was halted immediately & since Wednesday afternoon we've been sitting together hard at work – I've just dictated the first part to Landgrebe. I hope to have the thing at the printers' by Thursday. Although it's very taxing on me, especially with H. stubbornly insisting on his plans, we're both really very happy about this, our first real collaboration. H. is in very high spirits. I'm also glad that I can repay their hospitality a little in this way.

The private tuition Martin was giving the Japanese aristocrat Kuki Shuzo in Freiburg and Marburg provided him with a welcome source of additional income.

On 19 October he was finally promoted from associate to full professor of philosophy in Marburg.

My Dearest Soul!

I arrived here yesterday evening. This morning, when I returned from Mother's grave, your letter was already there. I could tell from your voice on the telephone the day before yesterday just how happy you were. The Minister's decision is a pleasing sign of objectivity. The Ministry itself must find it a relief to have solved the matter in a way that's satisfactory to all concerned. It's now even more to my advantage than if I had taken over Hartmann's post at once, almost mechanically. Clearly the reports turned out differently – & perhaps the Göttingen philology conference, where my book was on occasion a general topic of conversation, & which Becker & Richter attended, was what finally swayed them.

When you rang I was just on the point of going to see Finke & before that I had a very intense & at times heated – but friendly – philosophical talk with Husserl. The Hs were delighted beyond all measure. H. wants to propose me unico loco. I asked him to consider this plan carefully though, as such proposals can often prove damaging. Now I'm the successor to Natorp's chair, H. has another quite different ace up his sleeve.

I wrote a letter of congratulations to Mahnke this morning. –

That uncanny Heideggerian luck seems to be still alive after all. – I've written to Richter to say I'd like to have a discussion with him not only about the question of salary but also the question of the department, which you know is being expanded now following Hamann's departure. Concerning the salary, it depends in part on what Mahnke gets, and he of course was already a senior master. They can't put me below him again, & even with parity I shan't be satisfied.

Now we really will be able to breathe rather more easily & give ourselves the odd treat – but above all 'the house' now assumes a definite shape not only in our plans but in the possibility of becoming a reality.

It's sad that my dear Mother is no longer here to share all this & take pleasure in our boys as well. The grave is very nicely adorned & in a nice spot, which you already know of course.

The journey here through autumn on the Baar plateau & in the Hegau & along Lake Constance was quite wonderful. I've never enjoyed the landscape so much.

The bridge is indeed quite fabulous & it occurred to me that Jörg would certainly love to see it. It's splendid that you've now finally done the walk with the children after all. A pity I couldn't be there with you.

Finke was very pleased that I visited him – He & Honecker & Stieler ask me to convey their respects to you. –

All are fine here. Fritz looks very well & is contented. Little Thomas jumps around the house & is strong & cheerful. Liesl is well too.

Old cousin Karl has been very lonely since Mother's death. I'll call on him this afternoon. Mother's friend from her youth has put the picture of Mother at our disposal. We must see that we get a good reproduction of it. I'll bring it with me when I come.

I've asked Richter to arrange a date in the second week of November when I can speak to him. Before then I'll also need a coat. I saw a short, lined one for 85 mks on display at Müller's on the corner of Bertholdstr. & Kaiserstr. – but didn't risk buying it on my own.

The remaining days in Freiburg were very taxing, as Husserl has become incredibly clumsy in terms of literary representation & form; often the prolixity & repetition cannot be eliminated without making substantive interventions, so further discussions were required in between times. Malvine was really charming. But I often longed to be up at the Cabin.

I begin my lectures – according to the notificn. from Jakobsthal – on 1 Nov. Seminars on 4 Nov.

Ingarden's coming to Marbg. over November & December.

Would you let me know once again in Heidelberg (Plöck 66) when you're returning with the children?

I intend to leave here on Sunday & hope that at the Jaspers' I'll have the time & leisure to start concentrating on my own work again, especially my work for the semester, which is far from my mind at the moment. For Husserl's work isn't finished yet, I've brought part of the ms. along with me to finish it off.

Much love to you, my Dearest Soul, & a kiss for the boys.

Good-bye!

Your Little Blackamoor. Fritz & Liesl send their regards.

1928

After Christmas up at the Cabin, Elfride and the children moved into an area of Todtnauberg called Büreten, where they stayed with the Rotzingers, a peasant family. The boys attended the village school, while Martin returned to Marburg alone.

Marbg. 10. I. 28.

My Dearest Soul! Dear boys!

I've just returned from the lecture. Usually when I come up the stairs I can already hear the children's voices from the playroom. This time it was silent & dark – the three of you aren't there – It's good that I have quite a lot of work; when I arrived here yesterday after a happy journey there was a mountain of invitations & 'stuff' on the desk. They're discussing physical education this evening at the Co[mmittee]. meeting – tomorrow at the Faculty meeting: Löwith is also on the agenda. Furthermore a new ministerial decree has been received today, which Jaeck [?] clearly arranged with his friends, stating that the 'intention' is to introduce gym as a 'major' subject. But I don't think this is any reason to hold back with our conviction – on the contrary – even if it no longer does any good in practice. Jakobsthal has sent my memo to all the members of the Co[mmittee]. Elster is producing a counter-report.

Furthermore the political economist Köppe has been retired by the Minister – so a replacement required – as it's an important matter & fresh blood is needed here, they want me to work on the Co[mmittee]. too. I'd like to ask Walter Bauer for detailed information – which he'll certainly provide willingly & well. I don't have his address though. Please send it to me. The reimbursement for my trip on academic business has also come: journey 76.80, 2 days' expense allowance 14 mks

111

a day, one half day at 12 mks, overnight accommodation 10 & 9 mks, in total 129.80. –

Scheler's been offered a chair at Frankfurt & is going to accept. [. . .]

I feel extremely rested & fresh – even though I was dreadfully annoyed that all that lovely snow vanished the very day of our ascent & all those outings we'd planned & dreamt of came to nothing – all the same, when I look back it was wonderful as it was. I can still picture Christmas Eve in my mind when the boys were standing in front of the tree & you read the Christmas story & from time to time I sing to myself the children's lovely Christmas carol.

And I think that in spite of the disturbances in the next few weeks I shall make good progress with my work. Husserl had a nice talk with me & above all – like you – advised me against going to Berlin for now or in the next 10 years.

And this is quite right – for I'm just beginning now & all I need is concentration & passion for work, which is there but simply gets shoved to one side by the bureaucratic professor in me. [. . .]

I hope you're all well. Here the weather is lovely & warm & sunny. Though how long for is difficult to say. [. . .]

Do write & tell me straight away how you are & a little of what you've been doing.

[. . .] Bultmann has now himself written the 'Heidegger' entry in the dictionary of 'Religion in History & the Present' as Wünsch didn't dare.

Much love & best wishes to each of you
from your Blackamoor & Father.
Regards to Frau Rotzinger & Mathilde too.

Marbg. Jörg's birthday, [21. I.] 1928

My Dearest Soul!

Our letters have presumably crossed paths in the post. Thank you very much for yours. It's probably wonderful with you now – I haven't had proper powder snow in January & Feb. for a long time now. But the main thing is that the children & you enjoy it. Here the weather's very changeable – in the Sauerland 30cm. of powder. Moser wanted to tempt me with the offer of his 2nd pair of skis – but it's quite out of the question – partly because of external duties & partly my very close engagement with Kant, which has already led me over into my logic lectures for the summer. I'm expecting a lot from the coming months of vacation for my work. After the excessive pressure of the 'publication' came a rest period – I can tell that's all over with now & the Demon has already started harassing and badgering me again in its rather uncanny way. But at the same time I'm glad that I've recently been more involved than otherwise in outside life. After all I've learnt all sorts of necessary things about tactics & social interaction & 'judgement', which is important, although I don't have the slightest intention of ever becoming a 'faculty animal'.

The meeting with the ministerial undersecretary – the registrar – the rector & many others concerning physical education lasted from 10 a.m. until ½ past 2 in the afternoon. I spoke after Jaensch & in very fundamental terms & above all addressing the undersecretary – University, Youth Movement, Physical Culture. The penny dropped – although in practice nothing can be expected – because the ministry is infested with fundamentally wishy-washy educational ideals & is under pressure from the professional interests of gym teachers in all the schools. The whole movement is underpinned not only by the question of the replacement for military service – but rather the outburst of the masses against 'education', aristocracy of spirit, & rank. For only when one has this in a genuine way & from primordial [?] sources can one then incorporate physical culture into life – whereas otherwise the latter becomes a surrogate for everything under the most disparate interpretations. These debates & my own reflections have made it increasingly clear to me that what is taking place here is the onset of a new barbarism. And it's no coincidence that I often found myself thinking of our great neighbour in Basel, Jacob Burckhardt. / The final wording & editing of our statement was a lot of work; next Monday is probably the last Committee meeting. But then on Tuesday preparations for moving the department get under way.

So I shan't have any real work time free from disturbances.

I don't know anything about 'Freiburg'. Certainly the matter is developing more slowly, as this way the government saves on another semester just like that. So objectively, the best thing is if you stay up there with the children as long as possible. [. . .]

My seminar on Schelling is very gratifying – the papers & reports get better & better. In the lecture I have the audience right in the palm of my hand, even though the material is now becoming more difficult every day for them. [. . .]

Do write & tell me how Jörg's birthday went.

With best wishes & love to you, my Dearest Soul, & the little mites
Your Blackamoor

Regards to Frau Rotzinger & our acquaintances.

P.S. Tell me, did you order me a new pair of socks to go with the brown suit? Up to now I've always worn the 'long' ones.

Martin was keeping a close eye on the developments in Freiburg. On 23 January he wrote:

I've just received the following card from Husserl:
Saturday 21. I. 28.
Dear Friend,
Committee resolution: unico loco.
Absolute silence to be maintained of course.
Kindest regards from us both.
E. H.
On 1 February he again sent Elfride a copy of the latest news from Husserl: Dear Fr[iend]., At the last meeting (of the Co.) my outline for the proposal to be sent to the government was now also unanimously approved. This outline won't be submitted (as a Committee report) until 7 February at the next Faculty meeting. The government has requested proposals only from the <u>beginning of March</u>. So the offer of the chair probably won't be made until the vacation. It all went nicely & very gratifyingly for you & I imagine it will be likewise at the plenary meeting of the Faculty.

Further on in the letter he wrote: In the same post came a short letter from <u>Bonn</u>. Schirmer wants a confirmation for his assertion that though I'm 'officially' Catholic, I'm inwardly Protestant. I confirmed this for him by return of post & also mentioned briefly that though the theologians here pass me off as officially Cath., they make all the more vigorous use of my work in lectures & elsewhere. At any rate I seem to be an object of contention even in Bonn. So let's wait & see –

At the time, Elfride was taking a close look at ideas for educational reform, including those propounded by the teacher Gustav Wyneken, who also belonged to the Wandervogel *youth movement. She was equally interested in the new educational ideas of Maria Montessori, which were gradually becoming known in Germany, and in Todtnauberg she prepared a talk on the subject which she hoped to give in Marburg.*

Mbg. 9. II. 28.

My Dearest Soul!
I wanted to wait with this letter until there was some news from Husserl. It's just come. According to him I've been <u>unanimously</u> proposed unico loco by the Faculty. One citadel after another is thus being taken. Now comes the final one. Husserl's note is very short; he's been in Hinterzarten for a few days & is apparently not yet quite at his best again. – I'll be able to keep quiet all right. But it seems doubtful to me whether it'll ever remain a secret in Frbg. Besseler was dropping hints even in his letter. When Fuchs was here recently, he said he'd heard at the A[cademic]. A[ssociation]. that they wanted to have me in Freiburg by the autumn, or in fact as early as summer – but that it

wasn't possible yet. All this can only have got here via Revd Ritter & his brother in Frbg. So the matter will presumably leak out after all. Incidentally, [Gerhard] Ritter (Freiburg) has written a long and appreciative review of Kaehler in the Deutsche Literatur-Zeitung. Oncken (Munich) is going to Berlin as the successor to Meinecke. So there's a risk that Ritter in Frbg. will get away. The von Auwers have invited us to dinner on the 17th. I suppose I'll have to accept. Bultmann also went somewhere on his own recently when his wife was ill. Mother has very kindly sent me a whole packet of sweets.

I've spoken to Fräulein Krumsiek again: so far it's Fräulein Bornkamm, Krumsiek, Pose, the Oltmanns & Herr Weinmann who are going [up to the Cabin]; Fuchs will probably come too. I gave W[alter]. Bauer's seminar paper to the Dean to read; he said he'd never read such a brilliant report – not even from full professors. I've already made use of it as well. Indeed, the best are – Jews.

A red form came from the tax office – a tax return. I'll leave it here for the time being. Many thanks to Jörg for his card; he really did write very nicely. What do you have in mind as regards accommodation for everyone if Hilde comes? [. . .]

Yesterday I had [Hermann] Mörchen here, his thesis will be quite excellent. Jonas – according to Bultmann too – has likewise produced an excellent dissertation. [. . .]

In my short breaks I'm currently reading a lot of Jakob Burckhardt – & feel so powerfully the Alemannic air it exudes.

Otherwise everything's all right; Grete & Olga are thick as thieves – which I'm very glad about – ; my lecture's still a fair amount of work, as I'm right in the most difficult parts of the critique; each time I just about get the daily quota finished. I'd like to get quite far with it too, as I'll possibly finish somewhat earlier after all.

The whole of Sunday recently was really very lonely; but now it's the 10th already & so I'll hold out all right.

The weather's always indifferent in the unpleasant way – neither nice nor really bad – Is some proper snow lying up there now with a decent base so we latecomers benefit from it a little as well?

With best wishes & much love
to you all
from your
Blackamoor & Father.

So Martin was to go to Freiburg as the successor to Husserl. In the city and the surrounding area Elfride looked for a plot of land to realize a long-harboured dream and build a house of their own. She found what she was seeking on the Rötebuck in the district of Zähringen. They purchased the land on 16 April. 'The Heidegger family's moving into the country', joked Martin's colleagues. Elfride had a very precise idea of their future home; she planned the rooms for the furniture that was available, conceived the study to meet Martin's needs, and also designed the outside of the house. The building plans were executed by Eugen Vetter, a building surveyor who lived on the Schauinsland-Halde. The house was to be ready to move into by autumn. Elfride supervised the completion of the house in Freiburg and organized the removal. Martin remained with the boys and the housemaids up at the Cabin and prepared for the winter semester in Freiburg. In addition, he wrote a contribution to the festschrift in honour of Husserl's 70th birthday, 'On the Essence of Ground'.

Cabin, 27 Sept. 28

My Dearest Soul!

You made me very happy with your lovely birthday letter. Latterly I've been thinking a lot about 'our house' – & how in our hearts we're also renewing & enriching the old Freiburg edifice of our love. Thank you very much for showing me all the strength of your trust. I know that I'm only slowly really learning to live & basing my life on what my inner voice plainly tells me at any time. Though we must never rely solely on external support, I do believe that our house, because there is actually nothing external about it – especially since as a work it sprang from your motherly aspirations – will pervade our communion & that with the children in a completely new way.

Our journey is only now beginning, as I knew it would, to have an effect within me – in the sense that I've suddenly acquired a freer & more objective position towards my work. In the end, the <u>inner</u> harassment by the problems must also spring from a more manly calm & distance.

All in all, life is slowly beginning to dawn on me in its true colours & I'm certain that in your love you'll provide me with new opportunities.

And henceforth you too will now be able to bring all your powers to bear just as you wish & create an exemplary house for the young people in particular as well. However much & however valuable what I owe to my parental home, not to mention the sacrifices that were made for me – there were some things there that I couldn't assimilate & even less so in the years of boarding school existence, which took up such decisive periods of my youth. From all of this I am & have been only slowly finding my way into real freedom. –

I'm sleeping with Jörg in the little room – the hike on the Feldberg was wonderful – on the way down we each had two glasses of milk in the Wilhelmer cabin, which incidentally has a splendid parlour, to go

116

Christmas 1928

with the birthday cake we'd brought along with us. We accompanied Hermann & Aunt Lili [Szilasi] to the car – when Herm. was sitting inside he suddenly got back out again & silently came up close to me & put his little hand in mine. But then off he went, very proudly.

The wood is now getting sawn, we need the broad saw for it – On Sunday the Schneiders are celebrating their 30th wedding anniversary, to which I'll probably be invited, & I'd like to give a small speech. After lunch I like going with Jörg to the Holzschlagbach valley – it's so wonderfully isolated now & nature then feels so very close.

Tomorrow I'll write to Mother in Wiesbaden. She's written to me now too, saying that your parents will give me the desk. Fräulein Krumsiek & Fräulein Bornkamm have sent me an album with photographs of Marburg – including our house, my study & the view from it towards the Frauenberg.

But the nicest surprise was the little clock, which only last night before falling asleep I imagined having in my study – It's a double joy to me, as it's from you as well – & so there'll be nothing unfamiliar at all in my room. What you say about the stairs etc. solves all the problems. I'm really curious to know when we'll move in now. Grete does her job well – but I can't lock her in in the evenings. – I'll set Anz some written work, & then he'll get his reference after all. I'm making good progress with my Husserl article. Löwith wrote & said that last Sunday he'd wanted to pay an official visit to Mahnke, but he was met by the wife, who told him her husband was in bed – in a terrible state of nerves – it's uncertain whether he'll lecture at all this winter. Why, things could come to a pretty pass with philosophy in Marburg. But that doesn't matter at all.

Jörgele, who has only just fallen asleep, sends his best wishes – Much love & best wishes from me. Your Little Blackamoor.

On 20 October, just half a year after purchasing the land, the Heideggers moved into their new home at Rötebuck 47. The house was a mixture of bourgeois town house and Black Forest homestead. Inside it had wood panelling; outside it was shingled. Martin's room was the biggest one in the new house.

1929

The family soon felt at home in their new house, and the garden was freshly laid out. In January Martin gave a talk in Frankfurt, where he met Kurt Riezler, the registrar of Frankfurt University. They met again at the Davoser Hochschulwoche *(Davos University Week), a special event established with a view to promoting international understanding and science.*

Davos, 21 March 29

My Dearest Soul!

Yesterday we did the Parsenn tour; it was indescribably beautiful. Riezler was with us, as was Revd Stallmann, who has come over from Innsbruck.

We climbed to 2700 and had a descent to 800m. Now I could really give full play to my skiing technique. At the beginning I was rather anxious how it would go, but after the first 100m. I realized that I was superior to them all, even Riezler, who has skied a lot in the Alps. It's wonderful, the wealth of scenery, the views that change completely every 50m. – The ascent wasn't strenuous & it's quite unusually easy to go up to an altitude of 2500m.

Admittedly it's all rutted, as it hasn't snowed for weeks now. Today's heavily overcast now & we're hoping for fresh snow.

The courses themselves are fairly strenuous, but I skive off most of the things 'one' is supposed to go to. I think the non-Germans probably will be as impressed as you hope them to be. Cassirer fell ill after the second talk, he already had a cold when he came up. So for now it's uncertain when the discussion will take place.

Davos itself is dreadful; boundless vulgarity in the architecture, a completely random hotchpotch of guest houses & hotels. And then the invalids –

119

The students are all very happy to be able to be up here – though all these lectures are quite strenuous for them.

Today I give my last lecture – they're arranged so I have the rest of the time for skiing – ; I was supposed to give a few more talks, but I've turned them down. [. . .]

I haven't got together properly with my students yet – I hope to do so in the next few days. In the meantime I want to work some more on my Kant. I've been with Riezler a lot – he told me that now he really is hoping I get offered a chair in Frankfurt – it just takes time. –

If the boys don't want to go up any more, that's all right by me; for the final technical formulation of my paper I naturally also prefer to have all my stuff handy. Today I wrote a card to your parents in Wiesbaden. –

It'll be splendid when the boys can come up into the high mountains – You really must experience it some time too. As regards skiing technique you'll certainly keep up – It's just that the physical strain is rather great – but then one can take one's time.

With best wishes & much love to you & the boys
Your Little Blackamoor.
[. . .]

On 23 March, Martin wrote to Elfride: My third lecture, in which I spoke for 1½ hours without a manuscript, was a great success. Cassirer is going to try to get up today, so the 'study group' won't take place until Monday or Tuesday. [. . .] Although there's basically nothing for me to be learnt here – I'm still very glad to join in with such things now & again – one's versatility, one's handling of people & a certain outward assurance do benefit. But I often look forward to our house & my room. Only there can the things I have to do flourish. I also think that the young people sense that the roots of my work are to be found somewhere that today's city-dweller no longer has – indeed no longer even understands. [. . .] It's frightful how devious, uncongenial, & lacking in security & instinct the young people are. And can no longer find their way back into the simplicity of existence [*Dasein*].

And on 26 March he wrote: I've just got a two-hour public discussion with Cassirer over with, which went very well & – quite apart from the content – made a big impression on the students. [. . .]

The registrar, with whom I've become really good friends, would like to keep me on here afterwards. Perhaps he's the man I'm looking for as a friend – & if that were the outcome of this conference – it'd be a matter of great inner happiness to me.

Martin worked on his inaugural lecture 'What is Metaphysics?', which he was to give on 24 July in Freiburg.

120

The family spent the late summer together up at the Cabin until the beginning of the new school year.

Max Scheler had died in Frankfurt in May 1928. In October, Martin travelled to Cologne to help Scheler's widow sort through his unpublished works. On the way back he visited his parents-in-law in Wiesbaden, as well as Riezler in Frankfurt, where he completed a busy programme of visits and established a lot of contacts. As Jaspers was unable to return on time from a journey, he cancelled their planned meeting at short notice. Not until early December, when Martin was invited to Heidelberg to give a talk on the subject of his inaugural lecture, were they able to make good the meeting that had fallen through.

1930

From early to mid-March 1930, Martin stayed up at the Cabin without the family in order to prepare for the two lectures he was to give at a scholarly association in Amsterdam on 21 and 22 March: 'The Current State of Problems in Philosophy' and 'Hegel and the Problem of Metaphysics'. This was the outcome of a contact that had been established in Davos.

On 12 March he wrote: I'm quite immersed in work & yet do miss you all especially & having you all around me – for odd though it may seem, it's above all when working most intensely that I'm close to you & know how elementally you form a part of me. Not at all in seeing to & looking after my external needs & providing comfort. For in <u>material</u> terms I have these things now too & yet I do not possess them in an <u>authentic</u> sense. And so I'm rather sad that something's missing from my usual nice working weeks & I'm already looking forward to April.

On 28 March Martin received his first offer of a chair at Berlin. Before going there for negotiations, he paid a visit to Jaspers in Heidelberg. In Berlin he met his old friend Elisabeth Blochmann, known as Lisi.

Berlin, 6 April 30

My Dearest Soul!

I had a very good journey; Lisi was at the station, then we were together for an hour or so. This morning we went to the Wannsee with the Bauers, walked on the beach for 1½ hours – & then went to Potsdam – this time things worked out better – the 'New Palace' is splendid – all in all I now have a real impression this time – ; it was worth living in the vicinity of Old Fritz [Frederick II of Prussia, the Great].

Afterwards we went to the Bauers' for lunch, Lisi still has some proofs to correct & as she's rather tired anyway & has to go to Halle next week I've left her alone for this afternoon; I myself am having a rest in my room, which is very conveniently located. This evening we're all going to the theatre together.

W. Bauer is for accepting of course; he thinks I could demand to take sabbaticals at least every 3 semesters or at will, & suchlike. He thinks politically but not with regard to the history of spirit; to be sure, how & whether the two can be separated in this way, or how this is to be given the right new form, is unclear to me, because neither of them are fixed quantities, but change, & our epoch is bringing about this very change.

That my appointment coincides with the rise of the young generation of Brüning, Treviranus & even Grimme too – in its general spiritual direction – is no accident & this fact was very strongly felt & stressed by Jaspers too. J. says he would definitely go, but fully respects my innermost decision, although he hopes it isn't final.

Riezler telephoned me after consulting with Windelband (strictly confidential – and I'm not saying any more about it here) to report that the Faculty has <u>proposed Cassirer</u> unico loco & commented on Hartmann & me. This proposal is of course quite transparently, if C. came, the most convenient one – insignificant & superfluous; but <u>behind it</u> the confident calculation that he <u>won't</u> be appointed <u>at all</u> & in this way the whole affair is resolved.

Bauer considers it possible that Richter & Windelband are also <u>against</u> my appointment & will do their best to scupper it.

This will be interesting at any rate & I shan't commit myself to anything & shall negotiate purely to gain information.

To the city & everything I really am quite indifferent this time. The sheer groundlessness of the place is dreadful & yet it is <u>still</u> no genuine abyss for philosophy after all. Berlin must be <u>conquered from the outside</u>.

With Jaspers (& wife) there was much – too much – talk about the chair, & I've now realized how hopelessly stuck these people are, like many others, in the psychosis of 'professorships'. And all this unbearable chatter about 'human beings' & this person & that 'as a human being'. I think that from time to time I have to experience such things in order to get a clearer idea of how much we're growing towards something quite different.

Lisi, who is very much looking forward to Halle & the work with Frankenberger, & the Bauers send their regards to you.

Much love to you & the boys

Your Little Blackamoor. Regards to the Baumgartens & Fräulein Lina.

In May Martin turned down the professorship in Berlin.

After presenting a paper in Cologne, he went to Wiesbaden to visit his parents-in-law, who had moved house from Kaiser-Friedrich-Ring to Wielandstrasse. For the first time, Martin changed the way he addressed Elfride in his letters. There was tension between the two of them. His journey through Germany thus came at just the right time for him.

Frankfurt 2 Oct. 30

My dear Elfriede!

Many thanks for your letter. I came here yesterday via Wiesbaden. Your parents are very well. They send their best wishes. I thought Father & Mother looked well.

The flat certainly is quieter, healthier & above all sunny. Mother derives particular pleasure from it. Those gas heaters I do find somewhat disconcerting, especially when one thinks that at their age parents sometimes forget a tap. I happened to have a Völkischer Beobachter[9] with me. Father was very interested in it. The Leipzig Trial does seem to be recoiling upon its splendid prosecutors. There's a big Hitler rally here on Saturday; everywhere huge placards saying 'We're on the attack!'. In the Völk. Beobachter even Hindenburg is warned not to get too involved with Brünning. All in all, the front against the Centre is very fierce.

Cologne was fairly strenuous. Frau Scheler, who takes great pleasure in the child, who is now quite better, now has a definite directive for her work again after all. I'd like to send the mss I need for later on back to Frbg. from here; lugging them about is unnecessary. In Cologne the weather was foggy & damp; here it's better; I'm sure it's glorious weather up there now. I'm hoping for a few days of work & concentration here. I <u>certainly</u> shan't speak in Göttingen.

I'll write to Beuron again from Göttingen; but there's no danger of me not finding accommodation; for it's the very quiet time there at the moment.

As I'm only giving short lectures & seminars, I don't think there's any harm in me not beginning until November. [. . .]

There's something dreadful about these big cities & time and again I see what a precious thing we have in our house.

The other day Grimme spoke to the sociologists in Berlin – clever, over-clever, but disappointing in terms of content.

---

[9] The *Völkischer Beobachter* (*National Observer*) was the party organ of the NSDAP, the German National Socialist party.

Don't you want to go up to the Cabin again with the children in the glorious weather?

Best wishes to you all, my Dearest Soul,
from your
     Little Blackamoor
Regards to Fräulein Lina.

After his stay in Göttingen, Martin went to visit Heinrich Wiegand Petzet's parents in Bremen, became acquainted with the artists' colony at Worpswede, and developed a particular enthusiasm for the painting of Paula Modersohn-Becker on display there. On 8 October he gave a talk 'On the Essence of Truth', and wrote to Elfride: I'm taking a great deal with me from this stay. And even though it's a long path, I trust that I can go the distance. And I ask you, my love, for your trust or at any rate for your help.

After a stay in Freiburg, on 14 October Martin went to Messkirch to visit Fritz and Liesel for their wedding anniversary. By now they had three sons. From Messkirch he travelled on to Beuron Archabbey.

Beuron 19 Oct. 30

My Dearest Soul!
This is now my third day here, & quite different from previous stays; this time it's a settling of accounts with everything from before & a new awakening into the future. Only now am I capable of letting the full richness of the wisdom of this monastic existence take effect. Today the liturgy took the words of St Paul as its subject, Renovamini spiritu mentis vestrae et induite novum hominem – be renewed in the spirit of your mind & put on the new man.

Even though I cannot go along with the way of faith actually called for, it does all help me to reflect & find inner strength –

And only now am I again seeing that even work is not enough unless it is thoroughly pervaded in its sway by the right spirit.

Living with them in the monastery really is more strenuous than I thought. But I do want to hold out & there'll be time for recuperation another time.

We get up shortly before 4 o'clock & then there's almost two hours' divine office in church. At 7 o'clock breakfast – then time for working until ¼ to 9; then it's high mass. From 11 to 12 work time again; at 12 midday, I eat with the monks in the refectory; then recreation, when the monks are permitted to speak; then at ½ past 2 vespers; afterwards coffee; then work time until supper at ¼ to 7; then ½ hour recreation & before 8 o'clock – the compline – the evening prayer; at ½ past 8 everything is quiet; one can go on working in one's cell, but the first few days I've been too tired & I probably will be in the next few days as well.

Father Anselm is touchingly concerned; he'd already put all sorts of philosophical books in my cell to welcome me; Mörike as well – I've gained a lot from contact with him & have come to trust him.

Of the older monks I know, only the Dutchman [painter-monk] Verkade is there & he has a serious heart condition. The Archabbot is away too (in Palestine).

Each day now is more magnificent than the one before, the gold of the autumn leaves glows along the Jura cliffs between the stretches of pine forest. And below, the silent river winds its way through the meadows.

The more I truly collect myself, the more genuinely and simply I can again fill my heart with love for you. And it's strange – when here there isn't any cause for it at all, the autumn of 1915 has come right back to life in me – and I'm rediscovering all the moods & am confident that they'll consolidate to form the lasting & prevailing underlying mood.

It might seem as though all things worldly are left behind here – of course – but for this very reason the bonds of my heart to you & the boys come to life so very differently.

Little though I want to close my mind to all the powers that work their effect here, from the outset I've behaved in such a way that mere mood is not the prime thing – because it can easily turn into self-deception. –

I hope Hermann has recovered quickly so you can enjoy the glorious weather – why, it must be pure summer up there now.

Thank you, my darling, for your love. Best wishes to you and the boys

Your Blackamoor.

Kind regards to Fräulein Lina.

During his stay in the monastery, on 26 October, Martin gave a lecture on Augustine's reflections on time, 'Augustinus: Quid est Tempus? Confessiones lib. XI', in return for the monks' hospitality.

1931

By now the house on Rötebuck had some new occupants: Mohrle, a dog, and Hieronymus and Hieronyma, a pair of bantams.

Summer saw the inauguration of the new swimming pool in the garden, which by municipal order could only be filled with rainwater or pump water.

Over Whitsun, Elfride and Martin went on a canoeing trip on the River Werra.

In June, Elfride went alone to visit her parents in Wiesbaden.

In August, Martin returned to Amsterdam to give more lectures, while Elfride found accommodation on the North Sea island of Spiekeroog and relaxed there with the boys.

The tensions between Elfride and Martin continued. Elfride had good reason to suspect that Martin was regularly maintaining relationships with other women.

This was not explicitly mentioned in their letters and cards. Not until his return to Freiburg did Martin allude to the matter.

Freiburg, 17 Aug. 31

Dear Elfride!

Many thanks for your letter. Many thanks above all for your love – again & again I encounter its greatness & my smallness in the face of it, but I haven't yet learnt to see your love fully in your severity & hardness; I suppose because I still see myself too much & fall victim to admiration & that sort of thing.

I know deep down that I belong to you & that you alone can help me build my life anew. I'm only slowly learning to be hard towards myself & really bear & assume the burden of what is difficult in me – instead of forgetting it. And I know that all that matters now is action, the daily work I do to improve myself. The eyes in your heart will see whether I make progress or not. I've made you enough promises.

It disappoints me too that Fräulein Krumsiek didn't find the right word. Since her letter I've not written to her again or seen her either.

I'm happy for you that you can have such nice weeks with the children in your countryside – & they could be even nicer if I hadn't brought you such great inner suffering.

You wrote in your last card that Hermann was making a quick recovery; after your letter of today this doesn't seem to be the case after all. I'm surprised that Jörg's enjoying it all so much.

While the first week in Holland was unusually close, in the second it rained almost every day. Only Wednesday was nice, when we went to Noordwijk & The Hague.

I spent a whole morning with the van Goghs – almost the whole autumn exhibition is still there – where one sees the abrupt development from 1888 on. The paintings made a great and very deep inner impression on me. I went there again on my own one morning.

The most striking one is a cornfield in a storm & a swarm of ravens flying into the wind above it – an ultra-golden yellow, above it a garish bluey black sky, through the middle of the field a path of earthy heavy brown & at its edges streaks of bright green grass. Unfortunately there are no reproductions of it right now. Instead I'm sending you the iris; the card only roughly reproduces the colours.

You can only experience the full luminosity & life of these pictures if you see them after the gloomy grim ones from his Brabant time.

I had a really big surprise when I suddenly found myself in one room standing in front of one of Rodin's 'Burghers of Calais' – the one clasping the key in his hands.

The two mornings spent with these works were what was most rewarding & lasting for me.

Then one time I was with Pos out on the River Amstel – where he read to me from his writings.

One afternoon I went to see van der Horst's Psychiatric Clinic – with all its patients – ; one day we went to the big locks at IJmuiden, & then with van der Hoop for an afternoon in Zandvoort – where he likewise read to me from his writings.

The sea & the dunes – but the beach! You're right, I wouldn't have stood it for long & above all I wouldn't have got down to any work.

This time Holland in general made a much better & more agreeable impression on me.

Pos & the hosts were very nice; admittedly, van der Horst was kept very busy by the Clinic, so he was keen to spend his free time with his children, who are still on holiday. As I noticed that they were hoping to have the Saturday to themselves I left that day & sent a wire here to say I was coming.

Here everything's just fine. [. . .] The garden looks lovely & is full of fruit – the silence out here – after Amsterdam – quite incredible.

This morning I went to the first sitting at Vanoli's. He works in a small studio behind the greengrocer's at the Herdern terminus. He started with great energy & excitement. The main thing is that <u>he</u> should learn something in the process. In the next few days I want to arrange my manuscripts & gradually get down to work & for the time being stay down here; especially since on 20 Aug. Pos will be passing through for two days on his way to a conference in Geneva.

On 28 Aug. the van der Horsts intend to pass through, likewise on their way to a conference in Bern. They don't know the Black Forest at all; I'd like to go on a hike with them & then spend a night up at the Cabin. That's all right, isn't it, even if the Stephanis are there. We can have lunch in the 'Engel'. When did Lisi want to come? How are we off for bed linen up at the Cabin? And shall I put the van der Horsts in our bedroom if they have to stay the night here?

Brock hasn't said when he's coming yet; but he has sent his work; the Dean has likewise written to say that he's sending me the three reports. –

[. . .] The second vol. of Grimm's A People Without Sp[ace]., which you were looking for, was in my desk. –

All the money I took for the journey I've brought back again & I've used just about the rest of the fee for all the expenses. Van der Horst told me that as a young professor Pos wasn't particularly well off, so now & then I paid for journeys & meals; I also left him & van der Horst small presents of books. Shall I keep the guilders here?

The money matters I'll deal with. –

I've already written to Beuron to ask whether I can stay there again for a fortnight at the end of the vacation.

So I won't be going up to the Cabin until September or right at the end of August.

Perhaps Fräulein Lina could then come up too; I don't really want to leave her on her own here, especially as Rötebuck is pretty deserted too.

Fräulein Lina has just told me that while I was at Vanoli's this morning Lisi rang from Neustadt.

Shouldn't I send you some more money so you don't exactly need to live 'extremely frugally'?

I'm enclosing the letter from Scheirer [?] about Baumgarten. I intend to advise him along the lines I've signalled; especially when I now draw the comparison with Brock's achievement – a habilitation thesis 390 pages strong.

Perhaps you could write & tell me your opinion briefly & at once. (I'd like to have the letter back again).

I've rung Lisi, for 10 days now she's been at a guest house in Neustadt; in good hands & very much in need of a rest; the other places in the Black For. were all booked up. At the end of August L. wants to go to Wiesbaden & from there back home. Next week we plan to go on a little walk some time; for the time being she still feels too exhausted. Many thanks once again, dear Elfride, for your letter; best wishes to you & the boys

Your Martin.

Fräulein Lina sends her best regards

From Spiekeroog, Elfride and the boys went via Bremen to see her parents in Wiesbaden, returning to Freiburg on 6 September.

On 7 October Martin wrote from Friedrichshafen, where he had been out on several sailing trips with Herr Magirus, the husband of his ex-fiancée Margret. Born in Strasbourg, Marguerite Magirus née Weninger had been engaged to Martin in 1914–15: The Baumgart[en]. affair has continued to be on my mind a lot – at bottom it's actually crazy how they've tried to force us into a certain role, as the ones who have to apologize etc. This is not to mention what Ed[uard Baumgarten]. has had from me in the two years, which will give him superiority over the Americans especially if he goes over there & a position which – on the face of it – has long since paid dividends. And then the behaviour of the two of them – But enough of that – the matter must now take its objective impersonal course; as for the scandal-mongering at the Moe[öllendorffs]., I'll have to get to grips with that some time after all.

On 11 October Martin wrote from the monastery at Beuron: I now have an increasingly strong sense of a gradual transformation, which extends even into my way of working, of asking and saying. Even though I can only advance slowly & don't want to fool myself, in everything that happens I sense a great providence, which gives me faith & trust.

And with all this I'm also learning to understand your great love & this means being ready for it.

And on 19 October he reported: Up to now I've had a very quiet time here, which will help me progress in the sense of consolidation and lasting assurance; to this end, the daily routine & the isolation, the constant example of the monks is a great outward help. Though I must accomplish the main thing myself, I also need above all the outward conditions; & I see more clearly today how much you've arranged our house for this purpose – how much it will yet be able to give to me & thus to us all. Since yesterday and for the next few days there's a liturgical conference for clergymen on the premises here – so the peace & quiet is pretty well over with. But I'd still like to stay a few days longer. Perhaps I'll come on Saturday though. – What's going on outside I don't know, as I don't see any papers.

Hermann was often ill, so in November Elfride took him to the milder climes of the south, to the Swiss town of Brissago on Lake Maggiore.

Martin and Elfride were not affected by the depression that held sway in Germany, generating high unemployment and financial hardship among the population. The political situation does not yet feature in the letters available.

1932

At the beginning of June, Martin gave the lecture 'On the Essence of Truth' in Dresden and met up with Elisabeth Blochmann, who by now was a professor at the Academy of Education in Halle an der Saale. Elfride went with Hermann to Rantum on Sylt. Jörg stayed at home and was looked after by the domestic help.

Frbg. 9. VI. 32

My Dearest Soul!

I'm very relieved to hear you arrived safely. The weather's certain to be better now too. My letter, which I wrote to Rantum on the very evening I arrived, will also have arrived.

On Tuesday morning I had to go to bed straight away, I'd picked up the flu while I was away. I called off my lecture & seminar. Today my temperature has gone back down & tomorrow I'll be back lecturing. Fräulein Lina looked after me excellently. Jörgele's very well – though he <u>is</u> a little sad that he couldn't go with you to his beloved seaside. –

Yesterday Ed. Baumgarten came – wanted to talk to me on urgent personal business. He brought the English original of his letter to Melton, as well as an explanation written by B. which I was to sign – & 'urgently' too – as today he had to go on a train journey.

In the explanation it said that I (H.) took back my 'objections' as they were founded only on errors of translation & did not concern the original.

I asked for the original & showed him the door. Checking it revealed that there are no errors whatsoever – only an omission at one point – which does indeed produce the wrong meaning, so in one respect my correction is unfounded.

The music room and dining room in the house on Rötebuck

I've written a very forthright letter to B. about it. A nasty piece of work –

He also tried to whip up Vetter's feelings again. It would have been a good thing now if I'd been informed about B.'s grumblings in my seminars so as to reproach him for the behaviour with which on the one hand he acts against me but on the other uses me to acquire some standing. –

I must now slowly try to regain inner composure for the lectures – the journey & the last few days have made everything seem so remote to me.

Baeumler has disappointed me to the extent that philosophically he really is rather weak – good as a historian – excellently informed in the latest movements. According to his reliable sources, the Nazis are still very narrow-minded in all cultural-spiritual matters – technical college & school of character – this formula is meant to solve everything & of course means ruin. Krieck – is an upstart elementary schoolteacher full of resentment.

<u>Grimm</u> – unsure in his intentions now – he lacks the great <u>material</u> appropriate to his new novel. Everything rather gloomy – B[aeumler]. doesn't consider communism to have been repelled at all – only fragmented for the time being – if a man comes who pulls the cause together he'll be a terrible force; the whole Jewish intellectual world is going over to it now; the Berliner Tagblatt has been a communist paper for a year now.

133

Behind it is the systematic dialectic founded upon Hegel, which for the moment is still superior in comparison with all the vague & seething stuff of the Nazis.

Each week Trotsky has a 20-pfennig booklet published in Germany, in which he gives his opinion on the situation, makes observations & points the way ahead.

The best & most informed book on communism is said to have been published here by Herder.

What seems most dangerous & obstructive to Baeumler is the <u>Christian</u> affectations of the German nationalists. Yet we want to try to bring together the people who share an inner bond –

Baeumler has ordered the 'Jüdische Rundschau'[10] for me, which is excellently informed & of a high standard. I'll send you the issues.

Dresden isn't a fertile ground for my work. Herr Kroner and Tillich have left behind a nasty crop of seedlings.

Just before the train departed I briefly went to the gallery & saw some Schwind & Caspar Dav. Friedrich.

The whole area of Brühl's Terrace is splendid.

In Halle Lisi picked me up –; she looked pretty exhausted; her work isn't easy & the political events are very much on her mind. I've now gained rather more insight into this whole Academy business – which just amounts to a secret desire to give oneself university airs – the stuff these people read: politics & worldview; education theory & worldview etc. I think Lisi's the only one who maintains standards & at the same time keeps to the limits.

L. lives very well on the 4th floor of a new house. The housekeeper very nice – only she had an awful cough & I assume that's where my flu came from.

On Sunday we went to Weimar. Going from the Halle landscape past the Leuna works into the Ilm Valley was very nice.

In the Goethe House I didn't want to see all the curiosities & real-life objects – but capture the atmosphere & that I managed. The contrast between the reception room & the study & bedroom –

We passed through a narrow alley to Frau von Stein's house – then on to the summer house – through the park & then to Belvedere – where we had lunch. By this time it was pouring down. When the rain stopped we walked back into town – to the royal sepulchre – in the beautiful old graveyard – to Charlotte von Stein's grave. Then I went to the inn & had an hour's sleep.

In the evening I went to the Blochmanns. The old gentleman is charming – served in Mainz & would get on very well with

---

[10] The *Jüdische Rundschau* (*Jewish Review*) was a German Jewish weekly newspaper that appeared from 1902 until 1938.

Father; loves a good vintage & local liver sausage; to his delight I was able to join in. We said good-bye in the early evening – as Lisi was returning at ½ past 6 – the next day I was rather tired & clearly already 'fluey' – I stayed in bed & then returned to Frbg. at 12 o'clock.

[. . .] Such was the outward course of the trip – as for the inward one – well, sometimes I was seized with horror at the great masses of people who merely seem to live without any sense of purpose. And I thought about my own work. And it's becoming increasingly clear to me – the experience in Dresden confirms me in this – that what matters is to put all my strength into the success of my planned new work in all its depth, unity & forcefulness & <u>lasting</u> significance & as far as possible to avoid being worn out by my teaching activity, for in the end it's pure chance who happens to turn up here –

I'm very much looking forward to the next few months & feel certain that something is coming – not the work – I'm still a long way from that – but a gaining of ground & of the paths upon which to begin with the whole task. Others must attend to day-to-day effects & business. More essential is that we again find a great aim for our German existence [*Dasein*] & above all that this is well founded, clear & worked out to the last detail. –

Beumelburg's Bismarck is exceedingly stimulating & instructive.

Which books do you want to have? Wagner sent something for inspection – The Story of San Michele –

I'll write to Father. A card to Fabricius too.

I've had enough of travelling for now & in August don't want to go anywhere except Lake Constance or somewhere like that.

For Father's 80th birthday I was planning something on the interpretation of Plato's Republic or perhaps the lecture on truth. Whether I'll manage the former with 4 dissertations still waiting to be dealt with – I don't know.

Perhaps some time in August. –

The roses in the garden are wonderful & I'm only slowly getting used to the two of you not being here. Best wishes & much love

Jörg also wants to read Fabricius's history some time.

Your Martin

Fräulein Lina sends her regards as well.

Martin was slow to recover from the infection, as this was compounded by a bout of sinusitus. On 18 June he wrote: The German student body has invited me through Baeumler to their conference in Blankenburg at the end of June. But I can't possibly go now. In general it's becoming increasingly clear to me how necessary it is to undertake wholly primordial & appropriate reflection & work here & that the immediate necessities of the day – however important they may seem – must take second place. The 'standard' of the V[ölkischer]. B[eobachter]. is again beneath contempt at the moment – if the movement didn't otherwise have its mission, it'd be enough to fill one with horror.

The National Socialist Alfred Baeumler was professor of philosophy in Dresden and in 1933 became professor of political education in Berlin.

Frbg. 20 June 32

My dear Elfride!
The parcel didn't come until today (Monday). It was a long time to wait, as since your first letter I only received the short card. Many thanks for your letters. I think of you a lot & am happy for you that you can spend these weeks at the North Sea. I'm growing ever more certain that we'll rebuild things anew & I too shall make an inner contribution to the construction of our lovely home. The clearer it becomes to me where I belong & what I must still demand from my work & this time also from my innermost self – everything up to now has just been a prelude – the more lonely I feel. I've lost all contact with my youth – not as a straggler – but as one who runs on ahead – And perhaps it's necessary for this utter loneliness to come – it alone assures us of our own direction – In the end the things I have to do cannot have any effect at all through direct contact – but only through the proper intermediate stages. And these one can perhaps help prepare through one's teaching activity – But otherwise this is – especially today here in Freiburg – really just a matter of chance. Elsewhere of course equally so – Even though I have the large lecture hall firmly in my power, I cannot rid myself of the feeling that it passes them by and if it does hit the mark it's hardly worthwhile.

But the limited number of hours I teach permits my writing to take on a quite different form & inner elaboration – often I can rewrite the whole lecture once again during preparation in the mornings – not because of the lecture course itself – but for the sake of the subject matter.

From all this you may see, my love, that in spite of the circumstances I'm forging ahead. Perhaps even in defiance of them.

Even though everything runs more swiftly when you're here, letting my thoughts escape to the island in the North Sea like this also has its good side. I keep everything at arm's length & live with Jörg out here. In between times I often sit with him in the workshop, which he really loves.

He's now building a big watermill – I can't keep up at all even when he draws a sketch of the plans. [. . .]

I just had a visit from Messkirch which interrupted me – This morning I went to the doctor's for the last time – that irrigation was torture, my cranial nerves are rather on edge now – but it'll be all right. You needn't worry at all.

I haven't made my holiday plans yet. I don't want to risk a trip in a collapsible boat at the moment. In August I'd just like to have a complete rest in order to get slowly back into work. We can discuss it when you're here again. –

What shall I do with the bills – the telephone bill etc.?

Otherwise everything's fine – Fräulein Lina shows great concern. –

What you write about the Jewish paper & the tic [?] were my thoughts too. One can't be too distrustful here. I'm now reading Bismarck's Thoughts & Recollections – but above all Greek historiography – I constantly ask myself what we've come to –

not only that there's nothing great & essential here – but there's a lack – which naturally goes with this – of all feeling for standards & rank. – But as I've written before – however much of an effort the Nazis require of one, it's still better than the insidious poisoning to which we've been exposed in recent decades under the catchwords of 'culture' [*Kultur*] & 'spirit'.

Admittedly – it will also be difficult to establish anything else again. First it must already be there – for the University as a mere institution, for example, has today long since ceased to have any right to itself – as long as it doesn't change from within. And I no longer believe in that happening. –

Today it's turned thundery here. Let's hope it doesn't turn into a steady rain. Jörg's going on the school trip tomorrow. Then he'll write. At the moment he's busy hammering away in the workshop.

Many thanks to Hermann for the lovely detailed letter & the descriptions – now I really can picture it. I hope he also finds an egg for me. I had no idea they were so big. The animals are all well looked after; the strawberries are flourishing & everything is lush in the garden.

I hope you continue to have good weather. – I'll send more newspapers in a few days.

Much love & best wishes
Your Martin

At the end of June Elfride returned home with Hermann.

In the late summer the family went up to the Cabin together on holiday. The next semester, Martin was on sabbatical leave and he remained up at the Cabin until 22 October in order to be able to concentrate on his work. On 14 September he wrote: This morning

Martha and Richard Petri, on his eightieth birthday in front
of the house on Rötebuck

a snake of grey mist lay over Rütte & crept its way as far as the pass
– ; now there's a thick blanket & the bells of the herd are ringing
through the mist. I've got well into my work & live with the woods &
mountains, the meadows & brooks – which give me what I need.
Quite away from all contingency – in profound indifference to the
non-necessary.

Cabin, 6 Oct. 32

My dear E.
This working week lacks the joyful prospect of your coming. And the
Cabin will remain without the bustle & play of the boys.

So this letter really must be with you by Sunday. I am surrounded
here by your support & silent presence, which lets me discover your
heart afresh. And my gratitude can only fail to keep up with what you
are & bear.

Only within the harshest discipline of work, reflection & composure can I then find the appropriate mood.

You asked me: what do you actually do?

Gather & clarify my actual intentions & in addition prepare the blocks of the coming work. I'm already hewing one block into shape – ; I don't speak to anyone about it: it's the essence of <u>space</u> – I discover & suspect that it is more than & different from what it has hitherto been thought to be, the form & receptacle of things & their dimensions; it is that as well – wholly with respect to what is most outward & passable – but it's something else. And 'time' also changes as a consequence & everything is under reconstruction – & not one stone is left on top of another. New ones first have to be dug out & discovered. –

Yesterday the first hoarfrost arrived, making itself felt at once. In the early morning the meadows, pastures & wood were white. The air is hard – the sun's out – but the thin, smoky mist settles in front of its rays. The smell of the potato fires pervades the air – autumn's here in earnest. In the Alps there must be fresh snow. At night there are storms. Cabin existence has acquired its proper form. I've moved into the front room – as the 'rear wind' stops the study from getting warm. I'm also making progress with the wood & as I go along I think of the lines from Goethe: 'Dragging wood, with rapture be it done, 'Tis the seed of many an earthly sun.'

Professors & everything that goes with them – have come to seem so remote from me – & I don't feel the slightest need of their worries & machinations.

Today on the way from the village I met Old Brender tending his herd at the Hasenloch & invited him to share some of the bottle still remaining. Black Pius was constantly lurking around the Cabin with his two cows & with the cold wind blowing I ended up serving him a kirsch. He then told me some patent hunters' yarns about how many capercaillie he'd shot in the old days. During our conversation about the wood the adage came up: 'Beech wood is twice wood.' –

Unless you tell me otherwise, on Saturday the 15th I'll come to the Notschrei [Pass] for the 1 o'clock bus.

Best wishes to the boys & much love to you.

Your Martin.

Cabin 15 Oct. 32

My D. S.

The last few days the weather's been wild up here. Yesterday afternoon the storm got worse from one hour to the next – it was at its wildest at 10 o'clock – the Cabin was creaking at the joints – I sat in the study

139

& worked – sleeping was out of the question – as on the previous nights too.

Suddenly at ½ past 10 there was deathly silence & then came the snow – it's good to be close to nature like this. This morning everything was covered in snow. In the village it has thawed away now but from Rütte upwards it's still lying.

I didn't expect you to come up on these days anyway, even though Church Consecration Sunday will be lonely now – you'll have heard that Mother was kind enough to send me a new parcel of sweet things & sardines. I thanked her at once yesterday. I hope your cold goes away swiftly & properly. Twice this week I've eaten at the Schneiders' (freshly slaughtered pig roast) – a good job that afterwards there was beerenauslese [wine] & I helped it down with kirsch as well & came through it all fine; it worked out quite well that I didn't have to go into the village in the awful weather. I feel excellent & toughened up. The wood – as far as I can manage it alone – is chopped & in part already up here too.

To the accompaniment of the storm this week I've made very good progress with my work.

Weniger, who's been in Höchenschwand up to now, has said he's coming for a day at the beginning of the week. This is really important to me because of the 'Tat' circle & I've all sorts of things to discuss with him about other matters too. It really is quite unclear what is to happen as regards so-called cultural & educational policies. The constant invocation of the Good Lord is becoming too much even for the Christian Tägliche Rundschau [*Daily Review*].

We do have one pure reaction & the Jews are now all turning Christian. To be sure, the Nat. Socialists are failing everywhere. Yet I do find one thing correct about Rosenberg's answer to Grimme – that Gr. had chosen the wrong target group. But one's suspicion is confirmed that the Nazis don't have any trained & experienced people. I find the article by Zehrer [editor of *Die Tat*] & his criticism of Nat. Soc. very good.

Mother sent me the issue of Die Tat too. –

The bill is correct; the July bill will be in my desk; the work on art history for your birthday is there with it.

Many thanks for your kind letter & the food parcel. I've no post to be answered. The letter is from an over-excited – but also presumptuous student; whom I answer thus. I don't know what should be given for the newly qualified graduates, please put a figure in.

Get well again soon.

Much love & best wishes

Your Martin.

1933

Hitler's seizure of power also had an effect upon the professional and private life of Martin and Elfride. On 18 March Martin visited Jaspers in Heidelberg.

19 March 33

My dear Elfride

In memory of our wedding day & the Heidelberg days I must send my best wishes to you and thank you for the inner help you give me. This really came home to me when Jasp. said he thought that my countenance & general demeanour showed a quiet harmony as never before. Your love & my still growing commitment to the work will help me to go on. –

From the first moment we – J. & I – have had the old contact & are already immersed in all questions of concern. I find it unsettling how this man sees our destiny & tasks in a thoroughly German way & with the most genuine instinct & the highest demands & yet is tied down by his wife – who incidentally now makes a 'happier', i.e. more favourable, impression than back then.

J. is also quite receptive to the real happenings that constitute the current German Revolution – though with respect to specific decisions tied down by an 'intellectuality' [*Geistigkeit*] that hasn't yet quite shaken off the Heidelbergian in him.

On the inner failure of the university as a unified world capable of exerting an influence, we've been in agreement of course for some time now – though also equally at a loss in the positively practical (the immediate) sense.

Regarding Krieck – whom Jasp. has known since 1920 & for whom he procured an honorary doctorate from the Hdbg. philos. Faculty in

141

1924 – I really am horrified – much though he shows genuine instinct. Rothacker is said to be trying by hook or by crook to secure himself a post in Berlin – all this racing around will soon turn nasty anyway.

We also spoke about Baumg[arten]. – & Jaspers told me that he hadn't for a moment hesitated to reject him & knew B. only too well from his student days here.

Even the minutes of the discussion, which B. had written & wanted to give Jasp. to sign (!) the next day, were not only biased but downright distorted & J's rejection much firmer than B. portrayed it.

The whole business of keeping quiet about the funds J. finds outrageous & he'll also bring it to the attention of M[arianne]. W[eber]. some time. –

In the last few weeks & esp. on the occasion of the Frankfurt conference I've been constantly reflecting on whether & to what extent immediate intervention makes sense or has any value. I have an innermost aversion to the false topicality to which even Jasp. tends – he'd like to persuade me to write a pamphlet on the university – ; this aversion is founded on my fear of divulging so soon what I've recognized increasingly clearly in these months of leave to be my true creative task. I believe that only now have I found its most characteristic spiritual form – & on the great matters one must keep silence as long as possible.

Even though action must be taken as resolutely as hitherto – & more so – in all coming individual decisions in the university, I'm convinced I mustn't allow a type of action that is 'political' in the narrow sense somehow to become the yardstick for philosophical action. The appearance of being on the outside will stay & yet <u>only in this way</u> will it be possible for the metaphysics of German existence [*Dasein*] to become an effectual work in its original affinity with the Greeks. To be sure, precisely in this respect Jasp. thinks too much in terms of 'humanity' & must do so too unless he wants to negate himself. –

Much love to you & the boys
Your Martin.

On 21 April, Martin was elected Rector of Freiburg University. On 3 May, backdated to 1 May, Martin and Elfride joined the National Socialist party. On 27 May, Martin gave his inaugural address 'The Self-Assertion of the German University'.

On the occasion of his lecture in Heidelberg on 'The University in the New Reich', Martin met Jaspers for the last time on 30 June. In 1936 their correspondence also came to an end. Gertrud Jaspers was Jewish.

Martin turned down a second offer of a chair in Berlin as well as one in Munich.

In accordance with the new statute of the universities of Baden and the Technical College of Karlsruhe, on 1 October Martin was appointed Rector by the National Socialist provincial government. He in turn appointed deans who were not members of the Nazi party, including his neighbour Wilhelm von Möllendorff, who had been forced to resign from the rectorship in April under pressure from the National Socialists.

Elfride was one of the first women in Freiburg to take her driving test, and bought a car in order to drive Martin to the university each day.

1934

Seeing himself restricted in his capacity to put his ideas on university politics into practice, at the end of February Martin announced his intention to resign from the rectorship to the Baden minister of education and the arts, Dr Otto Wacker. He officially resigned on 23 April, and now had time for his philosophy once again.

Jörg was more interested in railway engineering and carpentry than the grammar-school syllabus. For this reason he was sent to Stuttgart to attend the first Waldorf School in Germany. At first he stayed at a teacher's house, subsequently living with the Magirus family, who were friends of the Heideggers. Hermann attended the Friedrich Grammar School in Freiburg.

Cabin, 11 Oct. 34

My D. S.

It was nice that you were here, albeit briefly – I suspected it would be a foggy journey. The next day the sun came out; today it's overcast again & drizzling. I've now started writing & – regardless of the lecture course & such preparations – I'd like to keep it up for as long as there's a storm blowing. In the months after the rectorship I felt drained & was afraid of a long barren period – But now it's there again & quite different too – quite free, simple & essential, I feel – & yet difficult to hold on to, because we need a new but unaffected language & what's worn out is no good any more & only leads one astray. But it will take time before this comes to have an effect; I'm glad that nobody worries about me & that I'm away from the literary prattle & others play the roles there.

It's difficult to be alone with Hölderlin – but it's the difficulty of everything great. I wonder if the Germans will ever grasp that this was not a weakling unable to cope with life who took refuge in verse, but a hero facing up to the gods of the future – without any followers, 'rooted fast to the mountains for days on end'. –

But as I've told you before, this time I won't yet be a match for him in thought, for <u>philosophically</u> he's far beyond even his friends Hegel & Schelling & in a quite different place which for us is still unspoken & which it will be our task to <u>say</u> – not to talk about. –

The newspaper is amusing; the way such things look when seen from up here. But the mediocre & petty is necessary, & only a fool would have it done away with, for how else is the great & primary to stand out – & indeed without the contrast people see neither the one nor the other. –

I'd like to stay until 20 Oct; I have easily enough provisions; the students have provided lunch twice. I'll come on Saturday at ½ past 1. –

I've drafted a letter to the student union; but I no longer know the dates. Perhaps you could quickly write them in. Konrad [Kempf] can then type the letter out on a signed sheet of paper.

Much love to you & Hermann.

Your M.

Regards to Konrad. As the Dresdeners have moved, the new Berlin address will have to be obtained from the Freiburg student union.

1935

At the start of the new school year Jörg changed to Bieberstein rural boarding school, a Hermann Lietz School.

In July, 14-year-old Erika Birle from São Paulo in Brazil entered the Heidegger family as a foster daughter, both her parents having recently died in quick succession. Erika was a distant relative of Elfride's, and her mother had been Hermann's godmother. She had already met her new family during a visit to Germany. She was expected to be grateful.

Cabin, 3 Oct. 35

Dear Elfride!

On the whole the gathering was a success. It was just a pity that most of them already had to leave on Tuesday afternoon. Bauch also took advantage of the opportunity. Perhaps the bad weather played a part as well.

The best is Heisenberg – he should have really been up at the Cabin; he comes from the Youth Movement; clear, simple, modest & reserved, & yet open & friendly. H. stayed on longer than the others of his own accord & I spent a few more pleasant hours with him. Only when I hear of such people & their colleagues does the full dreariness of Freiburg hit me.

The Heidelbergers – as I heard from Achelis [?] – always get anyone else we find in the way of good people.

In the very near future Heisenberg himself will be appointed to a chair in Berlin or Munich & leave Lpz. [Leipzig].

But perhaps the gatherings, as we continue & extend them, will be a sort of replacement. Ultimately, after all, everyone's on his own if he wants to do something real. Thank you for your birthday greeting too;

you're probably right, we should be satisfied if we have such opportunities.

The days were very strenuous for me, as it wasn't easy to provide such wide-ranging conversations with a ground & a direction, especially since these themselves first have to be created.

Yet the next day I made a bright start to work; my art lecture must now take on the right form once and for all & in addition the winter lecture still has to be done.

The weather really is terrible & I don't expect you to come up on Saturday/Sunday if it goes on like this.

I'll ring some time around noon on Saturday.

Hermann should collect the pine cones on the floor & not in my bed.

I've written to Jörg

Much love to you & best wishes to the children

Your M.

On 13 November Martin gave the lecture 'The Origin of the Work of Art' to the Freiburg Aesthetics Society.

1936

My dear E.

I hope to complete the Rome lecture in its structure in the next two days; I must make sure that it's quite simple & yet not shallow.

As I need all the volumes & other material as well for the preparation I'll come down on Tuesday evening or Wednesday. The weather also seems to be getting worse & heating is a palaver.

The Cabin was in splendid shape. It was very nice with Hermann. Bauch went down yesterday, he was rather restless.

B[auch]. brought the news that Bäumler has enforced Nic. Hartmann's transfer to <u>Greifswald</u> because H. refused to change a class that was scheduled at the same time as one of B's. –

The last few days we've done all the cooking ourselves – ; proper snow was only left in Wittenbach Valley – now it's wet even there.

Much love & best wishes to you & Erika

Your M.

In April Martin travelled to Rome with Elfride and the boys. On 2 April he gave the lecture 'Hölderlin and the Essence of Poetry' at the Italian Institute of German Studies, and on 8 April he spoke at the Kaiser Wilhelm Institute (Bibliotheca Hertziana) on the theme 'Europe and German Philosophy'.

Cabin, 11 August 36

D. S.!

As I climbed up alone from Todtnau on that last lovely Thursday I was very sad & it was some time before I felt at home again in the lonely Cabin. But you'd prepared everything so nicely for me again that even

With foster daughter Erika Birle

this was a sign of your presence. In the meantime my work has been continuing. Working is actually just the way I create the right opportunity for it to flood towards me – & sometimes it really is an almost uncanny flood – from which I can hardly escape – so I always just have to hold on tight. And that's just the way this loneliness <u>has</u> to be, even though it isn't always easy to bear –

But the simple things all around one provide for the continuity & steadiness of work & its broad direction.

Everything ordinary drops away.

This evening I'm sitting in the Cabin with the shutters closed, & outside there's a 'pig' of a storm raging once again. What's more, there must be something wrong with the standard lamp, yesterday it suddenly flickered & a fuse blew in the shed; I replaced the fuse – but I don't dare use the lamp any more. The new stove is very nice.

If you don't come in the next few days – i.e. within the week – do send me the following books:

1. the <u>Schiller</u> volume that contains the letters upon aesthetic education
either 9/10 or 11/12.

2. <u>Taine</u>, Philosophy of Art.
standing or lying in the <u>middle</u> bookcase (outside wall) <u>bottom shelf on the right</u>

3. Schopenhauer, the World as Will & Rep[resentation]. 2 vols. in the bookcase by the desk (halfway to the left below the middle) [. . .]

If you come by car you'll probably have to take the <u>old</u> road from Schindelbächle – as they're now – so I'm told – rolling the road between the village & Schi[ndelbächle].

Let's hope Jörg learns English as well as he's learnt to drive.

In the letter you sent, Pongs [?] says he'd like to have my Hölderlin lecture for his journal.

Has Hermann written again?

What is Fräulein Semmler's address? I'd like to send her a picture postcard some time.

With best wishes to you both & good-bye
Your M.

'Hölderlin and the Essence of Poetry' appeared in the journal Das innere Reich (The Inner Realm).

Elfride had succeeded in obtaining special permission for Jörg to take his driving licence at the age of 17.

She became friends with Erika Semmler, who as a member of the NS-Frauenschaft, *the women's organization in the National Socialist party, would go on to become head of the department of culture, education and schooling in Berlin.*

1937

Bieberstein, 25. II. 37.

D. S.

Jörg is now much better; he's still rather pale but otherwise fresh & cheerful. At the medical examination for Labour Service he was declared 'Fit 1'.

Things aren't so rosy with regard to his school exams however. He's probably stuck with his 4s in the languages & I fear that the same will happen with history; otherwise in mathematics, physics, chemistry, biology & German he has 2s.

The teachers are all very well disposed towards him – with the exception of the history teacher. But I've spoken with Jörg about the matter & he'll work flat out on this now.

He really is one of the boys who makes the best impression now. And barring really rotten luck they'll pass him. The place where he'll do his Labour Service is still uncertain; J. thinks it could be the Moselle region.

This evening I gave a talk to the pupils; at the request of [Headmaster] Andreesens on Dürer's hare; & I think the boys got something out of it.

It really is splendid here & the view from Jörg's room unrivalled; his roommate is also very nice.

The angina infection, which Andreesens suspects was brought into the school by a pupil following a medical-(military) examination, seems to have been pretty nasty. But they appear to have got over the matter now.

I'm very glad I was able to be here these few days, even though Jörg is rather preoccupied with school lessons & revision & homework. The Andreesens are very much looking forward to you coming in March.

There's approx. 10cm snow on the ground here now & from time to time the sun even comes out.

151

Frankfurt was not unpleasant; I got a thing or two out of Reinhardt. Now there's Weimar coming up, & then I'm looking forward to a few days' rest.

If I've had enough I'll come back as early as Sunday evening.

The schools seem to be still unaffected & the rush of new applicants is said to be very great.

Jörg says thank you very much for what you sent him & sends his best wishes to you all. Now we can only hope that he continues to be blessed with good fortune in this final spell of his schooldays.

Best wishes to you & Hermann & Erika

Your M.

Shortly after the ninth form, the eighth-form pupils at Bieberstein took their school-leaving exams the following March. Jörg passed this specially brought forward Notabitur *and afterwards was immediately called up for Reich Labour Service in Melsungen from April until October.*

Todtnauberg 2 July 37

Dear Elfride!

I wish you many happy returns of the day. Even though it's seemingly just a formality, I'm still sad not to be together with you on this day. You know that I'll perhaps never be fully able to make good the early suffering that came your way from me; and this pain grows greater by the year. But I can endeavour, with what remains to me, to do things right and thank you every day for your kindness & love. I don't want anything for myself, but everything for the task.

And if – as it appears – I now once again have to go through a spiritual crisis so severe that it even leaves its mark upon the body, here too you will be my strongest & most silent help, even without specifically involving yourself in philosophy.

Of course here too help & interest is possible, as the short question you asked recently has now proved to me; for the question about the relationship of truth and genuineness has suddenly opened up quite new perspectives to me & things that hitherto lay side by side have now come together. I've already drafted a certain amount. But I want to leave it in peace now, otherwise I'll immediately start working again. –

Today's a fine sunny day – though I doubt whether the weather will last.

Liesel [Schmid] is charming, quiet & careful, she tells me a great deal about plants, animals & stones; & I introduced her to Stifter for the first time as well, whom she didn't know at all.

152

I'm also writing to Soergel, asking him to let L[iesel]. stay until Thursday or Friday 9 July.

So I'll ring you again tomorrow evening around ½ past 7. If I can stay up here, you'll also have to send up the pills at once.

I hope you have a lovely time & send my best wishes to all. My regards above all to your parents in W[iesbaden].

Much love,

Your

Martin

Best regards to Janssen too.

Elisabeth Schmid was a relative of Martin's and would later become Professor of Prehistory and Early History and the first woman rector of Basel University.

1938

March saw the Anschluss, *the annexation of Austria by the German Reich. On 23 September, Elfride's father died of old age in Wiesbaden.*

[Freiburg] 24 Sept. 38

Dear Elfride,

I think now of the moment when the news of my mother's death reached me. You silently laid a kind hand on my brow and then left me alone with my pain. Today I'd like to respond with a similar silent sharing in your suffering, if only from afar.

You bear the unlosable figure of your father within your heart. And if what is fragile in the human being has now been taken from you, this only means that what can never be stolen from you will remain in your possession as all the more precious and radiant. For what belongs to you is not only the memories of the dear departed, but the whole living fabric of your own nature is filled with the constant presence of your beloved father. I often think, and in recent days especially, how ever since those moments when we first met one another the figure of your father, a small picture of whom was then on your desk, has been present as well.

You also know, without me ever having spoken of it a great deal, how dearly I've always valued the esteem it was given to me to receive – undeservedly – from this man.

His spirit and his image will now move anew into our house, and let us all foster the strength of this model of true nobility.

My thoughts are with you & I hold your hand & ask you to remember me to your revered Father as well.

Your Martin.

Dear Elfride!

Many thanks for your greetings. I hope you and your dear Mother are as well as you can be. It's almost a comfort to know that dear Father no longer has to endure all these confusions.

Jörg arrived safely (8.02). Otherwise everything's all right. But I really am very worried, not about particular things but about the West as a whole – even if the worst doesn't come to the worst – when I reflect upon the level on which everything now moves.

From time to time now I think of our peaceful days together up at the Cabin & yearn for the simplicity & silence & natural greatness of the mountains & woods & meadows under the glowing wide autumn sky.

What will the coming days bring? The Swiss, as ever, give very excited accounts of the situation in the neighbourhood: there are Papists yonder!

It was a very lonely birthday. Indeed, basically I didn't think about it at all; for such things are unimportant. A <u>very serious</u> letter came from Lisi. [. . .]

Janssen thinks it's important to stay here just in case. What is to become of Erika?

I've also sent a card announcing the death to the Schneiders in Todtnauberg & Adolf Kempf in Messkirch.

Best wishes to Mother from us. I understand entirely that you have to be there now.

I hope we see one another again soon.

Best wishes to you from us all.

Much love

Your Martin.

Frbg. 27 Sept. 38

Dear Elfride!

This afternoon Erika Semmler rang up from Munich; I told her of Father's passing away & gave her your address.

Körte & Bröcker are with me just now, very worried about what to do with their wives & children. The situation is getting much worse, and in such a way that we've no idea what it's about. France, England, Russia have all declared their solidarity & regard our intervention as an act of war.

I still can't believe that the worst will come to the worst.

But I think that given this critical situation it would be good if you didn't stay away too much longer. Can you ring up tomorrow between 2 & 4 o'clock or towards the evening? I'll stay here all morning & afternoon tomorrow.

Best wishes to you & Mother
Your [Martin] [a piece of the letter is missing]

*Germany was planning the annexation of the Sudetenland; mobiliza-
tion began on 27 September. On 29/30 September the Munich
Conference took place, which agreed to German control of
Czechoslovakia's Sudetenland with its predominantly German population and thus prevented the outbreak of war for the time being.*

The Heideggers' foster daughter Erika was attending the municipal
Frauenarbeitsschule (*a school of domestic science for girls*) *in
Freiburg, where she completed her course with an exam in house-
keeping in March 1939. Prior to this, she had completed her German
Reich Labour Service as a domestic help with a priest's family in the
Black Forest.*

*The escalating persecution of the Jews was not a theme treated in
the letters available.*

1939

Frbg. 19 Jan. 39

Dear Elfride!

I'd like to send my best wishes to you too for the twentieth birthday of our Jörg and say a simple thank you, which will always – as I know – fall short of what I have to thank you for.

I often think of you in Wiesbaden; & I'm certain too that this return really was & had to be different from usual. But now there remains the strength and the personal 'fortune' – if one may call it so – of <u>remembrance</u>.

I hope you and Mother are well. With every post I wait for news from you. I'm going through strange times at the moment with Hermann & Erika often away. The growing of the children into independence & a world of their own – this is a new task for us as well, to acquire the proper free attitude, yet indirectly still give them something on their way. Jörg's self-confidence is reassuring, & I have the impression that he's now also beginning, entirely in <u>his own</u> way, to think more deeply about certain things that go beyond a future profession. Hermann makes me very happy – he's now, I think, kindled an interest in philosophy after all – at any rate he understands that it involves something that cannot simply be equated with 'science' & 'worldview'.

As for 'the Lass' [Erika] – Hermann is busy teaching her things; I told him recently in a conversation one evening that we fail to take enough account of what an uncultured environment the child grew up in; for then there's so much more scope for inconstancy. –

I hope you also have time for <u>reflection</u>, so that you cope all right in Berlin with E[rika]. S[emmler]. A new issue of 'Die Frau' has come with a picture of Gertrud Baeumer. Shall I send it to you?

I've now read 'The Wish Child'; the final part is by far the best; but perhaps the difference from what comes before reflects an inner

157

artistic intention. The poet [Ina Seidel] herself must be a very 'troubled' character. We must speak about her work when you're here again; especially also because it touches upon questions concerning the meaning of folklore, symbol, heritage & blood. – one wonders whether I. S. is a solution.

Otherwise everything's all right here. Hermann returned very satisfied from the J.V. [Jungvolk][11] skiing competition; on the 28th/29th he wants to go to the University championships. My passport is ready already. The weather seems to be staying unpleasant even longer; one spell of foehn after another.

Much love from me & best wishes from us all.

Your Martin.

Best wishes to Mother from us.

Frbg. 26 Jan. 39

Dear Elfride!

Many thanks for your detailed letter. Now you'll have mine at last. I think it was simply the postman's obtuseness & not malice that caused this confusion.

Here everything's all right; I'm getting on well with my work; in the seminars the ones who matter are responding very well & even from a distance are really acquiring a more precise idea of Nietzsche's thought. When, in my preparation, I now consider this untimely meditation on history, it becomes clear to me how little is still actually known of the younger Nietzsche too, who even so is easier to grasp. Hermann listens attentively; yesterday I dealt with the concept of 'personality', with Kant's categorical imperative, according to which man must never be taken as a means but only ever as an end in himself, i.e. in his <u>essence</u>, through his respect for the law – with one eye on Scharnhorst – Clausewitz.

On Saturday–Sunday Hermann's taking part in the University championships on the Feldberg; he has accommodation at the Feldberger Inn; he isn't hoping for a victory, but wants to see what he can do. (Karljörg [Lieber] recently came 2nd & was in the paper!). Erika's working hard, & was yesterday invited to the 'Huberten' [student association of foresters] by Frau Hausrath; the parcel for Berlin will be sent today. (I'll be responsible for looking after the bees while Hermann's away).

Yesterday Bröcker was given his medical – two years ago of course he'd been declared unfit for service; today – after hardly a glance – fit

---

[11] The *Deutsches Jungvolk* was a subdivision of the Hitler Youth for boys between the ages of 10 and 14. Hermann was a *Fähnleinführer* or troop leader.

for service! Students from all these years are to be called up on 1 March.

The day before yesterday H. brought the following news item from 'Le Temps': les milieux compétents démentent de la façon la plus catégorique que le ministre Goebbels ait été cité devant un tribunal de parti. [The competent parties deny in the strongest possible terms that Goebbels has been summoned to appear before the party court.]

I mentioned this to Brö[cker]; whereupon he said I was apparently the only person in Germany who didn't know already. There's a lot of talk – but G[oebbels]. seems to have had it; in other areas too a reshuffling is said to be imminent. The internal situation worries me more than the external one – for the latter is but the consequence of the former. What's the point of things like 'customs' & 'symbols' any more in view of the actual realities and the inexorable dynamic of the military-technological organization of the people as a whole; why, they're just smokescreens [*Vor-wände*] – romantic – historicist – attempts at Romanticism – more academic than all that is 'academic' today, which after all is already working everywhere for the Four-Year-Plan. I don't think your discussions will lead to any decision unless E[rika]. S[emmler]. can find a way out of the context of her current position beforehand. Make sure your stay in Berlin is not too 'wild' & strenuous – even though I understand very well & hope that human help & support is available there. Let's hope you get your manuscript all wrapped up. If you're very tired after your days in Berlin, do travel back second class. –

The summer semester begins on 12 instead of 1 April. Lucas was here the day before yesterday & wants to finish the lamps before the week is out.

The weather is fresher again & up there there's snow again. On Sunday afternoon Bauch is coming; & Janssen said on the phone recently that he's still waiting for an invitation from you. Schwarzweber had to repeat his slide lecture; Körte talked about 'the Führer's roads'; only unfortunately it didn't fit into my time, as I'm still taking the study group on Hegel with the older ones. Steding's book – edited & with an introduction by Walter Frank – is said to be out now with the title 'The Reich & the Disease of European Culture'. Let's hope it isn't another – not Freudian but folk-political – psychoanalysis, like his dissertation on Max Weber. When St. last expounded his definitive plan to me up at the Cabin in 1934 (summer), I had a strong impression that he's still stuck in the sociological-psychological analysis of N[ietzsche]. & Jakob Burckhardt & can't find his way to a substantive & fundamental engagement at all. On a 'walk' at the time I had a very intense discussion with him on this point. He was always of course a very self-willed person, but also highly gifted & above all

<u>deadly serious</u>; yet he always – even in the seminars – evaded the fundamental substantive questions, perhaps because he sensed his limits there; his only interest was the philosophy & analysis of history & historical attitudes. Yet he never saw the great danger here: that for purely analytic criticism the differences of <u>rank</u> must disappear & any silly old Nietzschean is taken just as seriously as Nietzsche himself, & in such a way that N. is even made responsible for those who misinterpret him. But in a certain way this danger comes from Nietzsche himself & the manner of his analysis, if one takes this to be the only & essential thing, whereas to follow N's apt but perhaps unbridled will it should only be a necessary foreground & thoroughfare.

E[rika]. S[emmler]. presumably has the book already, as there's said to be a lot of official propaganda for it. One wonders if it will produce intellectual engagement. As far as I can see, it lacks the basic prerequisite for this: the clear separation of fronts which thereby call themselves into question & <u>want to</u> listen to one another; instead of this, convictions are merely confronted with other convictions, beliefs with other beliefs – & everything stays as it was – i.e. the 'reaction' feels that it's more & more in the right & <u>this</u> – as the alleged guardian of 'spirit' – is what most prevents any reflection. Yet perhaps there <u>have</u> to be these times without reflection, in which the lack of reflection is demanded & instigated by the conflicting attitudes. –

As long as there are just a few to safeguard the way into the German future not for what has existed hitherto, but for what is ever primordial & the yardsticks for this – & this means renouncing an effect in the present, in the knowledge that what is essential never 'exerts an effect' but only 'is' provided that something of its own kind comes to meet it from a deeper origin. Yet we cannot plan this, but only wait in silent readiness. –

The other day I was talking with Fräulein Riese at Albert's about Ina Seidel's new 'novel' [*Lennacker*] – she rated it even higher than the Wish Child. – I envy – albeit not wholly in earnest – such people, who from the assurance of their faith somehow cope with everything & from this attitude can create free of care.

And yet – these are not the true ways of the God that again & again transforms Being, letting the new depths & heights spring forth from the abysses. –

I think of you a lot & wish you & me a pleasant & contented homecoming.

Best wishes to you & Mother from us all.

Much love, your

Martin

Kind regards to Er. Semmler; & best wishes to Gertrud Baeumer.

On 1 September Poland was invaded by Germany, triggering the Second World War. Hermann reported to the Reserve Battalion of the Seventy-Fifth Infantry Regiment in Donaueschingen, wanting to become a regular officer. The Technical University of Karlsruhe was shut down, so Jörg continued his studies in mechanical engineering in Munich.

In Messkirch, Martin worked intensively through his manuscripts, which were then typed out by his brother Fritz. As Freiburg University was near to the border with France, it was to remain closed for the time being.

Messk. 6 Nov. 39

Dear Elfride!

In one's home town – and yet not at home, this is another of the many conflicting situations arising from the essential insecurity of the universally armed West. There's no hold to be found in what is present & what has hitherto been is finished, even though the outward circumstances may still be maintained a little longer. So all that remains is the only thing that can always be determining for us: what is yet to come, & the way in which we are there [*da-sind*] for it. Great transformations in thought & human existence are perhaps already preparing themselves, the contours of which we can hardly conceive. This & having the whole workshop at my disposal gives me the impetus to work. With each day that passes I find I'm making better progress.

The summary of course cannot be a mechanical one, but has the makings of a success in the simplest saying of what is essential. Along with this there's the other task of looking through & comparing the – extremely substantial – previous transcripts & the original manuscript in question.

This job will take quite a few hours & afternoons together with Fritz, but it helps me to recollect what I've attempted so far and make it my own & this makes the collection stronger & richer as a whole. Towards evening it's then time for our walk together on the paths through the fields and woods I frequented in my student days. The deer now come out into the snow-covered fields & meadows; with the restricted traffic the countryside has fallen quite silent again. I only allow myself visits to relatives on Sundays. On All Saints' Day we were up at the graveyard & also visited the older graves; the names provide a history of our youth. Most of the faces are already unfamiliar to me & at a glance one can only make a rough guess at the 'lineage'. As far as provisions are concerned, the people here still hardly notice this strange war. And many of them think it'll soon come to an end by itself.

In school, on the teacher's instructions, the boys now have to cross out the words 'Bolshevism, the world enemy' in their readers from 1938. Perplexity & refuge in the faith of the Church are equally prominent. And yet also a universal willingness to make the sacrifices that are necessary. –

It's Liesel's name day on 19 Nov.; I'd like to give her a special treat some time for all her trouble. I don't know anything suitable though.

I wonder if you're now gradually finding the peace & quiet to do some 'spinning'. I constantly find myself thinking about how you're alone in our house, no less conscious of how scattered we all are than I am here.

Where do you think Hermann will end up now? We'll probably be without any news for a while, there's talk here of a 3-week postal ban for these convoys.

In Munich the masses of students are said to be pretty unhappy, as they don't learn anything with all this commotion. – [. . .]

Fritz would like to read the book about Mad[ame]. Curie; but I'm not sure we have a copy; you sent Jörg the one from the reading circle, didn't you. –

Treat yourself to a little more outward rest now too after the constant exertions of recent months. Semester & university have turned into something unreal, less on account of the current events than the work in which I'm involved.

Best wishes & much love to you

Your Martin

Everyone sends regards.

In order to become more self-sufficient, Elfride had acquired a spinning wheel to process the wool from their Angora hare. Since the mid-1930s she had been working in an honorary capacity for the Nationalsozialistische Volkswohlfahrt (NSV) *or National Socialist People's Welfare Organization in Zähringen, Gundelfingen and Wildtal. She looked after mothers and children and organized regular get-togethers, known as 'Mothers' Evenings'.*

Erika was doing a practical at a residential school for foreign girls in Stuttgart.

On 22 November Martin wrote: What I'd most like is to return to Frbg. as soon as you're there again. Even though I'm in good hands here, I miss your silent presence, which after all is an integral part of my work. There's something I dread about this constant toing & froing – one feels as though one's been turned out onto the streets. And everything's growing more & more mysterious. And yet – & yet – we know something other than this & in this knowledge there prevails an

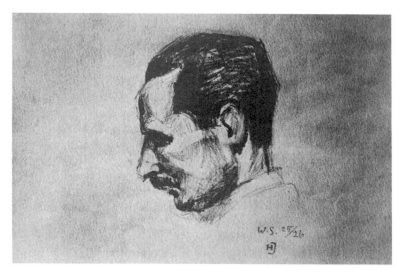

'This drawing (by Hans Jonas) from a Marburg logic lecture was duplicated by Fritz for my name day. Messkirch, St Martin's Day, 1939. Your M.'

unassailable belonging of hearts; the more boundless the chaos, the more single & solitary the true. Every day I think of Hölderlin's words:

'Long is the time, but the true comes into its own.' And we must now realize that for a long time to come the future will lack any space in which anything essential might take shape; indeed the very possibility of creating space is destroyed.

And nonetheless – the knowing closeness to Being [*Seyn*] is – & that we may do something small for it & in the process remain certain of the silent consent of a few gives the most inconspicuous activity its essential purpose.

Messkirch, 26 Nov. 39

Dearest Soul!

Many thanks for your kind letter and the card. I'm glad you can give Mother a treat. Why, this is the only thing that still contains truly effective strength now. At a time when the invisible devastation is more far-reaching than the visible destruction, even the paths of daily reflection must head in the direction of the invisible. In this realm there is a coming-together of the invisible & uniquely real few who have given man his grounding upon existence. Firstly, these are the individuals who are today involved in the immediate struggle of war & who find no support in anything present, not even in community and comradeship. In their way they must have a premonition of something

163

else for which they're willing to make the sacrifice, something they cannot say, yet only create in the sacrifice. How many such people there are out there, nobody knows. But that there are such people is certain. And then there are the women who out of an originary love keep secluded spaces ready for the soarings of what is noble & by virtue of this love are indestructible. Who they are eludes all publicity. And thirdly we may count those who, running on far ahead in their poetizing & thinking, belong to another history. Where they are & whether they are remains so well hidden that not even this questioning after them can awaken, let alone make itself generally heard. These three invisible and uniquely real figures prepare the 'poetic', upon the ground of which alone the history of man is founded. To these three figures belongs the gift of Being [*Seyn*] – that it is given to them, each in their different way, to be open to the coming of originary decisions & each in their way protect it.

What the philosopher must always already know, others too may now perhaps learn – that the invisible is more existent [*seiender*] than the visible. –

A card just came from Hermann; he has now received my parcel & the letter. He writes: one must 'draw thought from within oneself, I'm glad to be able to do this; so though I miss the spiritual encouragement, at the moment I'm replacing it myself' –

Yesterday I wrote H. another letter; at Adolf [Kempf]'s I read some cards from Konrad, who writes that in his btl. [battalion], which is in the same position as H.'s, 90% had volunteered for the western front.

Two days ago Schuchardt, who is standing in for the Dean, rang me about a PhD matter. He said that according to instructions from Berlin all the universities are to be opened again in January with the exception of Freiburg, but after the latest talks in B[erlin]. Frbg. too is now to be opened; I don't believe it; which of the students are supposed to come to Frbg. now? –

Liesel now sends the butter to H[ermann]. every Monday. Recently I've often thought how kindly fate treated the good gentleman [Elfride's father], allowing him to depart a year ago.

I had anticipated you'd stay away longer. I reckon to get the work sorted out by about 10 Dec. Comparing the transcripts where there's a lot of Greek text holds me up a lot; but I don't want to miss the opportunity of working together with Fritz. If you deal with matters in Berlin so quickly it'll be a strain on you & won't be worthwhile; surely you ought to be able to see G[ertrud]. B[äumer]. & A[lice]. R[ilke]. at leisure too.

Today I rang E[rika]. S[emmler].; I've come across a reference here to a manuscript I need for 'Art & Technology' and which I had no memory of at all; it's from 1927, when E. S. has a typed transcript of the lectures. But she doesn't seem to have the ms in question. To judge by her voice & everything she's obviously very low & is taking refuge in a 'job' that probably isn't one. But for the moment there's probably nothing to be done, even though the schools everywhere are on the lookout for teachers. So it'll be a good thing for you & for E. S. if you stay on a little longer – perhaps until 4 or 8 Dec. Above all, <u>don't stint on things</u>; & do you have any warm clothes? Here it's proper winter, very beautiful, but very cold & raw & it brings back again the winters of my youth. It's almost like up at the Cabin. But I have a nice warm study, even though the house is rather lightweight & of course not heated throughout; but in this we've been schooled by the Cabin, haven't we.

I've answered yes to the enclosed question from the Reich directorate & given Niemeyer the appropriate instructions. Perhaps it'd be good if you kept the letter. Perhaps you and E. S. could go over the outline I sent you & in this way both raise <u>questions</u> that may help me. Under the current circumstances of course there's nothing to be expected from E. S.

It's touching how Liesel continues to look after us – ; & my presence here seems reassuring to everyone. There's a dark weight on people's minds, quite unlike during wartime in the past.

I hope, Dearest Soul, that you have a good, quiet time together with Mother, & I send my best wishes to you both. Your Martin

What are Jörg & Erika up to?

I wonder if Jörg can go back to Karlsruhe again.

But I suppose it is out of the question.

Perhaps you could have a discreet look round E. S.'s some time to see how my things are being looked after there?

Martin was considering the possibility of teaching at the secondary school in Messkirch or the village school in Todtnauberg. He was very worried about his library and manuscripts.

In mid-December, Jörg in Munich was also called up for military service. He was just able to take his first diploma in mechanical engineering beforehand.

1940

*Freiburg University was reopened. In the Easter vacation Martin
returned to Messkirch to work for a few days.*

*On 10 May, on his way to Messkirch, Martin was informed that the
German offensive in the West had begun at 5.35 that morning:
German armed forces had invaded the Netherlands, Belgium and
France. Freiburg suffered its first air raid just before 4 o'clock in the
afternoon: three Heinkel 111 bombers from Combat Wing 51 stationed at Landsberg am Lech had lost their bearings in a storm and
inadvertently set their sights on Freiburg instead of the French airport
of Dôle-Tavaux. Fifty-seven people were killed and many more
injured. The people of Freiburg were allowed to believe that the air
raid had been the work of the western powers. (See 'Geschichte der
Stadt Freiburg', vol. 3, p. 358).*

Messkirch, 18 May 40

My D. S.

The storm that is now breaking over our enemies is fearsome. If we
older people tend, often reluctantly, to think of the charge forward in
the summer of 1914 & the standstill at the Marne, we're forgetting
that despite the strength of our adversaries the situation today is fundamentally different. Not only because such uncertainties & confusions as the mission of Lt. Col. Hentsch[12] are no longer possible & the
leadership is quite united, but also because our enemies, even though
they have their aircraft & armoured cars, still think along the old lines

---

[12] Lieutenant Colonel Hentsch was the German general staff officer commonly regarded as
responsible for the stalling of the initial German offensive in September 1914 of the First
World War.

& have to rethink matters from one day to the next. With us, however, the complete mastery of technology has in advance produced a quite different kind of strategic thought. In addition, the invasions are sufficiently well rehearsed. Now we will see how a breakthrough of this new sort can also be secured & its consequences turned to account differently from 1917 & '18. The ruthless 'operation' is in itself also an unconditional commitment to the inner lawfulness of the unconditional mechanization of warfare. The single person disappears as an individual, but at the same time he has the opportunity to be informed of how the whole thing stands in the quickest possible way at any day & any time. Of course, this knowledge gives the warriors increased certainty of really being led. Even so, yet other forces are necessary, especially those that prevent the war from becoming dependent [?] on the war, but find their way out of it to another beginning. Yet these forces are still without space & without shape; but I believe <u>that they</u> are there.

Many thanks for your letter. I'm glad you're not all on your own now. Here there were wild rumours & obvious exaggerations about the air raid going round. Yesterday I wrote letters to both the boys; at the same time, but separately, each of them was sent a bar of chocolate as a letter. We probably won't get any news for a while now.

This afternoon & tomorrow I'll be dictating to Fritz. I've written to Schuchardt to say I'll need next week for work. [. . .]

When I read Hölderlin each day now, I remember that you're reading with me.

Recently I've been reading the 'Archipelago'. That we possess such things, not as a past 'achievement' but as a work that even now is hidden, vouchsafes a German future towards which the paths must be <u>even</u> steeper & even more hidden than the tracks that must now be trodden in sacrifices & deeds. –

I'm delighted that Erika is so open to what you want to teach her. Here I've now got hold of a 'Hieronymus'[13] (not of my own, but to read), a description of the Baar & the Black Forest from last century; very simple & honest.

It's turned rather cool here; last night it snowed on the Heuberg. But the ground, which really was very dry, now has its rain, & the farmers are pleased about that. Some of the fields with winter seed look quite wretched. I want to get this letter finished for the afternoon post; perhaps you'll have it then by Sunday. I've also got hold of 100 bullets for the air rifle through Thomas. If you want to ring me (perhaps

---

[13] Lucian Reich, *Hieronymus: Lebensbilder aus der Baar und dem Schwarzwald*, first published in 1852.

because of University), the best time is in the afternoon between 4 & 6 o'clock; it's easy to fetch me then. Have the copies of the Potsdam speech on Fr[ederick]. the Gr[eat]. arrived? I hope to make some decent progress in the next week. Much love to you. Best wishes to both of you.

Everyone here sends regards.

Together with Erika Semmler, Elfride had been working on a small book about the leader of the German women's movement, Helene Lange, which she was now hoping to publish.

After passing her housekeeping exam in March, foster daughter Erika now wanted to go to the women's technical college in Freiburg. She prepared for this with help from Elfride.

Before returning to Freiburg on 26 May, Martin wrote on 22 May: My work continues to progress as usual; and if I could stay on now I'd get much further with everything than I'd myself expected; for of course it's always the final getting to grips with the whole thing that first leads wherever it wants to go, something which is never achieved during the stage of preparation. But these few weeks of lectures will pass as well; I consider the whole operation of the University (apart from medicine & nat. sciences) to be pointless. There's no knowing when the time will come for my work to have an 'effect'. But I believe that in the steps it takes & through the realms it enters, it will – one day in the future when 'philosophy' is essential again – have an effect, simply in the way 'philosophy' does have an effect, invisibly & indirectly; for the effect I was able to have in the past as a 'teacher' & 'professor' may have meant a certain amount, but it isn't the essential thing. For me myself it was an important spur; today I can manage without it, because the field that lies before me every morning is firmly bounded in itself & rich enough to give ever fresh impetus to my work. Teaching has now become a hindrance, at least until I decide to dispense with the preparation of new lectures.

1941

At the end of January, Elfride visited her mother in Wiesbaden. Elfride and Martin were hoping for German victory, but daily life was conditioned by their worries concerning their sons, both of whom had taken part in the campaign in France. They spent the summer up at the Cabin.

While Martin continued work in Messkirch in September, Elfride again went to visit her mother. No sooner was she back in Freiburg than she learnt that Hermann had sustained a serious leg injury in Russia and would be transported home.

Messkirch, 25 Sept. 41

My D. S.

We really can be very reassured by Hermann's handwritten letter telling us that he's an officer and that the transport back is clearly well organized. And perhaps it's particularly fortunate that he was injured now of all times, when in the south towards Kharkov things have intensified once more & further sacrifices are having to be made.

All this time I haven't been able to bring myself to write to Vienna. I have no desire at all to appear there & even less to go there on my own with things as they are at the moment.

We have to be there for Jörg & Hermann now.

Jörg of course is on his way northeast. But the danger isn't nearly as great for him, especially as he's with the [sound-ranging] analysts. And even the lookouts aren't that far forward. Claus, the son of Robert Vetter in Constance, is servicing the same weapon & has the same function as Jörg. Yesterday, Eugen Vetter (Baden-Baden) was here and told me about it. What's terrible is the actual street-fighting of the sappers & infantry there.

Together we must continue to make our contribution to what the boys and many thousands with them have to bear.

Even if our knowledge allows us to see & experience certain things more essentially & therefore as harsher & more fraught with consequences, we do also have an inner richness to give in turn, which lets us overcome what is horrifying.

Many thanks for your birthday letter. Your silent concern for my work is surely singular in its kind, as is the path I must take, knowing that genuine communication & indeed an effect are among the things I must renounce & am happy to renounce. Fortunately I was always fully aware of the illusory success of an earlier decade. Every day I gratefully submit to the inner law obeyed by the 'work', which of course is always a solemn celebration because the efforts involved are as nothing.

In these last three months I've never 'taken refuge' in the 'work', but have let my thought be affected by what the fate of every heart in these times leads us to fear but also to trust.

I was very happy about Jörg's letter. I'll tell you about my enquiries concerning the farms once I'm back.

Good that Erika's now finally with us for a rest.

Theophil's suggestion about the Stübenwasen Inn is perhaps the best thing if he isn't coming on his own. For you too, the Cabin bustle would be too much. And I don't want to interrupt work. After all, the semester will soon be engulfing everything in its educational bustle again.

Bauch has written a very short but very friendly letter, remembering the nice September day we spent together in '39.

I haven't read Janssen's letter yet, as I want to write to you at once so you have my letter by tomorrow.

Be sure to order a car in good time, as I'll be bringing a few lbs of apples as registered luggage.

Let's hope the weather stays reasonably settled. I hope the move to the Cabin goes well for you both.

I'm always here at work, & so easy to reach by telephone.

Much love to you, D. S.; & best wishes to you & Erika.

Your M.

Best wishes to Frau Winterer. And kind regards to Frau Ruch from me & from the people here.

1942

Hermann slowly recovered from his wound and attended lectures given by his father. Martin wrote a contribution for the volume commemorating the 100th anniversary of Hölderlin's death.

Princess Margot von Sachsen-Meiningen was one of Martin's students, and a close and long-standing relationship developed between them.

Messk. 14 Oct. 42

D. S.

Today your letter came with the little books. Many thanks. Yesterday evening I rang to find out about Jörg. The honey is ready for Frau R[?]'s sister. L[iesel]. has got some for the boys too. Rudolf's brother wants to be rid of one of the ducks <u>soon</u> because of the feed.

I haven't finished the letter to Theophil yet, as I've been busy with the Höld[erlin]. ms for the last three days because of Kluckhohn's letter. Some pages have been rewritten; a few things added. In your last post was the photocopy of the final stanza – quite wonderful. I've discovered a thing or two in it as well. In addition, I've made the beginning, which you objected to, easier to understand in some paragraphs. Fritz transcribes it all, then it still has to be corrected, so the whole thing is then presumably all right. I'm due to get the first set of proofs at the end of November.

Liesel will try to obtain the other things, it's difficult to get wine. One mother here, who in the last war lost her eldest son at the age of 21, has now also lost her youngest at the age of 32.

In the last war there were 98 killed or missing in action here, now it's 30. [. . .]

I'll send Gertrud Bäumer & Frau Rilke the allegory of the cave [Plato] from here. The Princess writes briefly to tell me that she plans to send the children to Birklehof [boarding school].

Good that you can still hear a decent concert.

Tomorrow I'm going to Constance to see Robert Vetter with Liesel & Fritz, who are celebrating their wedding anniversary. I'll go & see Jünger in Überlingen another day, as with the bad connections it isn't possible to do both without staying overnight.

Since yesterday the weather has been better again. Let's hope Hermann soon gets back into shape again.

Best wishes to you both.

Your M.

Everyone sends regards.

On 25 October, Elfride went to Berlin-Frohnau to celebrate Jörg's engagement to Dorothee Kurrer. On 17 December Dorothee and Jörg were married at such short notice that it was impossible for Elfride and Martin to get to Berlin.

1943

Elfride cultivated their large garden with fruit and vegetables, kept bees, spun the wool from their Angora hare and kept goats in the empty garage. The swimming pool was filled in, converted into a makeshift air-raid shelter and planted with potatoes.

Messkirch, 12 April 43

My D. S.

The parcel with your nice letter from Freiburg & the letter from Wiesbaden arrived today at the same time. Many thanks for them both. In the same post there was a card from Jörg to Liesel, in which he writes that from 15 Apr. he'll be back in Jüterbog. Liesel intends to send the Kurrers some more eggs she can spare here.

I'm well looked after here. Hermann is sending me two more things from Freiburg so I can prepare the semester at the same time. Don't rush yourself in Wiesbaden – you're bound to have quite a lot of running about to do now, which is always strenuous in town.

I can easily stay here until after Easter. I'm beginning the lectures on 4 May.

We're making good progress with the work. Unfortunately the weather isn't particularly nice.

I'm enclosing a copy of the letter from Baeumler. He's presumably basing his form of address on party membership. I wonder if this is now the sign of retraction.

I have no intention of getting mixed up in anything or indeed getting controls lifted on the banned writings at the expense of cooperation. To be sure, it's sad that real work in the western [*abendländisch*] sense isn't possible. We must not now make speeches & write articles about the West [*das Abendland*], but be western – for this it's enough to release the forces that are there.

173

The practical question is what & how I should answer. I don't want to do this without your advice. I'll also confidentially send a copy to Wolf in Freiburg & ask him for advice.

There's plenty of time.

Best wishes from us all to you & Mother.

Much love,

Your M.

Friedrich has written from Stuttgart saying he's heard from an acquaintance who often goes to Tübingen that several student transcripts of my Hölderlin lectures are in circulation there.

Messkirch, 20 April 43

My D. S.

I'm glad you're home again. Just you have a proper rest now! This morning I waited 2½ hours for the conversation, then suddenly had a call from the Rector. The University & the city are planning a Hölderlin commemoration, which is to take place in the Domed Hall. I accepted under the condition that I'm not expected to make a speech to the masses.

I can only see two possibilities, as I'm certainly not giving a standard commemorative speech with a biographical account & an 'overview' of the works: either an interpretation of a poem, so Hölderlin has a chance to speak, or a direct dialogue with the poet that makes it clear how we must listen to him in the times to come. This would make it an address concerning poetry and thinking. For this I have a large manuscript to hand. After all, in some entirely non-polemical form something must soon be said about what we have to be.

In the meantime, as I was expecting you to be staying longer in Wiesbaden, I've set to work going through a large ms. In the next few days I'd like to finish this off in the main, so as then to work through the mss. for the Hölderlin lecture; for I don't want to take them to Freiburg & as yet there are no transcriptions of them.

It would have been nice if Jörg could have come. But we can be happy that he's in J[üterbog]. What's his address? I forgot to ask the Kurrers to send the egg boxes back here again.

Congratulations to Hermann & many thanks for looking after the post. Please send me what has arrived in the meantime once more. What does the Lass write?

From Tübingen, Kluckhohn writes: 'the Party is planning a three-day Hölderlin celebration'. The academic ceremony takes place on 7 June.

On Sunday I went on a hike into the Danube Valley with Fritz & the two eldest. It was a magnificent day. We found the most beautiful flowers, corydalis & pasque flower, & the first sloes in bloom.

It'd be good anyway if you could ask Principal Weber to issue a written confirmation that I must immediately return to Freiburg on university business. Then I can leave here as soon as I'm ready with the work. Then we'd have a few days together as well before semester starts again. I give the first lecture on 4 May.

The rainy weather has now come back again; but the rawness & cold are gone. People are beginning to work in their gardens.

Best wishes to you & Hermann from us all.

Much love

Your M.

Regards to Frau Ruch as well.

Erika had been working since 1942 as a welfare worker in Stuttgart.

Messkirch, 5 Dec. 43

My D. S.

Your letter with the corrections came today. Many thanks. Every day I am grateful that I'm granted the time for thinking and creating. I have a very simple & regular daily routine. From 8–1 o'clock & from 3–7 o'clock I work. In the evening we then go for our walk in the lonely countryside. I've got into the swing of things more rapidly & better than I first thought.

At a time when everything is geared to utility & success, power & business, we must remember at every hour that 'life' finds fulfilment sooner and more purely if we bestow our attention upon the ownmost essence of things. This inconspicuous guardianship of the essential in silent commemoration, escorted by those entrusted to us, is the echo of the origin to which everything returns. The weakness of will that is everywhere around us is but the counterpart to the mastery of will, from addiction to which no good ever comes.

We who still know of the essential cannot just drift aimlessly along, because otherwise we would forget what is most important, which is that the greatest and most beautiful thing that falls to man finds its truth not in an effect, but only in this: that it is & thus accords with the everlasting. –

Things seem to be quietening down on the southern Russian front. The retreat from Melitopol [in the Ukraine], which I should think was hardly expected, probably means that urgent work is now necessary on their current positions.

Sometime soon a parcel will be leaving here for Hermann. [. . .]

I think I'll have finished what I set out to do by 18 Dec. Fritz is getting on just as well with the transcribing.

The boxes will also be ready this week.

Lots of love to you & Dorle
                    Your M.
    The whole house send their regards.

Jörg's wife Dorothee, known as Dorle, had by now moved in with her parents-in-law in Freiburg.

1944

In April Martin returned to Messkirch. On 13 April he wrote a letter describing the journey, which took him via Constance: The journey to Lake Constance was full of memories. The island of Reichenau lay beautiful in the calm lake under a high blue sky. The church in Mittelzell chimed across to us in greeting. Somewhere there in the lake the little ring lies hidden. Untouched by the troubled waters & storms, this is how our thinking and being towards one another is too.

Princess Margot von Sachsen-Meiningen was now living with her two children in a forester's lodge belonging to Graf Douglas, situated near the ruin of Hausen Castle in the Danube Valley. Martin was to be a constant guest there.

H[ausen]. 14 Aug. 44

Dear Elfride

Along with his regiment, which was unexpectedly given its marching orders during night-time exercises, Hermann has hastily been put on board a train in Storzingen, which is in a valley leading into the Danube valley. They're heading east. That Hermann is being taken from the midst of his native world, a good deal of which he's had the good fortune to see, and is imbued with a real task, makes me think of him each day with a trusting calm. Whenever his dearest wishes have demanded fresh sacrifice from him, things have turned out to his advantage.

I very much hope that you have detailed news from Jörg & Dorle. Each day now I have the feeling I may not see my homeland again for a long time. Yet everything I've searched for & found over many years is now to be preserved in good order here.

After a few days spent in part resting, I got into my writing so immediately that I'd like to spend the few remaining days doing the same. At the same time, from the most important manuscripts not yet transcribed, which are full of stimulation, I'm making notes to keep with me in the near future, just in case there's still any chance at all of doing any work.

But I can't exist without my thinking & should like to prepare myself inwardly for other situations too in such a way that I'm not entirely deprived of the tokens of thinking.

I think of you so often now & each day thank you for your silent love, which unobtrusively & graciously prepares the way for me on the long & varied paths I tread. I also thank you for letting me have these days. I shall be returning from clear reflection & confinement to the simple.

In midweek I'll travel back to Messkirch & stay there a few more days. I'd like to be in Frbg. by 22 Aug. unless you need me sooner or the situation changes.

Further restrictions on travel are said to be in store.

Best wishes to you, dear Elfride. I hope these days are not too troubled.

I've written to Hermann for his birthday.

With all good wishes,

Your Martin

After the Normandy landings, the Allies were on the advance, and Martin was very worried about his manuscripts, the closure of the University and his impending conscription. Among other things, he applied as a civilian employee for clerical work at Heuberg Military Training Area, but he was not required. In the meantime, he continued to put his papers in order and search for possible places to keep them safe. On 28 August he wrote from Messkirch: The only thing is that we're lagging behind with the time-consuming corrections. After all, even with the greatest care serious misreadings are often possible. My inner composure now almost exceeds my strength, and in spite of everything that weighs upon my mind I use the first fresh hours of the day for writing down essential things. I now often achieve a previously unattained simplicity –

During the night of 22 November Martin and others from Zähringen and from the University were called up for the Volkssturm, *the German Territorial Army, and taken to dig trenches in Alsace.*

Arzenheim, Saturday, 25. [11. 1944]

My dear Elfride!

This morning I went to see the doctor, Dr Villinger. I'm only allowed to do office duty & am to be <u>replaced</u> as soon as possible. For the time being it's still quiet here.

Engineer Captain Graumann, who's in charge of the Vst. [*Volkssturm*] battalion of the armed forces, is a comrade of Hermann's. I talked to him for 10 minutes a short while ago.

There are 50 of us stationed here on straw in a school hall without a heater; the conditions for writing are accordingly poor.

I need a pair of slippers & some boot polish. I don't know whether you've already received my forces' letter. Things are very war-oriented here, though there's no combat. We dug trenches yesterday, which didn't do me all that much good. Schuchhardt & Maunz are in the same hall. Everyone's worry of course is that we might yet cross the Rhine.

Today the landlord of the Castle is going back with a farmer from Wildtal & taking post with him. Please write & give him your letter on his way back.

I wonder how you all are. I often think of you over there. We're stationed just opposite Sponeck, 2km from the Rhine ferry, which is in constant use. I'm writing in the greatest haste. I'm very much looking forward to hearing from you – the slippers (not good ones) & boot polish you can give to the Castle landlord to bring.

Best wishes to you, dear Elfride, & Jörg & Dorle.

Your Martin.

The night of 27 November saw the Allies' heaviest air raid on Freiburg, which almost completely destroyed the old centre around the Minster, the Clinic and Institute district, and other parts of the city, but left the Minster largely intact. Almost 3,000 people were killed during the night. At the time, Jörg was in the military hospital above Freiburg-Herdern with hepatitis, and could see the city as it burned. In December, Martin was discharged from the Volkssturm. *On Jörg's bicycle, he rode to Hüfingen, where he took the train on towards Messkirch. He had the idea of having one of the towers of Messkirch Castle restored with a view to working there. Given the shortage of skilled workers and materials, it was never possible to put this plan into practice.*

Erika and Wilhelm Deyhle were hoping to marry in Nussdorf, where Wilhelm, known as Helm, worked as a parish priest. Yet they were not granted permission to do so because Erika, as an expatriate German, was lacking certain important documents.

Martin stayed in Messkirch over Christmas. Elfride did not want to join him there.

Dear Elfride!

I'm giving this letter to Fräulein Dr Husemann, whom I met yesterday here in Hausen, to take with her. She's been visiting the Princess's sister for eight days. I came here yesterday lunchtime & am returning to Messkirch today – even travelling this distance is quite an undertaking. I hope that post from you & Jörg & Hermann is there today. I'm constantly thinking about how you might be & what's going on now in Freiburg. In the last few days I've again tried to continue with the preparation of my lectures, but it still isn't really possible; my sleep isn't much use. Nor is it surprising. I still haven't got things sorted out with the distribution of the mss – the number which have still not been transcribed – Fritz himself now realizes too that it's no good leaving the main bulk in some kind of pile in Messkirch.

The day before yesterday I wrote you a letter which I wanted to bring to Frau Künz at the station; she was returning to Frbg., but unexpectedly took an earlier train – So I gave the letter to Dorle, who posted it in Sigmaringen. Yesterday, 29 Dec, there was still no post from Jörg. D. was thinking of taking a trip to Tübingen from Tailfingen.

It worked out quite well that we left as Liesel had earmarked yesterday & today as cleaning days; besides, there's also a friend there, though she's staying with her sister.

The house here is full & the Princess is without any help at all. But I myself had to make the selection from the mss that are here. I had fruitful conversations both yesterday & today with Prof. Schulz, who is also here over the holidays. But at the same time I also see how quickly I've got out of practice in certain respects & not yet regained the proper composure for my own things. I wonder if it'll come again. Indeed it must, for otherwise we'll be completely crushed by the fury of the mechanism.

A card to you came to Messkirch from Mother in Wiesbaden. Apparently my letter to Wiesbaden is still on its way too.

Leiner wrote telling me not to come with the mss until after the New Year. Perhaps I'll go with Dorle, who wants to be in C[onstance]. on 2 Jan.

Fräulein Dr Husemann says that our Faculty has arranged for its working premises to be in the 'Lamb' in Engen. She didn't know whether there are to be just seminars or lectures too for the examination candidates, who are the only ones supposed to matter as regards the continuation of teaching. Her own Science Faculty she said is being dispersed; she herself is going to join Prof. Schulz in Rostock.

Have you made a firm plan yet in case Frbg. is evacuated one of these days?

The Lass wrote once again & suggested she should stay a few days in Messkirch so as to be declared a resident there. I spoke once more with the compt. person; but it isn't as easy as that. I do hope that the petition to the Reich Ministry of the Interior is successful.

I wonder if you haven't been up to the Cabin after all in this nice weather. Here & in Messkirch there isn't much snow lying now. At times the east wind hasn't half been blowing through the little house.

Here in the 'Castle' Graf Douglas has made another nice garret available so as not to have to give it to anyone else.

In an emergency there'd be another refuge here too if it became too cramped [in] Messkirch. What with the cold the building work in the tower is making little headway.

From 1 Jan. they're <u>supposed</u> to be getting rid of the Kellers' tel. too, so it'll then only be possible to make calls through the local bank.

Since the line near Singen was seriously damaged, the Berlin fast train from Constance & other trains now pass through M. more.

But all this remains entirely external as long as we preserve our inner being. And this we will; & I am learning to do so more & more simply & clearly & gratefully.

Best wishes to you, dear Elfride. Constantly thinking of you,
Your Martin

Regards to Gertrud & Frau Ruch.
& Bauch.

On 28 December Erika and Helm were finally able to marry in Nussdorf.

181

1945

Martin stayed in Messkirch. Postal connections with Freiburg were unreliable: most letters were sent with acquaintances, and only rarely was it possible to make telephone calls.

Fritz was called up. Martin was writing longer letters to Elfride again. On 8 January he told her: I haven't managed to do any more 'work' as all my time is spent in ordering & making additional corrections to the transcripts. Besides, my sleep is very poor, so I'm not fresh enough for what even now certainly remains the most necessary thing; increasingly clearly I feel the need for simple saying; but this is difficult; for our language only applies to what has been up to now. [. . .] On Christmas Eve I went to Midnight Mass with Fritz, but I kept thinking of that early morning when we went to the Minster together & then returned across the Karlsplatz. I often wonder too how Jörg & Hermann might think back on the city in particular. It's all just memory – in it everything is more existent [*seiender*] than otherwise. Yet this memory must not induce us only to think <u>back</u>. Even if we're unable to intervene directly in what is spiritual & essential, the latter must still & nonetheless be preserved, tended, cultivated. This is often revealed even more brilliantly to me now through a poem of Hö[lderlin].'s – but I lack the time & lack the composure to hold on to it.

In fact Martin was supposed to be taking up his teaching at Freiburg again. At the same time he learned that the University was to be moved out of the frontier zone. The Philosophy Faculty was thus looking for a retreat in the area around Messkirch. On 10 January, Martin, who was still without news from Elfride, wrote the following: Kant wrote the Critique of P[ure]. R[eason]. at the age of 56, under what for him were quieter circumstances. I have the clear knowledge that I'm standing right on the threshold to a more experienced & simpler saying.

There will be no 'post-war' in the same form as hitherto. If any space for thinking remains at all & the outer conditions haven't vanished completely, we could still find ourselves entirely cut off from our own work – from the mss & other aids. For this reason I take the few opportune moments I can to concentrate upon the essential & reflect on the paths; for this vanishes from sight all too easily when our thoughts turn to our needs. In outward matters and in the course of my life I've experienced much favour & fortune, but it really isn't the case that I've never encountered need. And the innermost need of history & the West, don't you think, saps & strains one in quite a different way from social affliction & human suffering, which I by no means regard as insignificant.

Here at my birthplace, which now gives shelter to more than double its population in strangers, I have to search for home each day; this is how concealed everything is.

Eventually, Martin heard from Elfride, who had opened a small school for the neighbourhood children in their house and was expecting Martin to go back. Martin too was considering a return to Freiburg, and on 16 January he wrote: I don't understand what good I'd do the few girls with the Leibniz seminars. Sch[uchhardt]. says I'd find a new impetus for work there. Once I'm down now I shan't come back here any more. No one else can make everything safe here once and for all. But I can do without having to explain these things to other people. After all, I'm not here to get out of anything. But down there with you I can stay in our house once again & live from memory & perhaps help quite a bit. I understand very well the necessities of war & the current situation. All the same, thinking will come before any other activity for me right to the last, even if no one else comprehends this at the present time & what is essential remains unpublished.

Jörg went down with malaria, was admitted to a military hospital near Prague, and in January was granted leave of absence. Together with Dorle, he came to visit his father in Messkirch. Dorle was now working as a welfare worker in Constance.

On 22 January Martin wrote to justify himself for not returning to Freiburg: I'm occupied with my manuscripts day & night, i.e. busy salvaging the whole thing in a reasonably meaningful state at least. Other than this I no longer manage to 'work' – quite apart from the fact that I lack the strength to do so on top of the other task. But I've now traced the path & the relevant writings from 'Being & Time' until 1932 & indicated the references & connections between them. Now comes the time from 1934 to today; more difficult, more extensive & yet clearer & simpler in essence. Sometimes I despair of getting it done, because a great deal does need to be looked through – . Of course, my univ. colleagues don't have anything of this sort to bequeath & so it's easy for them to have other concerns & to believe 'the University' can still be rescued today after long since failing to do so.

On 15 January, Elfride's mother died of old age in Wiesbaden shortly after an air-raid in which their flat had also been hit. In the war-time turmoil, the news of her death was delayed in reaching Elfride. It reached Messkirch at the end of January.

Hüfingen, 2 Feb. 45

Dear Elfride!
You know where my thoughts are the whole time. With Hermann & Jörg & you. On Mother's passing I wanted to give you my hand in silence & say what you 'said' to me back on that May morning in Marbg. when after hearing the news of my mother's death you left me quietly on my own in the study. Even if we tell ourselves it is a blessing & a release, the pain still remains, & with it the memory of everything Mother has bestowed upon you and me & the children in the way of goodness & kind-heartedness. And as you duly sensed what was about to happen and made provisions for everything, the laying to rest of the deceased will also be properly taken care of by the two sisters. Indeed, the din of battle will probably soon be raging all around the place where you yourself spent happy years & now know your parents to be at rest.

In the last few weeks, which since the assault in the East have brought nothing but inner restlessness, I've been trying to do what I could on the mss despite further obstacles. Sometimes I've wanted to give the whole thing up; but I know of nothing more important for the future. Occasionally I've thought that out of self-deception I might be taking many things too seriously. But now that I've looked through older writings, some of which go back two decades, & recognized their intrinsic connection with what has now been achieved; now that I've looked back over the path on which I've been led with many a detour & deviation, & I draw comparison with everything else that is there, I cannot leave it all to chance. To be sure, I can't do more than what is humanly possible either. I'm still undecided about what is to be done with the iron chests. 'Burying' them is indeed too dangerous; for then it's quite some time until one can get at the stuff, which keeps on getting damp inside the chests as it is.

Transferring it all from Frbg to Messkirch, which I was hoping to do at first, is hardly likely to be possible now. And so I've tried to make headway on my own.

In the process I probably rather overdid it, as I was working at night again too, above all on the more external business of listing and collating the material. I haven't wanted to write to you about it up to now,

184

as I thought it was just temporary fatigue – but the insomnia is continuing, the faint spells & headaches & strange depressions. Since Fritz left, I have no one around me with whom I can talk or go for a walk in between whiles. Yet what really wears one down is the fate of this people, especially when thinking beholds it in its western essence & with a destiny such as this. A great deal from Hölderlin has only now become clear to me; but it's only through certain key words & hardly sentences that I can get a hold on these insights.

On the night journey here I wasn't particularly well – the next day I went to Marie's family doctor here, who showed touching concern for me & said that intellectual over-exertion was causing the symptoms and I was to rest for a while. Marie wants to keep me here too; it's touching & almost too kind how she looks after me –

but I can't sit around doing nothing in this state. The strafers are here morning & afternoon & drop their bombs; people don't bother too much about it.

I want to stay here a few more days & see how the situation develops. Tomorrow I'll write to Ziegler as well – the doctor here was regimental doctor with the 75th regiment in the France campaign & knows Hermann too.

I've brought two iron bars here. There's very little chicken feed here now.

Rudolf & Marie are quite well at the moment. This sort of life here isn't very strenuous & might almost be called comfortable. I often think – & thank you for it every day – of how much my outward life was already provided for so that the proper task could be pursued & thinking & its path could thus unfold – But when I think back over the long path, it sometimes frightens me, and the present implications of many efforts & reflections no longer surprise me either.

Suddenly all of this is then overshadowed by thoughts of the fate of our young generation, if one may still talk of such a thing. Historical comparisons are always erroneous. But even though we must not compare ourselves with Greece, not even with the late Greek civilization of Plato's time, I do believe that unknown paths of tradition & of reawakening will remain; that language in particular will awake as the abode for a new dwelling. –

We'd been hoping in Messkirch that you'd come to see Jörg after all. He was very composed and confident and almost touchily optimistic. What a good thing that D. & J. didn't meet in Berlin, otherwise Dorle would probably still be in Berlin now. Liesel took an almost motherly pleasure in looking after the two of them. The jam has still not arrived in Göggingen. I suspect Schneider is getting more enticing remuneration from Loch Farm & is doing everything for the Breithaupts so far as he has room. The cases that Fräulein Gisb[ertz].

brought are now well looked after at Adolf Kempf's; there's even more room there. Hermann's things here are also away at the parish house in Hausen vor Wald. I've talked to Liesel once more about you coming. You can always count on being taken in in Messk.

Erika has written me a short note too. From the letter to Dorle, I gather the wedding was very nice & rural after all. If only all this could remain. –

With regard to the allocation of troops in the East & West, you hit upon my thoughts entirely. Often it almost seems as though the course of 'events' were a mere mechanism.

I often now wonder how this spring will find the soil of the fatherland. No one can probably imagine what's going on in the East now. The transcripts in Gleiwitz have now gone too. The Cabin will perhaps be a refuge, at least in spring. I've paid the yearly rent for the Tower. The restoration work is to restart once the mild weather comes. No money has come from the savings bank yet. What was sent via Heidelberg hasn't arrived either.

I'll write to you from here again in the next few days to let you know what I'm doing depending on the situation. Best wishes to you, dear Elfride. Constantly hoping that you stay safe, your Martin. [. . .]

On 17 February Martin was back in Messkirch and wrote: Perhaps even now, in spite of the unspeakable misery, there is little pain in the world because everything is only hardened by power of the will. What is now taking place over the entire planet is of such a kind that an essential event must be concealed within, even if we cannot yet see it & cannot yet speak of it. For this reason, however, we must always remain close, in our thinking, to what is concealed, without wanting to force anything. But there are times when this steadfastness exceeds the capacity of any human being. I often think of how you're now on your own, looking after our home in Freiburg, where everywhere memories bear <u>that</u> part of the present that is dear to people. [. . .] You mustn't worry about me too much – together in enduring & remembering we try to live up to everything that is dearest & most worthy to us. Over everything there now lies a rubble of incongruity and strangeness, which is all the more disconcerting because it was heaped by one's own people over the hidden striving of its own essence to grope its way to its truth.

Hermann was in East Prussia, and Jörg once again in Olomouc [Olmütz], near Prague.

On 22 February there was an air-raid over Messkirch that claimed 35 lives and left more than 120 injured. The bank where Fritz worked was also destroyed, but the manuscripts Martin had deposited in a safe there remained unharmed.

Martin finally received post from Elfride again, and on 2 March he replied: I often now think of Grillparzer's words on the modern age: 'From humanity through nationality to bestiality.' But this process as a whole is already unfolding in subjecti[vi]ty, in that man has lost the proper relationship to the unnecessary, indeed perhaps never attained it. To be sure, this is difficult or even impossible to grasp for a world of achievement & work, power & success, which is why this must vanish too; but it won't have vanished by the day after tomorrow or the foretellable future. On the essence of the unnecessary (which is what I mean by 'Being') I recently found the short conversation between two Chinese thinkers that I'm copying out for you.

On 11 March Martin wrote from Messkirch: Nonetheless, I've got over the depression; I feel that my strength isn't at an end yet; perhaps the efforts of the last 7 years can resolve themselves after all into a quite simple saying. Without all my burrowing labours, which may have seemed obsessive, this would not have been possible. I've recently read Hölderlin's 'theoretical' treatises, which helped pave the way for the great elegies & hymns & are incomprehensible to common reason & set forth in sentences that run on for pages. It is indeed appropriate for the mind to keep waiting & to let itself be led, even though much remains painful & for a long time unilluminated.

The food situation in Messkirch was reasonably bearable thanks to Fritz's connections. Dorle had set off on the spur of the moment to fetch her sister and niece from Berlin, parts of which were now encircled and in flames. On 23 March, Martin wrote to Elfride: This Easter greeting is full of sorrow. And yet we mustn't yield to it. The fate of the fatherland is so mysterious in the midst of everything else that is happening that it must harbour within it something that towers far beyond our knowledge. From this painful secret comes wonderful strength. Even though my condition is still physically delicate, in the last few days I've gained such remarkable momentum that I'm almost completely oblivious to food & sleep. I suddenly found a form of saying I would never have dared use, if only because of the danger of outwardly imitating the Platonic dialogues. I'm working on a 'conversation'; in fact I have the 'inspiration' – I really have to call it this – for several at once. In this way, poetizing & thinking saying [*das dichtende und denkende Sagen*] have attained a primordial unity, & everything flows along easily & freely. Only from my own experience have I now understood Plato's mode of presentation, & in some form or other the Plato book intended for you must one day become reality after all. Of course, it's a struggle to collect my thoughts in the outward circumstances. For I must also consider how to go about salvaging & distributing my things, manuscripts & books.

Happily, Dorle had got her sister and niece out of Berlin and to safety, found accommodation for them in Kissingen, and returned to Constance. On 3 April, Martin wrote from Messkirch: When I think of Jörg and Hermann, the jitteriness about safety strikes me as strange. Thinking about the two of them has given me a strange strength in writing the conversation – whether I'll finish it completely I don't know; keeping my composure & withstanding the strain of writing is getting more difficult by the day. There are now more than 120 ms pages; Fritz has already begun transcribing them. [. . .] But thinking holds on to me; in spite of everything I trust in the higher future of our essence, though at times it looks as though all the Powers of Darkness have been unleashed even from within ourselves in order to block the path that leads there. [. . .] I often feel as though despite its dimensions this monstrosity suddenly ought to collapse in upon itself like an evil spirit because of its emptiness and vacuity. Soon now the pandemonium will be raging across the meadows of Hölderlin's homeland; and yet – the water and the groves, the breezes and the morning and the evening will rest within themselves & always be new signs.

On 10 April Martin wrote from Hausen. The Philosophy Faculty had found accommodation up at Wildenstein Castle, though teaching had not yet begun there: I think I'll find the right decision for the transition. The essential thing seems to me to be not that one is still here oneself, but that possibilities for a future are preserved. Mere gestures mean nothing one way or another.

Messkirch, 15 April 45

Dear Elfride!

Today your card came with the greeting from Bauch. I've sent you two letters through Picht in the last few days, telling you that Dorle received the latest news from Jörg dated 25 Mar.

Also that I met the librarian Dr Hoffmann from Stuttgart (National Library), who is in Beuron & was looking for somewhere to store the Hölderlin manuscripts. Together with a museum director, we had a look at the cave where my manuscripts are kept locked away in crates; both of them found the place excellent. Now two more vols. of letter manuscripts first have to be brought from Leutkirch in Swabia (Zeil Castle) & then the cave will be closed up & all traces leading to it removed. A precise map of the area will be produced & given to trustworthy people. As soon as the time comes I'll try to get one of these to you or the Pichts.

Thomas has to leave on Monday, Heini's in Ulm & will be joining a newly formed Inf. Div. Franz has his medical on Thursday. On Monday I'll be cycling to Wildenstein & Beuron.

Let's hope Jörg returns westwards some time. I think of Hermann with quiet pain.

My last letter to Erika was returned here the day before yesterday with the stamp 'access closed'.

In the last few days I've also been clearing up here with Fritz, who'll possibly be leaving as well.

In all the turmoil it's a pleasant thought to think that my work is allowed to rest together with Hölderlin in the cliffs by the Danube.

I trust in you making the right decision at the right moment.

I'm always thinking of you & send my best wishes with thoughts of the children & everything that belonged to their youth.

Your Martin.

Regards to Frau Ruch, Fräulein Schroth & Fräulein Gisbertz, Beringer & Janssen.

Thomas, Heini and Franz were Liesel and Fritz Heidegger's sons. On 17 April Elfride received another letter from Hausen: Although the future is dark & forbidding, I'm confident that there are opportunities to be realized, even if teaching is denied me in future.

On 8 May the German armed forces surrendered unconditionally. The Philosophy Faculty remained up at Wildenstein Castle; Martin lived in the forester's lodge.

Hausen, 14 June 45

Dear Elfride!

Each day I wait for the bus that is to take us from Wildenstein to Freiburg. Today I hear that some evacuees are returning to Freiburg. I'll try this way to send you a few lines.

Thank you for your note, which Büchner brought. Now at least I know you're safe and well & looking after the house and garden. We go about our daily business with great sorrow and the essential truth is still quite unutterable. But the thought of Jörg and Hermann is a boon to me, & I use the time for reflection and clarification.

From the conversations up at Wildenstein I can only infer that the 'University' continues to think in the old style. There's probably nothing to be expected from any institutions of this sort. Decisive alone is that one day we enter into conversation with others & have something substantial to say when we do so. I prepare for this every single day. I have a small garret here, & am well provided for. My sleep still isn't good & I have to conserve my strength. The hard thing is that I don't hear anything from you and Freiburg; the connection with Messkirch isn't easy either. Things there are relatively well. Thomas & Heini have presumably been taken prisoner. Fritz is at home.

I think that the waiting here will soon be over & that the University will make an effort to bring us back, even if everything is shut down there at the moment.

The news only comes from hearsay & reports are conflicting.

The garden will once again be a help now, & they say here that the fruit's growing well. Yet what with the essential truth and its misery we forget to think of the needs that do demand consideration in order to scrape a living, which in itself of course has always been pointless and is so now more than ever.

I'm working on a translation of Valéry together with [Prof.] Friedrich. Perhaps this will be a starting point for discussion.

Valuable though my earlier teaching activity was, it never really let the authentic heart of my thinking become properly free – the merely scholastic & scholarly would suddenly intrude & prevent or warp the simple and essential.

As long as the young men are missing from university, any work is only half done, with no opportunity for venturing another attempt at sowing the seeds of a real spiritual tradition. Perhaps we ought to try to bring people together in our own house, without falling prey to the usual culture industry. I often now think of the Marburg time, which in its way had a certain unity.

I very much hope to be in Freiburg for your birthday. I'd like to bring back the rest of my books and manuscripts with the Faculty transport too, as otherwise I don't see any chance of doing so.

Up at Wildenstein we've agreed that the Freibg. bus should come here from there & take all the boxes. As I'm expecting the bus any day now, I haven't been to Messkirch again either.

I wonder if you've been to the Cabin in the meantime.

Regards to everyone there.

With best wishes to you too, faithfully thinking of you,
Your Martin

Regards to the others in the house. To Beringer, Janssen, Wolf & Bauch.

Martin was unwelcome at the University and not allowed to hold lectures.

Martin and Elfride had still received no positive news whatsoever about Jörg and Hermann, who had gone missing in Russia and Czechoslovakia. On 28 September Erika gave birth to Martin, the first grandchild.

1946

Times were difficult for Martin and Elfride. A French family was billeted on the ground floor of the Rötebuck house. In addition, the newly widowed Elfriede Pagels, Jörg's wife Dorle and one of Theophil Rees's sons were also living with them. They continued to fear for the fate of their sons, both of whom they assumed were in Russian captivity. Furthermore, Martin's professional prospects were exceedingly uncertain: his future at the University hung in the balance. On top of this, he had to make a decision between Elfride and his mistress, Margot von Sachsen-Meiningen. All these factors together weighed upon Martin so heavily that he suffered a breakdown. Through acquaintances, he found help with the psychiatrist Viktor Emil Freiherr von Gebsattel at the sanatorium Schloss Hausbaden in Badenweiler.

Badenweiler, 17 Feb. 46

My Dearest Soul!

Many thanks for your nice letters: the first came on Friday; the second today Sunday. Hermann certainly had a hard time of it a year ago. But I'm confident for Jörg and him. Given the <u>essential</u> unfathomability & unpredictability of events today, one can never say for sure such things as that the officers have been kept behind. Herr v. Gebsattel too has said it ought to be possible to achieve something with my name, which it seems I myself still underestimate in the weight it carries. He will also try certain channels himself. It's good that news has now come of Thomas. I think we'd best send the letter to him to Herr von Naurois via Baden-Baden. All this week I've really been 'vegetating'; the first few days the exhaustion did eventually hit me, it wasn't anything special, but I was tired & lacked the drive to do anything. I then suddenly also felt depressed being surrounded by invalids.

191

So I put everything to one side & went out a lot in the mornings & afternoons, although the weather still wasn't good & at the altitude here there's hardly even a foretaste of spring. The letters are still unanswered & this letter today is the first time I've written yet. On the one sunny afternoon I climbed up to the Blauen, but soon turned round because I got too tired. I'm now feeling fresher each day. Every other day I get a glucose injection, which has a beneficial effect on one's overall health. Since yesterday I've again had the clear feeling that I'm getting back into thinking & will set to work with new vigour & new experiences. On my lonely walks I've thought a great deal about you & the children, & I must thank you in particular for the picture of the house. But I find the woods near the Cabin more beautiful, more magnificent & simpler; here everything is too reminiscent of the health business though the place clings to a Black Forest slope. How few people today know what 'the present' is; how few have any idea that everything is drifting along in outworn forms. I'm already looking forward to the coming weeks when we can be up at the Cabin. It's strange how much from my youth is coming to me at the moment; I've now also discovered a very cheerful nurse who lives near Messkirch. A few days ago Matron visited me in my room & we had a long talk about her brother & the old student days.

From the paths leading further up to the Blauen one can in places see the Rhine – but it's all very painful. And yet this earth remains the same old earth & those who inhabit it will awake once again; with us, fate takes very wild & winding paths; but poetizing & thinking, the things that last, cannot be a matter of chance or something of no avail. We cannot count the ages of peoples & do not know the measures with which what is now happening will itself be gauged. In front of me is the picture of the Parthenon & underneath the little pictures of Jörg & Hermann & the house. It belongs together after all.

It was a good decision to come here; for along with the distance from everything connected with Freiburg, the pleasant humanity & spontaneous friendliness of Herr v. G. is helping me greatly. He is 63 years old now, has experienced much, has come from philosophy & remains within it despite his basic theological orientation, which is by no means narrow. He knows my stuff in great detail & tells me how much he & his friends have for years been waiting & pinning their hopes on my thinking. He was in Paris together with Rilke, was also with Dilthey & the Yor[c]ks up at Klein-Oels – Yesterday evening we had a very good conversation; today I again accompanied him up to the Hochblauen, where he stays overnight to have a rest, he still has no help here & is rather busy. He thinks I should leave the University now whatever happens; for what is essential in my thinking, which he sees very clearly, will be constantly distracted & held back by didactic constraints.

Besides, he says the people who matter aren't there yet anyway. And after all, what lasts will be the created work. All things that I of course know & tell myself too – but in his way he sees it more directly & at the same time as a spectator; what's more, he himself is rather critically disposed towards psychology & its analyses. In his eyes, philosophy itself, & what I think & say & seek, is much too fundamental & central for him to assume the role of someone simply dealing with an interesting 'case' here.

So I think the days I spend here will be very invigorating & clarifying.

Herr v. Gebsattel is driving to Freiburg on Thursday & meeting Welte & Ochsner in the Caritas House there. Perhaps you could drop off some 'walking drops' there some time & 'Der Herr Kortüm' [novel by Kurt Kluge] (but this isn't absolutely necessary) if Fräulein Schroth, to whom I send my regards, can manage without it. The nurses' fare is rather conducive to constipation, & fruit & jam are rare. – I'll write to Fritz & the Beringers tomorrow. I'm nice & tired from the Blauen walk & it's 'already' 9 o'clock. Haven't you had any more news from the Lass & Helm? Helm's address?

I presume you've written to the Laslowskis to tell them to come sooner. I'm sure he'll find somewhere to stay in Frbg. among his circle of acquaintances.

How is Dorle? How are the exam preparations going? Are the two of you cramming already? [. . .]

Good night, my D.S., go to sleep well with quiet thoughts, best wishes

from your Martin.

Best wishes to Dorle & Elfriede.

Regards to Jürgen [Rees] & Frau Ruch & Frau Winterer & Frau Oertmann.

Since the end of 1945 Martin had been in correspondence with the French philosopher Jean Beaufret. On 4 March he wrote to Elfride: Of important Frenchmen, above all Prof. Beaufret from Paris, whom I don't want to miss under any circumstances, could be considered [for a visit]. He can easily come here. Perhaps one could even put him up overnight in Badenweiler.

On 6 March Martin wrote: I'm now in the process of tuning the instrument of thinking to its fundamental pitch & gathering all its essential relationships, and this calls for much composure & listening, as well as for noting things down in a way that captures what I have gathered with sufficient clarity for the moment when I get down [to] giving proper shape to it all. This moment is yet to come & for that of course I need to have my workshop around me. We've now talked

193

through some Heraclitus fragments & in the process much has become clearer to me, but also much that I was previously attempting has been corroborated.

Martin became noticeably more confident again and made a good recovery. On 10 March he wrote: You ask about the meaning of the final stanza of 'The Daily Work of Thinking': 'err uncommonly' – the 'uncommonly' is deliberately ambiguous; first it means: not common; the errancy [*die Irre*] is nothing usual or even just negative; it's the essential possibility of truth as unconcealment. Where there is concealment, there's the possibility of errancy (as in my Truth lecture); then it means: as you suspect: unusually great – the more man thinks, the greater the possibility of errancy – for the one thinking it is uncommon as such –

These are the errant [*Be-irrten*] in the proper sense, while the 'unerring' [*Unbeirrbaren*] are those who close their minds to truth & defy it in their uprising into a groundless self-assurance. –

He then summed up: M[argot].'s letter is calm & on the path of composure; but it will all take time. A very friendly greeting came from Heimpel. I don't want to go to Marburg now, important though the A[cademic]. A[ssociation]. may be. Klostermann would like to put all my Hölderlin essays & the others together in one volume. Von G. has once again tried to obtain glucose especially for me, so the treatment lasts as long as possible. I'm thinking of coming home around the 20th.

Eventually the first indication that Jörg was still alive reached Dorle. Like Hermann, he was in Russian captivity.

Badenweiler, 15 March 46

My D. S.

Our dear Jörg's lucky star hasn't deserted him, cruel though his fate still remains. But what he writes shows such immediate calm & goodness & alertness that we can hope with renewed confidence & think of him with all our strength and love. How I'd have liked to be with you when this liberating news came. But despite all the gloom hanging over the world he'll keep his bright and helpful nature & fill the house & garden & everything at home with new expectancy. I did imagine that you'd sent off the reply card straightaway, especially in the present circumstances. Of course, it still pains me that I couldn't write something as well. But perhaps this is all part of it.

Many thanks too for your previous detailed letter & the enclosed draft. I'm to blame too. And the reflection that my thinking is undergoing here is also constantly concerned with all that has happened & is to come. One thing clear to me is that in no way shall I live together with M[argot]. If I decide on Messkirch or my own home area, I'd like you to be there <u>with me</u>. It is also clear to me that I must get away from the university atmosphere entirely, so my thinking & the evolving work retains its clear style and grounding.

Messkirch, i.e. home, calls me for the single reason that I need this close environment as the supporting & driving element in the great loneliness of the work to come & I feel quite vividly that a collected, settled, rooted way of life for the years still remaining is part & parcel of the work. This leaves the Todtnauberg plan; but for all its beauty & simplicity, life there is perhaps too hard for the exertions of the work in store for me & the location too close to Freiburg – With the break in regard to the Univ. my relation to the city & everything else is also broken. Only our house & the children's home is enduring – but this after all, as we like to hope, is to belong to them. However, for you the move would be a great sacrifice, & furnishing a dwelling in Messkirch, if possible at all, a further strain with existence now strenuous enough as it is & the worry of the Freiburg house, which would somehow still be with us. And then M[argot].'s relation to Messkirch would also have to be defined & clarified in such a way that everything resolves itself amicably & for the better. Having Fritz nearby would of course be a <u>further</u> boon for me; for I can see from my work here how much I need this connection. On the other hand, I must also keep away from all other distractions (lectures, conferences & suchlike & empty visits) for the next few years for the sake of my composure. With growing inner clarity, each day here is becoming more fruitful for thinking too. The company of G[ebsattel]. is very beneficial; he helps me in a good way to grow into the atmosphere of thinking that I require. But what you sensed is correct; in the last analysis, he is <u>quite shackled</u> & secretly hopes that my path will lead back into his world. This all transpires in a very genteel fashion, and also forces me to engage in a good deal of analysis and clarification. In what is essential I must probably tread the path alone, without making anything special of this solitude. I have the clear feeling that in Messkirch it would become the 'natural thing' & the work would be part of the growth of the native soil precisely because it is growing into what is universal & is becoming something that could creatively incorporate 'the East' within its mysterious essence beyond the immediately apparent 'political' conflict. I often think it can be no accident that Jörg & Hermann are in Russia – a mysterious exhortation is concealed therein, a pain that leads into the open & permits both of them to share in the task assigned to me – quite apart from any anticipation of what may happen or not in the near future. Let us not be overhasty – I'd like to discuss everything with you; I can do so better when I'm quite clear about myself & about my work & above all again have a clear outlook on the work itself & the paths I must tread in future, so that what has long been prepared flows freely towards me. G. speaks in his way of an 'incubation period' which is now evidently coming to an end. In spite of all that is hard & confused & painful I sense a hidden injunction. The important thing now is to recover purely & well & gain strength for the transition – so I no longer <u>fall</u> from the thrust of work & out of the presence of what-is-to-be-thought. Each morning I already work in full swing now, & can sense its sustaining rhythm. The afternoon is for relaxation & in the evenings the conversations take place.

G. thinks I should on no account break off prematurely. Not until 8 April is he going via Freiburg to see his daughter in Überlingen & attend a conference in Salem with Weizsäcker (Heidelb.), Guardini & F. G. Jünger. He thinks I can easily stay until then, & he also wants to prolong the glucose treatment until then as a reserve for the scarce times to come. So if I weren't to come next week, I'd have to ask you to wait even longer while I submit myself to this solitary treatment.

I'll let work alone decide & the ever-growing feeling of freshness & inner consolidation. As the catering is still reasonable, it would perhaps also help to save on your own provisions. Yesterday G.'s son-in-law was here, a Herr von Gagern, who is an assistant with Beringer – he said that food was already in very short supply there.

Many thanks for the apples you sent me with Fräulein Mylius. She passed her exam pretty well. No doubt it's the last one I'll hold. After my return I'd like <u>to go up to the Cabin soon</u> so as not to be burdened with all sorts of functions in Frbg. again & so the break in my work doesn't become too great.

Best wishes to you now, my D. S. – in the hopeful joy we <u>share</u> for Jörg & Hermann, a joy which still has its pain & which through the work we do for the future in return must remain worthy of what our sons are enduring in the fate of our people.

An easier & freer closeness to you is awakening within me now that everything is progressing purely on the single path of the work, which I don't regard as <u>my</u> achievement & in which I don't see myself reflected either. Even one's anxiety about the task assigned can turn into something erroneous. But my freedom towards myself has emerged anew & for this reason I face everything more readily.

Perhaps we may expect greetings from Hermann & Jörg again before too long. [. . .]

Have a good rest & enjoy the prospect of us seeing one another again. Fondly thinking of you, your Martin

Contact had been re-established with the Szilasis, who had invited Martin to Brissago in Switzerland. On 20 March Martin wrote: Sz.'s

concern & devotion is touching. L[ili].'s letter is from a 'world' that has stood still in time & no longer 'is' at all. Whereas there the type-writers clatter away, here the hand with the pen falters in the face of everything dark & painful & unfathomable yet at the same time great & uncanny – & thought hardly dares turn itself to word. We've long since ceased to exist [*eksistieren*] in order to produce 'philosophy' & 'culture' – but rather to find the site where the dwelling human being is again touched by Being [*Seyn*] as what is whole and healing [*das Heile/n*], & disaster [*das Unheil*] does not lapse into a mere meaning-lessness to be ignored 'once the war is over'.

Martin was to be made a professor emeritus. Uncertain whether he would be given permission to teach, on 22 March he wrote a worried letter to Elfride: Well it did seem that calm was restored at the Univers.; now the pendulum's swinging to the other side & it'll go on toing & froing like this for a while yet; the best thing is if I have emeri-tus status; G[ebsattel]. says that some people in my Faculty (presum-ably including Friedrich) tried particularly hard to secure my return, but that it's better to go easy at present. Perhaps you could talk with Wolf or Bauch about it.

On 31 March the French philosopher Alfred (Frédéric) de Towarnicki visited Martin in Badenweiler. Towarnicki would go on to publish the article 'Visite à Martin Heidegger' in Jean-Paul Sartre's journal Les Temps Modernes. *On 4 April Martin reported:* I wrote Sunday's letter in great haste because of the unexpected visit, which gave rise to fairly long conversations; the misunderstandings really are very great; the interest is also frequently in the activist element rather than the genuinely philosophical moment, as I gather from the jour-nals Tow. left here.

Badw. 8. 4. 46.

My Dearest Soul!
Your letter from 3 Apr has constantly accompanied me since it came. I'm so pleased that for all the pain you're able once again to take plea-sure from its source & that everything around you and what is ours speaks to you again. The path of my thinking has passed through much that is erring and unfathomable, through much forgetting & neglecting & yet at the same time searching & liberating, and the more truly it finds its way into its own, the less it belongs to me or to anyone. A voice from deep within told me that everything will come good one day, will attain a <u>coming-good</u>, for here too, & here first of all, one must learn the genuine habit, which is to in-habit what is fitting [*das Schickliche*], which only gradually is able to grasp its fate [*das Geschick*] purely. The voice told me this & I trusted in a listening in

197

M[argot]. & in M. also delivering what is her own into the open [*ins Freye*] & simple and selfless. But at the same time I was also too unadvised & unaccomplished – & could only wait; I thank you for helping & ensuring that we now help ourselves into the open in unison, each of us giving the other what is one's own & receiving it from the other – so that henceforth everything may belong to us anew.

In everything dark & confused about the path a providence is concealed. The unthinkable destiny of our fatherland & the fate still in store for it is where we belong, in the most secret of workshops, gaining ever fresh heart from the growing knowledge.

And as the words now come to me again, newer every day, & my strength joyfully grows & the thought of my sons & all their brothers becomes more hopeful, I no longer shrink back either from the path into the work, which is revealing its outlines ever more clearly.

Together with your letter came a short note from M[argot]. in which she tells me she wants to give you her letters to me to read. –

Readiness for the unconcealed [*Unverborgene*], this I learn, is the pledge [*Bürgschaft*] for what is genuinely sheltered [*Geborgene*] & sheltering [*Bergende*]. The more purely we give, the more richly we receive & learn genuine poverty. And so I trust [that] the depth of your and M.'s hearts, each in its own underlying tone, will help the saying & release it anew & joyfully tend it. –

Here I hardly know the date & time & silently proffer myself to what is to come – Everything's gradually returning – as a result I forgot to send you the nice letter from [Rev.] Sander, which coincides strangely with the arrival of Jörg's note. When I read the sender's address I immediately assumed it was the student who'd sung with the boys in the morning. I'd like to send him some of my shorter articles. So far I've sent him just a short but cordial answer. Keep the letter, as I'd like to go into some of the questions some time.

Here everything is starting to flower now too, every day I go along my lonely path & each time the wood is more alive & gleaming & I think how in faraway Russia the birches will be gleaming now & greeting with homely memories those who are patiently awaiting their homeward journey in the knowledge that someone's thoughts are constantly greeting & visiting them. –

Thank you for the things Friedrich brought. He said you wanted to come on Thursday or Friday. On Thursday I'm going to the Chaplain's Hölderlin circle once again. So I'll expect you on Friday; unfortunately Gebs. won't be back yet. As Matron told me, he won't be coming till Sunday, as he has other patients in Überlingen. I'll come & fetch you in Badenweiler at 14.53; if you bring coupons you can have dinner with us; a junior doctor has been here for a few days now. Do bring the case with you & a white shirt & hankies & coffee. –

Fritz's question can only refer to the invitation from Rev. Krautheimer, who is a friend of his & Dr Welte's.

I'm really looking forward to seeing you again. Couldn't you come with the earlier fast train at 12.08? You have a connection in Müllheim & are here at 13.28 – I'll go for this train at any rate.

On 8 May Martin wrote to Todtnauberg: The 'lecture' from the 'Fundamental Concepts' was too difficult after all; you know it of course. I don't speak to anybody about my real concern; even G[ebsattel]. knows nothing of it. Up at the Cabin you'll be able to read quite a few things. I'm really looking forward to the solitude & simplicity. It's now time for me to break off here. I haven't heard anything more from Margot for weeks now. [. . .] I'm coming on Monday the 13th by car or <u>at any rate on Tuesday</u> somehow or other.

Up at the Cabin, the first meeting with Jean Beaufret took place on 12 September, the start of a lifelong friendship.

The following letter is written in a completely different, Latin script rather than the old-fashioned style of German handwriting:

Cabin, 24 Oct. 1946

My D. S.

This morning at 11 o'clock, just as I was coming to the final lines of the Pindar, there was a knock at the Cabin door & the nice Rotzinger girl brought me your note & the news of Jörg & Hermann's card. Perhaps we may put our minds at rest somewhat after all. Jörg will certainly do his work meticulously & thus make an impression. And if Hermann holds out with his willpower & knowledge, he too will come through.

Tomorrow I hope to finish the Pindar. Then it'll be polished up & then all the rest. At the same time I'm starting my next task so that I don't lose the thread. Yesterday evening I thought it would snow in the night. All we got was an icy easterly gale, which is still blowing. In spite of the sun the thermometer has been below zero all day long. I've wrapped myself up nice & warm & thought of Russia. The electric power is very low & the wind into the bargain & the Cabin cold besides. [. . .]

I took the post into the village after 6 o'clock so as to get some exercise. Frau Brender, who has hurt her leg, invited me to her bedside for a little chinwag, I also got two thick slices of bread & butter with honey & nice milk, so I was hardly hungry in the evening. In addition I got a piece of bacon fat to take with me too.

I've already started moving the books as well.

The death of Eva Eucken is very sad. The Biemels have written a very affectionate letter for my birthday.

I hope you don't have too much running around now. If M. Rovan drove up again it would be convenient for you, but I don't think it's necessary – he'd presumably like to hear about the translation, which is very meticulous & in many respects astonishing. In any case I'd like to go through it while I'm here, also in view of the others he's working on.

It's very lonely & severe up here now. I go to bed early in the evenings.

I'm looking forward to us being able to continue working together down there as we have up here in the last few months. At any rate I'm also preparing myself mentally not to let things disturb me.

With much love and thoughts of the two of them.

Your M.

At the end of December Martin was finally banned from teaching and removed from his post at the University. Wilhelm Szilasi occupied the chair in his place. Only once Martin had been pensioned off by the Baden regional government in July 1950 would he again be permitted to teach at the University.

1947

Erika now lived with her family in Birkach near Stuttgart. On 4 December 1946, she had a daughter, Ursula.
In September Hermann was released from Russian captivity.

Cabin, 8 Sept. 47

My D. S.

The hardest part is over now; for I'm confident inside that Jörg's homecoming will be easier, albeit slower. In its joyousness the news was so disconcerting that it took me a long time to regain my composure & the next two nights I could hardly sleep. On Friday evening when Bauch brought me the news I then found among the post at the Brenders' a card from Hermann himself in Ulm on 2 Sept.

We can't and aren't meant to appreciate what this return means all at once. It was painful to tell the Brenders about it.

I'm deeply relieved now I know that Jörg was able to escape the havoc in Czechoslovakia. Now we can focus all our hope on fetching him home, though it's also directed at all those still waiting with him. No one at all has yet returned from Russian captivity here in Todt.

Rotzinger didn't finish until Saturday morning. He took every other day off. Rita didn't come. R. wants to do the shingles too.

Albert wants to fell 2 steres of timber very near here this week.

Apart from this, the letter from Fritz and manuscripts came too; from Szilasi the proofs of the Cabin sheets. When I sent them back I announced Hermann's homecoming at the same time.

In addition, I had various French visits; even minus the customary politeness, still gratifying. Beaufret sent a card from Venice with the remark A bientôt. [. . .]

With fondest thoughts and best wishes, my D. S., and much love Your Martin.

The enclosed credit note comes just in the nick of time for Hermann's arrival. That I can't be down there is how it has to be now too. But what with looking after the Cabin it would be a lot of bother.

The chocolate in the Swiss packet is for Hermann.

1948

Martin was invited by the Krohns to go and stay in Badenweiler. Martin hoped that his stay with the bookseller and his wife would give him a rest and the chance to concentrate on his work. At home he rarely found such peace and quiet, as Lene and Ernst Laslowski, his college friend, were also taking refuge in the house on Rötebuck.

Jörg remained in Russian captivity. Hermann had taken up his studies in Freiburg once more.

Martin received a letter from his former student Franz-Josef Brecht and on 25 February wrote: The letter from Brecht is strange; these grades he gives – but it's probably well meant. What he says about Jaspers is interesting. Even before this letter here I occasionally wondered whether it wouldn't be a good thing if I made the first move off my own bat & set things straight again between the two of us. For what are we to say of the mutual disputes among Germans if their two philosophers live apart, instead of both of them, each in his own way, helping together as far as they can. I already thought of sending him the Cabin notebook simply with a greeting.

Badenweiler, 2 March 48

My D. S.

Many thanks for your two letters of 25 & 26 Feb. In the mornings I'm now working through from 8 o'clock until ½ past 1 & creating the base for the real thing up at the Cabin. I forgot to enclose Brecht's letter. The grade 1–2 he gives me is pretty fatuous. The comment about Jaspers re the 'Neue Zeitung'[14] is outdated in so far as on the day after

---

[14] The *Neue Zeitung* was a twice-weekly newspaper that appeared in the US-occupied zone from 1945 to 1955.

203

I wrote to you there was a long interview with a picture of Jaspers for his 65th birthday in the above-mentioned paper. In spite of everything one does not wish to give offence. The thought came to me simply because of the situation & state of German philosophy – without any reference to university matters & what had gone on there.

I feel more oblivious to this world by the day. But so far it has continued to bother me too much even in Frbg. I wish all relations were broken off. It's probably better if I leave things as they are with Jaspers. I don't intend to write to Brecht. [. . .]

I enclose the draft reply to the conference organizers.

Herr v. Gebsattel is expected at the end of this week. Herr Krohn recently told me how glad he is that I'm here because it means his wife has something to do & take her mind off things without overexerting herself; these weeks in springtime are always very critical. They get a lot of parcels & have old, good suppliers among the farmers all around.

I won't overdo my stay here.

Bröse dropped by & asked whether it was all right by me if a public campaign for me were mounted through the Swiss press; I advised him strongly against it, and asked instead for the matters of salary & accommodation to be sorted out – said that how the University dealt with its shame was its own affair. Br. will now discuss the matter directly with the finance minister. [. . .]

You don't write anything about whether your 'treatment' with Schilling is making any progress. At least it's some consolation that Jörg's now getting post more frequently. Many from around here are still in Russia.

Frau Krohn likes chocolate; though she has a lot of American stuff for cooking, she says she doesn't have any to eat. Could you send a bar for her, one of Boss's?

Let's hope the house remains empty. Rovan may come some time around Easter.

Regards to Inge [Schroth], the Laslowskis & Frau Ruch.

I think a great deal about you & the children. Best wishes to you & Hermann & Dorle. Your M.

Médard Boss was a Swiss psychiatrist with whom Martin formed a lasting friendship in this period.

In June, Martin worked up at the Cabin. Elfride had to look after the house and garden in Freiburg.

Martin spent August together with Elfride up at the Cabin, joined at times by Hermann and Martin's niece Clothild.

On 6 November, Christoph was born, the third child of Erika and Helm. Elfride went to Birkach to support the mother after she had given birth. Martin worked hard on the manuscript of Off the Beaten Track [Holzwege] *and on 18 November wrote:* By Saturday I'll have finished the rough copy. The fair copy I'll do in the first few days at Messkirch, so Fritz can get on with transcribing it. I'm going to Hüfingen with Clothild on Saturday afternoon & on Monday on to Messkirch. Niemeyer [publisher] has written a very meek letter & at the same time sent five copies of B[eing]. & T[ime]., which have arrived. I'll bring the letter with me. Each day now I'm expecting the proofs [for *The Pathway/Der Feldweg*] from Klostermann. [. . .] I hope the ms for Off the Beaten Track will be ready in December & it'll be out for Easter. In the last few days I've been noticing the foehn again, yet I can still work for 8–9 hours & think that after the current ms I'll be able to get down to looking through the dialogue once again.

1949

In March, the State Commissioner for Political Cleansing classified Martin as a 'fellow traveller', who would thus face 'no punitive measures'. His future at the University remained uncertain. At the beginning of April he again went to stay at Badenweiler on the invitation of the Krohns. The billeting of the French in the house on Rötebuck was now over, but the Laslowskis continued to live there.

In Badenweiler, Martin came to appreciate the Alemannic folk poet Lina Kromer, whom he met at a reading she gave in the health resort assembly room. On 10 April he wrote about a further meeting with her: I've just returned from a trip to Bürgeln Castle, where Krohn & I were with Frau Lina Kromer, whom we picked up from her home village beforehand. It would have been even nicer if I could have been alone with this quiet pensive woman; but all the same we spoke Alemannic; a simple, deeply reflective fellow-suffering with the times & a natural love for her home region are alive in this woman. This is the greatest gain from these few days.

At the end of May Martin went to Messkirch via Hüfingen. Elfride, who had driven Martin to the station, slipped and fell awkwardly on the platform. On Ascension Day Martin wrote: I'm constantly thinking of you, wondering how you are after that nasty fall. Do take care of yourself; I was going to ask you anyway to ease up a little in the next few weeks. It was enough for both of us, as was becoming clear to those around us. But perhaps this is a good thing; our path for the next few years, which must not lead us right out into the cold, thus comes to acquire a clarity of its own. Inside I'm constantly grateful to you for helping to bear everything so courageously and unassumingly. When we came up to the heights of the Black Forest yesterday, my only thought was of our coming weeks at the Cabin. If only Jörg were here.

206

At Freiburg University efforts were being made to have official emeritus status conferred on Martin. Financially too, his position was very difficult.

On 28 May Martin wrote from Hüfingen, where he was visiting his sister Marie and her husband Rudolf: Be sure to ease up now a little in the next few days, after the anxious and trying time we've had. There's no other course of action left for me than to break completely with the whole university atmosphere and keep my mind on the task at hand. As this must be self-sustaining & can have no outer form or support of its own, this isn't easy & thus constantly tempts one to seek helpers. I still haven't got the journal plan sorted out.

The Pathway had come out in Messkirch in the spring. Martin was working hard on his book Off the Beaten Track, *which was to be published the following year by Klostermann. On 2 June he wrote from Messkirch:* I collect myself again in thought; this way the other things vanish of their own accord. In the long run of course there'd be no circle to live among here; a great deal slips into trivialization in the little town; but the professorial environment is no longer a circle either; if indeed it ever seriously was. Once I'm back on the track of my thinking, steady and deliberate, we'll certainly pass the coming years fruitfully and in the appropriate style for ourselves and the few people around us.

Messkirch, Whitsun 1949

My D. S.

Thomas fetched your nice Whitsun letter from the post office today, otherwise it wouldn't have been delivered until the day after tomorrow. Today, as I lay awake in the early morning, I spent a long time thinking about the tower in Rottweil & our Whitsun trip into Swabian territory back then. You're right, little remains; but the feeling, which here makes the real difference, becomes more & more awake. What survives the test here will help us to pass the next few years quietly and fruitfully; as a result we'll also come to feel in harmony with those first years when the two of us set out on the long & winding path.

I have a desire to go rambling with you, above all we must go and see the Upper Rhine region which you liked so much in those days with Friedl Lieber. The area of Upper Swabia between the Danube & Lake Constance is also beautiful in a different way. The summer meadows with flowers in bloom are especially lovely here this year. Apart from the elderly, the people are quite foreign to one; also, there are a lot who weren't brought up here & overrun what is local.

But perhaps this steadiness has only ever existed in times that were lived more slowly & above all in greater isolation.

It's uncanny how radio & film are eating away at everything. I'm pleased that you could listen to the two nice concerts at Whitsun. The radio here is no substitute; I've had enough of listening to that box.

I wrote to Frau Senn right away. The meeting with Staiger will probably also materialize. I'm still appalled at the Freiburg business, even though it doesn't concern me at heart. Yesterday I happened to hear from the Kellers' brother-in-law, who works for the tax office in Stockach & knows Herr Kirchheimer, that the current head of department in the Ministry of Finance is a certain Dr Heiland (!),[15] Ki.'s closest colleague; it's clear that these people in their own way are getting their revenge; the nasty thing though is that the Christian Democrats are helping these gentlemen to get on everywhere. I'm not yet at all convinced there won't be a problem with the emeritus professorship; for these people will inform the Ministry of Education & the Arts & of Finance in great detail & in their way about the result of the Senate sitting. –

Reading Vietta's first letter I at once had the same impression as you; it was written immediately after mine had been received. I also think that he intends nothing malicious or underhand, but for all his genuine interest he's of course also concerned about keeping ahead as a journalist. I'm letting him keep the mss he borrowed before for further study; but once again I expressly wrote that he must never let them out of his sight to third parties.

The newspaper item is yet another sham; well meant but set about in completely the wrong way; I immediately sent off the corrected version by registered mail. –

Many thanks in particular, my D. S., for dealing with the proof-reading so quickly; it was a fair bit of work; I've now read them for the third time & found only a few more things; clarified a certain amount; Fritz is still at it now. I want to send them away on Tuesday or Wednesday. It's bound to be a lot of work for Elisabeth [Gerber]; but then again she's very attached to it & would be sad if I were to withdraw the proofs now. [. . .]

I wrote briefly to Dr Nebel from Hüfingen to tell him that the journal plan needs a much sounder foundation. I said the thing is absolutely necessary, especially given the decline of everything spiritual. Now that the basic reaction against the Hitler era has gradually worn itself out, no one has anything positive & forward-looking to propose. But whether they'll manage to pervade the whole atmosphere of public journalism is another matter. They certainly won't if the whole thing remains just a literary affair in which manuscripts get sent to & fro. – [. . .]

---

[15] The name means 'Saviour' or 'Redeemer'.

The weather here is unusually cold & raw; we have to heat every day. [. . .]

At any rate the organization of the Church governance has been reinforced incredibly; a lot has been learnt from Hitler. But the whole thing is accordingly hollow too.

Hermann will be turning up soon now from somewhere or other. Here one again hears nothing of homecomers.

Fondly thinking of you, with best wishes, my D. S.; I'm looking forward to coming home. Your M.

Regards to all. The Messkirchers also send their regards.

Martin went from Messkirch to Freiburg via Constance.

It was becoming increasingly plain that Dorle was mentally ill. Elfride and Martin felt at a loss in the circumstances. On 27 July, Dorle fell off her bicycle on the way from Todtnauberg to Freiburg. Elfride looked after her in Freiburg, while Martin remained up at the Cabin, proof-reading the printed sheets for Off the Beaten Track. *After completing her habilitation thesis, Liesel Schmid came up to the Cabin to help Martin.*

On 9 August he wrote to Elfride in Freiburg: I've written to Klostermann about the festschrift. Quite apart from Jörg I don't want to see anything done for my birthday. But I suppose one's defenceless against it. I find the whole University affair as nasty as ever. I don't want to have anything more to do with the whole atmosphere, & this is for the one positive reason that the only thing that matters is for me to get my stuff all wrapped up. It's a great nuisance that the proofs will coincide with the time at the Cabin. But I'm still hoping for some weeks when I can get down to the real thing. Otherwise I'm well & have got over my ill humour about the infuriating & yet useless wrangling from outside. [. . .] Every day I give silent thanks to you for the Cabin.

In February Karl Jaspers renewed his correspondence with Martin. Referring to a letter from Jaspers from 6 August, Martin wrote to Elfride on 11 August: Yesterday another letter came [from] Jaspers in St Moritz; it said an American friend had written saying I'd been offered & accepted a chair in Buenos Aires. You can read it when you're here. I'll write as soon as the proofs have gone; I don't do anything else. But Liesel & Friedrich are helping greatly.

In mid-November, after a visit to Birkach, Martin was back in Messkirch. He was preparing to give a series of lectures in Bremen in December. On 20 November he wrote to Elfride in Birkach, where she was helping Erika look after the children: Then we went down to Beuron, where I'd been in touch with F[ather]. Anselm the day before; the old gentleman is 75 now & was as pleased as Punch; he at once asked after Jörg & Hermann & you; he told me he thinks of me every day. We've known one another for 30 years. I took him The Pathway. For me it was an unforgettable encounter. He invited me to spend a few days in the monastery again some time in spring. It all made a great impression on Fritz, who had never been inside the cloister before. F. A. still works in the library & is very fresh in spirit – just his hearing is poorer.

This evening a small circle of my old classmates & friends want to hold a small celebration for me, which I can't get out of. [. . .] The fair copy of my lecture [*Insight into That Which Is/Einblick in das was ist*] will be ready tomorrow; I've worked eight hours on it every day.

Martin's sister Marie and her husband had just moved back into their house in Hüfingen, which had been confiscated by the French.

Jörg was finally released from Russian captivity. Before his return, he had been in Moscow, and he was relatively well.

Messkirch, 12 Dec. 49

My dear Elfride!

Your letter was there when I returned from my walk on the snow-covered pathway. We must be grateful that Jörg has been restored to us like this. At heart he has kept his style of existence even in the difficult years. The fact that he's now been released despite the agitation against me bears out my confidence that his life will follow a good course.

I find it particularly pleasing that the two brothers can really be together now after a long time. We'll find the ways and means to help both of them enter a profession that allows them to work in their own way.

It's good to see how everyone here shares the joy of Jörg's homecoming. Yesterday cousin Anton Braun was here (the carpenter, who also owns a large sawmill), he said he'd help Jörg any way he could, if it were necessary.

It's deeply regrettable & irresponsible of Dorle to spoil this harmony of joy & the will to make a new start like this.

Her foolish fantasies are just an escape from the serious path of life that is now beginning. I won't even mention her ingratitude towards us.

I'm coming on <u>Friday</u> evening with the Ulm fast train.

The Hüfingeners were very pleased about Jörg and about my visit.

The two of them have done a great deal; except for Clothild's room everything is back in order as far as possible. Both they & I would rather I came to visit with you later on for a few days to go rambling in the Baar.

I made the Messkirchers particularly happy by coming. At the actual ceremony I had the seat of honour next to the Mayor in front of all the others. A very nice museum of local history has also been opened. Fritz & Liesel are well. It's lovely wintry weather, which I'm using though to prepare the appendix to the new edition of the Kant book from older manuscripts. I won't finish this week, but I do want to return to Freiburg to see Jörg & be together with you all in the days leading up to Christmas.

There were some very nice letters in the post Hermann brought, especially from M. Schröter in Munich & from Boss in Zurich, who has invited us both up to Lenzerheide, where he has a cottage. –

I always think now with particular sympathy of the prisoners who must still remain behind. We're still 12 short here, and 60 are missing.

According to Niemeyer's letter, Regnery is in Germany after all. Hasn't Klostermann been in touch? I'm enclosing N.'s letter, so you can think about it. The question indeed is: <u>who</u> will translate it? <u>How</u> is the text to be dealt with?

With fondest thoughts & best wishes, my D. S. – regards to everyone and especially Jörg & Hermann.

Your Martin. The Messkirchers send their regards.

I've already sent the Care Parcel card to you from Hüfingen.

1950

On 7 February, Hannah Arendt visited Martin in Freiburg. Only shortly beforehand had Martin told Elfride of his love affair with Hannah, of which she had not previously been aware.

14 Feb. 1950

My dear Wife!
Thank you, simply for helping me again. A moment has come when I must tell you what has moved me particularly in the last few years. You mentioned it yourself in my study one morning last week: that something indestructible prevails and endures between us. Time & again it has been seriously jeopardized by my behaviour all these years. But time & again you've saved it, and each time I've been brought back into the constancy of this painful happiness.

But two things I've never been able to tell you properly until now. First of all, that despite frequent appearances to the contrary I don't see our love and marriage in terms of what is merely practical or indeed convenient, but on the contrary know how much everything you do forms part of our shared life & of my thinking, right down to the slightest and inconspicuous detail, essentially & not just as a mere external condition; & that this, your constant accompanying presence [*Mitdasein*], leaves a lasting mark on whatever may be lasting about this thinking; for this I also know – that every move & step you make is not only produced by your sense of duty, but borne by your inner belonging to my path.

I often think of what I promised you early on: that the work in which I deal specifically with Plato's thought is to be yours. If the world stays reasonably in order and I stay alive & keep my strength up, this work will one day be written.

Winter 1949/50

The other thing, inseparable in a different way from my love for you & from my thinking, is difficult to say. I call it Eros, the oldest of the gods according to Parmenides.

By this I'm not telling you anything you don't know on your own account; nonetheless I can't quite find the terms to express it suitably. It can easily sound too free and easy & acquire a form that gives an impression of seeking to justify what is wrong and inappropriate.

The beat of that god's wings moves me every time I take a substantial step in my thinking and venture onto untrodden paths. It moves me perhaps more powerfully & uncannily than others when something long intuited is to be led across into the realm of the sayable & when what has been said must after all be left in solitude for a long time to come. To live up to this purely and yet retain what is ours, to follow the flight and yet return home safely, to accomplish both things as equally essential and pertinent, this is where I fail too easily & then either stray into pure sensuality or try to force the unforceable through sheer work.

My disposition and the manner of my early upbringing, instability and cowardice in the ability to trust & then again inconsiderateness in the abuse of trust, these are the poles between which I swing & thus only too easily & only too often misjudge & overstep the measure with regard to Hera and Eros.

What I say in The Pathway about the Mother, you continue on another level and in other realms. I don't mean to praise you, but just tell you how over the last few years I've been trying increasingly hard to incorporate not only these years but the earlier decades of your closeness into my path.

Everything that has been finally turns into what in the end becomes & inheres [*west*].

Accept these lines kindly as an attempt.

Your Husband.

Martin offered Elfride the following poem, probably to celebrate their 33rd wedding anniversary:

To the Truest Companion

Shepherdess of my highest ways,
Mother, who by the purest grace
delivers yet Aphrodite's play
into the simple roun1delay,
when I stumbled, lifted me,
quietly bonding trust and bliss,
excelling in bestowing gifts –
Keep these words in memory:
    In every joy you are there.
    In all sorrow I'll be near.
    Inseparable in the right,
    incombustible in the light
    that kindled once a spark of souls,
    wherein togetherness resides.

March 1950.

In this poem Martin again refers to the Ganeisterlîn *or little 'spark' from the 1918 letters.*

Martin applied for an early retirement for health reasons.

In the summer semester, Jörg again took up his studies in mechanical engineering at Karlsruhe Technical College. Dorle's schizophrenia now made it impossible to live with her.

Hermann was working on his PhD thesis.

Elfride was suffering health problems, including a painful inflammation of the knee.

Messkirch, 4 May 1950.

My dear Elfride!

Our parting was so sudden under the blossoming trees among the flowers after these restless weeks. And yet the time we had was filled with growth in belonging and maturity in trust and the courage to resolve everything together, with the sons that have been restored to us, in the midst of bleak times. So with your healthy constitution you really must make a full recovery again. Once our external situation has improved, a certain alleviation & relaxation will then also be possible for you.

Our wonderful Cabin years remain in our memory & perhaps the best thing really is if we venture once more to preserve our inseparableness purely within its ownmost root – in order to be all the better able to do so. It gladdens me how in the last few years I've subsequently become increasingly fond of the Freiburg house too, in spite of its city location. –

The journey passed quickly & well through the cool and rainy evening. Today I'm still rather tired, but this comes from the weeks before. The air has a marvellous effect; at a height I really am free in a quite different way. It's quite still in the little house; otherwise too less company than I expected. Fritz & Liesel are well. Fritz still has a lot of work.

I haven't dealt with anything yet in the way of post. I want to install myself here first & have the necessary manuscripts around me.

Now I hope you don't go & do too much again when the workmen are there. Write soon & tell me how you are.

This note should reach you by Sunday.

I think of you a lot & take you with me on my walks among the seedlings in the sweeping fields. It's painful how much the wood really has been cleared. Looking out of the window too I suddenly noticed how a whole strip of the wood was missing on the horizon. Much love to you. Best wishes to you and Hermann.

Your Martin.

Regards to the whole house; also from Fritz & Liesel to everyone.

On 10 May, in answer to a letter from Elfride, Martin gave his views on historical research: I understand very well what you mean: genuine tradition that has evolved naturally contains the strength to gather and select what is enduring & present it to the future in ever renewable form. Yet tradition is not made by <u>historiology</u> [*Historie*], but at most disguised & confounded by it; especially by the research & archive activity of modern scholarship. That the human sciences – the philologies too – are unable to find or offer any real tradition is one of the main shortcomings of our university education & its whole activity. From the outset I've always selected essential thinkers & from these only essential writings & expounded them <u>in contrast</u> to every other form of activity. Of course tradition, even when great & simple, is nothing in itself if nothing answers to it & if it isn't brought to speak in action & thought. Today's youth & intermediate generation feel this immediately everywhere; but they cannot express it; no one helps them to; for if it were expressed, the whole elaborate apparatus of the professors would cave in on them & they'd be forced to think about things & not only go into what is essential, but <u>remain with it</u> all the time. They're afraid of this. And in these conditions anyone who pursues his own course is eventually worn down.

On 6 June Martin gave his lecture 'The Thing' at the Bavarian Academy of Fine Arts in Munich, travelling there with Elfride. As previously in Bremen, it was Heinrich Wiegand Petzet who had established the contact. For Martin, these lectures were a substitute for his teaching activity. On 13 July, Martin was pensioned off, his retirement backdated to 1 April.

From 26 October Martin stayed in Messkirch again and on 2 November he wrote: The only course for me is to maintain a quite loose connection to the Univ. & for the rest to stay entirely away from everything; for otherwise I'll always be used for something or other in some way or other, & substantive interests & tasks will no longer carry any weight at all.

Martin was now offering private classes for students in the house on Rötebuck.

1951

On 3 May, Martin and H. W. Petzet visited Bühlerhöhe, a mountain
spa hotel in the northern Black Forest, to attend a lecture by Kurt
Bauch. Afterwards they travelled on to Bremen, where Martin gave
his 'Logos' lecture.

After visiting Maria and Rudolf in Hüfingen, Martin was driven to
Messkirch by Jörg in Elfride's new car. On 15 May he wrote: In the
coming days I'd now like to draft the Darmstadt piece so I have an
outline & can talk about it with you. I think a great deal now of our
first walks here – though the country is still unspoilt away from the
public roads, the whole lifestyle has switched markedly from the rural
to the industrial. [. . .] I'll be thinking of you a lot as I work, especially
since in its subject matter too it's turning into a dialogue between us.

Martin was working on his lecture 'Building Dwelling Thinking',
which he was to give on 5 August as part of the Darmstadt Symposium
on 'Man and Space'.

The previous year in Munich Martin had become friends with the
secretary-general of the Bavarian Academy of Fine Arts, Clemens Graf
von Podewils, and his wife, Sophie Dorothee. Together with the
Podewils, Martin was invited to the castle Schloss Walchen in the
Austrian province of Salzburg by Sophie Dorothee's sister, Princess
Walburgis zu Schaumburg-Lippe, and her husband, Prince Albrecht.

Walchen, 24 Aug. 51

My D. S.
Your letter came today, so it again took 6 days coming. Many thanks
for your kind words. But I'm very sad that you aren't well. I hope
you've had some good days at the Cabin. The weather here has been
very dull, rainy & cold. On 27 Aug. we're going to Munich, the

Princess is coming too, as the sisters want to visit their mother, who is currently in hospital in Munich.

Graf Podewils has prepared a meeting with Heisenberg which I don't want to miss, as I'm not yet clear in my mind about the Bühlerhöhe lectures. Judging by his kind letter, Stroomann evidently doesn't have any real idea either. It seems to me he's now hoping more for Weizsäcker, especially since the latter didn't actually speak in Darmstadt.

I'll let Orff go if it proves not to be particularly convenient; likewise with Dr Münster of Bav[arian]. Radio.

I'll then come directly back to you in Freiburg on the 29th or 30th. Perhaps Messkirch can be done in the autumn. I'll need longer anyway to discuss with Fritz the transcription of the Schelling lectures, which I'm going through again here.

Would you be a dear & send a telegram to Haarsee [the Podewils' place of residence] just in case, so I know how you are.

The days here are quiet; we all work on our own, with little walks or games in the park from time to time. In the evenings Fr[iedrich]. G[eorg]. Jünger reads from his childhood memoirs.

I'm happy to tell you about the implications of the Darmstadt lecture within my thinking as a whole, in so far as I have it clear in my own mind. To me it seems it's the decisive step towards the positive overcoming of the essence of technology. In particular however I'm concerned by the essential origin of place & space & the different levels of things.

The Provincial Governor of Salzburg, who attended my lecture with his wife, has now sent me tickets for the Festival on the 29th & 30th – such tickets are impossible to come by otherwise.

With best & fondest wishes, my D. S. Your M.

Best wishes to Jörg & Hermann, as well as the Laslowskis

[. . .]

Regards from everyone here & the Gräfin sends particular thanks.

After being made an emeritus professor on 26 September, Martin was finally able to take up his lecturing at the University once again. To prepare for the winter semester, he went to Messkirch. On 24 October, he wrote: Every day I thank you for your unspoken love & especially for the last few years, when I've been less in the public eye. You've given me something I find it difficult to know what to call, & which alone now permits me to turn everything beautiful & pure, in the most silent congruity, into thinking and doing. So you'll be as great a help at my side with this newly beginning activity as you used to be in the days when I almost took it for granted. *Two days before, Martin had been in Beuron and in the same letter he reported:* During the liturgy

In front of the Cabin with Fips

in Beuron all sorts of thoughts came to me about the form & effect of the spiritual. *And on 25 October Martin wrote:* From the liturgy, which also made a great and clarifying impression upon the Gräfin [von Podewils], I again learnt how indispensable it remains to find ways & forms of working what has been thought in an essential way into the matter of dwelling. A dwelling within the praise of God transpires in the liturgy; but there's often also a doubt as to what extent a fruitful closeness is still alive. On the other hand, neither in the Catholic nor the Protestant Church can a creative or history-making piety be enforced by a liturgical movement – unless God speaks himself. This is why it may after all be a proper way to prepare us to hear what addresses us, to furnish a presentiment of its realm, & to arouse this in the individual.

On 1 November Martin returned home in time for the start of the semester. The subject of his lecture course was 'What is Called Thinking?' ['Was heisst Denken?'].

1952

On 12 January Martin was in Munich to give a lecture and attend preliminary discussions ahead of the conference of the Bavarian Academy. On 14 January he told Elfride: Yesterday evening went well. Above all I'm pleased that Guardini has been rejuvenated & is making another attempt. Perhaps I'll have another talk with him for longer this afternoon. Tomorrow we're all going to Haarsee with Graf & Gräfin P[odewils]. [. . .] Yesterday morning with Petzet I saw some really amazing Klee drawings in the Franke Gallery. Outside I want to continue my discussion with Podewils; perhaps Riezler can come after all.

There was a serious housing shortage. Lene and Ernst Laslowski therefore continued to live in the house. In addition, children from among their circle of friends were constantly being taken in.

On 24 April Martin returned to Munich to record his lecture 'What is Called Thinking?' for Bavarian Radio.

Munich 28. IV. 52

My D. S.

Yesterday Sunday I thought of you a lot, & altogether I feel an inner peace springing from the ever more precious sense that the heart of this indestructible belonging to one another rests on nothing contingent & can grow still further from our essential affinity to one another. This knowledge keeps everything fine & in order. Thus my days here will also be good & remain all right.

Yesterday from the morning on until around 9 o'clock in the evening I was at Petzet's, where we spoke with Helmken about Antigone [by Carl Orff]; 'Creon' [baritone Hermann Uhde] was briefly there too, but then had to leave for rehearsals. Orff is in England. Then

Petzet's young painter friend showed his latest pictures, which show good progress along his path.

Today it's my Zurich lecture; & I'm also supposed to be chairing the discussion myself; I think it'll be a seminar since simple ideas & the clarity that belongs to them are lacking everywhere.

I learnt some important things from my tour of the radio station; Münster wants to remunerate me directly this evening after the lecture.

Ernst Jünger has also said he's coming for the next few days at the Podewils'. Taking advantage of 1 May, P. himself has taken a holiday.

This way there'll be good conversations; we also want to get to see the deer, which over the winter have turned into sedentary game in the immediate vicinity because they feed there.

P. wants to take advantage of 1 May to extend his holiday until then. Guardini's supposed to be coming back on 1 May. I'll go to Messkirch either on the first or second of May. The weather's rainy, but not unpleasant, the wild cherries here are in blossom right now.

I hope you cope with workmen & clearing up without too much trouble. Tomorrow after the talk I'll get down to my lecture course.

In the April issue of the periodical Wort & Wahrheit [*Word & Truth*] now being published by Herder, Podewils showed me a long article by old Picht on 'Army without Pathos', which he considers excellent. I don't have time to read it now; but perhaps Ernst [Laslowski] could get the issue for Hermann.

A short time ago Benn passed through; the Ps spent an evening in his company. I'll tell you about it later.

Good old Petzet has become even plumper – almost everything has been cut down around the house; he still doesn't have a buyer.

We're considering mid-October for Bremen, & they think it's important to talk about Nietzsche.

Thinking of you with devotion and affection, I keep you constantly present in my mind.

Best wishes to Hermann. Your M.

Regards to Ernst & Lene.

Elfride suspected that Martin was having an affair with Sophie Dorothee von Podewils. On 29 April Martin wrote from Haarsee: My D. S. Everything is <u>very</u> quiet and peaceful – & your dream deceives you. The spirit of Artemis herself reigns so pure and severe that I myself am thankful for it & filled with joy that I may tell you this.

In June he stayed in Messkirch once again, and wrote these undated words: I'm constantly thinking of everything. I'll find my way yet after all. I ask you for your forbearance.

Unless such a destiny of such a sickness prevents it all & the soul can still be free, help must come.

Cabin, 8 August 52

My D. S.

It was a great disappointment yesterday when you didn't come. But even during the days of your journey I'd been uneasy & slept badly because I was afraid the trip would tire you out after all.

And now you won't be here <u>tomorrow</u> either, & dear Jörg is also leaving today. From Hermann came a note, which is in the post. And so I'll be on my own and very sad, most of all about myself, about all my erring ways and failings, the oppressive guilt & about the great pain I've inflicted on you time & again. So it will be a cheerless day of guilt, one that I dread. Nor do I want to say the word 'but' – for I've done little to prove to you that my heart belongs to you and cannot be without you. Many lovely and fruitful weeks here up at the Cabin remain, even though a shadow still hangs over them now and there is so little I can do to regain your trust. Perhaps the coming weeks up at the Cabin would have been quiet and good, filled with new confidence and fruitful work. Yet now I've no idea how things stand with your health, whether you can risk a stay here, whether it isn't all too tough and taxing here. Jörg said the Marburg doctor would call in again in Frbg. You must discuss everything clearly with her, also the possibility of your staying <u>here</u>. If the doctor were to advise against it, then of course I'll come down; I don't want to be up here on my own. If you were able to come though, dear Jörg would be willing to drive to Frbg. once again and bring you up. Here we are overflowing with people, & Wolf constantly out and about. Clothild came on Monday afternoon. She's cheerful & likes being here; takes good care of everything & at the same time has a rest herself. She can stay until Wednesday. Heini is supposed to be coming up over Sunday. Then they also want to discuss whether they'll live downstairs with us now that the Reck[endorfs]. unfortunately can't come. Recovery from this illness is obviously a very lengthy business.

On Wednesday there was a storm, & since then it's been rainy and foggy part of the time & always overcast – already rather autumnal.

Since Monday Gadamer has been with his wife at the 'Stübenwagen' inn, staying a good fortnight; they were here briefly on Wednesday; on Monday there was a good conversation with Nitschke. He wants to come again at the end of September. Otherwise there haven't been any other visits yet; the Heidelberg students have said they're coming on 16 Aug., they intend to camp.

The afternoon you drove away with Jörg, I at once got down to work to complete the lecture course and a few important additions; I finished on Wednesday; now I'm rather tired & am dealing more with the external aspects of the other work. As long as I don't know how you are & what's happening, I presume nothing will come good. I can't force things either, but in the next few days I'll try to get back into the preparatory work. No one can help me directly with the subject & there can be no corroboration. The path may be surrounded by error & guilt which I first have to deal with, but I won't abandon the task I have in mind even if I'm destroyed in the process.

Niemeyer is pressing for a new edition of B[eing]. & T[ime]., which is very inconvenient for me at the moment; for after all I have to go through all the required corrections myself.

I don't have a clear view of what I'll come up with for Bühlerhöhe either; I now just want to get back onto the path again.

I've written to Boss, also about Stuttgart. I'll send you all the post.

I hope Ute [Bogner] will drive into the village. There's a lot of traffic, especially on Sundays. Recently someone drove his motorbike from the Schneiderhof straight onto the Ratschert. But otherwise it's still very quiet back here; though the beautiful Holzschlagbach path now gets walked & driven along a good deal too. –

I keep sinking into deep sadness about myself: that my failure brings you the greatest suffering, and my strength is insufficient to bring the human dimension and the thinking into proper harmony with one another.

Yet I don't wish to lament this now & I'll be content to try once more, with what has been granted to me, to fulfil the task I've been assigned, without any literary ambition, without professorial craving for achievement, without help or approval, in a time that is as unpropitious for thinking as ever one was.

Everything wouldn't be so arduous now if you were here. But the most important thing of all now is that you should take care of yourself & above all find proper healing there where the cause of the pain lies.

I think of you a lot; & all the things in the Cabin and outside remind me of your presence. All this I owe to you & from amid all the ingratitude & inability I ask you still to feel my enduring sense of belonging to your heart.

With best wishes to you & many thanks for the lines you wrote.

Yr. M.

Clothild sends her regards. The Brenders' tea is undrinkable; Cloth. has got us some better stuff from the 'Sternen', so we're managing.

Thanks for the card, which was already here on Sunday.

View from the desk towards the fountain

On 12 August Martin wrote to Elfride to commemorate the 30th anniversary of the Cabin: I sensed your thoughts of here on 9 Aug. & helped myself over this solitude by starting work afresh on the morning of that day. It went well, so I'm already on my way now. But treading these paths always calls for reciprocity between being borne in one's soaring & being ready oneself & bringing something of one's own in turn. I don't need to tell you such things, because you know them only too well. I just have to tell myself that until now I have never

Cabin in the snow

been capable of receiving the soaring as essentially & purely as of con-
tributing the ceaseless exertion of my labour from the workshop. I
don't 'consent' to what is wicked, or so little that I struggle to bear
what has happened & cannot shake it off even with constantly
renewed effort. This remains inviolate in its necessity, just as <u>even
more</u> primordially my sense of belonging to you remains intact within
me through all confusion & failure. The misuse and the destruction of
trust are probably founded <u>amongst other things</u> in my inability to
receive within the genuine & thus guiding bounds the gifts of the
soaring and to be watchful & through this watchfulness to help others
in turn. *Martin and Elfride were constantly concerned with fundamental religious questions. In the same letter Martin thus wrote about
his reading:* The essay by M. Buber is excellent & when you're here
we'll have plenty to say about it. The diagnosis is very far-sighted and
of great wisdom – But the healing must start even deeper than he sug-
gests. And there remains a question of whether we mortals address our
eternal Thou (B. means God) <u>through</u> our mortal Saying-Thou to one
another, or whether we aren't brought into correspondence to one
another only through God's address. The question remains whether
this 'either-or' is sufficient at all or whether both the one and the other
have to be prepared even more primordially, a preparation which of
course again requires the behest and its protection. The final sentence
is beautiful and therefore essential: 'Reconciliation effects reconciliation'. Mere forgiving and asking for forgiveness is not enough.
Reconciliation [*Versöhnen*] belongs with 'atonement' [*Versühnen,
Sühnen*] & 'to atone' really means: to still – to bring one another into

225

Stove and cooker in the Cabin

the stillness of essential belonging. The genuine & fruitful & funda-mentally ceaseless conversation is the one where those conversing are <u>different</u> in kind and intuitively recognize this, neither in mere indif-ferent acceptance nor using a single yardstick & its doctrine.

In October Martin returned to Messkirch. On 16 October he wrote to Freiburg: But I'm inwardly freer and confident that I can do what is right. And the fact that I know you can be happy again in spite of the pain and that the two of us, helping one another, can together further the work in these decisive years makes me happier myself & reinforces my readiness for the path which still lies ahead of me & is probably the most difficult part. The Cabin cup is here beside me now & reminds me of so much, good and bad, joyful and painful.

On 22 October Martin told Elfride of his work with Fritz: I now live so quietly and simply & with no burden of what is feigned or unclarified & am glad that everything has been brought onto a good, though also painful, path in which you can trust. And I also think that S[ophie]. D[orothee]. has learnt a lot & is doing her utmost. Despite her quite different origins & background, she is a kind & open person,

Dining area

who in some sense, albeit with lesser powers, touches upon essential matters. First & foremost, for me it's decisive that all the desolation of discord is kept at bay & the relation can evolve on amicable terms, which alone can determine its duration. I wrote her a note in which I told her of my work here & my misgivings about the radio play, which isn't suited to her abilities. I also think that S. D. will reconcile herself to a more sparing correspondence.

At the end of October Martin and Fritz took the train to Darmstadt. In the course of the journey they were joined by Elfride, who had come from visiting Erika in Birkach. In Darmstadt they were greatly impressed by a performance of Orff's Oedipus. *On 3 November Martin wrote from Messkirch:* They were such lovely days together with you despite the moment of pain; I've become more confident again that I'll find my way into what is simple, a path on which thinking and doing are in accord, & from your true quiet love will also draw the strength to accomplish what I have in mind – however dark & forlorn the world may be. Fritz too is very animated, & thus the journey will be of benefit to our work too. If only we can find a simple form & the appropriate way of making the communication of thinking fruitful. The essential stimuli do come to me from people who – though not philosophers – are themselves creative. The bare hour at the breakfast table with Orff moved me most powerfully.

And on 4 November Martin again wrote about Darmstadt: Oedipus, the performance & the question of language, has been on my mind a lot. Looking back, the performance strikes me as still too 'Schillerian' & oriented only towards the realistic. On the other hand

227

there are opportunities concealed here, given the right approach, for affecting modern man in a quite different way. And how necessary this is is shown by the America book, which I read a little while in the evenings – atrocious, but in principle just the corroboration of the 'framework' [*Gestell*] – the essence of which is becoming increasingly clear to me. *The volume* Amerikakunde *('American Studies'), one of a series of 'handbooks of foreign studies', had appeared earlier in the year in a new edition revised by Eduard Baumgarten.*

Impressions from Darmstadt continued to occupy Martin's thoughts when he wrote on 6 November: It was so good to have your quiet presence here during the manifold conversations & the performances. 'Oedipus' & the conversation with Orff have made the question about <u>language</u> even more urgent for me; about its essence as well as about its probable capacity to prepare a turn [*Wende*] today against the raging of the technological world. Looking back, it seems to me that the event of disclosure and the play & counterplay of appearance, which all takes place essentially in the dialogue, did not come through strongly enough. Everything was transposed too much onto the characters, whose action however is purely & simply what they say – Apart from this nothing actually happens 'on stage' in the whole tragedy. My stay in Darmstadt brought home to me how much the atmosphere & the appropriate participants for conversations are lacking. Teaching & lecturing receive nothing back in return & of necessity become dependent upon the audience. I notice this now as I write up the 1935 lecture course, when I compare the accompanying notes, which suggest a different position. At any rate I'd like to ensure that the 1951/2 lectures appear as far as possible in <u>connection</u> with those from 35.

Martin stayed on in Messkirch until his name day and visited the Beuron monastery. On 12 November, shortly before travelling to see his friend Leiner in Constance, he wrote: The question of the manuscripts is now worrying me again, even more so than in 1938. But I can't find the time now to get down to this work here. The most important thing now remains for me to bring out the planned publications as soon as possible.

From Lake Constance on 14 November, Martin sent a postcard of the Island of Reichenau: This picture contains the loveliest & enduring memory – without many words may it tell you everything; & my sending you this particular picture today with all my fondest thoughts includes the request that you should trust what is indestructible about what is ours.

Jörg took his diploma. Dorle was very unhappy at the psychiatric clinic in Berlin, and Elfride and Martin tried to obtain a place for her at one of the Bethel Institutions.

1953

Martin went to Constance to visit his friend Bruno Leiner, who was seriously ill.

Co. 20 Feb. 53

My dear Elfride!
I'm always thinking of you. Through all the pain, may you feel ever more clearly that in spite of everything our love and our life are one, one also in your companionship, which I have <u>never</u> regarded merely as a matter of looking after my outward needs & relieving me of every-day concerns.

My constant thought is that we may work together for one another, the children & our tasks for the quiet years ahead. And I'm glad that you also share in the essential efforts of my thinking & can follow & understand them. –

The city's filled with memories of youth & on the journey I looked over in remembrance towards the avenue of poplars that leads to Reichenau.

Your Martin.

On 2 March Martin travelled on to Messkirch, and on 5 March he wrote: The world situation is tense on account of Stalin; but I don't think there'll be a war. But here we're greatly reminded of the years 1938/39 when we stand in front of the mss & iron chests. Fritz too thinks we should get as much as possible ready for publication our-selves.

On 23 March Martin was in Munich for meetings and again met up with Sophie Dorothee von Podewils, with whom he had now devel-oped an intense relationship. Sophie Dorothee was 44 years old, had been married to Clemens Graf Podewils since 1932, and was a painter and writer.

Munich, 24. III.

My dear Elfride!
Thank you for your letter and your hopeful, helpful love. I'm glad that everything is in the open – but at the same time I'm very despondent & sad at having caused you such pain once again. You say one thing that is hard – but it again concerns the very thing I'm striving to clarify & resolve. – As far as home is concerned – what is ours persists & has grown – even though at times I have seemed not to appreciate it. What I've tried to give S[ophie]. D[orothee]. takes nothing away from you & was never intended to impinge upon what is ours, let alone to forsake it.

Despite all that is difficult – thank you for your letter & for the hints.

M.

Haarsee, 25. III. 53

My dear E.!
I'm writing to you from here – after a sleepless night. But this I can tell you: here peace has come and great gratitude – a return to bounds & a reticence that watches over everything for the best – and – without a word about it being uttered – a rapprochement between S. D. & Cl[emens].

I'm writing briefly to tell you the essential & assure you that I myself am following your counsel & in following it find unspoken help through S. D. I know there's a long path ahead of me.

But thank you for waiting so faithfully.

I'll write to you again tomorrow. Your Martin.

H. 26. III. 53.

Dear Elfride!
These few words are to tell you that I reflect on your hints every hour & keep you in my thoughts, through all the pain I bring you.

But remember this – that the home that was founded through our marriage remains the point to which everything is related for both good and ill.

And remember this too – that in the three days here everything has remained quiet and within bounds, not just deliberately through care and prudence, but through a decision reached.

And without overhasty self-confidence I'd like to tell you that not only is all threat averted, but in a positive sense that an encounter prepared & grounded in what is beautiful and pure has unfolded & become stronger from the experience of the past.

I know you mistrust my language and power of expression.

But this loving friendship can withstand any test now & will no longer be able to do harm. – I had hoped for a greeting from you today. But perhaps I shouldn't do so now – after your last letter. The love for you within me is indestructible. Martin.

On 18 May Martin was driven to Messkirch by Médard Boss. He met up with Sophie Dorothee by Lake Constance in Altreute, above Bregenz.

A. 28. V. 53.

My D. S.

My thoughts are with you ceaselessly & my whole being here is contained therein – & is gratitude that you bestow this upon me – is confidence that after all this erring something helpful and fruitful is growing forth from it.

S. D. picked me up yesterday afternoon in Friedrichshafen, where we caught the boat to Bregenz, where her brother-in-law picked us up. After the great heat, today the weather changed completely. But there's great peace and pure restraint here. S. D. isn't feeling entirely well – cardiac asthma – but towards you and me there's a great sincere & earnest gratitude for the fact that I may be here.

I myself am peaceful in a quite different way & even closer to you now that the uncanniness of what was hidden, the unfreedom imposed by lack of openness has fallen away –

I think about you every hour & now you'll be in Wiesbaden after what I hope were pleasant days with Lotte Caesar.

In Messkirch, I worked very intensively on the mss up until Monday.

Fritz was rather busy just before Whitsun.

It was unusually hot & during the first thunderstorm that broke & lasted several hours a 52-year-old farmer was struck dead by lightning as he went reaping with his scythe.

As all the post here goes via the censors in Innsbruck I won't post these lines till I get to the German side. Thinking of you with affection & devotion, your M. S. D. sends her grateful regards.

Best wishes to Jörg & Hermann.

On 31 May Martin wrote from Altreute: As a 'token' I've taken the lovely picture of you looking up at little Joggelein [Jörg] as a young mother from the old photographs at Fritz's. It has accompanied me at all moments – And it's as though it's awoken the protective powers in S. D.'s nature even more powerfully too, and the days have thus been full of stillness, clarity, trust and gratitude towards you.

Messk. 1. VI. 53.

My D. S.

I've come back happy & grateful; because everything was free & open, quiet and thankful.

And I was able to help a lot simply by being there, reading aloud in the afternoon hours and talking about Hölderlin & explaining the basic concepts of thinking.

Your disquiet is not unjustified – but it has become all the clearer to me now in particular that the quietest restraint helps S. D.'s nature most of all, because it also corresponds to it. And my 'being in love' has now clearly and decidedly found the fitting path of affectionate friendship. And all are thankful that what was threatening and harmful was resolved last year. And although we've intentionally touched upon the matter only fleetingly: S. D. is deeply thankful that her relationship to Cl[emens]. has become close precisely as a result. – In the next few days S. D. is returning to Mu. with her brothers & sisters.

Thinking of you with devotion, I remain
Your M.

Messkirch, 4 June 53

My D. S.

This Sunday greeting comes with constant thoughts of you and the boys and is to tell you how seamlessly the workshop here is joined with the one in our house, which you've helped build for my work. The growing clarity and stillness, the consciousness of having come to feel at home within the bounds and the worthiness of the tasks still to be accomplished makes me silently glad within & wakefully sustains my closeness to you, which remains unshakeable.

Today we finished the WS [winter semester] 51/52 lectures, which, as I see it, do provide a conclusion. To be sure, they lack a clearer stance with respect to Nietzsche's thought, so the impression is often given that I identify with N. In addition, they also lack a clear connection to the new approach in the SS [summer semester] 52 lecture course.

I'd like to rectify both shortcomings by means of an 'appendix' which I've already outlined. Tomorrow we're starting on the summer

Elfride with a flycatcher on her sixtieth birthday

lectures, followed by the 'Basic Concepts'. Since Fritz has been on holiday we're progressing at quite a different pace.

Last week during the morning hours I made some important notes on the relationship between mod. tech. & mod. science, so I'll have this topic over and done with by autumn too. The work on the lectures on Parmenides & Heraclitus is the most laborious, but probably also the most important. Mind you, time & again I also see the need to make the essential features of my own path more clearly visible than up to now. But I'm still unsure quite how to go about this in the proper way.

I'm waiting to hear from Boss in order to plan a work schedule taking into consideration the exact date of my return home.

Leiner, whose wife I telephoned, is considerably better; & he's already out & about a lot again & almost too active; he's away now until next Tuesday.

Please write & tell me how you & Jörg & Hermann are. Have you started with the cherry harvest yet? Today Liesel brought the first ones from the little shop. The weather seems to be settling down; the traffic is also less noisy than usual.

Has the letter I sent you at Hedwig's address in Wiesbaden arrived yet?

Thinking of you with devotion, and best wishes to you and Jörg & Hermann.

Your M.

Regards to Ute as well.

Martin prepared his book What is Called Thinking? *for publication and dedicated it to Elfride: 'to my true companion for her sixtieth birthday'.*

On 28 July he was back in Munich for meetings and with the Podewils in Haarsee. He was looking for a publisher for his planned publications and consulted his Munich acquaintances on the matter.

On 1 August Jörg took up his first job as a mechanical engineer in Bad Homburg.

H. 7 Aug. 53

My Dearest Soul!
I'm very much looking forward to coming home to you and our house, after learning some very helpful and important things in the course of the various meetings and discussions, especially with regard to the further <u>presentation</u> of my thinking as well, & bringing to fulfilment a quiet, helpful and gratifying time spent within clear bounds.

Contrary to expectations, Heisenberg had to change his arrangements again & came <u>yesterday</u> afternoon for a three-hour talk, which I'll tell you about in greater detail later. In the course of it, it emerged that there are plans to locate the great nuclear power station for West Germany beside a large reservoir in moorland to the east of Munich & H. is now constantly being consulted on this. It's to be something similar, only on a smaller scale, to the station described in Jungk. Everything continues to drift in this direction with an uncanny inevitability; on the other hand, H. sets his hopes firstly on a mastering of technology in the future & also on religious help arising from a general renewal – Basically however there's no sign of any <u>inner detachment</u> from this whole research mentality. We only touched upon these points in the final half hour – before that we discussed questions of causality, temporality & the connections with the fundamental perspectives of mediaev. & ancient thought. This was exceedingly fruitful & stimulating for both parties & I came more & more to the conclusion that liberation from the basic technological mentality is <u>only</u> possible through <u>immanent</u> reflection, if at all.

H. is very impressed with my lecture & wants to talk to me specifically about it again tomorrow. He's letting me know from Munich today whether he can take time off from his regular consultations. If I'm not too tired & don't disturb the Sunday here too much, I'd like to return on Sunday. Otherwise I'll travel on Monday & stop off in Hüfingen. In any event you'll be informed of my arrival in good time. [. . .]

The author of the article in the Frankf. Allg. [*Frankfurter Allgemeine Zeitung*], Habermaas, is a 24-year-old student!!

Since then I deliberately haven't touched another newspaper. It seems to me that Vietta really hasn't gone about matters entirely successfully. But basically these things are of no consequence. [. . .]

I wonder if you've had the first reports from Jörg with his impressions.

I always keep with me the picture of you with the young flycatcher – it makes your nature & our house as immediately present to me as my own endeavours to repay your trust everywhere & at every moment. Let this be my fervent Sunday greeting to you. Perhaps the one after next will already see us up at the Cabin. With fond thoughts, I remain your gr[ey-haired]. Little Blackamoor. The Podewils send their best regards.

Regards to Otto & Ute.

In his article, Jürgen Habermas had undertaken a critical analysis of 'An Introduction to Metaphysics', the newly published version of Martin's 1935 lecture course.

After completing his teacher training in Lörrach, Hermann had obtained a post as an elementary school teacher in nearby Wieslet in the river valley of the Kleine Wiese, and become engaged to Jutta Stölting from Lower Saxony. Elfride and Jörg accompanied him to the engagement party on 10 October in Hemschehausen.

Martin was in Altreute, preparing for a conference of the Bavarian Academy. On 11 October he reported to Elfride from Messkirch: The two days of discussions were very satisfying. With Preetorius & Riezler I stayed at a very nice little guest house above Altreuthe on the Buchenberg. On the second day we were joined by Ernst Jünger with the publisher Neske (who brought out 'Wet Bread'[16]). The discussion & the meals were at the Schaumburgs', where the Podewils & Friedr. G. Jünger were also staying. On Thursday aftern. & Friday morning I presented two thirds of my revised manuscript. Preetorius was very taken with it, as were the 'Jüngers'[17] & Neske in particular. The two misgivings were exactly the same ones you voiced straightaway: firstly the Greek & then the frequent 'presencing' [*Anwesen*] & 'ordering' [*Bestellen*] – But I learnt a lot from the conversations & on the other hand clarified the outline of the whole conference. Heisenberg was unfortunately unable to come due to the demands of 'nuclear energy', & M. Schröter fell ill the day before leaving – he had to be aspirated because of a rupture & was running a temperature. His lecture is the most dubious as well. We've given up the 'round table'.

---

[16] *Nasses Brot* by Richard Hasemann.
[17] Heidegger puts Jüngers in inverted commas because the German word *Jünger* also means 'disciple'.

In addition, the participants were in favour, as initially planned, of not holding the talks until 16 Nov. For all of us – & especially I – need time to prepare the final version. [. . .] During the talks for the conference it again became clear to me that I must publish my writings on Greek philosophy in a separate & self-contained form as soon as possible.

On 12 October Martin replied to Elfride's objections: What you write about language hits the nail on the head. Of course the question about essence is just <u>one</u> way. But it seems to me that in the spiritual sense a relationship to technology must first be acquired. That this monster cannot be tamed overnight or with a few formulas is clear. Art too is basically characterless – as long as it's only backed by the culture industry & considered in aesthetic terms.

On 15 October he wrote from Messkirch: Fritz is delighted for me to speak for his 60th birthday – only he thinks it'd be difficult for me to 'climb down' far enough. We've now found an important manuscript on causality & freedom, which we're going through again together before transcribing it.

Martin met up with Sophie Dorothee and on 19 October gave a short account of their meeting: It was a quiet, healing time & for S. D. the peace and the trust that fortify her. [. . .] Fritz is now writing parts from my 'draft', from which I've also read excerpts to S. D. From the many suggestions & questions I've received since I read the text to you I think I've now found a simple guiding thread & also a style that allows the terminology to take second place.

On 24 October he reported an anecdote concerning Fritz: Today he came into the room & saw my sheets spread out & says: haven't you got a lot of 'martyrial' there!

Messkirch, 1 Nov. 53

My D. S.

I neither want to keep you away from our Munich trip, nor is there any special arrangement afoot, and above all there's nothing secret going on in the background. For the fact that it's come to this painful confusion it is I – and again my failure to talk – who am to blame. And with all my heart I beg you to forgive me.

When I was reading the additional parts of the draft to you in Frbg. and you were less & less in agreement, you suddenly said: '<u>I don't think I'll go to Munich with you after all</u>'. I can still remember exactly, because this refusal hurt me. At that point I briefly broke off my reading. Instead of immediately going into your comment & the reason behind it, I allowed myself to nurture a suspicion that the whole event was distasteful to you and you wanted to avoid meeting up with the P[odewil]s.

Up until your comment I took it for granted you were looking forward to our trip like all the other lecture trips and would be coming too.

Po. thought the same thing in Altreute too, until I said of my own accord that it was uncertain whether you'd be coming; of course I couldn't & didn't want to say the reasons that I myself wrongly suspected lay behind it, but said you were busy in the house. This was the position I took with S. D. too. But I also told her that I'd already read you the draft & you'd raised the same objections at almost the same points, that you'd read a draft of Heisenberg's talk & thought highly of it. S. D. knows from earlier conversations that through you & your friendship with Hilde we've known about Preetorius for quite some time & that you've been looking forward to meeting him.

I haven't mentioned any further details about Pr.'s friendship with Hilde, above all because I don't know anything about it. S. D. also knows that you think particularly highly of Friedr. G. Jünger's writings.

And above all else she knows what you are to me even for my work, not just in 'practical' matters. S. D. thus wrote her card quite spontaneously.

In Altreuthe the Ps invited me to go to Haarsee for a few days after the conference. Nothing at all was arranged in advance. Friedr. G. was also to be invited; but he still didn't know when he'd be able to come either; his wife was planning to go to Tunis with a friend from Meersburg for a few weeks.

You know that S. D. is happy and thankful for every day she can spend with me. Everything is calm & open & trusting. And I'm glad that I'm allowed to help and am now also capable of doing so in the nicest way.

With you I also know, & S. D. no less so, that any secrecy would be unworthy in every respect, but also that our meetings are permissible if they're openly discussed at all times. Even though we've not touched upon what is most personal, I do sense from it all that in part due to the clarity of our friendship the marriage is coming back to life. Once on a quiet walk towards Schloss Bronnen [Danube Valley], when the conversation turned to the fate of Dorle, S. D. intimated how she's sometimes seized by a profound fear she might meet with a similar fate, and that my being close to her is alone what saves her from the threat of despondency. These fears, rather than any dogmatic convictions, are probably also the innermost reason that she is so attracted to the vivid & engaging features of Catholic ritual.

I'm writing to tell you this because I still gather from your letter of yesterday, which made me feel very sad, how your ever willing heart

is opening itself up to S. D. again too, even though your character &
hers are quite different.

If you are looking forward to Munich and the talks, & your aversion to the draft, which was rightly to be criticized, was just a momen-
tary one, then I'll be all the happier if we can travel together & spend
the days together in Munich.

I would rather have postponed the conference once again so that it
could be prepared even more carefully & above all so that an architect too had a chance to speak among the 'arts'. But Preetorius didn't
want any further postponement. As it is, I'm afraid everything rather
falls apart & especially towards the end becomes too bland. I didn't
like the 'stock-taking' of the conf. at all. But there was clearly no
making Schroeter change his mind. So there may be a number of dis-
appointments, even with Heisenberg, which doesn't mean that my
own talk will be a pièce de résistance –

It is more likely to disconcert people. But given the dogmatism of
today it's no mean achievement if people are pushed into asking
questions.

Friedr. G. was like me, & for the same reasons as you, against 'free
admission'. But here too Preetorius insisted that the Academy should
not charge admission fees.

How they'll cope with the crowds, even for Guardini, is their
problem. It'll be like my Freiburg lectures. Po. writes that a lot of
bookings have also come from further afield.

Up until my own talk on 18 Nov, of course, I'll have to concentrate
as I did in Aachen – for as a result of the preceding talks by Guardini
& Heisenberg I'll probably think of some improved formulations &
amendments, which I'll then insert.

Otherwise, a lot of people will be getting together; in A[ltreute]. the
Schaumburgs said they'd be coming too, as well as Dr Marcic from
Salzburg, Günther Eich & Kästner if he's back from Greece, possibly
the Stroomanns too.

I'm still fiddling around somewhat with the 'Final Part' & haven't
yet found the final form for it. I'll leave the whole thing for a while
now & work on other matters. Fritz has drawn my attention to quite
a few details & over-concise passages. Otherwise he finds the thing
compelling & thinks I'll get onto the 'Index' at all events, one way or
another.

My D. S., the deepest wish of my heart, which is always near you, is
for all uncertainty & all grounds for mistrust & sadness to be kept at
bay, for us to spend this not unimportant conference happily together
too, & for everything to remain friendly & open towards our friends.

Up to now you haven't said anything to me about the lovely idea of
visiting your school friends in their exile. But that would work out

well, and as I'll certainly be getting the 300 DM as a 'net profit' you'll not only be able to pay for the stay with your friends, but perhaps even help them in other ways too. We could then travel back on the Tuesday or Wednesday, provided I can in fact stay in Haarsee from Sunday on & there aren't too many visitors there.

Fritz has to return to the office tomorrow in view of the start of the month. He's more rested; we're not finished though, & above all I still haven't got the material together for the Constance Gymnasium article.

Perhaps on the journey back I'll be able to stop off here again for a few days when Fritz is more likely to get time off again.

Perhaps I'll even manage it in the next few days if I drop everything else. I don't really want to break my concentration on the Munich double lecture though, & so I'll take it with me to Constance.

I also think Hermann will be relieved from his current post as soon as possible if the main point 'stands'.

Claus Vetter, who has a very tough job in Stuttgart as a qualified engineer, wants to change his profession & become a teacher of commerce like his father. [. . .]

I've hardly had time to rest either. And next weekend Boss will be taking it out of me with his new work (ms) as well; he'd like to stay for Monday too.

Tomorrow I'll write to Pod. in Munich to ask him to book us a double room & sort out the prices for the room & breakfast.

Today Marie and Rudolf came by car & are staying till tomorrow afternoon. Marie I think looks much better & is also fresher.

They've already been out & about here several times today, taking Rudolf's niece with them as a help again.

Everyone, Fritz & Liesel too, sends best wishes to you.

With fond thoughts and best wishes,

Your M.

On 18 November Martin gave his talk 'The Question Concerning Technology' in Munich. After Elfride had left, Martin stayed with the publisher Schnell and on 22 November wrote: My best wishes come to you this Sunday, arising as always from a thankful thinking [*Gedenken*] – which, as you know, is a thanking [*Danken*] – Everything is so balanced & free now that I can also be happy with you about the days we had. I believe they also brought you much gladness. The last day was much worse than I'd feared – Riezler almost spiteful towards me & Jünger; Schröter absolutely useless, he'd made his draft even worse. Pree.'s vanity unfortunately proved too great for him to thank Pod. publicly; his talk was disappointing overall.

Then Martin was invited back to Haarsee and on 24 November wrote: In spite of the dreadful two concluding talks, the young people have been <u>very</u> affected & would like to have an opportunity to ask questions. Depending on how the conversation here tomorrow turns out, we'll arrange a gathering in Munich again for Thursday or Friday. I'll then be staying in the Palais prior to my return. I hope you got back home safely. [. . .] – Yet the decisive thing is not the newspapers – but the fact that a horizon is opening up amongst the young people, one which announces itself from within technology while going beyond it.

1954

On 10 April, Jutta and Hermann were married in Eimbeckhausen in Lower Saxony. Hermann worked as an elementary school teacher in Gersbach in the southern Black Forest.

On 23 April, Martin was in Messkirch again. Elfride went to a class reunion in Wiesbaden and visited Jörg in Bad Homburg. On 28 April, Martin reported from Messkirch: In the last few days I've been working very intensively on the preface & epilogue & other sections of the 'Insight'. I do want to go over the whole thing one more time. Between 30 Apr & 3 May Fritz intends to transcribe what I draft so I have a better base to work from for the final version. [. . .]

Today I'm going to Altreuthe (post Lochau, near Bregenz) & staying until 3 or 4 May. I'm taking my work with me, for I'd like to use the mornings for myself. I'll write to you from there.

Martin stayed in Altreute with Sophie Dorothee for longer than expected and on 4 May wrote: My constant thinking of you and of our house and the children is not only a 'thinking', but an action too. My stay here is so serene and helpful and also through your love gives me such quiet goodness that I cannot thank you enough. Work on the 'Insight' is progressing well each morning; I've now run into just one difficulty, which is that a gap is produced by leaving out the difficult lecture on language, and the lectures on the λόγος & the 'poetical' are left without the necessary foundations. I'm thus considering whether I shouldn't add something about language after all. But I would like to save the conversation about language outlined in Freiburg, which has now progressed somewhat further, for a separate publication. As regards the transformation of the λόγος in Plato I've now made a decisive discovery, which gives me new heart to believe that I shall eventually produce the Plato book after all, which I still harbour as an early promise for you.

241

On 8 May Martin again wrote from Messkirch: What most concerns me is the question about language; & today I had another discussion about it with Fritz. It perhaps really is best if I just touch on the issue without yet discussing it specifically. It must come to light in all its significance through a publication of its own.

Messkirch, 13 May 54

My D. S.

My best Sunday wishes come to you with the same thankful sense of the belonging of hearts. This too, Dearest Soul, is presence. And I've often told you that I could never leave you – not because of the apparently merely outward things. I cannot, even though it may seem as though I am wholly withdrawn from you in utter forgetfulness. This <u>was</u> the case from time to time with M[argot]. I thank you for telling me again & again of your deep distress – it is no less painful for me than it is for you to endure & tell me of it. But it helps me in the way you quite clearly expressed – the fulfilment of the present – yet this is, especially now, not a matter of being swept away – the present remains & furnishes an inspiring element to what is required of me. And so my 'action' now is by no means restricted to what you mention & not only determined by what I can't help. On S. D.'s part & mine there's a real & <u>understanding</u> endeavour – a restraint that grows ever more pleasingly & securely in strength.

You're perfectly right, dear Elfride, I don't belong in this other world & I'm <u>never drawn to it</u> either; just as on the other hand S. D. senses more and more what is different about my & our world and secretly wishes for it. Only for her the outward milieu is more binding. And I therefore thank you once again especially for the days I spent in A[ltreute]. For they help S. D. to achieve growing independence in her affection. And every evening I hope & I ask that it might be granted to me to remove the bitterness from <u>your</u> heart too.

Today S. D. passed through on her way from Überlingen, where she'd spent a few days at the Jüngers'. I showed her the church & castle, took her along a stretch of the pathway; Fritz & I then went for a little walk in the country with her as well & then in the afternoon she went to Munich via Sigmaringen. She's genuinely grateful for such experiences, which release her & make her freer. I'm writing to you about it because the path & the encounter with S. D. is a different one – & to you too I can above all say everything freely & with trusting openness – for no longer is there the oppressiveness of secrecy, but only the pain of your bitterness. But I know that even in this your love & devotion are alive & because of this I hope I can ease your sadness.

With regard to the new edition of the essay 'The Essence of Reasons', I'm still considering whether I should write an 'Introduction' to it after all, connecting the question of 'reasons' with the theme of causality as I present it in the technology lecture. But first I must finish the 'Insight', where the individual pieces call for quite a few additions & deletions which Fritz transcribes anew. In addition, the Parmenides lecture (Muggenbrunn)[18] is still causing me trouble; you found it too difficult; I'm completely rewriting it all, making it lighter & more clearly connected with the rest.

The hardest part will be the last section, the fundamental features of which I've already drafted too; but as the introduction & conclusion are added last I can still use June to complete the final version.

I've already discussed my 'First Mass' speech with Fritz too. The speeches aren't supposed to be too long at all. Yesterday we had a look at the rooms for the banquet. I'm afraid it'll all be rather cramped. Next Wednesday Fritz wants to discuss it all with the parish priest & I'm supposed to be there.

I hope to be more or less finished by 22 May & return home to you that day. I phoned Rudolf again about Marie; he clearly doesn't like the idea of us going there of our own accord without him. He claims he doesn't know the name of the doctor in charge. I'll now wait for the address you are sending me through Peter, for we don't want to arrive there without writing first.

The business with Ute has taken me completely by surprise. I myself haven't given her the slightest grounds. And if you saw it coming, it would have been good if you'd drawn my attention to it; perhaps even the innocuous music evenings were too much. But I think it can all be easily sorted out with U.

I don't know what's being plotted in the Faculty. Presumably they are beginning to consider the question of a successor. I don't want to get in any way involved in these intrigues, even though I support Fink & [Max] Müller. If only Fink would at last publish something bigger. The deanship & Studium Generale public lectures aren't exactly ideal in this regard. –

Now with you too spring will be everywhere around the house & garden. Here the sloes & the first fruit trees are coming into blossom, & the east wind is invigorating for work.

Thinking of you with all my heart & saddened by your distress – & yet with enduring love – best wishes to you, as well as to Jörg & Hermann & Jutta & Erika. Your M.

Fritz & Liesel, who's completely taken up with preparations, send their best regards.

---

[18] Muggenbrunn is a small village near Todtnauberg.

On your advice Liesel Schmid has said she's coming to the First Mass. She would have been invited anyway.

On 19 May Martin wrote from Messkirch: I have indeed thought about dedicating my book to Fritz. While I have the long-standing plan of dedicating a Plato book to you more & more clearly in mind, I can dedicate the 'Insight' to Fritz. That will really delight & surprise him. [. . .] I've decided on a longer 'Introduction' for the new edition of the essay 'The Essence of Reasons'; but I need <u>time</u> for it, especially after looking – albeit only fleetingly – through old manuscripts here which are worth considering for it along with my more recent investigations into causality. The essay will thus strike readers in a new way, & as you rightly observe, it's also a good idea in publishing terms. I'll write to Klostermann some time. The Parmenides piece for the 'Insight' is still causing me trouble. I'll completely rewrite it. The other pieces have all been checked through, & in places additions & improvements made.

On Whit Sunday Martin's nephew Heini celebrated his First Mass. Elfride came to the ceremony, and Martin delivered an after-dinner speech. Afterwards he remained in Messkirch and from there on 8 June he went to Zurich, where he stayed with the Boss family.

On 28 June Martin gave the lecture 'Reflection' ['Besinnung'] in Constance, repeating it on 30 June in Meersburg.

On 12 July he was back in Munich and wrote to Elfride: All through the journey today our conversations from the last few days were on my mind – they'll remain so throughout my stay here. More than hitherto, I shall try and understand myself better & see myself more clearly. I thank you for still continuing to help me. I can feel how it is your love that binds us indestructibly. And if I forgot myself in forgetfulness itself and a helpless lack of trust and openness, then I want more than ever to take advantage of any help. [. . .] With S. D. I'll speak as we discussed. And I think that her affection is a help on the clear, good path – rather than a hindrance.

At the time, Martin was sitting for a bust by the sculptor Hans Wimmer.

On 24 July he again visited the Leiners in Constance. He was preparing his essay 'Heraclitus' for the festschrift to commemorate the 350th anniversary of the Heinrich Suso Gymnasium in October.

In Wiesbaden, on 12 August, Jörg was married to Hedi Veidt, the youngest daughter of Elfride's school friend Hedwig. The newly-weds spent their honeymoon at the holiday home of the Boss family at Lenzerheide in Switzerland.

On 18 August Martin wrote from the Cabin: I look back fondly on Jörg & Hedi's quiet wedding. The occasion has helped us too. Here there's a lot of time & opportunity for reflecting –

Back view of the Rötebuck house

In October Martin and Elfride spent some days together in
Constance for the Heinrich Suso Gymnasium jubilee celebrations.
Martin then went on alone to Messkirch and on 21 October wrote:
And now you've caught a small reflection of what surrounded me as
a little boy at grammar school; only you must imagine everything
much quieter & almost sleepy. For me of course they were the first
foreign parts I knew & seen from <u>here</u> a residue from them lies over
everything even now. Fritz finds it all much more threatening, but then

245

school & religion were more trying for him. From our conversations (yesterday & the day before) I can see that he really is far removed from formalism & such things.

On 27 October he wrote: As ever, work with Fritz is 'fruitful' & full of agreement. He isn't at all 'narrow' – He said it'd only be right if they placed me on the Index in Rome. Work on the 'piece' has again clarified quite a lot for me, but once more I see how much I need to present the essential thoughts in their own context without reference to history & with no intention of constructing a 'system'. Whether I'll yet find the strength & energy for that I don't know.

Jörg made up his mind to train to be a trade-school teacher in Stuttgart and with Hedi moved into his parents' house on Rötebuck in Freiburg.

Frbg [Messkirch] 13 Nov. 54

My D. S.

I arrived here somewhat late yesterday evening, weary and sad about myself – for I have stumbled again on account of something that didn't provide the slightest grounds for secrecy. –

I'm not gone from you; far from it; it is simply the indestructible closeness of those who are starting to 'age'.

But my character is more contradictory than yours; and I cannot prove to you by any arguments that I have to live in Ἐρωζ in order to give at least a preliminary & imperfect form to the creativity I still feel within me as something unresolved and ultimate.

There's nothing to be achieved here by mere 'willpower'. One could perhaps simply draw a line under things & renounce one's late works & devote one's time to the unpublished ones.

But I can't do that; indeed I'm not yet capable of the unbroken & free awareness & transformation of Ἐρωζ either; & I know I've abused your trust too much for you to be able to feel calm & assured about giving me free rein here. –

But in the next few days now I'll try to catch up on important work with Fritz; he's already made all the preparations. But I really must have a rest for one or two days. Work wasn't possible this morning; & I'm like a blind man. I hope you have a good time with Clothilde. With you in fond thought – best wishes, your Martin

Fritz & Liesel send their regards. The news has just come that Heini has been transferred to Steinach in the Kinzig Valley. [. . .]

On 11 December Martin's school friend Leiner died in Constance. Martin attended the cremation there and made a short speech.

1955

On 11 February, Jutta and Hermann's first daughter, Ulrike, was born. On 19 February, Martin again went to Messkirch, and on 25 February he visited the family of his late friend Leiner in Constance. Here he was picked up by Boss and driven via Zollikon to the holiday home in Lenzerheide. On 3 March, Martin gave the following account of his experiences skiing: The movement has done my arm & whole body a lot of good. You go with a lift not far from Sural up to a middle station; from there you ski to the next one, where the lift takes you up to 1800m. There we had lunch; Frau Boss had already 'floated' up on her own earlier – you don't actually 'float', but go up with your skis in worn tracks, two abreast; it takes a certain amount of practice the first time, & you can feel the strain in your calves. After eating I lay in the deck chair, Boss & wife then went up by lift to the peak (2300m) & were back in an hour; Frau Boss went straight on back to the house on the well-worn 'piste', while Boss returned with me over <u>un</u>used slopes with powder snow & in places a sheet of ice on top. It took me a while to get used to the descent again, but B. did everything very cautiously & carefully.

Fritz and Liesel were in deep mourning. Their youngest son Franz had suddenly and unexpectedly died as a result of a perforated appendix. Elfride and Martin went with Jörg and Hedi to the funeral in Messkirch. Martin stayed on afterwards. On 21 May he wrote: Silent but composed grief pervades the little house here. Liesel is much calmer & more collected than Fritz, who hides it all with painful humour.

On 3 June Martin wrote from Constance: I could feel you were sad yesterday as we were saying goodbye; and I was even more so, because I know how far I am from winning back your trust. And I shall think every day about what is contained in these two sentences.

From 9 June he was working in Messkirch again. On 17 June, Johannes, the youngest son of Erika and Helm, was born. On 23 June, Martin wrote from Messkirch about the lecture he was planning: Fink isn't moving a muscle. I've sent off the announcement for the one-hour lecture 'The Principle of Reason'. I only want seminars privatissime, if at all. Gabr. Marcel must have talked a fair bit of nonsense about me. *In the same letter he gave an account of a visit to Ulm:* On Tuesday/Wednesday I was at the Gunderts'; both of them (he's already 75) send their best regards & thank you again for taking in their son [Hermann] 10 years ago. I've rarely learnt so much in conversations as on this occasion. G. was also a German language teacher at a grammar school in Japan. He was able to give such precise answers to my questions; for the first time I've gained an insight into the structure of the Jap[anese]. language; of course, the interference of the Indo-Germanic categories & the corresponding grammar still gets in the way. In addition, we spoke about Zen texts & the problem of their interpretation. Gu. is a cousin of Hermann <u>Hesse</u>, old Swabian stock, & his wife a proper Swabian.

In 1954 West German security policies led to the signing of the Paris Agreements, and thereupon to admission to the North Atlantic Treaty Organization. A consequence of this was the establishment of West Germany's own armed forces, the Bundeswehr, *as the country's contribution to the NATO defence system. Hermann was asked whether he was interested in a military career.*

Messkirch, 28. 6. 55.

My dear Elfride!

Many thanks for your letter. I dealt with the enclosed post at once, have written to Larese to tell him I can't come, & asked Biemel to come. [. . .] I don't want there to be a 'philosophers' conference' in Cérisy with a lot of inquisitive onlookers.

I've arranged my return home for Friday evening (fast train). Fritz will probably have tomorrow off; today he's unavailable because of a visit from the head of the local banks.

I need Thursday to put things in order; I probably won't be able to transport everything at all. We've talked over various publication plans, some for Niemeyer others for Neske.

According to Leibniz, 'the principle of reason' is the principium grande – the major principle of all thinking & being, & it was first thought through by Leibniz at the watershed, as it were, between ancient, mediaeval & modern thought – formally it runs: 'Nothing is without a sufficient reason'; the principle is at the same time the basis for causality.

Hegel alone since Leibniz has systematically discussed the principle in his greater 'Logic' – in one of the most difficult texts in philosophy; I've been working on this as well here with the help of old manuscripts. But the title – as I've told you before – is chosen as a <u>camouflage</u> so the theme of '<u>language</u>' doesn't create an immediate sensation. In addition, with great enthusiasm & veneration I've been delving once again into W. von Humboldt's treatises on language.

Up to now we've had sometimes violent thunderstorms almost every day here; the haymaking is seriously behind. We thus don't get round to 'walking' as much either.

It's very sad that Fritz has nobody here to keep him mentally alert & at the same time take his mind off things. [. . .]

I also wrote to Theophil, as well as to the Schnells & to Cl. Podewils about the question of language. I sent the lecture announcement directly to the Faculty earlier. Now in the harvest time it's hard to find a car going to Frbg. from here. Couldn't Thomas go [cherry]-picking & then send them express?

I'm looking forward to coming home & spending time at the Cabin. Let's hope the visits don't mount up again.

With fondest love to you & best wishes to the children.

Your M.

On 6 August, I was born, the first child of Hedi and Jörg, in the Rötebuck house.

In September Martin and Elfride made their first journey to France. At Cérisy-la-Salle in Normandy, Martin gave the lecture 'What is Philosophy?' ['Was ist das – die Philosophie?']. The two of them visited his friend Jean Beaufret in Paris and Georges Braque in Varengeville.

In October, Martin's sister Marie was taken seriously ill, and Martin and Elfride travelled to Hüfingen. Elfride then returned to Freiburg while Martin went to see the Leiners in Constance again. On 6 October he wrote from there: I think I'm making good progress with preparing the lecture, as the meticulous outlines from those collected days at the Cabin make many things easier for me – as I'm now coming to realize. I'm more worried about the Messkirch talk – but I think once I'm there & breathing the air I'll find a proper form for the thing all right. It's good that you'll be there too. For it [is] also the 40th anniversary of our first meeting in that little lecture hall below the roof. And so this winter lecture course is especially one of remembering for me.

Elfride was away visiting friends and relatives as well as Dorle in Bethel. On 14 October, Martin reported from Messkirch on his preparations for the Conradin Kreutzer memorial: On Wednesday I discussed the programme again with the Mayor; today it's already printed. South-West Radio has declined – though why is not entirely clear to me. The thing probably isn't important enough for them.

I'm enclosing a copy for you, which also counts as an invitation as a 'guest of honour'. Fritz says celebrating the 175th anniversary is a bit 'far-fetched'. The address is causing me rather a headache.

On 16 October Martin wrote, again from Messkirch: I'm making better progress with the lecture course than with the Messkirch talk. But it'll be all right. Weizsäcker has sent me a very interesting but difficult manuscript about the logic of quantum theory. The problem of language has been ramifying constantly since I've begun to have some idea of the structure of the East Asian languages. I don't want to say anything premature in the talk here.

On 30 October, Martin gave an address on 'Composure' ['Gelassenheit'] at the memorial for the 175th anniversary of the Messkirch-born composer Conradin Kreutzer.

Messk. 4 Nov. 55

My D. S.

The Mayor has just brought me a programme for the radio broadcast of the Kreutzer memorial. It says: Tuesday 22 Nov. 19.30– 20.30, on the 2nd prog. FM. On the occasion of the 175th anniversary of the birth of C. Kr. (22 Nov. is the date of birth).

The Mayor has received a lot of enquiries from outside the town asking whether the address can be heard on the radio again or is being printed.

I presume now the radio in Frbg. will ask me about this – If so, you can give my consent under the condition that the address is reproduced unabridged, above all with the introduction, & a fee of 800DM is paid. Here they're still talking about the address. If you yourself have <u>serious</u> misgivings about the broadcast, turn it down.

One is indeed somehow at the mercy of the framework [*Gestell*] after all.

The first lecture I think now 'fits' properly. Now there's ms work to be done over the weekend.

Tomorrow we want to go for a walk in the wood once again –

And I think there'll be a note from you as well.

Much love to you, with best wishes
Your M.

Best regards to Jörg & Hedi.

Fritz & Liesel likewise send their regards.

Martin's letter from Messkirch dated 7 November includes a hand-written addition on one side from Elfride: from the journey to see Marl. [Marielene Putscher] in Tü[bingen].

Marielene Putscher, a medic and art historian, was 35 years old and had attended Martin's lectures in Freiburg. Martin had written a contribution for her book on Raphael's Sistine Madonna and its influence, published in Tübingen, and was having a relationship with her.

Hermann left teaching in order to work for the Ministry of Defence on the development of the West German armed forces.

1956

In mid-April Martin went to Messkirch to prepare his lecture on Johann Peter Hebel, while Elfride visited Erika and her family in Birkach. Elfride was very unhappy about Martin's continuing relationship with Marielene Putscher.

M. 18 April 56

My D. S.

The card announcing your safe return to Frbg. was there by Saturday. Thank you too for the packet, which arrived on Tuesday & which I can make good use of here as it's cold & snowing. There hasn't been a single fine day yet. The wheat seedlings have been killed by frost almost everywhere, & now the opportunity for sowing is being delayed again.

And today your sad note came – which really did make me sad, as I'm already sad enough anyway. I didn't want to send you the letters & poems from M[arielene]. or my poem with the quatrain on the days you were visiting. You say such things 'help' you – may it be thus, yet don't harden your heart in brooding, but let this be the beginning of a return of trust –

For surely this is founded upon a readiness for whatever may come, which can never bring down what has once been fated with regard to our bond. A love that has worked for decades & evolved from a shared life cannot be destroyed – There's no place for trust where one knows everything already & can imagine & control this in advance. Trust is strength in the affirmation of what is concealed & what we leave unspoken in its hiddenness. Thus was my yes back then – when you told me about Hermann.

Let this most profound trust come to you – I know this is made

252

terribly difficult by me; but my secrecy will fade away now if you give me your trust, as I've said & long considered in these days here.

And for me, the fact that you immediately felt a sort of elective affinity with M. is a pledge that my love for you, irreplaceable & enduring as it is, can incorporate my fatedly other love for M. Once I'm released from the burden of what is unfree I have powers of love which cannot let your heart turn to stone & are capable of ensuring that M. continues to grow and does not waste away.

All this, because it is fated to be, cannot be guided by resolutions, but only awoken by free trust and delivered safely into lasting form.

From every relation every human being gains something fruitful & helpful in the sphere of such freedom. But in every relation there remains the pain – and the joys are but the transitions from one pain to the next.

Believe me, I am & remain one who searches, & am searching for a form of belonging for man from within which not <u>he</u> but a coming God will establish new bonds and dispensations – Such searching sounds presumptuous & yet it is the greatest fore-running [*das Vorläufigste*] & the greatest holding back that is possible for thought today.

In connection with the Hebel talk I'm reading Goethe now & then; & I enclose a couple of sheets for you that say a great deal. – [Goethe's two short poems 'Whatever you think Truth. . .' ('*Was auch als Wahrheit*'); 'One and All' ('*Eins und Alles*')]

I've now read the whole thick vol. of Hebel's Letters & the Treasure Chest closely. I have a lot of material, but it's a slow & difficult business finding the right form.

On Saturday at noon I'm going to Co[nstance]. & I'm coming on Tuesday at 16.40 – Frau Leiner writes that this train is by far the most convenient.

Best wishes to you, D. S., whom I shall not leave, with constant & heartfelt trust, your M.

Best regards to the children. I'll write to you again.

On 3 May Marie died. Elfride and Martin attended the funeral. Afterwards Martin gave the lecture 'The Principle of Reason' in Bremen.

On 19 June he was back in Messkirch to work. Elfride had taken him by car. In his letter to her, he reported on his first attempts to incorporate his fundamental ideas into a larger work: I'm now thinking of working the Principle of R[eason]. & the Principle of Identity 56/57 together with other essential stuff into a single appropriate essay, so that the answer to the question of B[eing]. & T[ime]. becomes clear &

my path – if not reaching its goal – still finds and keeps its direction even so.

And on 22 June he wrote: I've now set up the workshop and got into my work as well. I immediately found the ms on Fichte's Science of Knowledge, which that Novalis fragment I showed you has to do with. There's also quite a lot there that I can use for the question concerning ground, the principle & fundamental proposition of sufficient reason. With Fritz I've now arranged the Nietzsche lectures that have been transcribed. There are 923 typewritten pages. Just one important seminar from S.S. [summer semester] 37 on 'Being & Seeming' ['*Sein und Schein*'] is still to be transcribed. I'm considering whether I shouldn't publish these Nietzsche lectures next, in <u>summarized</u> form, with Niemeyer – and <u>wait a little longer</u> with publication of the most recent lectures.

M. 23. VI. 56

My D. S.

It wouldn't have taken your note, rightly so sad, to make me even sadder. But I thank you – for this too is a help. And I won't write words of which you're distrustful. But I'm nonetheless striving to cope with the demon; perhaps the only word you have for this is 'weakness'. However, here too I understand your judgement – and only ask you, even now, after such a long time to no avail, to give me time.

If my existence is without passion, my voice falls silent & the source does not spring forth. You rightly say: what is this, if so much untruth is involved? I do believe though – without wanting to make excuses – that the question of truth & lies isn't that simple.

But I'm telling you this only to say that I'm thinking about myself – & in spite of everything will remain with what was once established – even though for you and me it's overgrown with much that is painful. And that I'm keeping no more secrets. Thank you for the little picture – from which <u>you</u> are looking at me.

Liesel would like to have one too.

Best wishes to you from my searching heart,

Your Martin

[. . .]

Elfride suffered greatly as Martin continued to get involved with younger women and work with them. Even though she had a good deal of company through Jörg, who lived with his family in the Rötebuck house, she felt spiritually and emotionally isolated. Martin often remained away for several weeks at a time, and to Elfride their estrangement was becoming more and more palpable. She felt jealousy towards any young woman in their circle of acquaintances, lacked anyone in whom she could confide, and revealed her deep distress neither to her friends nor her sons. Instead, she was forever at pains to maintain the outer façade of their marriage, expressing her disappointment in letters which, like this one, she never sent:

28 June 1956

Dear Martin

Thank you for two letters and for the nice cards by Braque. I hope by now you've made a good start with work – yes, you have your work, which is the centre of your entire life, – but then what happens on the sidelines anyway! This is why you cannot understand how – through you – I've been cast out from my centre.

In your first letter there were words from a quite shallow sphere, 'weakness' & 'excuse', oh no – that just won't do. For I <u>know</u> of what you do, of the inspiration you need, & even now I've striven once more to see what makes you happy & her as the one who can give it. But that all this should be bound up not only with '<u>lies</u>' – no, with the most inhuman abuse of my trust, this still fills me with despair. – Please imagine (I've said it before but you've already forgotten) just what it would be like if M. were <u>now</u> – while she seems so bound to you in this great love & in your letters you speak as one heart to another – if she were now to deceive you with another & only your mistrust revealed her deception to you. Where would this leave your love for her? What would you do? How would you bear it? And I'm supposed to be able to endure it – not <u>once</u> – but again & again throughout 4 decades? can any human being do so if he isn't superficial or made of stone? Time & again you say & write that you're bound to me – what is the bond? It isn't love, it isn't trust, you look for 'home' in other women – oh Martin – what is happening to me – this icy loneliness.

But I won't write anything more; you don't like hearing it anyway; there are many letters I've started here, but I haven't posted any. – Have you ever thought about what empty words are – hollow words? What <u>is lacking</u> in such words?

Elfride put this letter, as well as the following undated transcript, with the letters from Martin, and for this reason they are inserted here. The transcript is an extract from the birthday letter that Martin had written to her in 1918 entitled 'In the Thou to God'. Elfride gave the original to the German Literature Archive in Marbach, and in 2004 it was published by the Verlag Karl Alber (Freiburg/Munich) in the Heidegger Jahrbuch I, *the first volume of the Heidegger yearbook:* The state of things [*Zuständlichkeit*] was broken by the primordial [*Ursprünglichkeit*] – not as though a breaking forth of the primordial would have ever been possible <u>within</u> the prevailing state of things. The state of things was bypassed as if it did not exist, & the self was struck with elemental force on a new & originary path. The 'Thou' of your loving soul had struck me.

The experience of <u>being</u> stricken was the beginning of the break-out of my ownmost self. My direct and unmediated belonging to your 'Thou' gave me to myself as a possession.

New, living being & the old state of things initially sought a balance; the dimension of the state of things could not suddenly be pushed aside, given the burden of its own heaviness. Hidden influences of its typic continued to flourish, & only slowly did its shattered remnants fall away. – The fundamental experience of the 'Thou' then became a totality flooding through existence . . . The fundamental experience of living love & real trust has made my being blossom & intensify. It has had a creative effect in the sense that the basic patterns of my inner working, which initially yearned only for a <u>return</u> to the soul's primordiality, have broken out <u>from</u> the primordial origin.

On the back Elfride noted: From a letter from Martin in 1918, the model for all his love letters to his many 'loves'

Messkirch, 30 June 56

My Dearest Soul!
I know this will be a painful day for you; and my letter is filled with pondering on what I've done to you. And I'd like to avoid the grand words you – rightly – fear and simply offer my silent thanks to you for having always lovingly been there, and being there still & helping me merely through this.

A lot of time in our life has gone by and even so I ask you once more, give me time to find the path and regain my inner peace and composure.

And what is indestructible about our love, which has come to fulfilment in our shared life & activity, even though some things have militated against it, will again sustain you & keep you open for the many beautiful things that are still in store for us.

I know my birthday greeting to you can only be the willingness really to win back your trust.

Until yesterday I was in Lindau i.e. Bad Schachen – it was all very overcrowded but one could go unnoticed as well; the most significant lecture was the one by Dirac, who's working in the same direction as Heisenberg; the latter is obviously wholly taken up with organizational matters.

With Gertrud at the spring by the Cabin

The tendency among the younger physicists moves even more radically in the direction of resolving everything into purely functional terms & no longer allowing for anything object-like to exist. In the fundamentals I found unambiguous corroboration of the framework [*Ge-Stell*] everywhere – But this radicalization still cannot be expressed in philosophical terms at all, but only represented in a mathematics that is entirely new & of which I understand nothing.

On 2 & 3 July I'll set aside some time here to be quiet & close to you – to relieve your pain. I hope the parcel arrives on time if there's no delivery on Monday.

If you drive to the meeting with Frau Z[enk]. perhaps you could take the Finks with you. Here after the one fine day – on Saturday – it's dull & muggy again. The hay harvest is only making slow progress.

Keep your free nature – I beg you – & I'll help you & get things straight with myself. Otherwise this will prove a great hindrance to the work as well.

With fondest wishes, I'm still there –
Your Martin

Send my regards to the children & Hedwig.
Fritz & Liesel send their best regards

On 3 July Elfride celebrated her 63rd birthday without Martin, and the following day Friederike, the second daughter of Hedi and Jörg, was born in the Rötebuck house.

Before his return, Martin visited Frau Leiner in Constance, not arriving back in Freiburg until 21 July.

At the end of August, Martin was up at the Cabin without Elfride and was looked after by Liesel Schmid, while Elfride helped Jörg and his family move from the Rötebuck house into a three-room apartment in the Zähringen district of Freiburg.

In September, Elfride and Martin travelled round Provence. Elfride also accompanied Martin to Vienna, where he gave his lecture 'The Principle of Reason' on 27 October.

From 1 November, Martin was back in Messkirch. On 4 November the popular uprising in Hungary demanding democratic freedom was brutally crushed, and on 6 November Martin wrote: The world grows darker – but I myself am striving & can see things ever more clearly & am certain that our inseparability will once again be just as it should. If I should see M[arielene]., I'll write & tell you openly – & then I too shall make headway & resolve everything in a cordial manner.

9. XI. 56

My D. S.
I'm meeting M[arielene]. here over the weekend.

I won't forget you. And I implore you, keep <u>your</u> love for me, which has accompanied me for decades through everything difficult & will receive me into a good, all-vanquishing ending.

I'm thinking of you –
dear Elfride

your Martin

Regards to all

On 12 November Martin wrote: Many thanks indeed for your letter – and even though it's slow progress with me after everything that has gone before, I do now see everything in a different light & from the point of view of responsibility. Not only do I realize your love and absolute loyalty throughout everything most difficult – I feel your closeness, which has not abandoned me even now; & M[arielene]. sees things more calmly & maturely; up to her trip to America in April she'll be helping at her parents' & preparing her lectures, which begin in the summer. The strengthening of her ties with home & with a task that suits her gives her strength & peace of mind. And that M. is ready for a marriage is something she knows herself. This was a serious time, and what for you was a great sacrifice became a means of healing after all.

M. 19 Nov. 56

My D. S.

Many thanks indeed for your kind, magnanimous & helpful Sunday letter, which I was eagerly awaiting. And you understood my little message with the Cézanne card! And the hand that was holding you at that moment <u>will remain with you</u>, will come closer, & will allow you to feel the gratitude of decades.

The more thoroughly I look through the manuscripts here & am able to think through much of it afresh, the more clearly I see that a summary really will require a guiding & gathering intuition – just shoving fragments together won't do the trick, especially since these in themselves always refer to the same thing – even the most remote matters spontaneously evoke one another – ; I've taken on rather too much with examining these earlier, partially untranscribed notes; so I've been out relatively little – ; and I haven't got down to the printed manuscript with Fritz until the evenings. And I'm not used to night work any more. The cold is still lurking in my sinuses. On no account do you need to worry.

From the first lectures on the Pr[inciple]. of R[eason]. we still have to transcribe some passages that were in brackets in the manuscript & were skipped according to Fritz's earlier custom. We've now gone through the whole thing looking at the parts which Fritz had queried & duly corrected them. Now we have to read through the whole lecture sentence by sentence, Fritz with the transcript & me with the text – then the Greek texts still have to be entered.

Neske is delighted we're coming. About being picked up, I still wasn't able to say anything definite. At the end of the work here I'd have liked to go to the Leiners for a couple of days & then from Constance either to Stuttgart or Freiburg. But I don't think I'll be ready by Thursday – as the 'additions' are turning out more difficult than I thought. I've even considered printing the additions as a supplementary vol. <u>later on</u>, but don't know whether this is convenient in publishing terms.

With the state of the world ever more impenetrable, I'd also like to select the most important pieces of all & put them in a <u>special</u> box. I'd like to discuss all this with you. I'd thus be grateful if you could phone the Walters' house (Messkirch tel. 418) on Thursday 22 Nov. between

259

4 & 6 pm; I can keep myself busy there with my printed manuscript while I'm waiting for your call. We'll take full advantage of the holiday on Wednesday for work; then I'll see how far we've got. I think we can afford the expense of the train journey all right, so you don't have that exhausting drive at the weekend. Next year it'd be nicer to take a trip through Upper Swabia & its Baroque parts at a more suitable time of the year. If it isn't too much for Erika we could stay there for three days & reduce our participation in the celebrations to the bare essentials – though there are presumably some quite worthy people to be met there.

The envelope with the Trakl things for Dr Hering is next to the pile on the left on the top shelf of the bookcase by the door; I had the envelope in my hands only the other day.

A very reassuring card – in its handwriting too – came from Buchner in Frbg., where my letter had been sent to him. He asks to be allowed to help with the proof-reading again. I then also have to play through some tapes of the lecture with him, as the spoken version – according to my notes – in places says more than the written.

On Friday afternoon S[ophie]. D[orothee]. dropped in by car on her way to see Ernst Jünger & read me her latest play – real peasant theatre – similar in content to the little novella. It was all very calm & peaceful. S. D. is going to see her sister in Altreute, while Clemens is coming to Stuttgart on 25 Nov on behalf of the Academy. I've only just read the enclosed reports about Hungary, which Jörg sent me by post.

Today I gave Liesel your present for her name day, which she was <u>particularly</u> pleased with; I myself gave her something to read for the winter days: Marie Langewiesche, the Novel of a City[19] – (Venice – where of course they went in spring).

M[arielene]. writes from Bremen to say that she's preparing for the work at the Academy & is very busy owing to the alterations to her parents' house as well.

I'm looking forward to the quiet winter weeks at home – my composure is already there. And however much pain the past months have brought, the experience and the responsibility now remain; & I take & bear everything differently from before.

The Jubilee lecture will be a difficult matter – but I'd like it to be a milestone in my teaching & my path.

With best wishes and grateful love,
Your Martin
[. . .]

[19] Marianne Langewiesche, *Königin der Meere. Roman einer Stadt* (1940).

After going to Stuttgart with Elfride for the Eugen Gottlob Winkler celebrations, Martin returned to Messkirch until the end of November in order, among other things, to prepare his lecture 'The Principle of Identity' for the 500-year jubilee of the Albert Ludwigs University of Freiburg.

1957

On 14 February, granddaughter Almuth was born, the second daughter of Jutta and Hermann.

On 24 February in Todtnauberg, Martin gave the lecture 'The Onto-Theological Constitution of Metaphysics'.

On 24 March, Martin was driven by Hermann to Darmstadt, where he stayed with his old acquaintances the Viettas. On the initiative of Egon and Dory Vietta, he held a seminar there for selected students, with Alfred Guzzoni, Kôichi Tsujimura, Hartmut Buchner and Hildegard Feick taking part.

On 7 April, Martin was driven by Jörg via Hüfingen to Messkirch. Together they visited the grave of Marie and her husband Rudolf, who had died in January, barely a year after Marie.

At the end of May, Martin went to Lindau to meet Clemens von Podewils, Carl Friedrich von Weizsäcker and Martin Buber.

In mid-June, Martin once again visited the Viettas in Darmstadt, this time to prepare his lecture for the 500th anniversary of Freiburg University. He gave the lecture 'The Principle of Identity', which was so important to him, on 27 June.

On 22 September, Martin was driven by Dory Vietta to Aix-en-Provence. They stayed at a small hotel run by the Gaudins, where Elfride had also been with Martin the previous year. Martin sat for a bust by the sculptor and stonemason Louis Chiarelli. The landscape of Provence, and in particular of Mont Sainte-Victoire, so frequently painted by Cézanne, again made a deep impression on Martin.

Jubilee procession at Freiburg University

Aix en Prov., 25 Sept. 57

My Dearest Soul!

When I came back from Chiarelli with Beaufret at lunchtime today, your lovely birthday letter was there. Thank you for everything. You say the simple: the inseparable. And you aren't at all far away now. You're all around here, especially in my room, where we stayed, & where I now work quite undisturbed. Yesterday & today the work with B[eaufret]. really has been very fruitful; he's very pleased; in the summer in Frbg. too he indirectly found a lot of stimulation. He'd brought along his friend, whom we met after Cérisy at his house in Paris the evening before we left & neither of us liked. He's left again for somewhere near Marseille. Frau Vietta was appalled – but otherwise she finds B. very nice & understanding. There's a lovely sobriety about Frau Vietta – which makes her so assured & is pleasant at the same time. She understands more than she shows. Egon's coming today. Frau V. is staying here too & looks after us men – these arrangements would have been impossible with B[eaufret]. as Mad[ame]. is very 'penible' – he's rather overtired & needs to take things more easy. Clearly from all that building – which he's done himself. The whole beautiful front of the house is ruined by the porch; but otherwise the two of them are as delightful as last year & are happy to get the money for the third guest.

I've arranged the work with B. in such a way that we work from 9 am to 1 pm, in fact in Chiarelli's studio – Ch. is particularly keen on this as then the thing doesn't become 'posed'. Frau V. finds his 'heads' very good; he has a new girlfriend, a small black Frenchwoman who teaches Italian here.

The aged parents send their best regards. The father has already prepared le dejeuner, which is fabulous. But Frau V. takes care of the simple things: fruit – cheese – bread – melons – particularly nice ones.

The weather is very summery; overcast for the first time today, as it never was during our stay last year.

But the mistral is blowing. So it'll turn nice again.

Sometime towards evening today we're going to Bibémus [quarry], & I'll be thinking of you especially –

I'm pleased about your pleasure in the children; I'll write to Jörg & Hermann individually some time.

I'm close to you & thinking & reflecting on everything. Take care of yourself.

With all best wishes,

Your w[hite]. Little Blackamoor

B. & Vietta send their best regards.

On 5 October Martin was driven back to Freiburg by Frau Vietta.

On 19 November he was in Messkirch for a few days and wrote:
This morning I did find part of the ms I'm looking for; now there's one important section still missing. If I don't find it I'll have to select something else from what's stored here. All this searching has given me new insight into the materials collected here. For the winter Fritz wants to start on transcribing the major lectures from 1928/29 & 29/30. The Nietzsche lectures & seminars are all ready now too. Fritz is in good working form, unfortunately somewhat hampered now by the death [of Anton Braun] & preparations for the general meeting of the bank. But he'll get the ms for Gebsattel ready in any case.

1958

At the beginning of January, Elfride looked after her granddaughters Ulrike and Almuth so Jutta and Hermann could have a few days' holiday up at the Cabin. In the meantime, Martin was working hard on a Hölderlin lecture.

On 21 January, Martin again travelled to Darmstadt to spend a week there working on a reading of Plato with Hildegard Feick, Dory Vietta and her son Silvio.

Elfride and Martin were in Messkirch to celebrate the 60th birthday of their sister-in-law Liesel on 15 February. Afterwards, Elfride went on to Birkach to help Erika with domestic matters. Martin remained in Messkirch and on 28 February travelled to Munich for discussions at the Bavarian Academy of Fine Arts.

Martin again sat for a bust by the sculptor Hans Wimmer.

On 20 March he gave the lecture 'Hegel and the Greeks' in Aix-en-Provence. Elfride was there with him.

On 21 April Martin once again visited the Viettas in Darmstadt. He was working particularly intensively with Hildegard Feick, who had typed up his manuscript on nihilism.

Elfride found out about a further affair of Martin's, with the neurologist Andrea von Harbou. The two women met on 23 April. Not for the first time, Elfride attempted to fight for her marriage by taking up personal contact with Martin's mistresses and asserting her own position.

[Darmstadt, 28 April 1958]

Your grieving letter has just arrived
Dear Elfride!

I wrote the enclosed letter in pencil [see below] yesterday evening when for a long time I couldn't sleep.

265

Now I'll simply enclose it & tell you everything when I can come again.

Stay there & help me, now that – more knowing and more resolute – I'd like to come out into the open & into responsibility.

Accept this greeting – Elfride.

Your Martin

At Easter last year she quite unexpectedly dropped by in Messkirch

My D. S.

Now I'd like to tell you this as well. On Tuesday a telegr. from Badenweiler was phoned through from Frau Dr Harbou enquiring whether she could speak to me here during the week. How she knew my whereabouts made me wonder. I hadn't written to her for a year – In spring last year she suddenly came to Frbg. – where I then spent some hours together with her & she put me under great pressure. On the day of my Jub[ilee] lecture she waited for me in front of the department as well; but I asked her to stay away. I wrote to her at once from here saying that I was very much immersed in work & that a lot of things had changed with me. [*Inserted with an asterisk at the end of the letter*: Because the woman is a difficult person & her letters passionate [. . .?] I think she's capable of breaking away – at the same time I must accept the fact that however insistent these women are, I was still to blame – Because – even in their own right – there's nothing sustaining or really significant about these encounters.]

The clear recognition of what still remains for me to do, the unpublished texts, the lectures – the real task – has been helping me increasingly for months – to live calmly for work & break free from earlier bonds of the past.

All this will also make me quite free again for you for the important years we may yet have in store.

Darmstadt, 28 April 58

My Dearest Soul!

Oh, I don't deserve all this – your loving, grieving letter comes today before the lecture – And so you're closer to me than I can tell you. I mustn't waste words – but simply thank you every hour for your help and unutterable love, while also recognizing that only the severity of work, the responsibility for it & for the whole path & the abundance it has brought can give me the measure & composure for how I am to be myself.

All these months now I've been on my way there, and it will be a good, purified time for me with you. That you aren't well is a terrible worry to me, but perhaps the children will help you much more than I am capable of doing. But nonetheless I must come to you soon.

I'd just like to bring the work with my two assistants to a certain conclusion. For this I'll need tomorrow, Tuesday, & will return home on Wednesday afternoon with the Roland [train]. It's been a fruitful few days because my path is becoming present to me in quite new ways – but I've also had to converse with myself a great deal. While I had the cold I didn't get the lecture into as tidy a form as I require; I thus had to spend rather more time on it after all. It's remarkable how Frau V[ietta]. makes it easier for me – one might almost say – to keep a distance – and this matter-of-factness of the two women & their harmoniously coordinated work is a gift. And they both themselves regard it in this way too & are constantly grateful to you. – I've just had a look at the hall with Herr Michel; he told me that the publishers no longer want to reprint his father's Hölderlin book, which is out of print in its 3rd edition. I'd like to do something to help. In the old days up at the Cabin you were very fond of that book.

With all best wishes, constantly thinking of you, your w. Bl. – white, but not yet wise – regards to Jutta & sweet Ulrike; Jörg & his family.

Frau Vietta & Frau Feick send you their best regards.

At the end of April, Andrea von Harbou wrote to Elfride to say that she intended to break with Martin.

On 5 June, Martin met up for three days in Würzburg with his Badenweiler doctor, von Gebsattel, whose 75th birthday was being honoured by the University. Martin then went on to Darmstadt to continue working with Dory Vietta and Hildegard Feick, while Elfride took over Erika's household tasks in Birkach.

At the end of July, Martin went to Darmstadt again, passing through Heidelberg on the way.

Darmst. 27. VII. 58

My D. S.

I arrived here safely yesterday evening; the Feicks were very pleased & Frau V[ietta]. seems to be calmer, so I hope we can make a good start on the work tomorrow. Today I'm taking a day off.

The seminar with Gad[amer]. taught me one important thing; the people all think technically; & as Gad. suggested before, there is a regression to neo-Kantianism everywhere. They don't know much about my stuff.

The Academy lecture – if I may say so – was a great success & there's never been such a big audience in the Academy; but the nicest thing was: Richard Benz, who's a member of the Acad., postponed his holiday to be at the lecture. It was very pleasant to meet him again. Achelis [?] was there too, Schadewaldt, among others Ritter too, who said for the first time he'd now understood something. There was no discussion, but afterwards Academy business. The elder Bornkamm was elected new president with 20 votes, Gadamer got 12. After lunch we, i.e. Günther Bornk., first drove Benz home, then we drove out to G. Bornkamm's, where it was quite charming, the children all very pleasant & the wife very nice, rather like Paulus Fabricius's wife. The elder Bornkamms came as well & the Gadamers. The elder B. had made a sudden recovery – but his brother said he still found him very shaky; the doctors weren't able to establish what was wrong with him; they talked of an 'infection' but didn't do anything with drugs.

Everyone asks about you & the boys & their families; they send their best regards. The conversation kept coming back to the Cabin.

I liked G. Bornk. very much; but he's very busy as well; they have more than 700 theology students from all over the place. They – the professors – are still very much occupied with exams & meetings at the moment so in fact it wouldn't have been possible to take advantage of a prolonged stay, which I had considered briefly.

The city, as I wrote before, is hideous.

Out here, by contrast, it's quite silent. One afternoon Herr Feick wants to drive us into the Oden Forest some time. Today I feel quite rested & this evening I'll reread the Academy lecture, a good way of preparing for work tomorrow.

Let's hope the good weather lasts now, so visits to the Cabin are also possible for you. I hope you have a proper sleep too now that pestering spirit Hegel has been placated. But the work was worthwhile; during the lecture I could tell that everything does fit together after all. The Academy was unanimous in asking me to publish it in their minutes as this would be the best introduction to the new direction that the Acad. proposes to take. The elder Bornkamm seems to me to be the right man. Gadamer is to be the Rector next year. Kuhn! has got the chair in Munich, but they say Schulz will be appointed to a second. – But compared to the work which in its essential character now has me wholly in its grip – these are superficial matters.

That you've helped me through these long difficult years into this final stage & that you now completely understand & foster everything necessary – this closeness becomes clearer to me every day –

And I thank you for it every working hour & see in this the pledge that the years to come will be vouchsafed to us in the very way the task requires & in accordance with your nature. And everything will be set straight as well.

With best wishes and many thanks, & thinking with you of the children & the house – of everything you've built.

Fondly your w. little Bl.
Kind regards to Gerta & the children.
The Feicks & Frau V. send their very best regards to you.
They're also off to Sic[ily] in spring.

On 23 August Martin went to Lake Chiem in Bavaria, where he continued to work with Dory Vietta, who had moved there following her separation from her husband. From September, Elfride and Martin spent five weeks together up at the Cabin, and from 17 October Martin was back in Munich for discussions and preparations for his lectures. He wrote from there on 18 October: At 4 pm I went to see Weizsäcker in the M.-Planck Institute – built in a modern style by Sep Ruf – but not yet finished; we had a good conversation until about 7 pm; then in the sleet & storm we walked to an old inn, where we continued talking & had dinner & as he drank his Moselle W. produced a goat rhyme: 'A Bernkastler is good for a Kernbastler'.[20] After the meal, at ½ past 8 we went to see Heisenberg – twenty minutes in the sleet across meadows & fields; Frau Heisenberg was in bed with flu – H. himself was very pleased to see us; & the conversation got off to such a lively start that H. agreed to collaborate with us. Then we got onto Heisenberg's 'world formula', on which he's been working for 10 years; but he hasn't reached his goal yet. Incidentally, in the Institute W. showed me the great computing machine operated by women (physicists) who treat this 'thing' like a living being.

Martin met up with Dory Vietta in Grünwald and was also able to inspect the now completed sculpture by Hans Wimmer.

In this time, Elfride was visiting Hermann and his family in Koblenz, Dorle in Bethel, and school friends in Wiesbaden.

On his return journey, Martin stopped off in Messkirch on 22 October.

Messkirch, 24 Oct. 58

My D. S.
I just want to send you Sunday greetings in joyful anticipation of doing some good work in the quiet house. The weeks at the Cabin still linger on in my work; & I don't want to lose this mood for the 'composition' of the lecture, which is what it all depends on. Because of this I work on the manuscripts here only in the afternoons; there's much more there than I thought; and first I'm going to get a proper overview of it all again.

---

[20] A *Kernbastler* is a nuclear handyman or tinker (Weizsäcker himself, among other things, was a *Kernphysiker* or nuclear physicist). Bernkastler is a German Riesling wine.

Whereas in Munich it was really bad weather, here it's fine & there's an autumn chill.

Fritz has a holiday till Monday; Liesel is rather pale, & suffers from arthritis (feet) – but otherwise they're well. –

Here I often think now of the long path I've trodden & am grateful for the clarity & the simplicity of the abode in which my path has arrived.

Your loyalty & quiet help has never been <u>so</u> clear to me as it is now. And the weeks at the Cabin were a lovely token of this.

And that I've been granted the collaboration of D[ory]. and Frau F[eick]. is both an alleviation and an inspiration which gives me heart to put the essential into words. So let this greeting be a deep thank you.

Your w. little Bl.

Fritz & Liesel send their best regards.

Unless there's a telegram from you, I'll come on Monday afternoon.

1959

On 7 March, Martin returned to Messkirch to sort and edit manuscripts that he still kept stored there. At this time, Elfride went to see
Clothild and her family.

On 5 April, Martin went to Stuttgart-Stammheim to visit the architect Hans Bernhard Scharoun, whom he had met on a visit to Berlin
in January. He then paid a visit to Erika and her family in Birkach. He
was also given the opportunity to read original Hölderlin documents
in the Manuscript Room of the State Library in Stuttgart. As Martin
was also keen to work with the first editions of Hölderlin's work in the
nearby Bebenhausen Archive, on 26 April he returned to Stuttgart to
prepare his lecture 'Hölderlin's Earth and Heaven' for a conference in
Munich in June. When Martin arrived home on 30 April, Elfride had
gone to Wiesbaden with Jörg to see her school friend Hedwig.

After a class reunion in Constance, on 18 June Martin arrived in
Messkirch. The town was proposing to make him an honorary citizen.
On 19 June he wrote: I beg you to forgive me for being so silent; I've
been thinking a lot about myself & my work. I suppose I must simply
accept that no further productive encouragement will now come my
way. It may be enough if I maintain the strength to give some proper
shape to what I have begun –

Messk. 23 June 59

My D. S.

I shall thank you for your letter by thinking everything over & striving for the return of trust. –

Fritz & I work every morning & afternoon on comparing the transcripts; the texts are written in a small hand & abundantly interspersed with Greek quotations – this slows the work down. In between

With brother Fritz

times I go through the accumulated mss; I've already rediscovered quite a few things for the Hölderlin paper.

I've written a very circumspect letter to Berlin to say that I can't come, pointing out both that I don't wish my name to cause any confusion or prove a burden to the Academy and that the chosen topic is perhaps too narrow for the occasion anyway – & the preparation too difficult for me. I've also written to Flensburg to decline & dealt with the rest of the post. I haven't yet written to D[ory]. as I'd like to wait until you have more detailed news from Frau Feick – 'that the operation went well' – but such news <u>after</u> your visit does indeed indicate a more serious business. Thank you for showing D. this kindness. I'll also put things straight with V[ietta]. some time. But this will take time.

I inwardly broke with the University as long ago as 1934 after my resignation from the rectorship – this is nothing to do with hubris. Looking through earlier lectures now, I see how much energy was put into the lessons in purely didactic terms – at the expense of the work on what still concerns me equally essentially.

But there's no longer any use for 'thinking' now; which doesn't exempt one from pursuing it. [. . .]

The holiday weeks up at the Cabin will presumably bring better weather than we have now. Here it's muggy & damp; my cold is slowly going.

Thomas was here on Saturday/Sunday. The Stuttg. Lib[rary]. Soc. is paying a lump sum of 500DM for the talk. I've ordered five

272

tickets to be sent to Freiburg, as well as ones for Erika & Helm & the Leiners.

The business about honorary citizenship is to be discussed tomorrow or Friday; I'd like to keep everything quite simple.

At the moment there's much less traffic than before. The cornfields are looking magnificent.

We go for our daily walk on the pathway. I'd like to establish a more extensive work schedule for Fritz. I'd be interested to know whether we'll get an invitation to the Husserl commemoration.

Constantly thanking & thinking of you, with greetings from what endures,

Your w. little Bl.

Best wishes to the children & grandchildren.

Fritz & Liesel send their best wishes.

Dory Vietta was diagnosed with a brain tumour.

Messkirch, 1 July 1959

My D. S.

From the midst of my work I'd like to wish you many happy returns of the day. My dearest wish is that joy should return to your heart and that everything you have done and created for me and the children out of your love and devotion throughout these years should come together for you in a beautiful picture that casts light into your years to come. I know that a lot depends on me for this to be so.

A lot of reflection and renewed scrutiny of my path tells me that it is work that helps me most and gives me constancy, especially now my character has become calmer.

When I saw the Rembrandt in the gallery, I thought that this should greet you on your birthday.

One of the greatest gifts is perhaps that in autumn I'll be speaking in your homeland from the realm of my homeland. We could possibly spend a few days there and go walking through the Seven Mountains some time, couldn't we?

I haven't heard anything from Berlin yet.

On your birthday I'll go for a pensive walk on the pathway, which has unfortunately become a road in places thanks to the tractors. The joy of the children and grandchildren will be around you in the lovely house, where I'm looking forward to returning home. And then on Sunday we'll all be together to celebrate and listen to great and joyful music, which I particularly miss here. –

Because the older lectures are written in a very small hand & use abbreviations, quite a few misreadings have crept into the transcript.

273

Sixty-sixth birthday with (from left to right) Almuth, Gertrud, Ulrike, Friederike

I often have to break off after just three pages of ms because despite the magnifying glass it's too much of a strain on the eyes. Because there's a lot to do, I've fallen rather behind with the other jobs. Since yesterday we've been exclusively collating texts from morning to evening.

In addition, I've worked through the ms sent by Dr Pöggeler, which is to be the basis for our conversation. P. is arriving at Frbg. on 6 July at 3 pm. Neske is very interested in the work. P. has clearly also been given more detailed information on the early Freiburg years & the initial stages of B[eing]. & T[ime]. by Osk. Becker.

I haven't written to Boss yet; I'm making everything dependent on the course of my work & whether Jutta goes away for a rest. – The cherries have been very good here.

Holding you to my heart, Dearest Soul, and thanking you for your loving presence

Your Martin

My best wishes to the children & grandchildren. – I'm arriving on Sunday 5 July on the noon fast train from Ulm & will wait with my luggage <u>on the platform</u>.

But I'll write again briefly beforehand.

On 14 July, Martin gave his lecture at the Hölderlin Society in Stuttgart. He stayed with Margret Magirus. Dory Vietta died and was

*buried on 15 July. Afterwards Martin again worked in Bebenhausen
and went to Pfullingen to see his publisher, Neske. Meanwhile Hedi
and Jörg's third child, Burghard, was born on 18 July. On 24 July,
Martin was in Freiburg for a few days to prepare for his stay in
Messkirch. Friederike and I went down with whooping cough and had
to be kept away from our newborn brother. Elfride therefore came up
to the Cabin with Jörg and us children.*

Messk. 29 July 59

My D. S.

I arrived here safely; in the Black Forest it was raining. Here it's chillier; but in the attic still rather hot.

This will be a good, reflective period of work; & I live in the confident hope that your sadness will fade away & that good years are yet to come for the two of us.

Death is a great admonition to me. Tomorrow I'm going to Sigmaringen with Fritz – he's looking for theological material in the monastery library at Gorheim.

I think it will be a fitting birthday party.

I hope the children get well quickly now; & that you too have a restful stay at the Cabin with our Jörg until we meet again.

I'm very much looking forward to the days at the Cabin, which will be relaxed & freely affectionate.

With best wishes, my D. S., and grateful love,

Regards to Jörg & the children, as well as to the farmers up there.

Fritz & Liesel send their best regards.

They went on a staff outing to the Säntis [in the Swiss Alps] with the 'bank'.

*In Messkirch Martin worked hard on the proofreading for his book
On the Way to Language [Unterwegs zur Sprache], helped by Guzzoni
and Pöggeler. Preparations were also in progress for the celebration of
his 70th birthday and conferral of the honorary citizenship of
Messkirch. Martin was worried that the ceremony would be expensive
and that particular inns in Messkirch might feel hard done by. At the
same time, he began to edit his Nietzsche manuscript with Fritz. On
the afternoon of 10 August he was visited by the young Catholic theologian Karl Lehmann, who was writing a PhD thesis 'On the Origin
and Meaning of the Question of Being in the Thought of Martin
Heidegger'.*

*On 27 September Martin was made an honorary citizen of Messkirch.
At the ceremony he gave the speech 'A Thank-you to my Home Town*

Honorary citizenship ceremony in Messkirch

of Messkirch', and, as a present to his father, Jörg showed his 'Cabin film' with texts from The Thinker as Poet *[Aus der Erfahrung des Denkens].*

On 17 October, Martin went to see his former students Marly and Walter Biemel in Cologne, while Elfride visited Dorle in Bethel. On 20 October, he met up with a number of Marburg students for a conference in Höchst in the Oden Forest, and on 23 October he was in Darmstadt to work with Hildegard Feick.

On 2 November, Martin went to Zollikon near Zurich to see the Boss family. This was the start of a fruitful collaboration with Médard Boss and young psychiatrists with an interest in philosophy. The 'Zollikon Seminars' would continue until 1969. Martin returned to Freiburg on 7 November, but by 11 November he was back in Messkirch.

Martin's friend Theophil Rees died after a long illness.

Hermann and his family moved to Freiburg.

1960

From January Elfride suffered from a severe depression which confined her to bed. Martin gave her a transcription of Hölderlin's poem
'Encouragement' ['Ermunterung']. In spite of Elfride's illness, he travelled to Heidelberg, where he enjoyed a number of stimulating conversations with Gadamer and others. On 18 January, he wrote: I'm
thinking of you all the time. The sign was meant more <u>for me</u> than for
you as well; I can hear it more & more clearly. Let the joy within you
reawaken.

At the beginning of February, Martin visited Médard Boss, who
gave him advice for Elfride's recovery. She was given sleeping pills and
psychiatric drugs and was looked after by the domestic help Frau
Schuler and her own cousin Gerta. Martin wrote on 1 February: And
now this my love: one of the main remedies is me – in which everything will be all right – and the good years are still ahead of us, when
I hope to succeed in producing the counterpart to B[eing]. & T[ime].

Martin held a seminar and a colloquium in Zollikon, and wrote on
5 February: This evening the theme is: <u>'Consciousness' & 'Dasein'</u>; in
a very close circle the participants are more daring. Tomorrow B[oss].
would like to talk over some questions with me about <u>Indian</u> thought
& its relationship to my own. I haven't got around to my own work,
which I was initially hoping to do; & next week it's the seminar in
Hdlbg.; but it's all an opportunity for clarification again anyway.

On the evening of 7 February, Martin arrived home again. But by
11 February he was off to Heidelberg once more for Gadamer's 60th
birthday. On 12 February he wrote: I'm always thinking how you are;
I know that 'I myself' can & will be the best remedy. I often now have
a sense of returning to our earliest days & with it also the confidence
that I'll succeed yet with what is essential & you yourself will be
involved in everything in your so naturally loving way. I'm already

looking forward to 'coming home', but the work with Frau F[eick]. is necessary; & I again saw in yesterday's seminar how necessary publication of the lecture is.

In mid-March Martin went to Tübingen and then on to Messkirch. On 19 March he replied to a letter from Elfride: That <u>you</u> were able to give me the lovely news about being awarded the Hebel Prize lent a special sheen to my joy. Perhaps in its own way 10 May in the Wiesental really will be a special day. Many thanks for your letter of today; indeed, you've complied with the saying about the 'comrade-in-arms' as lover in quite a different way. I'm becoming ever more clearly and enduringly aware of what my 'works' owe to your closeness and foresight. Such awareness will reawaken trust, and this will be the place of composure for what I still hope to achieve.

Elfride went to stay at Hinterzarten in the southern Black Forest to recover from her depression. On 21 March Martin wrote to her: And I always think now that the Hebel Prize is a thank-you to <u>you</u> for bringing the Cabin into being and our lovely neighbourhood with the farmers of Todtnauberg, some of whom we really ought to invite to the ceremony.

Martin returned from Constance to Freiburg on 1 April, as Elfride was also home again.

On 13 April Martin held an address in Innsbruck to mark the 80th birthday of Ludwig von Ficker. For Elfride he brought home a cowslip from the grave of Georg Trakl.

On 10 May ('Hebel Day') in Hausen, Martin was officially awarded the Johann-Peter-Hebel Prize bestowed by the state of Baden-Württemberg.

On 14 July he returned to Messkirch, while Elfride helped Hermann and family with the household tasks, because Jutta, who was pregnant, had gone down with whooping cough. Martin worked hard collating his Nietzsche lectures with Fritz and sorting out manuscripts, while Fritz also transcribed the Wesselburen lecture on 'Language and Heimat'. Major roadworks were being carried out on Rötebuck, and because of the noise Martin did not return to Freiburg until 2 August.

On 6 October, Jutta gave birth to the twins Detlev and Dietrich.

Martin returned to Messkirch on 18 October. In Freiburg Elfride proof-read the Nietzsche book, which once again provided her with a challenge and made her feel involved in his work.

1961

At the beginning of March Martin once again visited the Boss family in Zollikon and held seminars at the Burghölzli psychiatric clinic.

On 17 May in Kiel he gave the lecture 'Kant's Thesis about Being' ['Kants These über das Sein']. Elfride accompanied him there, reawakening memories of the summer semester of 1914, which she recalled as the happiest and most carefree time of her life, a time of lively social life and many sailing trips. She went and visited the thatched farm in Heikendorf where she had lived with two friends. Afterwards Elfride went on alone to St Peter-Ording for four weeks' rest. In her youth she had enjoyed drawing and painting, and now she rediscovered this talent during the peace and quiet of her holiday. Martin travelled on to Bremen to hold private seminars there.

To the delight of the grandchildren, the swimming pool in the garden of the Rötebuck house was dug out again, and a paddling pool added.

Their niece Elfride and nephew Walter Presting and his wife Herta lived in Jena in East Germany. They were only allowed to leave the country to visit relatives, and Elfride invited them to spend their holidays up at the Cabin.

Messkirch, 4 July 61

My Dearest Soul!
On the morning of your birthday I spent two hours at Benz's, who was still simply delighted that I'd come to his celebration in Pforzheim. He's found a new lease of life; I told him how we'd read his Romanticism book & the other volumes up at the Cabin. Only he has a lot of trouble with his publishers, who haven't paid him for years. So the prize is a help from a practical point of view as well. You were

279

present throughout our entire conversation; I also had the pleasure of seeing Frau B., a splendid old lady, half Italian. She particularly sends her best regards to you. The daughter's husband was a violinist & was killed in the war. The one granddaughter is highly gifted artistically, a very quiet creature; in the ceremony I sat next to her. She lives most of the time in Florence, where she works as a restorer. From B.'s I went to the station. Frau Gadamer had already caught a cold on Saturday (the sinuses) & had to go to bed yesterday. From Karlsruhe on, the train was almost empty in 1st class, I had a compartment to myself & on the journey through the Black Forest could quietly think of you. Our Cabin & its location really are incomparable. Heini was at the station in Imdg. [Immendingen] & brought me here. I'd hardly been here an hour when the Mayor appeared. He's invited us to dinner this evening. A few hours <u>before</u> the Folkloric Evening is the unveiling of the bust of Archbishop Gröber – mounted against the Church. Welte is making the speech.

On 10 or early on 11 July the Mayor is going to the regional council at Frbg. Fritz & Liesel are travelling via Basel on 9 July. I'm now studying a few things in the Zimmern Chronicle[21] & a fairly long treatise on the history of the town. I think I'll come up with something suitable all right, & people are by no means expecting anything merely 'popular' either. Since yesterday evening it's been thundery-muggy here – everyone is just waiting for rain.

Tomorrow & Saturday we're eating in the 'Hofgarten'. Fritz & Liesel send their thanks for the gifts. Of course I must also pop into Heini's parish house some time. The cornfields here are looking magnificent; but the farmers are very worried about hailstorms, which can easily occur here around this time of year.

Do have a rest from bottling the fruit now, so when Hermann's daughters are there the work isn't too much for you. – It's lovely to think of that happy crowd of children. Gadamer said – he was in Berlin for a week – one should go there again & again – it's a badly wounded city – he knew Berl. well from his time at Breslau. He said the people really are at their wits' end & long for an echo from us.

Yesterday evening we heard Jasper's latest lecture on Swiss radio; he spoke about the 'Jew Jesus', the greatest man in Western civilization & the founder of its history. –

I'm so glad you came home feeling so refreshed & more relaxed; the days at the Cabin will be all the nicer for it.

---

[21] The *Zimmerische Chronik* or Zimmern Chronicle is a history book written by Count Froben Christoph von Zimmern in the mid-sixteenth century. The counts of Zimmern had their residence in Messkirch from the fourteenth century until the lineage died out in 1594. See also the letter of 13 December 1915.

Thinking of you a lot, with fondest & grateful best wishes.

Your w. little Bl.

Fritz & Liesel send their best regards. As do the Gadamers. In the next few weeks Frau G. has to go to Sylt with the little girl. [. . .]

On 22 July in Messkirch Martin gave a speech at the town's 700-year jubilee celebrations. Elfride attended as well.

Messkirch, 26 July 61

My Dearest Soul!

It was nice that we were here together for the celebrations. I must thank you once again for your useful hints for the speech. Only through them did it take on a suitable form. People everywhere are very pleased and grateful. And our walk on the pathway is now an eloquent memory for me for all the walks to come.

Fritz is still out of sorts. I have the impression there's something wrong with his health.

Yesterday evening we went to the Rural Evening, the Göggingen lot took the biscuit with their village music & the choral society & stage productions.

The prologue was composed by the 'Black Uncle' – 'Being & Time' was mentioned too, & that without the farmers' blessing it wouldn't have been possible. The whole thing was very pleasant.

The Mayor's always on hand in his usual way. The last two days the weather has been very muggy; today it's fresh again, & work is going correspondingly well. I keep discovering new things in the mss. But first I'd like to finish writing out an improved fair copy of the jubilee speech & also go through the Kant lecture once again. Tomorrow we're going to the Danube Valley with the Mayor. If the weather stays like this, the Baroque trip could prove very nice. Every day now I meet new old acquaintances. There are more here than there initially seemed to be.

I hope you had a nice time with the Reckendorfs.

Thinking of you with much love & best wishes

Your w. little Blackamoor

Best regards to the children, Frau Schuler & the two young people. Fritz & Liesel send their best wishes.

Martin spent the first week of November in Messkirch working with Fritz, while Elfride looked after four grandchildren to enable Jutta and Hermann to sort out the removal to their newly-built house in nearby Attental.

On 18 November, Martin flew to Berlin, where a discussion was taking place in the Academy of the Arts on 20 November.

From 26 November to 1 December, Martin was again at Boss's for a seminar in Zollikon.

Martin spent mid-December in Darmstadt, together with Hildegard Feick editing the final Marburg lecture course from the summer semester of 1928 for publication as a book.

1962

On 29 January, South-West Radio recorded the talk 'Time and Being' ['Zeit und Sein'], which Martin also gave on 30 January in Freiburg as one of the public lectures of the Studium Generale.

The book Being and Time *was published in an English translation.*

With his friend Petzet, Martin went to Bremen, where, on 9 February, he was invited as guest of honour to the 'Schaffermahl', a long-standing annual fraternity meal for ship-owners, captains and merchants. With Senator Helmken he discussed the trip to Greece they were planning to go on together in April. Through the good offices of Petzet, Martin then paid a visit to the poet and art collector Hertha König, who had been a friend of Rilke's, on her estate Gut Böckel in Westphalia.

On 25 February, Martin flew from Frankfurt to Berlin to give a speech at the Max Kommerell memorial service two days later. On 28 February, he attended a discussion at the Academy of the Arts.

On 12 April, Elfride and Martin set out on their first trip to Greece, a present from Elfride to her husband: Martin had long since had a desire to visit the country. They were accompanied on the journey by the Helmkens with their daughter and Ingeborg Schroth. The cruise on M/S Jugoslavija *began in Venice on 15 April and took them to the Greek islands, on to Athens and back via Dubrovnik. On 28 April they reached Venice again. Elfride captured her impressions of the landscape in a number of watercolour paintings.*

In May Martin took advantage of his days in Messkirch to prepare a new edition of Being and Time *with Fritz. On 11 May he wrote:* On the journey here through the Black Forest and Baar I was with you in Greece the whole time. How completely different the country, the sea, the islands are there. This fortnight has been an inexhaustible gift.

*At Whitsun, Elfride went to St Peter-Ording with her grand-
daughter Ulrike, while Martin stayed on for a few days in Freiburg.
On 14 June he returned to Messkirch again.*

My D. S.

Thanks for your card. I'm pleased you're both so well. Here, it's high-
pressure weather, but in between times very muggy. The hay harvest is
under way. On the pathway there are hardly any larks now. So far I've
only seen or heard one. Neske came on Thursday evening at 7 pm. We
had a little snack in the 'Hofgarten' & then joined Fritz. N. didn't
want anything particular – he showed us the cover for the Opuscula
series, beautifully designed by his wife; my technology lecture is to be
the first booklet, then Schulz and Jens; I think it'll be decent. I'm to
read the Hebel poems at the beginning of August, when the studio's
most likely to be free.

Next week it's the physicists' conference in Lindau; on Monday,
Niels Bohr from Copenhagen is talking about 'Nuclear Physics &
Human Knowledge'. Neske is picking Fritz & me up tomorrow
Sunday at around 3 pm – then we're driving to Dornbirn, where
Hämmerle has invited us, staying overnight in the hotel there &
driving to Lindau on Monday morning. Neske has bought three
tickets for Hämmerle & us at Prince Bernadotte's on Mainau. After
lunch Hämmerle's chauffeur will drive us back to Messkirch. This
evening I'm meeting up with the Mayor. The booklets should be ready
in the next week. The final proof-reading for Niemeyer is progressing
well. I hope I can get it finished here. I'll write to you in Frbg. to let
you know if I'm staying on for the music festival & so not coming until
the afternoon of 1 July.

I hope the stormy weather has died down by now, so you have some
warm days to finish.

This Sunday greeting will be late now. But I'll be thinking of you
and our granddaughter. I'll also write to Jörg & Jutta some time.
Unfortunately I don't have Hermann's address.

Much love – and best wishes to you & Ulrike
Your w. Bl.
Fritz & Liesel send their best wishes.

*At Jörg's request, on 18 July Martin gave the lecture 'Traditional
Language and Technological Language' at a training course for trade
school teachers at Comburg near Schwäbisch Hall, and was afterwards
driven to Wiesbaden by Jörg. The Feicks had now moved to Wiesbaden,
and Martin again worked intensively with Hildegard Feick.*

At the end of July, Elfride went to Bethel to visit Dorle. With his friend Beaufret, Martin made a tour of Swabia, taking in Tübingen, Nürtingen, Marbach, Laufen and Maulbronn. They were driven by Jörg.

The Cuban crisis sparked new fears of a nuclear war. On 28 October, Khrushchev declared that the USSR would be dismantling its missile installations in Cuba.

In November, Martin was taken seriously ill with infectious jaundice. He was nursed back to health at home by Elfride.

Hermann had been transferred to Koblenz. For the time being his family stayed on in the house in Attental near Freiburg.

Shortly before Christmas, Jörg and his family moved into their newly-built terraced house, still in Zähringen.

1963

In April and May, Elfride and Martin went on a trip to Sicily with Médard Boss and his wife, gaining a great deal from the experience and returning home rested.

Hermann's family completed their move to Koblenz.

After visiting them in Koblenz, at the end of May Elfride travelled on to St Peter-Ording with Almuth. Martin had to stay in Freiburg as Liesel had been taken ill in Messkirch. Elfride's cousin Gerta thus came to look after him. Elfride returned home from the sea in time for the fruit harvest in the garden.

On 3 July, Elfride celebrated her 70th birthday. As a memento of their trip to Greece the year before, Martin gave her his travel notes, Sojourns [Aufenthalte].

In mid-July, Martin went to Messkirch to prepare for a gramophone recording. On 23 July, he read from Hölderlin in a studio in Tübingen. The record was being released by Neske.

From now on, Martin stayed at the 'Hofgarten' hotel in Messkirch to take some of the strain off Liesel.

From Messkirch Martin also went to see Erika Leiner and relatives in Constance, and he was visited in Messkirch by his friend Beaufret, whom he showed round the local area and took to Beuron Archabbey.

Elfride and Martin spent the autumn up at the Cabin.

In October, Fritz and his family travelled to Rome for the ordination and First Mass of Karl Lehmann. On 11 November, his name day, Martin arrived in Messkirch again. Liesel and Fritz were delighted with their trip to Rome, and Liesel's health was better again. Nonetheless, Martin stayed at the hotel this time too. Looking through his things, he kept on finding manuscripts and notes of which he had no memory, and for this reason he started to compile an index.

One person not in Martin's good books was Günter Grass, who had parodied his style in the novel Dog Years, *which appeared in 1962.*

Messkirch, 20 Nov. 1963

My D. S.

Thanks for your letter and the enclosure. Now it really was a good thing that you went to the doctor, giving you the opportunity to counteract those tiresome complaints.

I wrote to Zurich yesterday. On 1 Nov, when you went to bed with flu, I then forgot about the question Larese had asked in passing of whether I would agree to make such a contribution. Your suggestion (Hebel) is very good. After the Zurich letter I did wonder whether it wasn't necessary & possible to read a <u>purely philosophical</u> text – I thought of Hegel, but that's probably too difficult. In any case, I've postponed the thing till January. On Sunday Neske was here, he came about 12 o'clock and drove back again in the afternoon. The Hebel vol. is out of print. The Hölderlin record isn't ready yet. When asked about Grass, he said that that was the record with several poets & had been recorded years ago. He and his wife were with the 'Gruppe 47'[22] at Saulgau – where Grass was too & Augstein – the relationships seem impenetrable to me. Then he's planning a talk about Marxism with Bloch, Hans Mayer & Lukaz [Lukács], & would I take part? I declined at once. Likewise with the plan for exhibiting various authors' mss next year at Dokumenta III in Kassel – could I put the ms of B[eing]. & T[ime]. at his disposal? I said no. He goes more & more for 'wilfully modern'.

I also said that I don't want any function for my 75th bday. Here I haven't been able to find out anything yet; the Mayor was going to invite me over, but at the moment he has a great deal to do because of negotiations for a by-pass. The traffic in the town is becoming a disaster.

Liesel was very pleased with your present. I gave her a little volume of novellas by Th. Storm. Heini took some photos in Rome, incl. one where Liesel is being greeted by the Archbishop of Frbg. [Hermann Schäufele]; she's quite transfigured. All in all, this Rome trip – she still complains of neuralgia; but her spirits are quite all right again. [. . .]

Today we're going to Heini's, where the plan is to celebrate my name day once again & show photos of the Rome trip.

---

[22] Gruppe 47 was a loose association of authors that came into being in 1947. Founded by Hans Werner Richter and Alfred Andersch, it was also attended regularly or occasionally by such writers as Heinrich Böll, Hans Magnus Enzensberger, Siegfried Lenz, Martin Walser, as well as Günter Grass.

Fritz has had a bad cold in the last few days so he's been unavailable for work. But I'd like to finish the thing off in the next few days. Today he's better, so we still have tomorrow & Friday for work. So I'll come home again for Sunday. I'll return on Saturday 23 Nov with the usual Ulm train from Tuttlingen. If Jörg still has a cold I'll take a taxi. After all, the suitcase isn't as heavy any more. I'll get the mss ready here. They can be transported in spring some time.

The weather's awful & the foehn's blowing. I'm coping well with the food. I drink wine only rarely & in small amounts.

In this constant blustery weather we go for walks in the Hofgarten park, where the paths are nicely done up now that everything's owned by the Council. They just don't know what on earth to do with the castle building. It needs thoroughly renovating inside & out, which costs millions. Instead of an industrial company, I'm going to suggest to the Mayor that they locate a research institute there; this would also ensure the peace & quiet in the Hofgarten, which is much frequented in the afternoons by young mothers with their prams. –

My work is still under way. I'm looking forward to coming home. I hope you soon get the Christmas shopping over & done with. I've written to Lene [Laslowski] & Carvallo.

With fond thoughts & best wishes

Your w. Bl.

Fritz & Liesel send their best wishes. Regards to Fräulein Bork.

1964

While Elfride was taking part in a reunion of school friends in Wiesbaden, on 2 May in Messkirch Martin gave the speech 'On Abraham a Santa Clara' to an audience of 700 at a school reunion for alumni born before 1894. As a 20-year-old theology student, Martin had already presided over the commemoration of the 200th anniversary of Abraham's death and written an essay to mark the unveiling of his statue in nearby Kreenheinstetten in August 1910.

On 8 May, Elfride and Martin flew to Athens on their second trip to Greece, subsequently spending a fortnight on the island of Aegina.

Together with the housemaid, Roswitha Thielen, Elfride spent the end of May looking after her grandchildren in Koblenz, while Hermann and Jutta in turn went on a voyage to Greece.

In Messkirch again, Martin worked on his notes from Aegina and prepared the Zollikon seminar.

Theodor Adorno's pamphlet against Heidegger, The Jargon of Authenticity, *was published, and Martin suspected that there were links between Adorno and Grass.*

Messkirch, 14 June 64

My D. S.

Thanks for your nice letter, which came a few hours after I'd posted mine. I'm pleased things continue to go well with the children. But in the last few days I imagine the heat has been even more oppressive there. If Jörg calls in on Dorle, you really should consider whether you can still make that difficult journey. Yesterday it was so oppressive here that I also had to stop work in the attic.

It's good that Herm[ann]. & J[utta].'s trip is going so smoothly & well. The noise here is less now – but the previous days it was bad because there were manoeuvres & from 7 o'clock in the morning until around noon there were helicopters constantly circling low over the little town. Sethe hasn't approached me again recently. I'm enclosing for you a report by the same writer on Grass's stay in the USA. No explanation is required.

It now seems clear who is behind the nastiness of the 'Dog Years'. I'd better get the presents for Pö[ggeler]. & Bu[chner]. in Frbg.

And now another dreadful thing. During the night from Friday to Saturday at about 12 o'clock between Immendingen & Möhringen, Gretl (& Konrad) Kempf's son Jörg, who studies in Freiburg & was cycling home, was hit by a coach & sent flying 20m through the air. He broke his neck & was dead immediately. The body hasn't been released yet; he was 22. The funeral isn't until Tuesday, so I won't be able to be there. I'm going to have a wreath sent. Now there's just a daughter left, who at the moment goes to grammar school in Sigmaringen. –

I've written to Pö. & Buchner & asked B. to pick me up in Bonn on 17 June at 18.17. On Friday afternoon I'll then come to Koblenz.

There's not been any more post from Frbg.

With best wishes

Your w. Bl.

Best wishes to the children, & also to Fräulein Rosw[itha]. [. . .]

On 15 June Martin returned to Freiburg and on 17 June he went to see Buchner and Pöggeler in Bonn. Here he visited the Hegel Archive and then met up with Elfride in Koblenz.

In July, Martin again stayed in Zollikon for the seminar with Boss. Franz and Dino Larese of the Erker publishing house in St Gall had invited Martin to nearby Amriswil. On 3 October in St Gall, Martin gave the lecture 'Comments on Art – Sculpture – Space' ['Bemerkungen zur Kunst – Plastik – Raum'] at the inauguration of a sculpture exhibition by Bernhard Heiliger.

Amriswil, 4 Oct. 64

My D. S.

The lecture evening at 8 pm in the church went well. Above all there were a lot of young people in the audience. The ambassador from Bern & his attaché put in an appearance on behalf of Bonn. Boss arrived just before the start; so did Sepp Ruf, who had been visiting the unwell G. Schmid in Basel; Neske came from Zurich; in addition roughly 15 students of Staiger's & young theologians.

Yesterday afternoon was the opening of the exhibition by the Berlin members of the Academy. Heiliger, the most distinguished of them, modelled me in clay in two hours in the morning at the request of the Lareses; he made heads of Heuss, Reuter & Chairman Martin; it was astonishing how he worked in such a short time; today I have to sit for him again. The Hämmerles & Neskes are enthusiastic about the head; the Lareses want to give a reproduction to Constance University for its inauguration.

Sepp Ruf & others asked me to say a few words about art after the opening speech by the gallery director; I'll bring the text with me; they wanted to tape it, but this I declined; however, the Zurich studio has recorded the Hebel speech. Yesterday morning I had a talk with Boss about the seminar which is to take place in the week starting 15 Nov. Boss had to return at midday, because he had to attend a legal hearing regarding his land. Frau Tugendhat was also at the lecture; I could only talk briefly to her during the evening; but longer yesterday with K. Victorius before the opening of the exhibition. Her son [Ernst Tugendhat] has been offered a visiting professorship in the USA from January to May & will finish off his habilitation after his return.

From Constance only a Frau Dr Wagl was there, the owner of the Südkurier's publishing house; the Leiners are said to be away.

In the evening there was a reception in Hagenwil Castle in honour of the artists, but I soon returned here in Frau Tugendhat's car.

A very stressed Hämmerle came zooming over here yesterday from Salzburg. This afternoon we're driving to Dornbirn – which is just an hour's drive away.

Tomorrow we're then supposed to be off up to the mountain house, where the Neskes are coming too; he has to go to Zurich again first.

I'm coming home again on Wednesday via Lindau-Basel. I don't fit in with this modern art business – although the people are very approachable; there were also Italian & French artists there who 'read' my stuff.

Larese also showed me the grounds, for which they have all sorts of plans. But he didn't come back to the Heidegger-question [?] again. It's a mixed business with these two brothers – on the one hand very interested & solicitous & at the same time vigorously business-minded.

I'm looking forward to coming home. Heiliger & Sepp Ruf told me there have been very fierce clashes in the Academy about Grass. Jens is said to have come out very firmly & fully against him. Since Buttlar's departure they also say the connections between the individual departments have disintegrated.

I told them I wouldn't be going any more.

The weather here is indifferent; a lot of mist from the lake; hardly an hour of sun.

291

It would be nice if we could go up to the Cabin once again. But you shall decide yourself, depending on how things are going with Fräulein Gertrud.

I'm constantly thinking of you & of my return. With best wishes & fond thoughts,

your w. Bl.

Regards to Jörg & his family too & to Fräulein Gertrud.

[. . .]

Boss continued to provide Martin and Elfride with sleeping pills and sedatives. Both of them were increasingly noticing the infirmities of old age. In spite of their helpers, work in the big house and garden became a burden to Elfride. Fräulein Gertrud was one of their domestic helps.

Elfride spent the autumn holidays with Jörg and the grandchildren up at the Cabin. Martin stayed behind in Freiburg and at the beginning of November again went to Zollikon for a seminar and then on to Messkirch.

Elfride took advantage of a visit from Hermann to go up to the Cabin once more before the snow came.

1965

At the invitation of Karl Vötterle, the founder of the Bärenreiter publishing house, Martin travelled to Kassel for a meeting of the Brothers Grimm Society at the beginning of January. In mid-January he visited the Boss family in Zollikon, where Boss and he worked on the problem of time-consciousness with the aid of psychiatric literature.

On 20 January he wrote about the seminar in Zollikon: I'm constantly learning something new & the people are very keen & grateful & can see more & more clearly how much they are caught up in the web of scientific thinking.

In Freiburg Elfride looked after the 4-year-old twins Detlev and Dietrich, while Martin once again visited Boss and on 10 March reported: It isn't possible to hold the seminars in Burghölzle because then all the assistants want to take part & can't very well be turned away, though B. doesn't want to have them there. Other places are already booked up for months to come. So that just leaves the possibility of here in the house. [. . .] B. is bent on keeping me here until midday on Monday, partly because of the sem. report, but above all because one week in April he's due to speak in East Berlin about the relationship of Daseinsanalysis to the positivism of the psychiatry over there.

Martin had advised Boss to accept the invitation to East Berlin.

The planned trip to Greece failed to materialize. At the end of March, Martin went to Messkirch without Elfride, who had gone down with flu. He stayed at the 'Hofgarten' and worked on his manuscripts.

While Elfride visited Hermann's family in Koblenz, Martin again went to stay with Boss in Zollikon. On 6 July he wrote: I've spoken to him about your memory; he says there isn't a lot one can do about it. But he'll look into it.

At a ceremony in honour of the Swiss psychiatrist Ludwig Binswanger in Amriswil on 30 October, Martin gave the lecture 'The End of Thinking in the Form of Philosophy' ['Das Ende des Denkens in der Gestalt der Philosophie']. Afterwards he rested in Messkirch and worked with Fritz. Elfride went to Meckenheim, where Hermann and family had moved.

Zollikon, 27 Nov. 65

My D. S.

Thanks for your letter. The second seminar also went well; I gave a 'Collegium logicum' course on the formation of concepts, for which people were extremely grateful. They now only know & pursue their science as a technology and yet are hungry for real horizons. This purely technological-practical attitude is said to be even more exclusive in the really young students. Then I read from the Amriswil speech. B. himself is very eager to learn 'thinking', but is often over-hasty in applying it, thus exposing himself to the criticism that he merely mixes Heideggerian philosophy into psychiatry – the philosophical aspect and his rich medical experience have not yet been brought into balance. He said very interesting things about Argentina, some of which I can tell you when I see you. I'll write to Jutta & Brock some time today. I'm sending Jutta a Cézanne card which is meant for you, for I haven't made it into town all this time. We just go for daily walks in the woods above Zollikon. What with the foehn & the rain all the snow has been obliterated again. [. . .]

Poor old Brock – I'll probably have to visit him some time before Christmas.

B[oss]. is going to give me something for your signs of old age, which are quite natural; they don't get rid of the defects, but halt the process. On no account is the Dor. [a sleeping pill] to blame.

As planned, I'll be arriving on Monday at 15.31 on the Rheingold [express train]. I don't need to change at Basel & in Frbg. the train stops on platform I, so it's just a short way to the telephone. In the next few days the intention is to talk through the book B. is planning (Outline of Medicine) & the report for the current seminar.

I'm very much looking forward to coming home, with best wishes and fond thoughts,

Your w. Bl.

The Bs send their best regards. They're going to the Lenzerheide from mid-Dec to mid-January, as their help is in Italy then.

1966

At the end of February Martin again went to stay with Boss in Zollikon. Martin and Elfride were planning another trip to Greece together. On 3 March, Martin wrote: You shouldn't skimp with the Dor; [B. says] these doses are <u>far below</u> the limits of what is addictive or harmful; there's no question of it making you stupid; on the contrary, it's during sleep that the brain cells regenerate.

We go for a walk every day, & I can just do with the coat. The Tuesday seminar went very well; and I hope it'll turn out well today too.

So I'll be coming on Sunday afternoon. The next few days we're discussing the reports for the two seminars & the book B. is planning.

In April, Elfride and Martin, together with Boss and his wife, went on their third trip to Greece, which included a cruise of Asia Minor.

On 6 July Martin wrote from Zollikon: In the afternoon we laid down our work schedule at once. He [Boss] is still awkward in his thinking about the fundamental questions, but I do think I'm making some progress with him. Next week he's going to the Lenzerheide on his own for a quarter of a year.

Martin returned to Messkirch, and on 21 July wrote: This reminder of Greece is to send you best Sunday greetings. My mind – even while I'm working – is often there. The text for Japan isn't too easy, because I'd like to avoid saying anything <u>about</u> Zen as I'm not properly acquainted with the sources; on the other hand, my text is meant to intimate a sort of possible dialogue. I often think that such endeavours are bound to be of no avail, at least in their immediate effects, owing to the technological revolution in the Far East.

On 30 July Martin made a speech at the village festival in Todtnauberg.

On 30 August he was picked up in Freiburg by François Fédier and François Vezin. The three of them drove through Burgundy, joined by

Le Thor

Jean Beaufret in Lyons, to the first seminar at Le Thor in Provence. Here Martin met the poet René Char, with whom a close friendship was to develop.

Le Thor, 5 Sept. 66

My D. S.

I've finally found time to write. The journey here from Malaucène was especially beautiful, because passing through the mountainous country the light and landscape of Provence gradually opened up more & more clearly. On our arrival at the hotel, which is very nice and clean, the young poet Fourcade and a young, highly gifted Italian from Rome were waiting on the patio – with a bottle of champagne to welcome us. After a little while we drove to see R. Char, who lives outside L'Isle sur Sorgue – in the country, at 'Les Busclats' i.e. in the bushes – he approached me & my companions so amicably, & at once the right spiritual atmosphere was created, as indeed only those French know how; he was very pleased with the presents – he asked after you and immediately announced that he'd be giving me herbs from his enchanting garden to take to you as well as the cooking essences.

He lives in a simple country house with lovely old things; he must be very rich. He has very painful problems with his spinal cord from the war, & the struggle against the nearby missile base has taken it out of him a lot, especially as it will all be in vain. Towards evening we drove back to the hotel, where Fédier very kindly always thinks of everything for me – ; altogether, these young people, with whom I always read Heraclitus in the mornings – with Monsieur taking part in his own intense way – it's an elite.

At table much eating is done & just as much talking about la cuisine; but I keep a low profile; I have a lovely room facing south. The next day – in the afternoon R. C. came & we visited an old castle nearby, then we drove to an estate run by Frau Mathieu with her three sons, the husband is dead. You'd enjoy meeting this woman; she has a simple country house in Lagnes as well, where R. Ch. has spent a whole summer working; she's invited me too; Fédier is going to take a photo of her.

In the evening she came with us in her working dress to the hotel, where we had dinner together with Char. On Sunday afternoon beneath a great plane tree in R. Char's garden Fédier read his translation of my Hölderlin lecture on 'Greece' – R. Ch. was very moved, & there was a good conversation about the technological world of today & saving the countryside. He's full of despair. One of the finest things was the walk along the Sorgue, towards its source – deep, calmly flowing, clear water which feeds the whole area through small channels & makes it marvellously productive; twenty km further in the direction of Avignon all that's left of it is a little rivulet; as R. Ch. said, it has a marvellous but short life. Yesterday the weather suddenly turned dull & now there's a glorious sky again like every day – & cool at night – ; some time we want to go up Mont Ventou & also to Aix.

I think of you a lot & hope your trip goes as well as you desire it to.

Although the Greeks were here very early on, the absent gods are missing, & so the stay is <u>different</u> from in Greece.

But the intensity of the questioning & thinking, the sense of poetry of the young people are astonishing & give me great pleasure; perhaps some recreation is lacking, but this will sort itself out at some stage.

The days pass by quickly, & I have in mind to be back home with you on 15 Sept.

In the hotel they also have the bowls for playing boules – though we haven't found time for this as yet.

As Beaufret says, the food no longer has the specific character of the landscape – by agreement of the hoteliers there are internationally uniform regulations – but there are melons & grapes in abundance & the plain table wine.

With best wishes, thinking of you with much love –
I often recall the voyage among the Aegean islands.
                              Your w. Bl.

On 23 September Martin gave an interview for Der Spiegel *with Rudolf Augstein and Georg Wolff. This was not to be published until after his death.*

                              Messkirch, 19 Oct. 66
My D. S.
Now I am pleased you can go to Badenweiler for a few days & along with the bathing also have the chance for a rest. [. . .]

In the afternoon it rained as well; otherwise the weather's foggy all the time. I've written to Silvio [Vietta] to say that I'm returning in the evening on 27 Oct; I won't be ready any earlier. Frau Feick asks whether she can take part in the seminar, which of course I'm happy to allow. But I don't know if she'll then be returning the same day.

The shirts were there on Monday morning; they fit well. Thanks for your parcel. My cough is slowly going away.

Fritz is still bad-tempered; I have the impression he doesn't feel well; at times he's quite pale.

The transcript of the Sp[iegel]. text will soon be ready; I'll bring it with me.

I'm now busy with Heraclitus & everything connected with this. I've given Fritz Jörg's number.

In the hotel it's very quiet & warm.

It was a pity we couldn't go walking because of the Sp[iegel]. business.

Today Aler is coming from Sigmaringen at 11.21 & he's going back to Tübingen just after 2 pm so as to return to Amsterdam from Stuttgart tonight.

Have a good rest & give my regards to Gertrud too.

Much love & best wishes to you,
                              Your w. Bl.
[. . .]

Jan Aler was an art historian who had studied under Martin in the 1930s. On 20 October Martin reported: Aler's visit was very nice; he wanted to see everything that I talked about in the 'Pathway'; we walked as far as the wood & then ate in the Hofgarten; at 14.20 he returned to Tübingen i.e. Stuttgart; he's invited us to the seaside in Holland next summer in the 2nd half of June; I am to give a colloquium there to a small private group.

On 5 November Hedi and Jörg's fourth child, Imke, was born.

Martin wrote from Zollikon on 11 November: B[oss]'s work contains 500 typed pages – in its rough draft – yesterday I immediately discovered some fundamental methodological discrepancies – it'll take some work.

I have the Dorid. for both of us. Yesterday evening we watched all that election to-do from Bonn on German television; Kiesinger extremely unpleasant; Brandt & Mende very tight-lipped & annoyed; Schröder no less so. Let's hope the SPD & FDP stick together so the conservatives don't make any headway.

Strauss wangled the electoral procedure. He appeared too; nasty –

The seminar on 'Heraclitus' given by Eugen Fink and Martin in the 1966/67 winter semester was published the following year by Klostermann.

1967

Carl Friedrich von Weizsäcker, who was now Professor of Philosophy at Hamburg, invited Martin to seminars there.

Hamburg, 26. I. 67

My D. S.

This morning your nice letter came. I hope you haven't taken on too much since then.

The seminars are going very well; in addition I have private conversations with W[eizsäcker]. as well. He sees the uncanny, but as always with him – it's a case of both/and – he says one can 'help' things within the technological world & using its means – e.g. famine in the world, the population explosion. But this of course isn't decisive. You see, he also has a private edifice: his faith. He admits that when the unity of physics is attained intellectually & scientifically, it will be necessary to integrate it into a world that is not merely technological. But he still doesn't see the fatefulness [*das Geschickhafte*] of destroying the humanity of man by biophysics.

Some of the younger people are philosophically more advanced and more astute than their boss.

Wagner's [?] efforts are to be highly respected as 'commitment' – but one wonders whether this helps now or leads anywhere at all?

Yesterday evening there were some nice colleagues there; including a Swabian, the professor of English here, who is very fond of Hebel. Then I read from the poems & from the Treasure Chest. Frau W[eizsäcker]. is a doctor of history; some of the younger guests are regulars who also help out in the household.

Tomorrow I'm on my own with the young people in the morning & then leave again from Dammtor S[tation]. I've written to Gadamer.

Family celebration of the golden wedding anniversary

So I'll be coming home again on Saturday evening.

The seminars always last from 10am to 1pm – but I have a long rest in the afternoons, so I hold out well. Afterwards at 6pm I'm taken to [Hermann] Noack's, whose son brings me back here again at around 10pm. The weather is awful & it's almost always semi-dark. The Ws send their regards. He's still busy with a variety of things. Regards to Jörg & Hermann too.

I'm looking forward to coming home. A lot has become clear to me through the conversations.

Much love to you, your w. Bl.

On 18 March, Elfride and Martin celebrated their golden wedding anniversary among friends and relatives in Freiburg.

Martin flew to Athens without Elfride and on 4 April gave the lecture 'The Origin of Art and the Destination of Thinking' ['Die Herkunft der Kunst und die Bestimmung des Denkens'].

Athens, 4/5 April 1967

My D. S.

The journey went very well; up in the Black Forest it was snowing; Fritz came to Sigmaringen, very cheerful. In Messkirch they thought our golden wedding anniversary wasn't till May. So I put him right. The weather during the journey to Munich very windy & rainy; in Ulm the fast train was waiting – the trains were overcrowded. When

301

I got off, I met Prof. Matern (architecture at the Techn. Univ. of Berlin). He suggested taking the taxi to the airport (8 mks) – the bus he said was unpleasant. At the airport we met the Scharouns; everything went smoothly. As we were boarding the plane Neske turned up – notified by Sepp Ruf. Despite the bad weather the flight was nice – far better than with the Caravelle. 10,000m altitude – through gaps in the clouds parts of the Adriatic could be seen from time to time, the island of Kérkyra – smooth landing – but cold & overcast.

A lot of acquaintances from the Acad. – the hotel as per usual – I was cold in the night – but the next day the sun was out. Very solemn in the Academy – full up with all the Academy members; Gadamer's friend, Theodorakopoulos, chaired the meeting – he did a PhD under Rickert in Heidelberg in 1927. The lecture went down well. Afterwards personal introduction to all the Academy members of Athens. As we were leaving the Academy – a massive popular gathering by the Communists in front of the University against the new government. The King seems to be tottering.

Afterwards with Sepp Ruf & Scharoun in a simple fish tavern with a fabulous fish dish & retsina & fruit – Sepp Ruf & Linde show great concern for me, as do Dr Löffler & the secretary Fräulein Lübold in the hotel – nicely located by the sea, opposite Aegina, somewhat further away than our hotel back then. Then sleep & in the evening reception at the ambassador's – a lot of people – Cunze was there too – it gave me a shock to see how he looked – he must be very ill – he's returning to Germany in June. He sends his best regards to you; (as do the Scharouns – he drinks & smokes an awful lot)

We're not flying back until Sunday morning, as no Lufthansa fly in the afternoon; just <u>2</u> hours; I don't yet know the time – but perhaps it'll be in time for the afternoon train to Frbg. Otherwise I'll stay overnight in Munich with Matern, who knows about it; Sepp Ruf came here by car & Linde is flying to Constantinople. At midday today government reception & lunch; in the evening lecture by Linde; I'm very well; & I constantly think of our coming journey. There's supposed to be a postal strike here, so this letter will perhaps reach you later. But you are constantly close by. Tomorrow morning Acropolis & museum. Have a nice rest. I'm taking good care with the food & drink. The city is dreadful.

Much love to you & best wishes; regards to Jörg & family & to Hermann if you ring.

Your w. Bl.

An awful lot of people want to talk to me. The lecture is to be published as one of the Academy treatises in German & Greek. I'm visiting Cunze on Friday or Saturday.

On 16 April Martin was in Zollikon, where he wrote Elfride a letter expressing his pleasure at the prospect of their trip to Greece together: I've been thinking ahead to our trip to the islands all the time, & I'll be glad once I've got the seminar week over & done with. Mind you, B. has described three young people to me who he says are very gifted & want to get away from exclusively scientif. thinking. But on the whole there really is no direct way of coping with these forces.

On 19 April he reported: The seminar went well; there were & still are some very gifted younger people taking part, with whom I immediately found it easy to get into conversation. They have stopped providing us with wine, which also benefits concentration. The simplest things are concealed from people by 'science', but the participants are not only ready & willing, but full of enthusiasm. I keep learning new things too. Tomorrow we'll continue with our discussion of the difference between causality & motivation & lead onto the question about freedom – a difficult matter given the determinism prevalent in the sciences. B[oss]. is still <u>lagging</u> a long way behind with his work in some parts – often the simplest things are still foreign to him – in general a lack of 'culture' – which of course is on the wane now everywhere. *He continued:* A[denauer]'s death evidently couldn't be dragged out any longer. No one here sees what he's to blame for as regards 'reunification'. People are so completely numbed by Western i.e. American 'thinking' that no discussion of the world situation is possible.

From 13 to 21 May, Elfride and Martin went on a cruise in the Aegean with Luise Michaelsen, who had been living in Athens for five years. After Elfride's birthday, Martin returned to Zollikon on 4 July to hold seminars and help Boss with his book. Elfride, who had brought Martin to the station, had a nasty fall on the platform, making walking and going upstairs increasingly difficult for her in future.

In September, Martin went to Lenzerheide for a week with Boss. At the end of the month he met up with Jean Beaufret in Messkirch. The two of them went on an excursion to the island of Reichenau.

While Elfride spent the end of October recovering in Badenweiler, Martin was in Messkirch, working with Fritz.

In mid-December, Martin again went to Hamburg for seminars there. On 13 December he wrote: He [Weizsäcker] has to go from one meeting to the next because (& this is confidential) the Max-Planck-Society is founding a new institute for planning the future on a scientific basis, of which W. will be the director. The institute will be in Heidelberg & is to be opened next summer. W. wants to work there with Picht, is giving up his chair here; he's taking some of his assistants with him – a big change, which appeals a lot to him; & international staff are to be involved – something that has been demanded for some time now by 'Atomzeitalter' [Atomic Age], a periodical W. also regards very highly. The whole thing is to have a philosophical foundation & not be a merely technical matter.

1968

In March Martin went to Lenzerheide with Médard Boss and his wife. His health was not particularly good, and he no longer went skiing either. He thus took advantage of the time to work with Boss on his book.

Following this stay in Lenzerheide, Martin and Elfride went to Badenweiler to recuperate.

By this time, the student revolt had also reached Freiburg.

Messkirch, Easter Sunday 1968

My D. S.

Now I hope my letter did arrive on Saturday after all; I posted it here on Thursday afternoon. With spring so hesitant in coming I will get to our garden in time to see the trees in blossom after all. Here there's still a raw east wind with clear skies. And I go for my walk in the Hofgarten, where I've now also discovered a squirrel in the area near the wall. In addition, wild pigeons can be heard, which I see from my bed in the morning as they sweep past. Otherwise nothing is moving yet – the pathway has become a proper road with cars now. Visits to Göggingen and Constance are unwelcome as both places are in the grip of illness. So I use the time to work with Fritz, who had a cold – through not dressing warmly enough – but is all right again now.

That the young people turn up to see me perhaps has something to do with the fact that their 'chief ideologue' Marcuse was a student of mine. I'll hear what they put forward of course. The start of the semester will certainly be a lot of 'fun'. The whole situation is impenetrable. M. Müller, who before my arrival passed through here on his way to Breitnau, told Fritz that he's already been warned of disruptions to his lectures; he's passing through on his return journey on 18 April. Trautel has given away the coat; I presumably won't be needing it.

On Good Friday at 3 pm the Mayor drove us to the cemetery. At my parents' grave, which is – still – without a stone, places for us & Fritz & Liesel are assured. We've left the arrangement open for now. The gravestones have to be a specified height (I'll enquire about the measurements some time). I wonder if we shouldn't ask Rickert or Kock for a design. – The Mayor wants to build a full grammar school here – on the 'pathway' – opposite the trade school (4 million). In November next year it's the elections for Mayor for a further 12 years.

I thought the Keats volume might make you happy – people who know about these things always claim that English lyric poetry is of a high standard. With K. there are genuine connections with Greece.

'Monsieur' [Beaufret] is up at his castle in order to supervise repair work. The festschrift is to come out at the end of May & a celebratory meal for a few close friends to take place in Paris in June. Fédier would like to pick us up for it. The journey to Provence is to begin on 23 August & the return to finish on 5 Sept, the day lessons restart. If you can't go up to the Cabin now, we could wait until a convenient time in June for a stay there, couldn't we?

The noise from the building work will possibly start opposite us within the next few months. Over Easter I was the only guest in the hotel. I wonder if it's still quiet in Meckenheim. I'll ring tomorrow over midday some time.

Liesel's sister is laid up in bed & will presumably have to go to hospital again. One of our cousins in an old people's home will be 90 at the end of the month. The Mayor hasn't mentioned anything about my birthday. – I'm using the remaining days for working with Fritz. I can tell that the inactivity in Badenweiler, which just came about naturally, was very beneficial to me.

I'm coming home on Friday with the usual evening fast train. Until then, best wishes to you and much love. Your w. Bl.

Best wishes to Jörg & Hermann's family & Erika.

Fritz & Liesel send their regards. Liesel is in noticeably better shape & in cheerful spirits.

On 24 April Jutta and Hermann had their fifth child, Arnulf. Dorle, Hedi and Jörg's fifth child, was born on 15 May.

Elfride continued to have severe pains in her knees, and, as swimming was particularly good for her, she and Martin had a heater for the swimming pool installed. Martin went to visit the Bosses in Zollikon and on 12 May wrote: It's good that the heating for the pool was finished so quickly & you can go swimming. B. wonders whether you shouldn't get them to give you a jab again after this break. Let's hope Frau Maier is fit to work again. Yesterday morning at B's request I <u>didn't</u> go to his lecture in the Burghölzli after all. On Friday we'd gone over the lecture once again. At my suggestion B. changed quite a lot & gave it a simpler form. He was typing half the night. The text will go in his book. The publisher's very impatient to go to press now. I must restrict myself to corrections of <u>content</u>. Questions of <u>language</u> are to be dealt with by a talented assistant from Germany.

Frau Maier helped Elfride with the housework over many years.

On 3 July Elfride celebrated her 75th birthday and was given the text 'On the Islands of the Aegean' by Martin.

With the invasion of Czechoslovakia by Warsaw Pact troops, the 'Prague Spring' came to a close.

At the end of August, Martin was driven to Le Thor by François Fédier and François Vezin, while Elfride remained up at the Cabin.

Le Thor, Sunday 1 Sept. 1968

My D. S.

Your nice letter from the Cabin came yesterday. I'm pleased you've been having at least some restful and half-sunny days.

There'll be no stopping the disfigurement of the village.

Here in France I was soon struck by the increased traffic – but how largely unpopulated & beautiful the countryside is. Admittedly it was all on display in dull rainy weather. As we left St Lattier on Thursday at 2 pm it was pouring with rain, & the clouds were low. It became appreciably darker; we decided to take the motorway from Valence, which goes as far as Montélimar (150km). We drove into a heavy thunderstorm, which then gradually faded away near Orange; we then turned off the main road (in the direction of Mont Ventoux). It became brighter & brighter, & when we arrived at Le Thor after 5 pm the sun was shining from a sky with just a few clouds. After an hour's rest we drove to see R. Char, who was very pleased to see us again & sends his very best regards to you. An hour later J. Beaufret came – he was presented with the festschrift. He was very surprised & delighted. In the hotel I have the same room as before. On the journey here we saw the cars from Paris streaming back on the main road – queues kilometres long in the 2nd & 3rd lanes all moving very slowly.

The first seminar was on Friday afternoon from 5–7 pm; there are 12 participants; & how highly stimulating I always find everyone's bearing & behaviour – as you know too, exceptionally alert & charming & genuinely reverential on account of the matter at hand.

It's touching how Fédier & Vezin look after me.

On Saturday morning Roger Munier from Paris was here, who asks me especially to convey his respects to you. He still recalls every little detail of his visit to the Cabin & your hospitality – he even remembers 'Fips'. He has to return to P. tonight. The second seminar was from 10 – ½ past 12; in the afternoon with Munier, J. B., Féd. & V. at R. Ch.'s again. Frau Mathieu was there; she is thin & rather careworn – the farm is going badly – she'd just brought some fresh figs for R. Ch. – a delicious fruit – ; we then drove her to her estate, where there was another delicious wine & an invitation for the coming week; all in all, eating takes up a lot of time for the French – but I go to bed at 10 in the evening – On Friday morning it was blue sky – since then – after a brief period of mistral – it's been the nicest weather. Today there was a seminar again from 10 – 1 pm – as time is always required for the translation, things aren't too strenuous for me. On Tuesday we're having a rest day & travelling to 'Upper Provence' – the loneliest region, for which R. Ch. has worked out an itinerary. He was very pleased with the book & gave me one of his most recent poems.

It will be a nice stay, & the work is doing me good & helping a lot to clarify matters.

With fondest regards and best wishes for a nice time with Hermann, to whom I also send best regards, as well as to Jörg & family.

Your w. Bl.

Regards & best wishes from everyone here who knows you.

On 14 September Martin wrote to say that on the spur of the moment he had withdrawn to Lenzerheide with Boss: His manuscript is considerably expanded & improved – I leave a few hours in the morning free for my own work. If the weather were to turn really bad, we'd return to Zollik.

While Elfride was giving the house a thorough cleaning in November, Martin went to stay in Messkirch and on 8 November wrote: I'm only making slow progress with my text. I'd like to restrict the problem of space in art to the plastic arts and choose the sculptures of the Temple of Zeus in Olympia as a paradigm, also as a contrast with the problem of space in modern physics. In order to see things even more clearly in this regard, I've suggested the second week in December to Weizsäcker for the seminar & sent him a copy of the Beaufret festschrift; here I do learn much more than in the conversations with 'philosophers'.

Hamburg, 12 Dec. 1968

My D. S.

Your letter with the little volume was here by yesterday afternoon. Thank you for carrying out my request so quickly. The conversations are very lively – above all it's becoming increasingly apparent that the participants don't just have 'intellectual' interests – they're all aware of the threat of science & technology, but they're also motivated by the insight that there's nothing to be achieved by appealing to additional constructions derived from some worldview or other. I've already learnt new things about the problem of space. At the same time I notice that people fail to grasp Husserl's idealistic-theoretical way of thinking – because it has no bearing upon them. I feel very fresh & in good form in this clear weather. Each day is nicer than the last; of course, the hours of sun are short in December – but the cloudless sky is certainly a boon. Yesterday & today it was minus 11 in the morning, during the day minus 3.

Tomorrow we're invited to visit their friend the professor of English (a Swabian), who lives just 10 minutes from the Weizsäckers'. The day before yesterday Aubenque & Noack were here.

I heard from Aub. that the dialogue between Cassirer & me in Davos is now to be printed. He wants to translate it. Frau Cassirer's 'memoirs' haven't been printed because no publisher has accepted the ms.

It's quite quiet in the house because there are no other occupants & no visitors. The seminars last from 10 – 1 pm each day. After a short rest at lunchtime I go for a walk & then get down to preparations for the next day. I don't eat too much. What a good job your heel is getting better. I don't want to press you about 'Greece'. Perhaps another stay would no longer turn out as well as the previous ones. [. . .]

The Black Forest honey, which Frau v. W. was <u>very</u> pleased about, doesn't get put on the table. Both of them send many thanks. Today & tomorrow afternoon W. has his lecture & seminar. On Saturday he's quite free. We want to discuss one of his mss on cybernetics & biology in private.

I'll be arriving on Sunday at 20.41 with the Helvetia [express train]. It isn't necessary to pick me up. My cold's quite gone. The Ws send their regards.

The last thing Karl Barth wrote was an '<u>Epilogue</u>' to a selection of Schleiermacher's writings. Frau W. gave it to me to read.

I'm looking forward to coming home – With fondest love
    Your w. Bl.

1969

In March Martin again worked with Boss in Zollikon.

At the instigation of Franz Larese, Martin had the previous year met the Spanish sculptor Eduardo Chillida. In St Gall Martin wrote the text 'Art and Space' directly onto stone with a quill, Chillida producing seven litho-collages to go with it. This was published in October by the Erker publishing house.

Following a serious bout of flu, Elfride and Martin decided to have a kind of 'retirement home' built in their back garden. As with the Cabin and the house itself, Elfride had a good many practical ideas for its construction. The plan was for a single-storey flat that would be easy to look after.

In May Martin worked on the transcripts and prepared for a colloquium in Heidelberg.

In June he went on his own to Kiel to hold seminars and visit the Bröckers. At Kiel University there were violent student disturbances. On 10 June Martin wrote: At the moment there's a big strike at the University – today it'll perhaps be closed for the S.S. [summer semester]. [. . .] If the disturbances go on like this Br. too intends to call it a day in the spring.

At the colloquium in Heidelberg on 20/21 June, Martin met Karl Löwith.

During a stay with Boss at Zollikon Martin was visited by his former student Hans Jonas. On 17 July he gave an account of their meeting: Yesterday at 3 pm Jonas rang to say he'd be coming at 4 pm. He's completely abandoned the theolog. philos. problems & turned his attention to the fundamental questions of biology. He clearly wants to regain a positive relationship to my thinking; he's now 66 & was with me in Frbg. back in his first semester in 1921. My response was cautious; B. said we should speak on our own. We only spoke about

Martin, Jean Beaufret, Patrick Lévy, François Vezin, Barbara Cassin (from left to right)

the situation of philosophy & the sudden change in attitude towards my thinking in the USA.

Through the offices of Hannah Arendt, in August Martin established contact with the National Schiller Museum in Marbach, as he wanted to sell the manuscript of Being and Time *in order to finance their retirement home.*

The original plan was for Elfride to accompany Martin to the third seminar at Le Thor.

Le Thor, 5 Sept. 69

Dear Elfride,

Thanks for your letter. I'm thinking of your pain. But I also know that this is not enough. And so every day and the hours awake at night I'm sad about myself & what I've done to you. As a result, even the landscape doesn't speak to me this time, quite apart from the fact that it's mainly dull weather, interspersed with thunderstorms. The three seminars so far have been very lively, & the preparation takes up rather a lot of my time. A good thing is that only Beaufret's students are involved, so the conversations make good progress.

The talks with René Char are valuable to me – I understand a thing or two more about his poetry. In between times we go for little trips in the immediate vicinity. We've already been to see Madame Mathieu

Eightieth birthday celebration in Messkirch

too; had a look at the business, 35 workers, a real fruit factory; the apples are picked 10–15 days <u>before</u> they're ripe & then artificially ripened according to demand. The farmers spray the fruit just before the harvest –

Today we're going to Luynes to see Fédier's cousin. Each day I also have special questions to discuss with J. B. concerning his work. My post is limited to the letters to you, & in the next few days I'll write to the children & grandchildren.

Larese is returning today; he has offered of his own accord to ring you up today. Though I feel well outwardly, inside me everything is agitated.

Tomorrow Munier is coming for two days. On Fri. 12 Sept. we're leaving here again, staying the night in Arbois & arriving in Frbg. in the afternoon on 13 Sept. The letter you enclosed for me was an enquiry by a Swiss photographer – the sort of thing we will hear more of in future.

The days here gave me the chance to prepare inwardly for my birthday, which I would have rather celebrated in private – or not at all. Apart from your letter there was no post, nor will there be. With grateful & sad best wishes to you, & hoping that you're well 'otherwise' & have a time of outward rest too. Your Martin

I've asked Larese to get his brother to send us the guest list. Next Sunday Mitscherlich is due to speak in Amriswil.

Best wishes to all the children & grandchildren. Let's hope your proposal for Messkirch is successful.

312

Celebrations for Martin's 80th birthday were held in Messkirch.
Subsequently there were further birthday celebrations at the castle
at Amriswil.
On 30 September Liesel died of heart failure after a brief illness.

Messkirch, 14 Nov. 69

My D. S.
dull, cold and wet November weather – as though it belonged with the
changed mood in the little house, with dear Liesel's final absence still
unfamiliar. Fritz looks exhausted & his 'speech' is more laboured than
otherwise, and every day he sees more clearly what is missing and
what was there before. Otherwise though, everything is carefully
arranged. While Fritz was in Bonndorf, Frau Keller & her husband put
in the double windows & saw to a lot of other things. Really a loyal
neighbourhood. A proper electric stove is in the kitchen & easy to
operate.

The gravestone tends not to be put in place until after a year –
because only then is the ground firm & no longer subsides. The
Walters are calmer now & are at their work. I hope Fritz becomes
more active again too – which isn't all that easy when it's just reading
& excerpting. Up to now he's been busy with the thank-you letters.
[. . .]

My D. S. I don't forget – and the present atmosphere is right for
keeping me in constant reflection & properly appreciating every day
of life I've got left and taking stock of myself. I'm working through
some of the festschrift articles so I'll be better prepared to answer my
colleagues. I slept badly on the first night; but it'll work out. I'm thinking a lot about myself & so about you – you must rest – let us prepare
quiet winter months for ourselves, and I'll make up for much that I
have left undone – I thank you for the trust you constantly bestow on
me anew – undeserved as it is.

With best wishes & thoughts of our often buried originary love – of
our originary belonging-together   Your w. Bl.

Fritz sends his regards & so do the Kellers.

1970

On 9 April Martin gave the lecture 'The Question about the Destination of Art' ['Die Frage nach der Bestimmung der Kunst'] at the Bavarian Academy of Fine Arts.
   He wrote Elfride an almost illegible letter which provided the first signs of his impending stroke.

Munich, 10. IV. 70

My D. S.
Everything went well, the journey and the stay [?] at Rotsee
But got <u>severe rheumatism</u> at Rotsee – in the
right wrist. But it'll get better.
20 cm of fresh snow on the morning of 9 April.
I'm staying at Pension Gräfin Harrach – quite quiet.
Today a rest day. Tomorrow Heisenberg & Georgiades
Sunday Weizsäcker, who's moving house
Monday Messkirch.
My wrist very painful
Already bought & rubbed in Rheumasan.
Ina Seidel was there too; & very grateful
Otherwise I'm very well.
Much love
Your w. Bl.
Preetorius seriously ill

Added by Elfride:
<u>last letter</u> (before Augsburg)
his collapse there finally brought everything out into the open – afterwards we were never separated again.

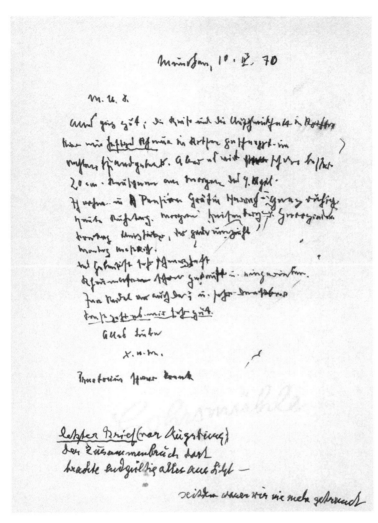

Heidegger's letter of 10 April 1970

In Augsburg, where he had a rendezvous, Martin suffered a stroke which paralysed the right side of his body and temporarily affected his speech. He was brought to Freiburg by ambulance and nursed back to health by Elfride in the Rötebuck house. He made a complete recovery, and only his handwriting remained affected.

1971 saw the publication of Médard Boss's principal work, An Outline of Medicine and Psychology, *the writing of which Martin had followed intensively.*

Martin's eighty-fifth birthday

At the beginning of September 1971, Elfride and Martin moved into their 'retirement home' in the back garden of the Rötebuck house. From now until Martin's death, they were separated only on rare occasions and for brief periods. There are no further letters from Martin to Elfride.

In the spring of 1976, Martin's health deteriorated, and he knew that death was near. On the morning of 26 May, he died in his sleep. The following night, Elfride slept one last time in the marital bed, beside her dead husband.

On 28 May, Martin was buried in Messkirch alongside his parents and his sister-in-law Liesel.

Elfride died on 21 March 1992. Three days later, she was laid to rest next to her husband in Messkirch.

Afterword by Hermann Heidegger

Martin Heidegger's understandable desire that the paths of his thought should be followed rather than his private life made public contrasts with his granddaughter Gertrud Heidegger's rightful desire to pay a more just tribute to the personality of her grandmother Elfride through the publication of this book.

On this occasion my niece has offered me the opportunity to say a few words about myself.

Born in 1920 as the legitimate son of Martin and Elfride Heidegger, at the age of just 14 I was told by my mother that my natural father was a friend from her youth, my godfather Dr Friedel Caesar, who died in 1946.

My mother made me promise at the time to mention this to *nobody* except my future wife, as long as she herself was alive. I have kept this promise.

Now I am grateful to my niece for allowing me to make this declaration, in so doing freeing myself from a burden that has weighed upon and tormented me for 71 years and confessing the historical truth.

Attental, Sunday, 3 July 2005,
On the 112th anniversary of the birth of our mother
and grandmother,
Hermann Heidegger

Life of Elfride Heidegger, née Petri (1893–1992)

3 July 1893	Birth of Elfride, the daughter of Captain Richard Petri and his wife, Martha Petri, née Friedrich, in Leisnig (Saxony)
1905	Move from Chemnitz (Saxony) to Wiesbaden, where Elfride attends the girls' high school
Winter 1907/08	Period spent in Nice with her parents during her father's convalescence
1908	Elfride stays with her parents in Paris
Autumn	Return to the girls' high school in Wiesbaden
Summer 1909	On her own to a language course in London
1909–13	Elfride attends the *Oberlyzeum* or upper high school in Wiesbaden
1913–14	Teacher training course in Wiesbaden
24 March 1914	State teacher training examination
Summer semester	Advanced teacher training course at Kiel University
August–October	Social work with National Women's Service first in Berlin, subsequently in Wiesbaden (day nursery)
March 1915	Supplementary exams in Latin and mathematics at a Kassel grammar school to achieve university entrance requirements
Summer semester	Studies in Berlin and continued activity within the National Women's Service
Summer	Harvest help on an orchard on Lüneburg Heath
Winter semester	Elfride studies economics in Freiburg Membership of the 'Freiburg Sorority' and the 'Cabin Guild'

December	First meeting with Martin in his seminar on Kant's *Prolegomena*
March 1916	Secret engagement with Martin
August	Official engagement on the island of Reichenau (on Lake Constance)
20 March 1917	War wedding at the registry office, Freiburg
21 March	Catholic wedding in the university chapel of the Minster with no family present
25 March	Protestant wedding in Wiesbaden with a reception attended by neither the bride's father nor the bridegroom's parents
August	With her friend Friedel Lieber she attends a meeting of the *Freideutscher Bund* or 'Free German Association' on the Lorelei
	First visit with Martin to Messkirch to meet her parents-in-law and the relatives
Autumn	Elfride and Martin move into their first flat together at Lerchenstrasse, no. 8, in Freiburg
1917–18	Teaching post first at a boys' elementary school, then at a girls' high school in Freiburg
Summer 1918	Rambling excursion with Friedel Lieber along the valley of the rivers Main and Tauber
October	Leave of absence from teaching work on the grounds of pregnancy
21 January 1919	Birth of their son Jörg
	Acute hardship in the post-war period, with shortages of foodstuffs and fuel for heating
20 August 1920	Birth of their son Hermann
	Financial problems owing to inflation and low income
Winter semester 1921	Elfride takes up her economics studies again
13 March 1922	Death of Elfride's half-sister Else Presting
	Planning and construction of the Cabin at Todtnauberg
9 August	The Heideggers first move into their almost complete Cabin
1923	She gives up her studies due to the pressures of domestic work, health problems and the shortages of provisions
November	Move to Schwanallee, no. 21, in Marburg

1925–7	Private tuition of her sons, as well as of children afflicted with polio, in Marburg
August 1926	Another move, this time within Marburg, to Barfüssertor, no. 15
1928	Planning and construction of the house in Freiburg-Zähringen, Rötebuck no. 47
October	The Heideggers move into their new house
1931	Construction of the swimming pool in the garden
August	With Jörg and Hermann on the North Sea island of Spiekeroog
November	With Hermann for a period of convalescence in Brissago in Switzerland
June 1932	With Hermann for convalescence in Rantum on the island of Sylt
3 May 1933	Membership of the NSDAP, the National Socialist party, backdated to 1 May
	Elfride takes her driving test and buys a car
1934–45	Active for the *Nationalsozialistische Volkswohlfahrt* (NSV), the 'National Socialist People's Welfare Organization', in Zähringen
July 1935	Arrival of their 14-year-old foster daughter Erika Birle after the death of both parents in São Paulo, Brazil
1936	Connections with the *NS-Frauenschaft*, the National Socialists' women's organization, in Berlin (Erika Semmler and Alice Rilke)
23 September 1938	Death of her father, Richard Petri, retired colonel, in Wiesbaden
December 1942	Marriage of Jörg and Dorothee Kurrer in Berlin-Frohnau
December 1944	Marriage of Erika and Wilhelm Deyhle
15 January 1945	Death of her mother, Martha Petri, in Wiesbaden
	School lessons for the neighbourhood children
	Severe marital crisis on account of Margot von Sachsen-Meiningen
	Both sons are reported missing and taken prisoner by the Russians
	A French non-commissioned officer is billeted in their house

September 1946	Birth of their first grandchild, Martin Deyhle
	Financial difficulties due to lack of income and food shortages
September 1947	Return of son Hermann from captivity
Summer 1949	Serious mental illness of their daughter-in-law Dorle
December 1951	Return of son Jörg from captivity
	New car purchased
April 1954	Marriage of Hermann and Jutta Stölting
August	Marriage of Jörg and Hedi Veidt
September 1955	First trip to France with Martin
January–March 1960	Severe depression and health cure in Hinterzarten
May–June 1961	Visit to Kiel and four weeks' convalescence in St Peter-Ording
	Successful attempt at taking up painting again
April 1962	First trip to Greece with Martin (subsequent trips in 1964, 1966 and 1967)
June	Holiday with granddaughter Ulrike in St Peter-Ording
Autumn	Martin suffers severe jaundice and is looked after at home by Elfride
April–May 1963	Trip to Sicily with Martin
June	With granddaughter Almuth in St Peter-Ording
18 May 1967	Golden wedding anniversary celebrations in Freiburg
1968	Gives up driving because of age
1969	Plans for a retirement home in the neighbourhood
10 April 1970	Martin suffers a stroke and is looked after at home by Elfride
September 1971	Martin and Elfride move into their retirement home, Fillibachstrasse, no. 25
26 May 1976	Martin's death at home
	Publication of further volumes of the *Collected Works* and ordering of the unpublished works and letters
October 1978	Final visit to the Cabin with great-grandson Florian
Autumn 1979	Hermann takes on the publication of the *Collected Works*
1983	Ninetieth birthday celebrations in the family circle

November 1987	Admission to an old people's home in Freiburg
21 March 1992	Elfride dies in the home
24 March 1992	Funeral in Messkirch

Life of Martin Heidegger (1889–1976)

26 September 1889	Birth of Martin, son of Friedrich Heidegger, master cooper and sexton, and his wife Johanna Heidegger (née Kempf), in Messkirch (Baden)
1903	Leaves the local *Bürgerschule* or citizens' school at the end of the eighth year and attends the humanist grammar school and the Catholic seminary, the Konradihaus, in Constance
1906	From the eleventh year on he attends the Berthold Gymnasium in Freiburg im Breisgau, in order to continue receiving a scholarship
1909	After his school-leaving exams, Martin enters the novitiate with the Jesuits in Tisis near Feldkirch (Vorarlberg, Austria)
	Discharged after two weeks owing to heart problems
	Application for admission to the theological seminary in Freiburg
	With financial support from the Church, he takes up his studies in Freiburg, initially Catholic theology and philosophy, under Carl Braig and others
1911	Discontinuation of his clerical training
	Martin now focuses on philosophy, mathematics and the natural sciences
1913	Doctorate, with a thesis on 'The Doctrine of Judgement in Psychologism. A Critical-

	Positive Contribution to Logic', supervised by Arthur Schneider (chair in Christian philosophy)
1913	Volunteers for military service, but in October is discharged for health reasons
1914	Habilitation thesis supervised by Heinrich Rickert on 'Duns Scotus's Doctrine of Categories and Meaning' under the influence of the historian Heinrich Finke
November	Enlisted for military service in a limited capacity (assigned to the postal supervision centre in Freiburg)
1915–16	From the winter semester onwards, lectures and seminars at Freiburg University, focusing on transcendental philosophy, in particular the problem of value, phenomenology and the category of 'life' and the hermeneutics of 'existence'
March 1916	Secret engagement with the economics student Elfride Petri
August 1916	Official engagement on the island of Reichenau (Lake Constance)
1917	Marries Elfride Petri
1918	Considered fit for active service: conscripted into the regional weather station command on the Heuberg, in Berlin and near Verdun
1919	Breaks with the system of Catholicism
1920	Private assistant to Edmund Husserl, who had come to Freiburg in 1916 as the successor to Rickert
1922	Construction of the Cabin in Todtnauberg in the Black Forest
1923	Offer of associate professorship with the status of a full professor of philosophy at the University of Marburg. Martin turns to the philosophy of Immanuel Kant. Those in attendance at his lectures in Marburg include H.-G. Gadamer, K. Löwith, H. Arendt, H. Jonas, W. Szilasi and H. Weiss. Fruitful collaboration with the theologian R. Bultmann
1 May 1924	Death of his father, Friedrich Heidegger, in Messkirch

3 May 1927	Death of his mother, Johanna Heidegger, in Messkirch
1927	His major work *Sein und Zeit* (*Being and Time*) is published in Husserl's *Jahrbuch für Philosophie und phänomenologische Forschung* (*Annual for Philosophy and Phenomenological Research*).
	Establishment of 'fundamental ontology', which is to supersede traditional ontological systems from Plato onwards. The problem of subjectivity is central here: the search for the synthesis of knowledge and object with the question about the meaning of Being.
	Promotion from associate to full professor of philosophy at Marburg
1928	Appointment to the full professorship for philosophy at the Albert Ludwigs University of Freiburg as the successor to Husserl
	The Heideggers move into their own house in Freiburg-Zähringen
1929	Inaugural lecture entitled 'What Is Metaphysics?'
	Three lectures on Kant at the Davos university week: 'Kant and the Problem of Metaphysics' (subsequent debate with E. Cassirer)
1930	Turns down the offer of a chair in Berlin
	Beginning of late work with his paper 'On the Essence of Truth': the constitutive place of truth is no longer seen in *Dasein* or existence, but a metaphysical understanding of *Sein* or Being comes to the fore. Expresses the growing homelessness of modern man in his *Seinsvergessenheit* or 'oblivion to Being'
21 April 1933	Elected as rector of Freiburg University
3 May	Membership of the NSDAP, the National Socialist party, backdated to 1 May. From the Nazis he expects a 'new beginning to German destiny'
27 May	Inaugural address on 'The Self-Assertion of the German University', in which he draws

	parallels between the way the scholar serves knowledge, the soldier serves in the army, and the worker at his workplace.
	Again turns down the offer of a chair in Berlin, as well as in Munich
1 October	Appointed rector by the Baden regional government
1934	Resignation from the rectorship on account of differences with the Faculty and with government and party authorities
	He dedicates himself completely to philosophy once again
1936	Lectures in Rome on 'Hölderlin and the Essence of Poetry' and 'Europe and German Philosophy'
	Starts preparation (through to 1938) of his second major work, the *Beiträge zur Philosophie*, or *Contributions to Philosophy*, which remains unpublished until its posthumous publication in 1989
	Painstaking analysis of the philosophy of Nietzsche (until 1940)
November 1944	Conscripted into the *Volkssturm*, the German Territorial Army
1945	The manuscripts in Messkirch are sorted out and safely stored away
	From April to June the Philosophical Faculty is moved to Wildenstein Castle (in the Danube Valley)
1946	Martin is banned from teaching
1947	In his letter 'On Humanism' to Jean Beaufret, he associates humanism with metaphysics and the revolt of man merely going round in circles.
	His works influence the French existentialism around Jean-Paul Sartre, the humanities, as well as the development of the psychiatric school of *Daseinsanalyse* or existential analysis.
1949	Series of lectures 'Insight into That Which Is' (in Bremen), four lectures in which he portrays and criticizes the connection between technology and modern science
	End to the ban on teaching

1950	Retirement
1951	Conferment of emeritus status
1951–3	Numerous lectures given at Bühlerhöhe, the Bavarian Academy of Fine Arts in Munich, and in Darmstadt
1955	First trip to France
1957	Lecture on *Der Satz der Identität* (*The Principle of Identity*) to celebrate the 500th Jubilee of Freiburg University
	Admission to the Heidelberg Academy of Sciences and the Berlin Academy of Arts
1959	The Zollikon Seminars undertaken in conjunction with the Swiss psychiatrist Médard Boss (until 1969)
	Appointed honorary citizen of Messkirch
1962	First of five trips to Greece
1966	Interview with Rudolf Augstein for the *Spiegel*, which at his own request is not published until after his death
	First seminar at Le Thor (continued in 1968 and 1969, and in 1973 in Zähringen)
1966–7	Works together with Eugen Fink in the winter semester at Freiburg University, organizing a seminar on Heraclitus
	Planning the *Collected Works*, which comprise more than 100 volumes
10 April 1970	Martin has a stroke, but makes a good recovery
1975	Volume 24 is the first of his *Collected Works* to be published
26 May 1976	Martin dies at home
28 May	Funeral at his birthplace Messkirch

Heidegger Family Tree

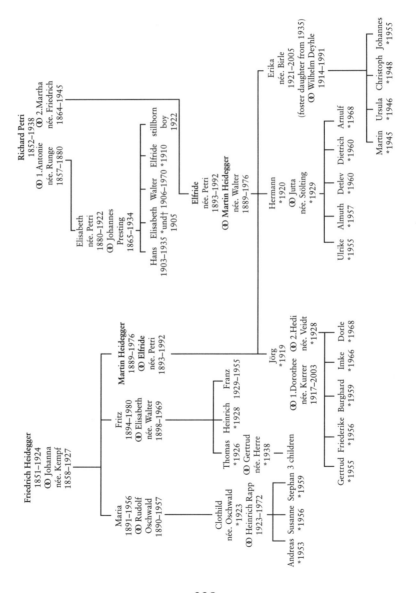

Annotated Index of Names

Abraham a Sancta Clara (1644–1709), preacher, lay name Hans U. Megerle

Adenauer, Konrad (1876–1967), politician (Christian Democratic Union), Federal Chancellor 1949–63

Adorno, Theodor Ludwig Wiesengrund (1903–69), German philosopher, sociologist, musicologist and composer

Aegina, nymph in Greek mythology, Greek island

Allemann, Beda (1920–91), literary theorist

Anz, Wilhelm (1904–94), philosopher, student of Heidegger

Aphrodite, Greek goddess of love

Arendt, Hannah (1906–75), political philosopher and friend of Heidegger

Artemis, Greek goddess of the wild and the hunt, daughter of Zeus

Aubenque, Pierre (*1929), French philosopher

Augustine (354–430), Doctor of the Church

Auwers, Karl Friedrich von (1863–1939), chemist, director of the Institute of Chemistry in Marburg

Bäumer, Gertrud (1873–1954), writer and politician, leading figure in the women's movement

Baeumler, Alfred (1887–1968), philosopher, professor of philosophy in Dresden and Berlin, from 1933 professor of political education, National Socialist

Barth, Karl (1886–1968), Protestant theologian from Switzerland

Bauch, Kurt (1897–1975), art historian

Bauer, Walter (1901–68), economist

Baumgarten, Eduard (1898–1982), philosopher, sociologist, specialist in American studies

Beaufret, Jean (1907–82), French philosopher and friend of Heidegger

Becker, Carl Heinrich (1876–1933), Orientalist and Prussian minister of education and the arts 1925–30

Becker, Oskar (1889–1964), philosopher, logician and mathematician, professor in Bonn

Benn, Gottfried (1886–1956), doctor, poet and essayist

Benz, Richard (1884–1966), writer

Bergson, Henri (1859–1941), French philosopher, 1927 Nobel Prize for literature

Beringer, Kurt (1893–1949), medic, representative of the 'Heidelberg School' (drug research)

Besseler, Heinrich (1900–69), music researcher at Freiburg University, subsequently professor in Heidelberg and Jena

Beumelburg, Werner (1899–1963), writer

Biemel, Walter (*1918), philosopher, student of Heidegger

Bismarck, Otto Eduard Leopold von (1815–98), major German statesman and politician of the nineteenth century

Bissier, Julius (1893–1965), German painter

Bloch, Ernst (1885–1977), German philosopher

Blochmann, Elisabeth ('Lisi') (1892–1972), educational theorist and friend of Martin and Elfride Heidegger

Boehlau, Johannes (1861–1941), director of the Fridericianum Museum in Kassel

Bohr, Niels (1885–1962), Danish physicist, Nobel Prize winner 1922

Bornkamm, Günther (1905–90), Protestant theologian ('the Younger'), professor in Heidelberg

Bornkamm, Heinrich (1901–77), Protestant theologian ('the Elder'), professor in Heidelberg, president of the Heidelberg Academy of Sciences

Boss, Médard (1903–90), Swiss psychiatrist

Braig, Carl (1853–1923), Roman Catholic theologian, professor in Freiburg

Brandt, Willy (1913–92), politician (German Social Democratic Party), Federal Chancellor 1969–74

Braque, Georges (1882–1963), French Cubist painter

Brock, Werner Gottfried (1901–74), philosopher and assistant of Heidegger

Bröcker, Walter (1902–92), philosopher, professor in Kiel

Bröse, Siegfried, philosopher

Brüning, Heinrich (1885–1970), politician (Centre Party), German Chancellor 1930–32

Brunner, Emil (1889–1966), Swiss Reformed theologian, professor in Zurich

Buber, Martin (1878–1965), Jewish philosopher of religion

Buchner, Hartmut (1927–2004), philosopher, student of Heidegger

Büchner, Franz (1895–1991), pathologist, director of the Pathology Institute of the University of Freiburg

Bühler, Hans Adolf (1877–1951), painter and professor of art in Karlsruhe, 1933 head of the German Art Society

Bultmann, Rudolf Karl (1884–1976), Protestant theologian, professor in Marburg

Burckhardt, Carl Jacob (1891–1974), Swiss diplomat, historian and writer

Burckhardt, Jacob (1818–97), Swiss historian of art and culture

Buttlar-Brandenfels, Herbert Freiherr Treusch (1912–76), secretary-general of the Berlin Academy of Arts

Caesar, Friedrich ('der Friedel') (1892–1946), medic, friend from Elfride's youth

Caesar, Lotte, teacher

Cassirer, Ernst (1874–1945), political philosopher, professor and rector of Hamburg University, emigrated to Sweden in 1935, to the USA in 1941

Cézanne, Paul (1839–1906), French painter

Char, René (1907–88), French poet

Chiarelli, Louis, French sculptor and stonemason

Chillida Juantegui, Eduardo (1924–2002), Spanish sculptor

Clausewitz, Karl von (1780–1831), Prussian general and military writer

Cohn, Jonas (1869–1947), philosopher, professor in Freiburg

Creon, Greek mythological figure, uncle of Antigone

Curie, Marie (1867–1934), chemist and physicist, 1903 Nobel Prize winner for physics and 1911 for chemistry

Descartes, René (1596–1650), French philosopher

Dilthey, Wilhelm (1833–1911), philosopher

Dirac, Paul Adrien Maurice (1902–84), British physicist

Duns Scotus, John (1265–1308), Franciscan scholastic theologian

Ebbingshaus, Julius (1885–1981), philosopher

Meister Eckhart (*ca.* 1260–1327/28), mystic and theologian

Eich, Günther (1907–72), writer

Eros, Greek god of love

Fabricius, Ernst (1857–1942), historian

Fédier, François (*1935), French philosophy teacher and translator of Heidegger's writings

Fichte, Johann Gottlieb (1762–1814), German Idealist philosopher

Ficker, Ludwig von (1880–1967), writer and publisher, friend of Georg Trakl

Fink, Eugen (1905–75), philosopher

Finke, Heinrich (1855–1938), Roman Catholic historian

Fourcade, Dominique (*1938), French poet and friend of René Char

Frank, Walter (1905–45), head of the 'Reich Institute of History' in Berlin, 1935–41
Friedländer, Paul (1882–1986), classicist
Friedrich, Caspar David (1774–1840), German Romantic painter
Friedrich, Hugo (1904–78), Romance scholar
Fuchs, Ernst (1903–83), Protestant theologian and student of Heidegger
Gadamer, Hans-Georg (1900–2002), philosopher and student of Heidegger
Gebsattel, Viktor Emil Freiherr von (1883–1976), psychiatrist, doctor at the Schloss Hausbaden sanatorium, Badenweiler
Geiger, Afra, philosopher and student of Heidegger
Georgiades, Thrasybulos (1907–77), music researcher
Geyser, Joseph (1869–1948), Roman Catholic philosopher
Gisbertz, Therese, student and assistant of Heidegger
Gluck, Christoph Willibald (1714–87), composer
Gogh, Vincent van (1853–90), Dutch painter
Grass, Günter (*1927), writer and Nobel Prize winner for literature 1999
Grillparzer, Franz (1791–1872), Austrian dramatist
Grimm, Hans (1875–59), writer and Nationalist journalist
Grimm, Jacob (1785–1863), philologist and fairy-tale collector
Grimm, Wilhelm (1786–1859), philologist and fairy-tale collector
Grimme, Adolf (1889–1963), politician, Prussian minister of education, science and the arts 1929–32
Guardini, Romano (1885–1968), Roman Catholic philosopher of religion
Gurlitt, Willibald (1889–1963), historian of music
Guzzoni, Alfredo, graduate student under Fink
Habermas, Jürgen (*1929), philosopher and sociologist
Haecker, Theodor (1879–1945), philosopher of culture
Hamann, Richard (1879–1961), art historian
Harnack, Adolf von (1851–1930), Protestant theologian
Hartmann, Nicolai (1882–1950), philosopher
Hauptmann, Gerhard (1862–1946), dramatist and novelist
Hebel, Johann Peter (1760–1826), poet
Hegel, Georg Friedrich Wilhelm (1770–1831), German Idealist philosopher
Heimpel, Hermann (1901–88), historian
Heisenberg, Werner Karl (1901–76), physicist
Heitmüller, Wilhelm (1869–1926), Protestant theologian
Helmken, Ludwig, senator in Bremen and friend of Heidegger
Hera, Greek goddess, wife of Zeus, protectress of marriage
Heraclitus (*ca.* 550–480 BC), Greek philosopher

Hermelink, Heinrich (1877–1958), Protestant theologian and Church historian

Herrmann, Wilhelm (1846–1922), Protestant theologian, professor in Marburg

Hindenburg, Paul von (1847–1934), field marshal and German president

Hölderlin, Friedrich (1770–1843), German poet

Hoffmann, Wilhelm (1901–86), director of the National Library, Stuttgart

Honecker, Martin (1888–1941), Christian philosopher

Humboldt, Wilhelm von (1767–1835), Prussian politician, educational reformer, philologist and philosopher

Husserl, Edmund (1859–1938), philosopher (Göttingen Philosophical Society/School of Phenomenology), Rickert's successor at Freiburg: Heidegger was his private assistant, and his major work was published in Husserl's *Jahrbuch für Philosophie und phänomenologische Forschung* (Annual for Philosophy and Phenomenological Research)

Ingarden, Roman (1893–1970), Polish philosopher

Jacobsthal, Paul (1880–1957), archaeologist

Jaensch, Erich (1883–1940), philosopher and psychologist

Janssen, Sigurd (1891–1968), pharmacologist

Jantzen, Hans (1881–1967), art historian

Jaspers, Karl (1883–1969), philosopher

Jens, Walter (*1923), classicist

Jonas, Hans (1903–93), philosopher

Jülicher, Adolf (1857–1938), Protestant theologian

Jünger, Ernst (1895–1998), writer

Jünger, Friedrich Georg (1898–1977), writer

Jungk, Robert (1913–94), journalist and writer

Kaehler, Siegfried August (1885–1963), historian

Kästner, Erhard (1904–74), writer

Kant, Immanuel (1724–1804), philosopher and critic of metaphysics

Keats, John (1795–1821), English poet

Khrushchev, Nikita Sergeyevich (1894–1971), Soviet politician and premier

Kiesinger, Kurt Georg (1904–88), politician (Christian Democratic Union), Federal Chancellor 1966–9

Klee, Paul (1879–1940), Swiss/German painter

Kluckhohn, Paul (1886–1957), literary historian

Kock, Hans (*1920), sculptor

Kommerell, Max (1902–44), literary historian

Körte, Werner (1905–45), art historian

Krebs, Engelbert (1881–1950), Roman Catholic theologian and friend of Heidegger

Kreutzer, Conradin (1780–1849), German musician, conductor and composer

Krieck, Ernst (1882–1947), teacher, from 1932 attempted to provide a philosophical foundation for National Socialism

Kroner, Richard (1884–1974), philosopher

Krumsiek, Elisabeth (married name Gerber) (*1904), grammar school teacher and student of Heidegger

Landgrebe, Ludwig (1902–91), philosopher

Lange, Helene (1848–1930), feminist and teacher

Laslowski, Ernst (1889–1961), archivist and friend of Heidegger from Silesia

Leibniz, Gottfried Wilhelm von (1646–1716), German philosopher and scientist, mathematician, diplomat, jurist, physicist, historian and doctor of secular and canon law

Leiner, Bruno (1891–1954), pharmacist and school friend of Heidegger from Constance

Lieber, Elfriede (married name Daniel) ('das Friedel'), friend of Elfride Heidegger

Linde, Horst Eduard (*1912), architect

Löwith, Karl (1897–1973), philosopher and student of Heidegger

Lotze, Rudolf Hermann (1817–81), philosopher

Lukács, Georg (1885–1971), Hungarian philosopher and literary historian

Mahnke, Dietrich (1884–1939), philosopher

Marcel, Gabriel Honoré (1889–1973), French philosopher and dramatist

Marcuse, Herbert (1898–1979), sociologist and assistant of Heidegger

Maunz, Theodor (1901–93), professor of constitutional law

Max, Prince of Baden (1867–1929), German Chancellor

Mayer, Hans (1907–2001), literary historian

Meinecke, Friedrich (1862–1954), historian

Mende, Erich (1916–98), politician (Free Democratic Party)

Mitscherlich, Alexander (1908–82), psychologist

Modersohn-Becker, Paula (1876–1907), painter

Montessori, Maria (1870–1952), Italian doctor, educational reformer, philosopher and philanthropist

Müller, Max (1906–94), Roman Catholic philosopher

Munier, Roger (*1923), French translator of Heidegger's writings

Natorp, Paul (1854–1924), philosopher

Nebel, Gerhard (1903–74), writer

Nelson, Leonhard (1882–1927), philosopher

Nietzsche, Friedrich Wilhelm (1844–1900), philosopher

Nohl, Hermann (1879–1960), philosopher and educational theorist

Novalis (Friedrich von Hardenberg) (1772–1801), German romantic poet

Ochsner, Heinrich (1891–1970), Roman Catholic philosopher and friend of Heidegger

Oltmann, Käthe (married name Bröcker) (1906–99), philosopher and student of Heidegger

Oncken, Hermann (1869–1945), historian

Orff, Carl (1895–1982), composer

Otto, Rudolf (1869–1937), Protestant theologian

Parmenides of Elea (*ca.* 500 BC), Greek philosopher

Pfeilschifter, Georg (1870–1936), Church historian

Picht, Georg (1913–82), classicist

Pindar (*ca.* 500 BC), Greek poet

Podewils, Clemens Graf von (1905–78), secretary-general of the Bavarian Academy of Fine Arts

Podewils, Sophie-Dorothee Gräfin von (née Baroness von Hirschberg) (1909–79), writer and friend of Heidegger

Pöggeler, Otto (*1928), philosopher

Pos, Hendrik Josephus (1898–1955), Dutch medic and philosopher

Preetorius, Emil (1883–1973), illustrator

Pushkin, Aleksander Sergeyevich (1799–1837), Russian poet

Reinhardt, Karl (1886–1958), classicist

Richter, Werner (1887–1960), head of department in the Prussian ministry of education and the arts

Rickert, Heinrich (1863–1936), philosopher, responsible for the expert's report on Heidegger's habilitation thesis

Riezler, Kurt (1882–1955), philosopher and registrar of Frankfurt University

Rilke, Rainer Maria (1875–1926), German poet

Ritter, Gerhard (1888–1967), historian

Rodin, Auguste (1840–1917), French sculptor

Rosenberg, Alfred (1893–1946), National Socialist politician

Rothacker, Erich (1888–1965), philosopher

Rovan, Joseph (1918–2004), French historian and journalist

Ruf, Sep (1908–82), architect, e.g. of the Chancellor's Bungalow in Bonn

Sartre, Jean Paul (1905–80), French philosopher

Schadewaldt, Wolfgang (1900–74), classicist

Schaefer, Clemens (1878–1960), physicist

Scharnhorst, Gerhard von (1755–1813), Prussian general

Scharoun, Hans Bernhard (1893–1972), architect

Scheler, Max (1874–1928), philosopher

Schelling, Friedrich Joseph Wilhelm von (1775–1854), Romantic philosopher

Schirmer, Walter-Franz (1888–1984), English specialist
Schlegel, Friedrich von (1772–1829), cultural philosopher
Schleiermacher, Friedrich (1768–1834), Protestant theologian and philosopher
Schopenhauer, Arthur (1788–1860), philosopher
Schröder, Gerhard (1910–89), politician (Christian Democratic Union)
Schröter, Manfred (1880–1973), philosopher
Schroth, Ingeborg (married name: Krummer) (1911–98), art historian
Schuchhardt, Walter Herwig (1900–76), archaeologist
Schulz, Walter (1912–2000), philosopher
Schwind, Moritz von (1804–71), Austrian painter
Seidel, Ina (1885–1974), writer
Sethe, Paul (1901–67), journalist and political writer
Soden, Hans Freiherr von (1881–1945), Protestant theologian
Sohm, Rudolf (1841–1917), professor of canon law
Staiger, Emil (1908–87), literary historian
Steding, Christoph (1903–38), student of Heidegger
Stieler, Georg (1884–1954), philosopher and educational theorist
Stifter, Adalbert (1805–68), Austrian regional author, painter and educationalist, major Biedermeier writer
Storm, Theodor (1817–88), poet
Strauss, Franz Josef (1915–88), Bavarian politician (Christian Social Union)
Stroomann, Gerhard (1887–1957), physician and writer
Switalski, Bronislaw W., philosopher
Szilasi, Wilhelm (1889–1966), Hungarian philosopher
Taine, Hippolyte (1828–93), French determinist theorist
Tauler, Johannes (*ca.* 1300–61), German mystic theologian
Tillich, Paul (1886–1965), Protestant theologian and philosopher, professor in Dresden, Leipzig and Frankfurt am Main, emigrated to the USA in 1933
Trakl, Georg (1887–1914), Austrian pharmacist and major Expressionist poet
Treviranus, Gottfried (1891–1971), politician (German Nationalist), Reich minister for the occupied areas
Trotsky, Leon (1879–1940), politician (Marxist), founder of the Red Army
Tsujimura, Kôichi (*1922), Japanese philosopher, student of Heidegger
Uhlenhuth, Paul (1870–1957), bacteriologist, professor in Marburg and from 1923 in Freiburg
Vezin, François (*1937), French philosophy teacher and translator of Heidegger's writings

Victorius, Käthe, Swiss psychologist, student of Heidegger
Vietta, Dorothea Bernhardine (née Feldhaus) (1913–59), jurist, friend of Heidegger
Vietta, Egon (1903–59), travel writer (pseudonym of Karl Egon Fritz)
Weber, Marianne (1870–1954), writer, friend of Gertrud Jaspers
Weber, Max (1864–1920), economist and sociologist
Weiss, Helene, philosopher, student of Heidegger
Weizsäcker, Carl Friedrich von (1912–2007), physicist and philosopher
Welte, Bernhard (1906–83), Roman Catholic theologian, student of Heidegger, subsequently professor in Freiburg
Weniger, Erich (1894–1961), educationalist
Windelband, Wilhelm (1848–1915), philosopher, professor in Zurich, Strasbourg, Freiburg and Heidelberg
Winkler, Eugen Gottlob (1912–36), writer
Wolf, Erik (1902–77), jurist, professor in Freiburg
Wünsch, Georg (1887–1964), Protestant theologian
Yorck von Wartenburg, Paul Graf (1835–97), philosopher

Index

Page numbers in italics refer to a photograph

Academic Association 95, 99, 194
Adenauer, Konrad 303
Adorno, Theodor 289
Aler, Jan 298
Andersch, Alfred 287n
Anselm, Father 126, 209–10
antagonism 4, 11–12, 15–16
anti-Semitism xii, 28, 77, 80, 99, 115, 133, 137, 140, 156
Anz, Wilhelm 117–18
Arendt, Hannah xiii, 212, 311
'Aristotle and Scholasticism', lecture 20, 90
art 164–5, 236, 290, 301, 310
'Art and Space', text 310
'Art and Technology', lecture 164–5
Athens 301–2
'Atomzeitalter', periodical 304
Aubenque, Pierre 309
Augstein, Rudolf 287, 298
'Augustinus: Quid est Tempus? Confessions lib. XI', lecture 126
Austria 154

Baden University 143, 144
Bärenreiter, publisher 293
Barth, Karl 101, 309
Basel University 153

Bauch, Kurt 146, 148, 159, 170, 188, 197, 201, 217
Bauer family 122–3
  Walter 87, 111, 115, 123
Bäumer (Baeumer), Gertrud 157, 164, 172
Baumgartem, Eduard 129, 130, 132–3, 142, 228
Bäumler (Baeumler), Alfred 133, 134, 135–6, 148, 173
Bavarian Academy of Fine Arts 235, 238–40, 265, 314
Beaufret, Jean 193, 199, 201, 249, 286, 296, 303, *311*
  building work 263, 306
  festschrift 306, 307
Becker, Carl Heinrich 103
Becker, Oskar 102, 109, 274
bees 158
Behring, Frau von 95
being 160, 162–3, 164, 187, 197
'Being and Seeming', lecture 254
Being and Time, book 105, 108, 205, 253, 274, 281
  manuscript x, 106, 287, 311
  new edition 223, 283
bekennende Kirche viii
Benn, Gottfried 221
Benz family 280
  Richard 267–8, 279
Bergson, Henri 71
Berlin 42–4, 45, 122, 123, 280

Berlin Academy of Arts 281, 283
Berlin University viii, 136
  offer of chair 122–4, 142
Berliner Tagblatt, newspaper 133
Besseler, Heinrich 87, 114
Beumelburg, Werner 135–6
Beuron Archabbey 74, 125–6, 130–1, 286
Bieberstein (rural boarding school) 146, 151
Biemel, Walter 199, 248, 276
Binswanger, Ludwig 294
Birle, Erika (later Deyhle) 146, *149*, 155, 158, 170, 189
  children 190, 201, 204, 248
  education 156, 157, 162, 167, 168
  marriage 179, 181, 186
Bismarck, Otto Eduard Leopold von 137
Bissier, Julius *35*
Bloch, Ernst 287
Blochmann, Elisabeth (Lisi) 60, 122–3, 130, 132, 134–5, 155
Boehlau, Johannes 101
Bogner, Ute 223, 243
Bohr, Niels 284
Böll, Heinrich 287n
Bolshevism 162
Bonn University 114
Bornkamm, Günther 268
Boss, Médard 204, 211, 223, 231, 233, 274, 290, 291
  medical help 277, 292, 293, 294
  Outline of Medicine and Psychology, 239, 294, 305, 306–7, 308, 315
  philosophy and psychology 294, 303
  Zollikon Seminars 276, 277, 293
Boss family 244, 247, 286
Brandt, Willy 299
Braque, Georges 249, 255
Braun, Anton 210, 264
Brecht, Franz-Josef 71, 203–4
Brender family 105, 139, 199, 201
  Pius (Black Pius) 85, 139
Brock, Werner 129
Bröcker, Walter 101, 155, 158–9, 310

Bröse, Siegried 204
Brothers Grimm Society 293
Brunner, Emil 102
Brüning, Heinrich 123, 124
Buber, Martin 225, 262
Büchner, Franz 189
Buchner, Hartmut 260, 262, 290
Buenos Aries 209
Bühler, Hans Adolf 26, *35*
Bühlerhöhe lectures 218, 223
'Building Dwelling Thinking', lecture 217
Bultmann family 102
  Rudolf 98, 99, 112, 115
Bundeswehr 248
Burckhardt, Jacob 113, 115, 159
Buttlar-Brandenfels, Herbert Freiherr Treusch 291

Cabin, Todtnauberg ix, 85–6, 89, 139–40, 186, *224*, *225*, *226*
  memories of 104, 165, 192, 215
Cabin Guild 7, 18, 36
Caesar, Friedel 64–5, 317
Caesar, Lotte 231
Cassin, Barbara *311*
Cassirer, Ernst 119, 120, 123, 309
censorship 231
Cézanne, Paul 259, 262
Char, René 296–7, 307–8, 311
Chiarelli, Louis 262, 263–4
Chillida, Eduardo 310
Christian Democrats 208
Clausewitz, Karl von 158
cognition 68
Cohn, Frau 82
Cohn, Jonas 60
Cologne 124
'Comments on Art – Sculpture – Space', lecture 290
communism 133–4
'Composure', lecture 250
computers 269
'Concept of Time', lecture 98, 99
consciousness 11, *57–8*
Constance, Lake 23, 177, 228
Constance Gymnasium article 239
Constance University 291

cowslips 278
creativity 8, 142
Cuban crisis 285
'Current State of Problems in
    Philosophy', lecture 122
Czechoslovakia 156

'Daily Work of Thinking', poem 194
Darmstadt 268
Darmstadt Symposium 217, 218,
    227–8
Das innere Reich, journal 150
Daseinalalysis 293
Davoser Hochschulwoche (Davos
    University Week) 119–20
death masks 107
Der Spiegel, newspaper 298
Deutsche Akademische Freischar
    (German Academic Volunteer
    Corps) 57, 80
Deutsche Literatur-Zeitung 115
Deutsches Jungvolk (Hitler Youth)
    158
Deyhle, Christoph 204
Deyhle, Johannes 248
Deyhle, Martin 190
Deyhle, Ursula 201
Deyhle, Willhelm (Helm) 179, 181,
    193, 273
Die Tat, periodical 140
Dilthey, Wilhelm 101, 192
Dirac, Paul Adrien Maurice 256
Dokumenta III (Kassel) 287
Dostoyevski 11, 48, 72–3
Dresden University 134–5
'Duns Scotus's Doctrine of Categories
    and Meaning', thesis 25–6, 27
Dürer's hare 151
dwelling 217, 219

East Berlin 293
Ebbinghaus, Julius 87
Eckhart, Meister 61–2, 64
Eich, Günther 238
Encyclopaedia Britannica 108
'End of Thinking in the Form of
    Philosophy', lecture 294
England 6, 155

Enzensberger, Hans Magnus 287n
Erker publishing 290, 310
Eros 213
Erzberger, Matthias 59
'Essence of Reasons', essay 243, 244
Eucken, Eva 199

Fabricius, Ernst 135
Fédier, François 295, 297, 306, 307
Feick, Hildegard 262, 265, 267, 270,
    276, 284, 298
Fichte, Johann Gottlieb 254
Ficker, Ludwig von 278
film 208
Finance, Ministry of 208
Fink, Eugen 243, 248, 299
Finke, Heinrich 25, 26, 41–2, 60, 109
Fips, dog 219, 308
'First Mass', speech 243
First World War 7, 17, 28, 37–44,
    58–9, 166–7
    food shortages 43, 69
    hardship 36, 53
Fourcade, Dominique 296
France 155, 249, 262
Frankfurt University 112
Frauenfrage (women's rights) xii, 7
Frederick II, Grand Duke of Baden 22
Freiburg 55, 166, 179
Freiburg Aesthetics Society 147
Freiburg Sorority 7
Freiburg University 6
    500-year jubilee 261, 262, 262
    cultural and educational policies
        140
    and Elfride viii, 7
    First World War 7
    and Husserl 32
    influence of politics 141–2
    Second World War 161, 163–4,
        166–7, 180–1, 183–4
    see also Heidegger, Martin: Freiburg
        University; Wildenstein Castle
Freideutsche Jugend (Free German
    Youth) 57, 80
Freideutscher Bund 36
Friedländer, Paul 83, 84
Friedrich, Hugo 174, 190, 197

Friedrich Grammar School, Freiburg 144
Fuchs, Ernst 114, 115
'Fundamental Concepts', lecture 199
'Fundamental Problems of Phenomenology', lecture 69

Gadamer, Hans-Georg 93, 103, 222, 267, 268, 277, 280, 300
Gadamer family 95
Gebsattel, Viktor Emil Freirherr von 191, 192, 193, 194, 197, 198, 204, 264, 267
German Literature Archive x, 255
German National Guard (Landsturm) 7, 37
German Nationalism 134
German Supreme Army Command 59
Germany
   depression 74, 80, 87, 89, 92, 94, 131
   political situation 133–4, 155–6, 159, 299
Geyser, Joseph 27, 28, 91
Giesert, Fräulein 34
Goebbels, Joseph 159
Goethe, Johann Wolfgang von 134, 253
Goethe, Katharina Elisabeth (Madame Councillor) 85
Gogh, Vincent van 128
Göttingen philology conference 109
Göttingen University 87, 88
gramophone recordings 286
Grass, Günter 286, 289, 290, 291
Graumann, Engineer Captain 179
Greece 185, 283, 302
Greifswald University 148
Grillparzer, Franz 187
Grimme, Adolf 123, 124, 133, 140
Gröber, Archbishop 280
'Gründerzeit' woman 74–5
'Gruppe 47' 287n
Guardini, Romano 196, 220, 221, 238
Gundert family 248
Günther, Agnes 3

Gurlitt, Willibald 87
Guzzoni, Alfredo 262, 275

Habermas, Jürgen 234, 235
Haecker (Häcker), Theodor 79
Hamann, Richard 87, 109
Hamburg University 300–1
Hämmerle family 284, 291
happiness 4
Harbou, Andrea von 265–7
Harnack, Adolf von 79
Hartmann family 95, 99
   Frau 93, 95
   Nicolai 103, 123, 148
Hauptmann, Gerhart 79–80
Hebel, Johann Peter 252, 253, 287, 300
   Hebel Prize 278, 279
Hegel, Georg Friedrich Wilhelm 21, 33, 122, 134, 145, 249, 287
   Hegel Archive 290
'Hegel and the Greeks', lecture 265
Heidegger, Almuth 262, 274
Heidegger, Arnulf 306
Heidegger, Burghard 275
Heidegger, Detlev 278
Heidegger, Dietrich 278
Heidegger, Dorle: daughter of Jörg 306
Heidegger, Dorothee (Dorle): Jörg's wife 172, 173, 176, 180, 183, 187, 188, 191, 210
   mental health 209, 214, 228
Heidegger, Elfride
life
   early life viii, 2, 6–7
   meets Martin 7
   engagement 9, 23
   marriage 31–2, 32
   sunflowers picture 47, 48
   birth of Jörg 60
   birth of Hermann 77, 317
   builds the Cabin 85–6
   and family 117, 149, 213, 219
   flycatcher picture 233, 235
   house at Rötebuck 115–16
   learns to drive 143
   mother's death 184

grandchildren *274*
70th birthday 286
Golden Wedding anniversary 301, *301*
on Martin's 85th birthday *316*
old age ix, 292, 293, 294, 295, 306
death x, 316
and Friedel Caesar 317
career
  involvement in Martin's work 208, 278
  teaching 7, 36, 183
  welfare work 18, 162, 175
  writing 168
children *81*, 107
  and Erika Birle 149
  Hermann 71, 77, 78, 317
  Jörg 44, 53, 60, 172
education 7, 18, 83, 92
First World War 7, 18, 25, 36, 44, 92
health 140, 206, 214–15, 217, 222, 277–8, 287
  fall 303
  following birth of Hermann 80
  influenza 58, 83
  old age 292, 293, 294, 295, 306
  pregnancy problems 71
interests
  drawing and painting 279
  education 114
  Frauenfrage (women's rights) xii, 7
  love of rambling 36, 46
  skiing 7, 85–6
  spinning 162
and the letters ix–x, xii
and Martin's infidelities 254–6, 311–12
  Andrea von Harbou 265–7
  birthday letter 255–6
  jealousy xiii
  Marielene Putscher 251, 252
  Princess Margot von Sachsen-Meiningen 191, 194–5, 196, 197–8, 242

Sophie Dorothee von Podewils 221–2, 236–8
nationalistic and anti-Semitic views x, 28
politics 36, 142
Protestantism 13, 18, 19, 49
relationship with Martin
  dedication of *What is Called Thinking* 234
  and Friedel Caesar 64–5
  Martin's love 6, 9, 10–11, 13–15
  poem from Martin 21
  see also Heidegger, Elfride: and Martin's infidelities
Second World War 162, 172
travel 283, 289, 295, 303
Heidegger, Elisabeth (Liesel): wife of Fritz 109, 180, 211, 233
  anniversaries 125, 162, 172, 260, 265
  death 313
  death of son Franz 247
  family 164, 165, 171, 185
  health 270, 286, 287
  marriage 103
  visit to Rome 286, 287
Heidegger, Franz: Fritz's son 188–9, 247
Heidegger, Friederike 258, 274, 275
Heidegger, Friedrich: Martin's father 5, 26, 38, 91, 92, 97
Heidegger, Fritz: Martin's brother 35, 38, 92, 109, 211, 272
  childhood 245–6
  death of father 97
  death of son Franz 247, 249
  health 281, 288, 298
  and Liesel 103, 125, 313
  and Martin
    as brothers 78, 162, 174, 195, 210, 236, 244
    other help with work 208, 238, 243, 273, 275
    transcribing lectures 175, 218, 259, 264, 271, 278
    transcribing manuscripts 78, 161, 164, 171, 180, 205, 229, 236, 241, 243

Heidegger, Fritz (*cont.*)
  personality 72–3, 77
  Second World War 182, 187, 189
  visit to Rome 286
  work at bank 186
Heidegger, Gertrud ix, 249, *257, 274,*
    275
Heidegger, Hedi: Jörg's wife viii, 244,
    247, 249, 258, 275, 299
Heidegger, Heini: Fritz's son 188–9,
    244, 287
Heidegger, Hermann: Martin's son
    281, 289
  birth 77, 317
  career in Ministry of Defence 248,
    251, 285, 286
  career in teaching 235, 239, 241
  childhood 81, 89, 98, 101–2, 117,
    117, 137, 147, 148
  children 247, 262, 306
  education 144, 214
  and Erika Birle 146, 149
  health 126, 128, 131, 169, 171
  interest in philosophy 157, 158,
    171, 173, 174, 203
  marriage 235, 241
  Second World War 161, 162, 164,
    169, 171, 177, 186, 189, 194
    captivity in Russia 190, 191, 199,
      201–2
  skiing 158
Heidegger, Imke 299
Heidegger, Johanna: Martin's mother
    38, 97, 107–8
Heidegger, Jörg 247, 288
  birth 60
  career in engineering 234
  career in teaching 246, 284
  childhood 63, 69, 72–3, 75, 76,
    77–8, *81, 85, 89, 98, 117,* 132,
    135
    love of his workshop 136, 137
  children 249, 258, 275, 278, 299,
    306
  driving 150
  education 144, 146, 150, 151–2,
    161, 165, 214, 228
  and Erika Birle 149

  health 151, 179, 183
  house move to Zähringen 285
  interests 136, 137, 144
  Labour Service 151–2
  marriage viii–ix, 172, 210, 214, 244
  Martin's honorary citizenship and
    70th birthday 276
  Martin's prenatal interest in 44, 45,
    48, 49, 56
  personality 136, 137, 157
  Second World War 161, 165, 169,
    173, 174, 179, 185, 186, 188,
    189
  captivity in Russia 190, 191, 194,
    199, 201, 203, 204, 210–11
Heidegger, Jutta née Stölting:
    Hermann's wife 235, 241, 247,
    262, 274, 278, 281, 289
Heidegger, Martin
  life
    childhood 5–7, 245
    meets Elfride 2, 7
    engagement 9, 23
    27th birthday 25
    marriage 31–2
    birth of Jörg 60
    birth of Hermann 77, 317
    search for chair 82, 87, 88, 89,
      90–1, 95, 106
    associate professorship, Marburg
      92
    Japanese job offer 98, 99
    proposed as successor to
      Hartmann 103
    Christmas (1927) 112
    Berlin University, offer of chair
      122–4, 142
    monastic life at Beuron 74,
      125–6, 130–1
    Munich University, offer of chair
      142
    appointed Rector of Freiburg
      University 142
    breakdown 191–4, 195–6
    applies for early retirement 214
    33rd wedding anniversary 214
    private teaching 216
    professor emeritus 218

sits for bust by Chiarelli 262
sits for bust by Wimmer 265, 269
Messkirch honorary citizenship
    271, 275–6, *276*
Hebel Prize 278
gramophone recording 286,
    287
sits for Heiliger 291
interview for Der Spiegel 298
Golden Wedding anniversary
    301, *301*
80th birthday 312–13, *312*
85th birthday *316*
old age and death ix, 306, 316
appearance 9
clothing 91, 94, 110, 113, 298
fatherhood 61, 83, 98, *117*, 157,
    213, 219
    Erika Birle 157, 167
    Hermann 77, 101–2, 117, 157
    Jörg 44, 45, 48, 49, 56, 62, 157,
        244
    see also Heidegger, Jörg:
        childhood; Heidegger, Martin:
        Second World War
finances
    cost of living 43, 94
    difficulties 80, 82, 207
    extravagance 44, 87–8
    fees 94, 129, 250, 272–3
    practical matters 111–12, 137,
        140
    salary 36, 85, 96, 99
First World War 13–14, 35, 37–48,
    49, 51–4, 58–9
    German National Guard
        (Landsturm) xii, 7, 26, 28, 34,
        37–44
    meteorology course 44
food 43, 48, 49, 93, 193, 199, 297,
    308
Freiburg University 7, 41–2
    500-year jubilee 260–1, 262, 263
    breaks with 192–3, 195, 200,
        204, 206, 216
    chair 28, 109, 113
    cultural and educational policies
        140

elected Rector 142
    inaugural lecture 120
    lectureship post 20, 27
    lecturing 16–17, 20, 21–2, 60,
        61, 67, 90–1, 136, 158
    professor emeritus 197, 207, 208,
        209, 218
    rectorship xii, 143, 144
    retires 216
    Second World War 183–4, 188,
        189–90, 191, 192
    students 68–9, 70, 74, 90
    voted onto faculty 84–5
health 45, 137, 185, 214, 298
    breakdown 191–4, 195–6
    dental 39, 67, 68
    influenza 83–4, 134–5
    jaundice 285
    old age 292, 305
    stroke 314–15
infidelities
    Andrea von Harbou 265–7
    birthday letter 255–6
    Hannah Arendt xiii, 212–14,
        214–15
    Marielene Putscher 251, 252–3,
        258–9, 260
    Princess Margot von Sachsen-
        Meiningen 171, 177, 191,
        194–5, 197–8, 199, 242
    Sophie Dorothee von Podewils
        221–2, 229–32, 236–8, 241,
        242, 244, 260
influences
    Augustine 88, 126
    Hebel, Johann Peter 252, 253,
        287, 300
    Hegel 33, 134, 145, 287
    Heraclitus 194, 233, 297, 298
    Leibniz, Gottfried Wilhelm von
        248–9
    Lotze, Rudolf Hermann 26,
        40–1
    Parmenides of Elea 213, 233,
        243, 244
    Pindar 199
    Plato 187, 212, 241, 244
    Schelling 145, 204, 218

Heidegger, Martin (*cont.*)
    see also Hölderlin, Friedrich;
        Kant, Immanuel; Nietzsche,
        Friedrich Wilhelm
    Marburg University
        associate professorship 92
        chair of philosophy 103, 108,
            109
        lectures 98, 99, 282
        physical education 111, 113
        salary 99–100
        search for chair 87, 89, 106
    opinions
        on historical research 215–16
        on Jews and anti-Semitism xii,
            28, 77, 80, 99, 115, 133, 137,
            140, 156
        on lecturing 168
        on marriage 34, 77, 83, 84
        on nationalism viii, xii, 142
        on Orff 228
        on professorial gossip 123, 139
        on sacrifice 164
        on Steding 159–60
        on students and 'youth of today'
            120
        on winter/snow 13–14
        on women 10, 74–5, 83, 164
    personality
        absent-mindedness 42, 93
        manuscripts, concern for 228,
            229, 259–60
        practical matters 87, 149
    philosophy 11–12, 21–2, 53, 136,
        168, 175, 182–3
        antagonism 4, 11–12, 15–16
        being 160, 162–3, 164, 187, 197
        cognition 68
        consciousness 11, 57–8
        creativity 8, 142
        dwelling 217, 219
        happiness 4
        language 228, 235, 241–2, 249,
            250
        metaphysics 120, 122, 142
        mysticism 67
        phenomenology 33, 64, 69, 75–6,
            80, 108

    reflection 3, 160
    social values 55–6
    space 308, 309
    technology 233, 234, 236,
        239–40, 300, 309
    time-consciousness 293
    value philosophy 62
    politics 133–4, 137, 141–3, 155–6,
        159
    reading tastes 79–80, 115, 135,
        137, 167, 193
        Dostoyevski 48, 72–3
        Eckhart 61–2, 64
        Seidel, Ina 157–8, 160
    recreation
        art 125, 128, 134, 220, 273,
            283
        games 80, 98, 297
        music 227–8
        skiing 82, 83, 112, 119–20, 219,
            247
        walking 36, 116, 207, 215
        see also Heidegger, Martin:
            reading tastes
    relationship with Elfride
        meets Elfride 7
        courtship 3–18
        Elfride's birthday 22–3
        engagement 18, 23
        following engagement 19, 20–1,
            29–31
        Martin's birthday 25
        marriage 31–2, 84, 95
        army life 43, 45, 48–9
        after Jörg's birth 62
        on death of her father 154–5
        on death of her mother 184
        poem for 33rd wedding
            anniversary 214
        flycatcher picture 235
        on her 70th birthday 286
        difficulties in relationship 22,
            64–6, 124, 127–8, 136, 152
        Elfride's mental health 277–8
        love of Elfride 39, 56, 126
        penitence at infidelity 221–7,
            247, 254–7, 311–12, 313
        religious differences 13, 18, 19

spiritual closeness 79, 104, 122, 177, 229
thanking for her support 101, 138, 141, 152, 157, 178, 206, 218, 268
see also Heidegger, Martin: infidelities
relationship with Fritz
as brothers 78, 162, 195, 244
other help with work 208, 238, 273, 275
transcribing lectures 218, 259, 264, 271, 278
transcribing manuscripts 161, 164, 171, 180, 205, 229, 236, 241, 243
other relationships 79
Elfide's parents 115, 117, 124, 135, 140, 154
Günter Grass 287, 289, 290
Jaspers 86, 106–7, 123, 141–2, 203–4, 209
Marguerite Magirus 130
with parents 69, 107–8, 109, 154
see also Beaufret, Jean; Boss, Médard; Husserl, Edmund
religion/spirituality 39–41, 49–51, 67, 69, 114, 218–19, 225–6
Second World War 161–2, 163–4, 175, 186
clothing needs 179, 198
comparison with World War I 166–7
concern for library and manuscripts 164–5, 178, 184, 186, 187, 188–9
effects on work 173–4, 180, 187–8
Hermann 162, 169–70, 172, 174, 189, 191, 195, 196, 199, 201
Jörg 169–70, 171, 185, 189, 191, 194, 195, 196, 198, 199, 201, 210–11
secondary school teaching 165
in Volkssturm 178–9
travel
France 249, 295–7, 296, 297, 307–8

Greece 283, 286, 289, 295, 301, 303
Sicily 286
Zollikon Seminars 276, 277, 279, 289, 290
Heidegger, Martin: works
books
Bodenseebuch 23
Introduction to Metaphysics 235
Off the Beaten Track 205, 207, 208, 209
On the Way to Language 275
The Pathway 205, 207, 210, 213
What is Called Thinking? 234
see also Being and Time, book
essays
'The Essence of Reasons' 243, 244
'Heraclitus' 244
'On the Essence of Ground' 116
lectures
'Aristotle and Scholasticism', 20, 90
'Art and Technology' 164–5
'Augustinus: Quid est Tempus? Confessions lib. XI' 126
'Being and Seeming' 254
'Building Dwelling Thinking' 217
'Comments on Art – Sculpture – Space' 290
'Composure' 250
'Concept of Time' 98, 99
'Current State of Problems in Philosophy' 122
'End of Thinking in the Form of Philosophy' 294
'Europe and German Philosophy' 148
'Fundamental Concepts' 199
'Fundamental Problems of Phenomenology' 69
'Greece' 297
'Hegel and the Greeks' 265
'Hegel and the Problem of Metaphysics' 122
'Hölderlin's Earth and Heaven' 271–2

Heidegger, Martin; works (*cont.*)
  'Insight into That Which Is' 210, 241, 243, 244
  'Introduction to the Phenomenology of Religion' 80
  'Kant's Thesis about Being' 279
  'Language and Heimat' 278
  'Logos' 217
  on Nietzsche 232, 254, 264, 275, 278
  'On the Essence of Truth' 125, 132
  'Onto-Theological Constitution of Metaphysics' 262
  'Origin of Art and the Destination of Thinking' 301
  'Origin of the Work of Art' 147
  'Principle of Identity' 248–9, 253, 260–1, 262
  'Principle of Reason' 258, 259
  'Question About the Destination of Art' 314
  'Question Concerning Technology' 239
  'Reflections' 244
  'Self-Assurance of the German University' 142
  'Thing' 216
  'Thinker as Poet' 276
  'Traditional Language and Technological Language' 284
  'What is Called Thinking?' 219, 220
  'What is Metaphysics?' 120
  'What is Philosophy?' 249
  'Wilhelm Dilthey's Research and the Struggle for a Historical Worldview' 101
  other works
    'Art and Space', text 310
    Constance Gymnasium article 239
    'Duns Scotus's Doctrine of Categories and Meaning', thesis 22, 25–6, 27
    'Evening walk on Reichenau', poem 23, 24, 27
    'First Mass', speech 243

Heraclitus, seminar 298, 299
  'In the Thou to God', letter 255–6
  index to works 286
  'Kant's *Prolegomena*', seminar 7, 99
  'On Abraham a Santa Clara', speech 289
  'On the Islands of the Aegean', text 306–7
  Sojourns, travel notes 286
  'Time and Being', talk 283
  'To the Truest Companion', poem 214
  Valéry, translation 190
Heidegger, Thomas: Fritz's son 109, 188–9, 191, 207
Heidegger, Ulrike 247, 274
Heidegger Jahrbuch I 255
Heideggerus, Joh. Henricus 6
Heidelberg University 22, 82, 142
Heiland, Dr 208
Heiliger, Bernhard 290–1
Heimpel, Hermann 194
Heinrich Suso Gymnasium 244, 245
Heisenberg, Werner Karl 146, 218, 234, 235, 237, 238, 256, 269
Heitmüller, Willhelm 102
Helmken, Senator 283
Hentsch, Lt. Col. 166
Heraclitus 194, 233, 297, 298
'Heraclitus', essay 244
Herder, publisher 134, 221
Hermann Lietz Schools 146
Hermelink, Heinrich 102
Herrmann, Wilhelm 73
Hesse, Hermann 248
Heuss, Theodor 291
Hieronymus and Hieronyma 127
Hilde, friend of Elfride 78, 237
Hindenburg, Paul von 124
historical research 215–16
Hitler, Adolf 124, 141, 208–9
Hoffmann, Dr Wilhelm 188
Hölderlin, Friedrich 49, 80, 144–5, 163, 167, 182, 185, 187, 188
  'Encouragement', poem 277
  gramophone recording 286, 287

348

lectures about 148, 150, 171, 174, 271–2, 297
manuscripts about 171, 188–9, 194, 271–2
Hölderlin Society 274
'Hölderlin's Earth and Heaven', lecture 271–2
housing 36, 43, 65, 92, 93, 105
  see also Cabin, Todtnauberg; Rötebuck, house at
Huberten (student association of foresters) 158
Humboldt, Wilhelm von 249
Hungary 258
Husemann, Fräulein Dr 180–1
Husserl, Edmund 27, 32, 33, 71, 116, 309
  Martin working with 62–4, 70, 75, 90, 91, 108, 110, 118
  support for Martin 25, 73, 92, 99–100, 102–3, 109, 112, 114
Husserl, Gerhard 54–5
Husserl, Malvine 73, 87, 108, 110

'In the Thou to God', birthday letter 255–6
inflation 87, 89
influenza epidemic 55, 58
Ingarden, Roman 110
Insight, book 241, 243, 244
Introduction to Metaphysics, book 235
'Introduction to the Phenomenology of Religion', lecture 80
Italian Institute of German Studies 148

Jaensch, Eric 94, 102, 107
Jahrbuch für Philosophie und Phänomenologische Forschung 73
Jakobsthal, Paul 99, 103, 111
Jannsen, Sigurd 153, 155, 159, 170
Jantzen, Hans 87
Japanese language 248
Jaspers family 106
  Gertrud 141, 142
  Karl 71, 86, 103–4, 121, 280

and Martin 106–7, 122–3, 141–2, 203–4, 209
Jens, Walter 291
Jews see anti-Semitism
Jonas, Hans 115, *163*, 310–11
Jüdische Rundschau, newspaper 134
Jünger, Ernst 221, 235, 260
Jünger, F. G. 172, 196, 218, 235, 237, 239

Kaehler, Siegfried August 115
Kaiser Wilhelm Institute (Biblioteca Hertziana) 148
Kant, Immanuel 7, 17, 88, 112, 120, 158, 182, 267
'Kant's *Prolegomena*', seminar 7, 99
'Kant's Thesis about Being', lecture 279
Karlsruhe, Technical College of 143, 161, 214
Kästner, Erhard 238
Katterbach, Prefect of the Vatican Archives 99
Kaufmann, Fritz 103
Keats, John 306
Keller family 208, 313
Kempf, Adolf 155, 164, 186
Kempf, Konrad 145, 164, 290
Kiel University viii, 7, 90, 279, 310
Kiesinger, Kurt Georg 299
Klee, Paul 220
Klostermann, publishers 194, 205, 207, 209, 244, 299
Klübchen ('Little Club') 36
Kluckhohn, Paul 171, 174
Kluge, Kurt 193
Kock, Hans 306
Kommerell, Max 283
König, Hertha 283
Körte, Werner 155, 159
Krebs, Engelbert 18, 31, 60
Kreutzer, Conradin 249–50
Krieck, Ernst 133, 141–2
Krohn family 203, 204, 206
Kromer, Lina 206
Kroner, Richard 134
Krumsiek (later Gerber), Elisabeth 115, 117, 128, 208

Kurrer, Dorothee *see* Heidegger,
    Dorothee (Dorle)
Kurrer family 173, 174

Landgrebe, Ludwig 108
Lange, Helene 168
Langewiesche, Marie 260
language 228, 235, 241–2, 249, 250
'Language and Heimat', lecture 278
Larese, Franz and Dino 248, 290,
    291, 310, 312
Laslowski, Ernst 21, 221
Laslowski family 193, 203, 206, 220
Le Temps, newspaper 159
Le Thor, Provence 296, 307–8, 311–12
Leber, Frau 89
Lehmann, Karl 275, 286
Leibniz, Gottfried Wilhelm von 248–9
Leiner, Bruno 180, 228, 229, 233,
    244, 246, 247
Leiner, Erika 258, 286
Leipzig Trial 124
Lenz, Siegried 287n
Les Temps Modernes, journal 197
Lévy, Patrick *311*
Lieber, Friedel 16–18, 23, 26, 30, 60,
    67, 80
    and Elfride 28, 29, 36, 46, 78, 207
Lieber, Gertrud 29, 30, 70
Lieber, Karl 26, 29, 30, 34
Lieber, Karljörg 158
Lieber, Revd. 31
Lina, Fräulein 129, 132, 137
Lindau physicists' conference 284
Linde, Horst Eduard 302
Logos, journal 59
'Logos', lecture 217
Lotze, Rudolf Hermann 26, 40–1
Löwith, Karl 84, 85, 90, 95, 111, 118,
    310
Lukács, Georg 287
Luther, Martin 67, 77

Magirus, family 144
    Marguerite 130, 274
Mahnke, Dietrich 102, 109, 118
Maier, Frau 306–7
Marburg 93, 95

Marburg University 111, 113
    see also Heidegger, Martin:
        Marburg University
Marcel, Gabriel 248
Marcic, Dr 238
Marcuse, Herbert 305
Martin, Chairman 291
Mathieu, Frau 297, 308, 311–12
Maunz, Theodor 179
Max-Planck Society 303–4
Mayer, Hans 287
Meinecke, Friedrich 115
Mende, Erich 299
Messkirch 182, 195, 287, 289–90,
    305–6
    700-year jubilee celebrations 281
    honorary citizenship 271, 272,
        275–6, 276
Messkirch Castle 179, 181, 186, 288
metaphysics 120, 122, 142
meteorology 44
Michaelsen, Luise 303
Michel, Herr 267
Modersohn-Becker, Paula 125
Mohr, J. C. B. (Paul Siebeck) publisher
    25
Mohrle, dog 127
Möllendorff, Wilhelm von 130, 143
Mondorf, Gertrud (Trudchen) 23, 38,
    60, 68–9
Montessori, Maria 114
Montmédy 46–7
Mörchen, Hermann 115
Müller, Max 243, 305–6
Munich 90–1
Munich Conference 156
Munich University 142, 161, 162
Munier, Roger 307–8, 312
Münster, Clemens 218, 221
Mylius, Fräulein 196

National Schiller Museum 311
National Women's Service 7
Nationalsozialistische Volkswohlfahrt
    (National Socialist People's
    Welfare Organization) 162
NATO 248
Natorp, Paul 87, 93, 98–9, 100

Nazi Party viii, 133, 134, 137, 140, 143
Nebel, Dr Gerhard 208
Nelson family 75
Neske, publisher 235, 248, 274, 284, 286, 287, 291, 302
Neue Zeitung, newspaper 203
Niemeyer, publishers 108, 165, 205, 211, 223, 248, 254
Nietzsche, Friedrich Wilhelm 158, 159–60
  lectures 232, 254, 264, 275, 278
nihilism 265
Noack, Hermann 301, 309
Nohl, Hermann 87
Novalis (Friedrich von Hardenburg) 254
NS-Frauenschaft 150
nuclear power 234

Ochsner, Heinrich 21, 26, 27, 30, 67, 68–9, 193
Off the Beaten Track, book 205, 207, 208, 209
'On Abraham a Santa Clara', speech 289
'On the Essence of Ground', essay 116
'On the Essence of Truth', lecture 125, 132
'On the Islands of the Aegean', text 306–7
On the Way to Language, book 275
Oncken, Hermann 115
'Onto-Theological Constitution of Metaphysics', lecture 262
Orff, Carl 218, 220, 227, 228
'Origin of Art and the Destination of Thinking', lecture 301
Oschwald, Clothilde 91, 97, 204–5, 210, 222
Oschwald, Marie: Martin's sister 38, 72–3, 91, 97, 185, 207, 210, 239
  death 253
  health 243, 249
Oschwald, Rudolf 97, 171, 185, 207, 210, 243, 262
Otto, Rudolf 57, 67, 103, 107

Pagels, Elfriede 191
Paris Agreements 248
Parmenides of Elea 213, 233, 243, 244
Pathway, the, book 205, 207, 210, 213
Petri, Adam 61–2
Petri, Elfride *see* Heidegger, Elfride
Petri, Martha: Elfride's mother 7, 9, 27, 31, 124, *138*, 140, 184
Petri, Richard: Elfride's father 6, 9, 85, 124, *138*, 154–5, 164
  career 7, 27, 31
Petzet, Heinrich Wiegand 125, 216, 217, 220–1, 283
Pfeilschifter, Georg 35
phenomenology 33, 69, 75–6, 80, 108
philosophy *see* Heidegger, Martin: philosophy
physical education 111, 113
physicists 257
Picht, Georg 188, 221, 303
Pindar 199
Plato 187, 212, 241, 244
Podewils family 219, 220, 235
  Clemens Graf von 217–18, 221, 230, 232, 249, 260, 262
  Sophie Dorothee von 217, 221, 226–7, 229–32, 236, 242, 260
Pöggeler, Dr Otto 274, 275, 290
Poland 161
Pos, Hendrik Josephus 128–9
postcard 46
Prague Spring 307
Preetorius, Emil 235, 237, 238, 239, 314
press/media 58
Presting, Elfride 279
Presting, Else 31, 85
Presting, Walter and Herta 279
'Principle of Identity', Jubilee lecture 253, 260–1, 262
'Principle of Reason', lecture 248–9, 253, 258, 259
Putscher, Marielene 251–3, 258–9, 260

quantum theory 250
'Question About the Destination of Art', lecture 314
'Question Concerning Technology', lecture 239

radio 208, 218, 220, 221, 250, 280, 283
Rees, Theophil 40, *55*, 60, 61–2, 74, 103, 118, 191, 276
reflection 3, 160
'Reflections', lecture 244
Reich, Lucian 167
Reich directorate 165
Reichenau, island of (Lake Constance) 23, *24*, 25, 62, 64, 82, 177, 228, 229, 303
Reichsmark 96
Religion in History & the Present, dictionary 112
religion/spirituality 39–41, 49–51, 67, 69, 114, 218–19, 225–6
Rembrandt 273
Richter, Werner 99, 109, 123
Richter, Hans Werner 287n
Rickert, Heinrich 22, 27, 32, 35, 61, 107, 306
Riese, Fräulein 160
Riezler, Kurt 119, 120, 123, 220, 235, 239
Rilke, Alice 164, 172
Rilke, Rainer Maria 192, 283
Ritter, Gerhard 115, 268
Rodin, Auguste 128
Rohden, von, brothers 95, 99
Rosenberg, Alfred 140
Rötebuck
    house at ix, 115–16, *133*, 195, 215, 245, 246
    retirement flat x, 310, 311, 316
    swimming pool 279, 306
    tenants in WWII 191, 203, 206, 220
Rothacker, Erich 142
Rovan, Joseph 200, 204
Ruf, Sepp 290, 291, 302
Ruhr refugees 94
Runge, Antonie 85
Russia 155

Sachsen-Meiningen, Princess Margot von 172, 180
    Martin's affair with 171, 177, 191, 194–5, 197–8, 199, 242
Salzburg Festival 218
Sander, Revd 198
Sartre, Jean-Paul 197
Schaefer, Clemens 103
'Schaffermahl' fraternity 283
Scharnhorst, Gerhard von 158
Scharoun (Sharoun), Hans Bernhard 271, 302
Schaumburg-Lippe, Prince Albrecht and Princess Walburgis 217, 235, 238
Scheler, Frau 124
Scheler, Max 90, 112, 121, 149
Schelling, Friedrich Joseph Wilhelm von 145, 204, 218
Schiller, Friedrich 149, 311
Schirmer, Walter-Franz 114
Schlegel, Friedrich von 42
Schloss Hausbaden sanatorium 191
Schmid, Liesel 152–3, 209, 244, 258
Schneider family 117, 140, 185
Schnell, publisher 239, 249
Schopenhauer, Arthur 149
Schröder, Gerhard 299
Schröter, Manfred 211, 235, 238, 239
Schroth, Ingeborg 193, 283
Schuchhardt (Schuchardt), Walter Herwig 164, 167, 179
Schulz, Walter 180, 181
Schweitzer, carpenter 85
Second World War 161–89
    casualties 171
    food shortages 164, 170, 171, 173, 185, 187, 196, 198
Seidel, Ina 157–8, 160
'Self-Assurance of the German University', lecture 142
Semmler, Erika 150, 155, 157, 159, 160, 164–5, 168
Sethe, Paul 290
Shuzo, Kuki 92, 108
Sicily 286
Silberberg Guild cabin 7, *8*, 18

social values 55–6
Soden, Hans Freiherr von 102
space 308, 309
Stalin 229
Stallman, Revd 119
State Commissioner for Political
    Cleansing 206
Steding, Christoph 159
Stein, Charlotte von 134
Stein, Hedwig (later Veidt) viii–ix, 71,
    106, 244
Stifter, Adalbert 152
Strauss, Franz Josef 299
Stroomann, Gerhard 218, 238
student revolt 305, 310
students 68–9, 70
Studium Generale 283
Stuttgart National Library 188, 271–2
Südkurier, publisher 291
Switalski, Bronislav W. 99
Szilasi family 70, 71, 82, 83, 87, 89,
    90, 95, 196–7
  Lili 117, 197
  Wilhelm 200

Tägliche Rundschau, newspaper 140
Taine, Hippolyte 149
Tanabe (Japanese student) 96
'Tat' circle 140
tea 37, 49, 93, 100, 223
technology 233, 234, 236, 239–40,
    300, 309
Theodorakopoulos 302
'Thing, the', lecture 216
'Thinker as Poet', lecture 276
Tillich, Paul 134
'Time and Being', talk 283
time consciousness 293
'To the Truest Companion', poem 14
Towarnicki, Alfred (Frédéric) de 197
'Traditional Language and
    Technological Language',
    lecture 284
Trakl, Georg 278
Treviranus, Gottfried 123
Trotsky, Leon 134
Tsujimura, Kôichi 262
Tugendhat, Ernst 291

Uhlenhuth, Paul 94
university closures 161, 164

Valéry, Paul 190
Vanoli (artist) 129
Veidt, Hedi see Heidegger, Hedi
Veidt, Karl viii
Vetter family 60, 62
  Claus 169, 239
  Eugen 116, 133, 169
  Robert 172
Vezin, François 295, 307, 311
Vietta family 262, 265
  Dorothea Bernhardine 263–4, 267,
    269, 270, 272, 273, 274–5
  Egon 208, 235
Villiez, Baron von 38
Villinger, Dr 179
Vogel family 94
Völkischer Beobachter, newspaper
    124, 136
Vötterle, Karl 293

Wacker, Dr Otto 144
Waldorf School, Stuttgart 144
Walser, Martin 287n
Walser Valley 82
Walter, Elisabeth (Liesel): wife of Fritz
    see Heidegger, Elisabeth
    (Liesel): wife of Fritz
Walter family 313
Wandervogel movement 36, 114
Weber, Marrianne 107, 142
Weber, Max 107, 159
Weizsäcker, Carl Friedrich von 101,
    196, 218, 250, 262, 269,
    300
  Max-Planck Society institute
    303–4
Welte, Dr Bernhard 193, 199, 280
Weniger, Erich 140
What is Called Thinking?, book
    234
'What is Called Thinking?', lecture
    219, 220
'What is Metaphysics?', lecture 120
'What is Philosophy?', lecture 249
Wildenstein Castle 188, 189–90

'Wilhelm Dilthey's Research and the Struggle for a Historical Worldview', lectures 101
Wimmer, Hans 244, 265, 269
Windelband, Wilhelm 27, 62, 123
Wolf, Erik 174, 197, 222
Wolff, Frau 43
Wolff, Georg 298
women's rights *see Frauenfrage*
World War I *see* First World War
World War II see Second World War

Wünsch, Georg 112
Wynkenen, Gustav 114

Yorck von Wartenburg 103, 192

Zehrer, Hans 140
Zen 295
Zimmern Chronicle (*Zimmerische Chronik*) 280
Zollikon Seminars 276, 277, 279, 282, 289, 290, 292
Zopke family 94, 95, 96

JHMun   2/6/2009   (R25)